EUROPEAN PAINTINGS 15TH–18TH CENTURY

Copying, Replicating and Emulating

EUROPEAN PAINTINGS 15TH–18TH CENTURY

Copying, Replicating and Emulating

CATS Proceedings, I, 2012

Edited by Erma Hermens

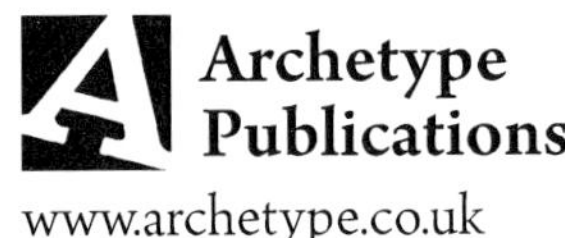

www.archetype.co.uk

in association with

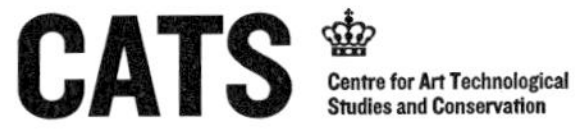

First published 2014 by Archetype Publications Ltd in association with CATS, Copenhagen

Archetype Publications Ltd
c/o International Academic Projects
1 Birdcage Walk
London SW1H 9JJ
www.archetype.co.uk

The Centre for Art Technological Studies and Conservation (CATS) was made possible by a substantial donation by the Villum Foundation and the Velux Foundation, and is a collaborative research venture between the National Gallery of Denmark (SMK), the National Museum of Denmark (NMD) and the School of Conservation (SoC) at the Royal Danish Academy of Fine Arts, Schools of Architecture, Design and Conservation.

ISBN: 978-1-909492-06-6

British Library Cataloguing in Publication Data
A catalogue record for this book is available from the British Library.

Front cover illustrations: (*top left*) Jan Massys, *Holy Family*, oil on panel, 101 × 73 cm, Antwerp, Koninklijk Museum voor Schone Kunsten, signed and dated 1563. (© Koninklijk Museum voor Schone Kunsten, Antwerp); (*bottom left*) detail from Quinten Massys, *Virgin and Child* (*Butter Madonna*), oil on panel, 135 × 90 cm, Berlin, Gemäldegalerie. (© UGent, Gica&s); (*top right*) detail from Jan Massys (attr.), *Virgin and Child*, oil on panel, 84.5 × 74.5 cm, Brussels, Musées royaux des Beaux-Arts. (© UGent, Gica&s); (*bottom right*) Jan Massys, *Virgin and Child*, oil on panel, 78 × 60 cm, Genoa, Galleria di Palazzo Bianco, signed and dated 1552. (© Maria Clelia Galassi)

Back cover illustration: Dieric Bouts workshop, *Virgin and Child with a Rosary*, after *c.*1459, oil on panel, 42.5 × 27.5 cm, Copenhagen, Statens Museum for Kunst, inv. DEP2. (© SMK.)

Printed on acid-free paper

Designed by Marcus Nichols at PDQ Digital Media Solutions Ltd.
Typeset by PDQ Digital Media Solutions Ltd, Bungay
Printed and bound in Great Britain by Latimer Trend & Co. Ltd, Plymouth

CONTENTS

FOREWORD

Whether you are reading this online or in a printed format, we are pleased to present the proceedings of the conference *Copying, Replicating & Emulating Paintings in the 15th–18th Century*, organised by the Centre for Art Technological Studies and Conservation (CATS), which took place at the Statens Museum for Kunst (SMK), the national gallery of Denmark, 21–22 May 2012.

SMK, the National Museum of Denmark (NMD), and the School of Conservation (SoC) at the Royal Danish Academy of Fine Arts, Schools of Architecture, Design and Conservation (the three partners of CATS) all have a long tradition of organising conferences, symposia and workshops on topics of interest to an international audience.

This conference was co-organised with the Technical Art History Department at the University of Glasgow and was made possible thanks to a substantial grant from the EU Culture Fund Programme (Strand 1.2.1 Collaborative programmes). The theme was inspired by the project *Tracing Bosch and Bruegel: Four Paintings Magnified*, a pan-European research project investigating four Netherlandish paintings from the 16th century depicting *Christ Driving the Traders from the Temple*. The paintings are currently in the collections of the Kadriorg Art Museum, Tallinn, SMK, Copenhagen, the Glasgow Museums, as well as in a private collection, and the research results are presented in the publication *On the Trail of Bosch and Bruegel: Four Paintings United under Cross-examination* (edited by E. Hermens, London 2012, Archetype Publications in association with CATS), the first in the *CATS Series of Technical Studies*.

In connection with this international and interdisciplinary project, the conference explored how the methodology of technical art history can be applied successfully to examine aspects of meaning, materials and manufacturing techniques, and can act as a catalyst for fresh perspectives on prevailing European workshop practices in the 15th to the 18th century.

From a large number of submitted high quality papers the scientific committee made a representative selection that covers more than three centuries, thereby illustrating a vast range of artists and workshop practices. Thirteen peer-reviewed papers plus one invited paper on two intriguing Boutsian versions depicting *The Virgin and Child*, are presented in these online and print-on-demand conference proceedings, carefully and eloquently edited by Dr Erma Hermens.

We hope you will find the proceedings enjoyable and enlightening and that the information contained therein will stimulate further research into aspects of copying, replicating and emulating paintings of the past.

On behalf of the organisers
Prof Dr Jørgen Wadum
Director of CATS

Dr Erma Hermens, editor
Lord Kelvin Adam Smith Senior Lecturer
in Technical Art History
College of Arts, University of Glasgow

Organising committee

CATS
Miriam Watts; Anne H. Christensen; Hannah Tempest; Jack Johnsen; Per Ingemann Hansen; Manuela Vernaccini; Mette Kokkenborg; Sarah Ferry; Sanne Capion Hansen; Sara Cadinanos; Kamila Marta Korbela; Ylenia Praticó; Marion Limbrecht; Jørgen Wadum

GLASGOW UNIVERSITY
Erma Hermens

This publication is also available online: www.cats-cons.dk/cats-conference-2-3-june-2014/conference-proceedings/

Scientific committee

VILLUM FONDEN VELUX FONDEN

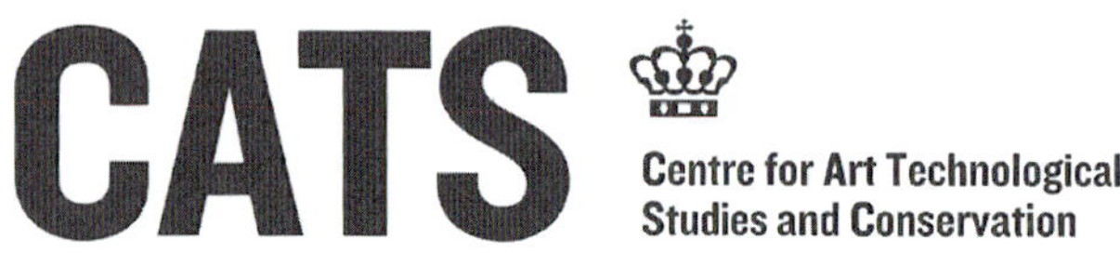

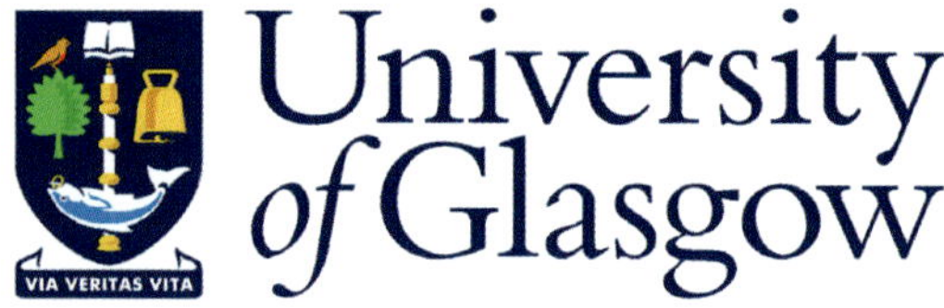

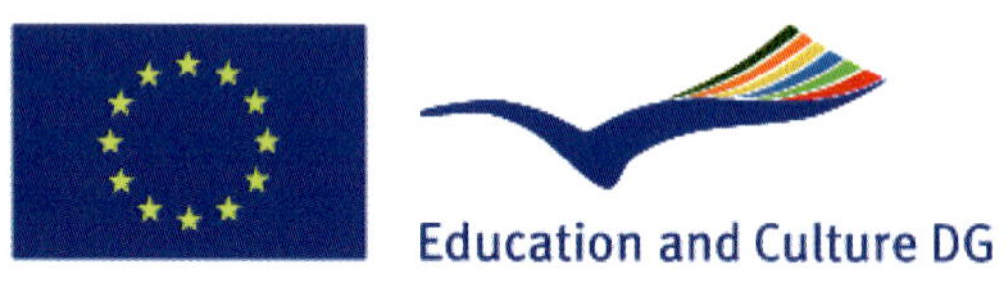

Culture Programme

PIETER BRUEGHEL AS A COPYIST AFTER PIETER BRUEGEL

Christina Currie and Dominique Allart

ABSTRACT A long-term technical study of Pieter Brueghel the Younger's replicas after his father has led to a deep understanding of his studio practice and copying process. This paper summarises the major findings, including the type and preparation of his panel supports, the materials, function and style of his underdrawings and the systematic build-up of his paint layers using identical reserves for copies of the same composition. Brueghel's design transfer technique – using pounced cartoons – is positively identified in one painting using infrared reflectography and inferred in his other copies through the use of reconstructions and overlaying tracings of multiple copies of the same compositions. That several hands contributed to the production is shown through stylistic analysis. Most of the signed paintings, however, seem to betray the work of a single hand at both the underdrawing and painting stages. This hand is likely to be that of the master himself. Finally, evidence from Pieter Bruegel the Elder's original paintings, reconsidered in the context of the technical examination of the copies, suggests that this great master himself had recourse to pounced cartoons for the transfer of certain of his compositions to panel.

Introduction

At the end of the 16th and the beginning of the 17th century, Pieter Brueghel the Younger emerged as the legitimate successor and copyist of his father, the celebrated Pieter Bruegel the Elder. He signed his paintings differently to those of his father, adding an 'h' after the 'g'. Working together with his studio, he supplied the market with hundreds of copies and pastiches of variable quality after his father's work.

The major part of Brueghel the Younger's output consisted of amazingly faithful copies after the originals. This is all the more surprising when we remember that he was only four or five years of age when his father died in 1569 and that his father did not train him. Indeed, he began his own career when Bruegel the Elder's originals were scattered in diverse and often inaccessible collections. He was therefore not always able to examine the models he copied.

This paper gives an overview of some of the main results of an in-depth study on this subject.[1]

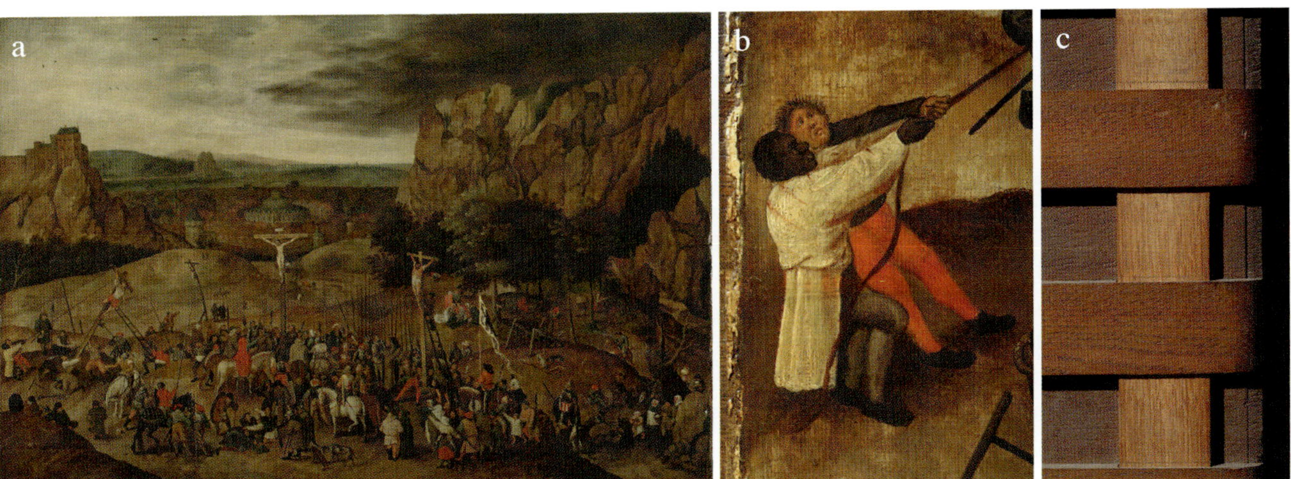

Fig. 1 (a) Pieter Brueghel the Younger, *Crucifixion*, oil on panel, 98.9 × 147.9/ 148.1 cm, signed and dated 1615, Coppée-le Hodey collection; (b) ungrounded and unpainted lateral border; (c) rebate cut into reverse of the panel. (© KIK-IRPA, Brussels.)

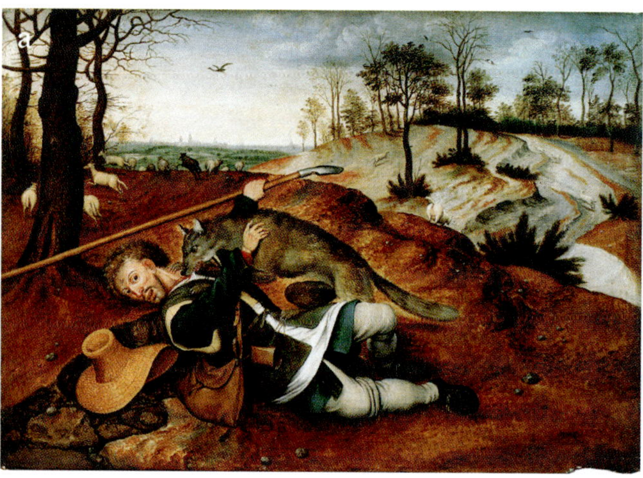

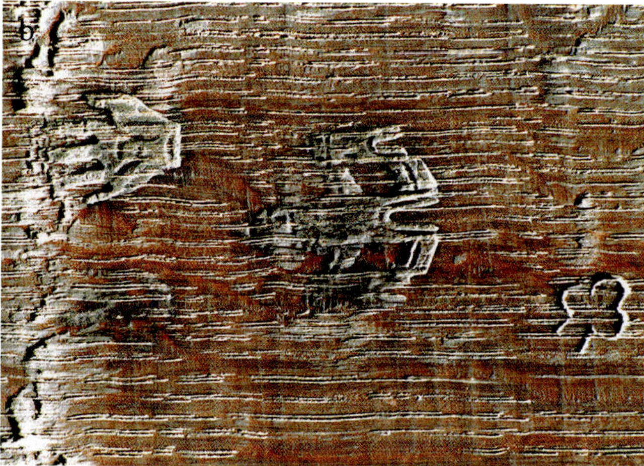

Fig. 2 (a) Pieter Brueghel the Younger, *Good Shepherd*, oil on panel, 41.2/ 41.3 × 56.8/ 57 cm, signed and dated 1616, Brussels, Musées royaux des Beaux-Arts de Belgique/ Koninklijke Musea voor Schone Kunsten van België; (b) Michiel Claessens's clover stamp on the reverse. (© KIK-IRPA, Brussels.)

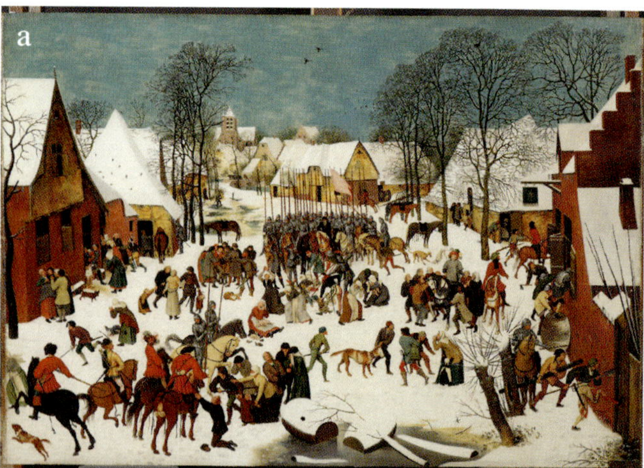

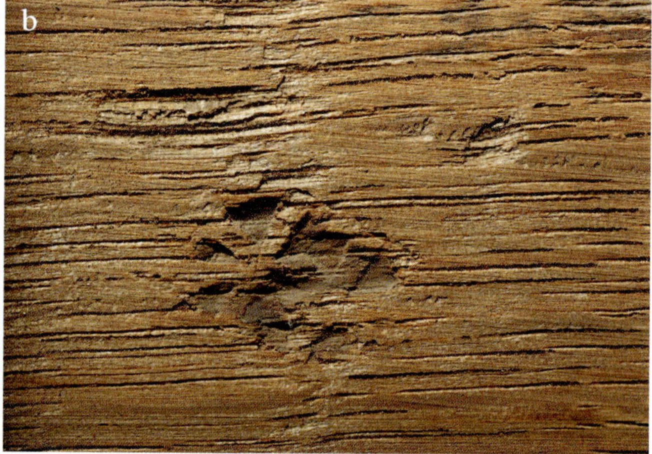

Fig. 3 (a) Pieter Brueghel the Younger, *Massacre of the Innocents*, oil on panel, 115.2 × 163.7 cm, signed, Sibiu, Muzeul National Brukenthal; (b) panel-maker's mark on the reverse. (© KIK-IRPA, Brussels.)

Technical characteristics of paintings produced in Pieter Brueghel the Younger's workshop

Supports

Brueghel the Younger painted mostly on oak panel and occasionally on canvas or copper. In the case of large-format works, there are almost always ungrounded and unpainted lateral borders, separated from the paint layer by a small ridge of raised ground known as a *barbe* (Fig. 1). These borders invariably correspond to rebates cut into the reverse of the panel. These redundant features probably accommodated temporary grooved battens, sometimes described as channel edge supports, which would have been slotted onto the sides of a panel at right angles to the grain of the wood before the ground was applied, and removed just before framing. Their purpose would have been to prevent warping and to make the panel easier to handle during painting, as well as providing provisional reinforcement for the newly joined planks.

In cases where panels have not been planed and cradled, the maker's mark can sometimes be discerned on the reverse side. The most commonly noted mark in the work of Pieter Brueghel the Younger is that of Michiel Claessens (working dates 1590–1637), whose clover stamp often appears on small-format works, for example on a version of the *Good Shepherd*, signed and dated 1616 (Brussels, Musées royaux des Beaux-Arts de Belgique/ Koninklijke Musea voor Schone Kunsten van België) (Fig. 2).[2] A more unusual mark, rarely seen on Brueghel's panels, was found on the Sibiu version of the *Massacre of the Innocents* (Muzeul National Brukenthal).[3] The mark is not accompanied by the Antwerp brand, and features three unevenly sized cross-bars (Fig. 3). It has been struck twice, the second time more firmly and partially overlapping the first. The mark remains unidentified, though it may be that of art dealer and panel-maker Hans Van Haecht, active in Antwerp from 1589 to around 1621. His symbol appears beside his name in a list of panel-makers from the Antwerp City Archives, dated 1617. Jørgen Wadum has found another example of this mark on the back of a version of Brueghel's *Procession to Calvary* (Copenhagen, Statens Museum for Kunst) also without the Antwerp brand.[4] It is possible that in both cases the lack of branding may indicate a date prior to the new rules of 1617 governing panel-makers.[5]

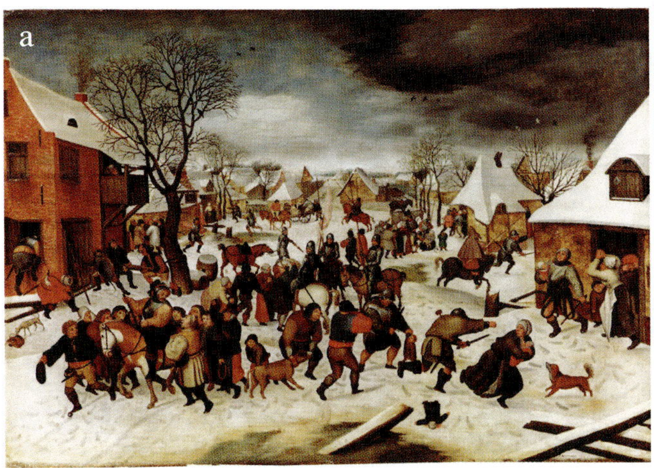

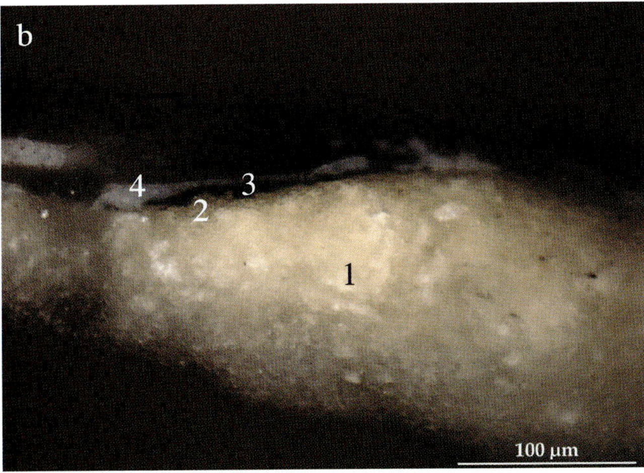

Fig. 4 (a) Pieter Brueghel the Younger, *Massacre of the Innocents*, oil on panel, 73.3 × 105.1 cm, signed, Antwerp, Koninklijk Museum voor Schone Kunsten; (b) cross-sectional sample from the snowy rooftop to the right, showing chalk ground (1), lead white and chalk *imprimatura* (with carbon black particles) (2), graphite underdrawing (3), and lead white-based snow paint (4). (© KIK-IRPA, Brussels.)

Pascale Fraiture (Koninklijk Instituut voor het Kunstpatrimonium/Institut royal du Patrimoine artistique (KIK-IRPA), Brussels) carried out dendrochronology on more than 20 works in the study. She discovered that for Brueghel's larger format panels, Baltic oak was predominantly used, whereas for smaller format works, oak from the Meuse and Moselle river valleys was more common.[6]

Preparatory layers

All Brueghel the Younger's panels in the study are prepared with chalk grounds. This is followed by a thin, tinted, oil-based *imprimatura*, usually containing lead white, chalk and carbon black. It is on this sealing layer that Brueghel applied his underdrawing, as in a version of the *Massacre of the Innocents* (Antwerp, Koninklijk Museum voor Schone Kunsten) (Fig. 4).[7]

Underdrawings

Works from Brueghel's studio, without exception, were painted with the guidance of detailed underdrawings in a dry medium. The underdrawings were carried out freehand in a carbon-based medium, the artist indicating folds and contours of figures with a vigorous well-practised touch, as in his copies of the *Wedding Dance in the Open Air* (Fig. 5).[8] Buildings were underdrawn in a similar linear style to figures, as in the background of the only known copy of Bruegel the Elder's *Magpie on the Gallows* (Georges De Jonckheere collection) (Fig. 6).[9]

Whether these underdrawings were executed in black chalk or graphite remained an enigma for a long time, and one that is almost impossible to solve from the appearance of the drawings in infrared. However, in three paintings, cross-sections could be taken that included the underdrawing. One such case was a version of the *Crucifixion* (Budapest, Szépmüvészeti Múzeum), where the paint layer is so abraded along the right edge that the underdrawing lies exposed on the surface of the preparatory layers.[10] Analysis of the cross-section using scanning electron microscopy with energy dispersive X-ray spectroscopy revealed the drawing layer lying directly above

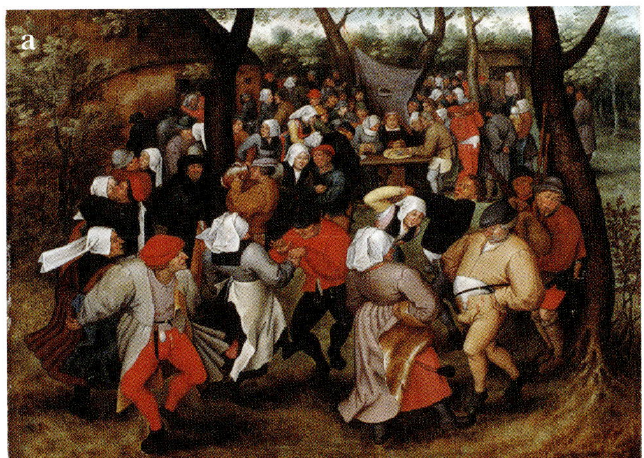

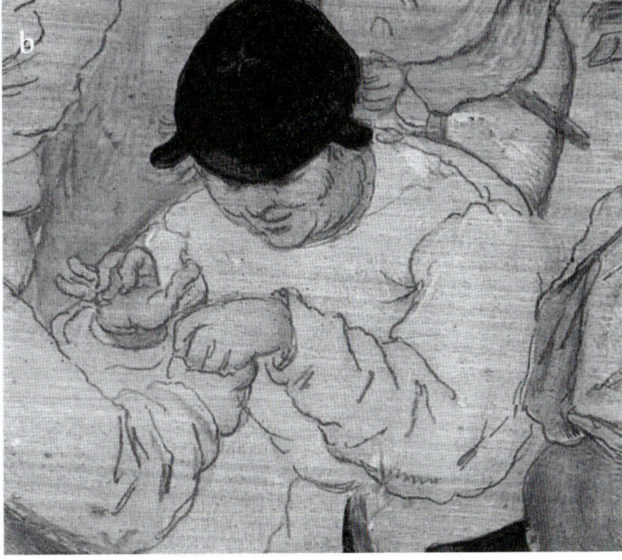

Fig. 5 (a) Pieter Brueghel the Younger, *Wedding Dance in the Open Air*, oil on panel, 38.5 × 51.5 cm, signed and dated 1607, Brussels, Musées royaux des Beaux-Arts de Belgique/ Koninklijke Musea voor Schone Kunsten van België; (b) detail, IRR. (© KIK-IRPA, Brussels.)

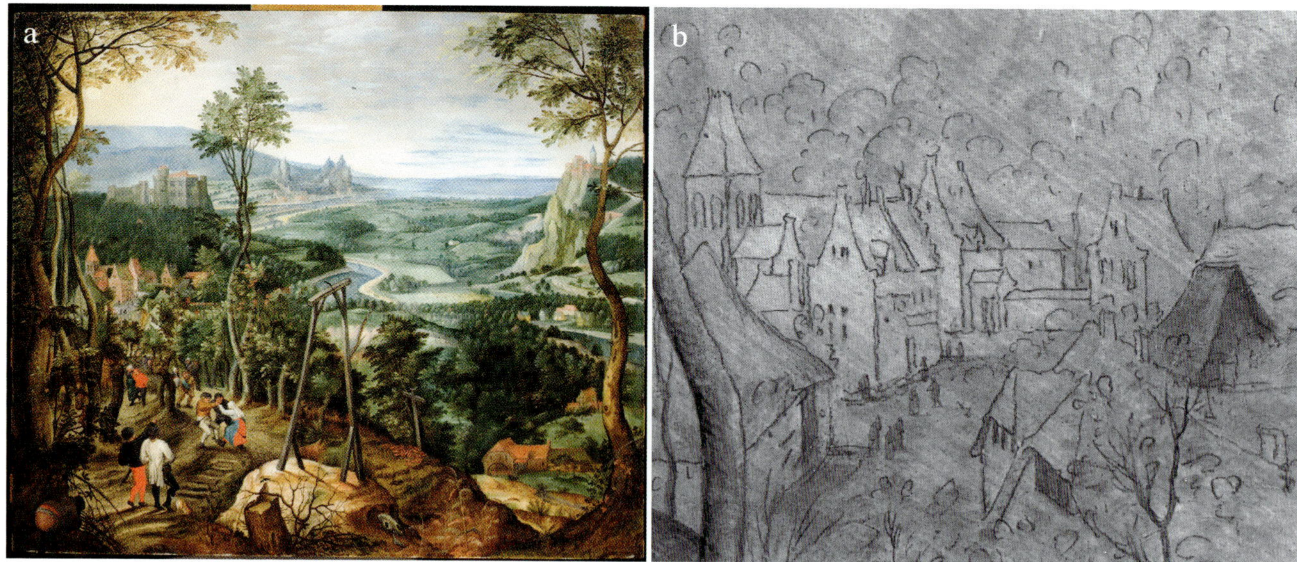

Fig. 6 (a) Pieter Brueghel the Younger, *Magpie on the Gallows*, oil on panel, 66 × 76.8 cm, unsigned, Georges De Jonckheere collection; (b) detail, IRR. (© KIK-IRPA, Brussels.)

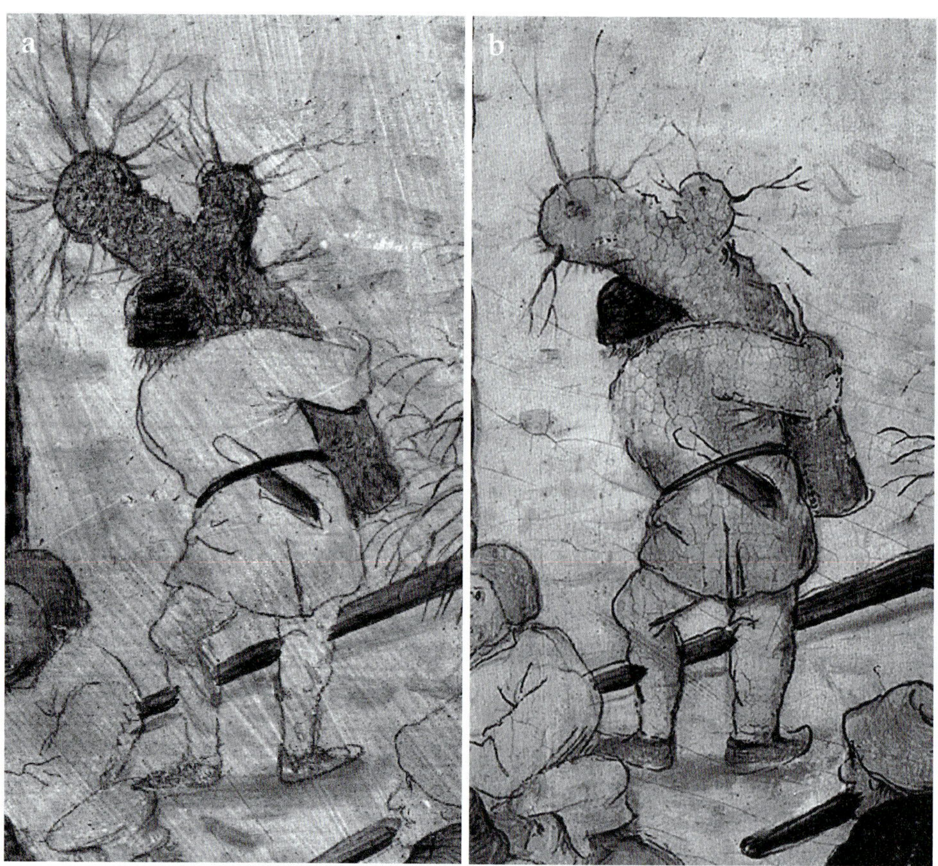

Fig. 7 (a) Pieter Brueghel the Younger, *Census at Bethlehem*, oil on panel, 108.5 × 160.5 cm, unsigned, Caen, Musée des Beaux-Arts: detail, IRR; (b) Pieter Brueghel the Younger, *Census at Bethlehem*, oil on panel, 115.3 × 164.5 cm, signed and dated 1610, Brussels, Musées royaux des Beaux-Arts de Belgique/ Koninklijke Musea voor Schone Kunsten van België: detail, IRR. (© KIK-IRPA, Brussels.)

a lead white and chalk-based *imprimatura*, and identified carbon as the dominant element. Micro-Raman spectroscopy (MRS) of the cross-section identified the drawing material as graphite. The other cross-sections of underdrawings were taken from two paintings of different formats, one small (*Wedding Dance in the Open Air*), and one medium (*Massacre of the Innocents*, see Fig. 4): both underdrawings also proved to be graphite, the identification made with MRS.[11]

It was also possible to conduct MRS directly on the underdrawing of the Sibiu *Massacre of the Innocents* during its recent conservation-restoration at the KIK-IRPA (see Fig. 3a). This analysis was carried out without sampling on an underdrawing

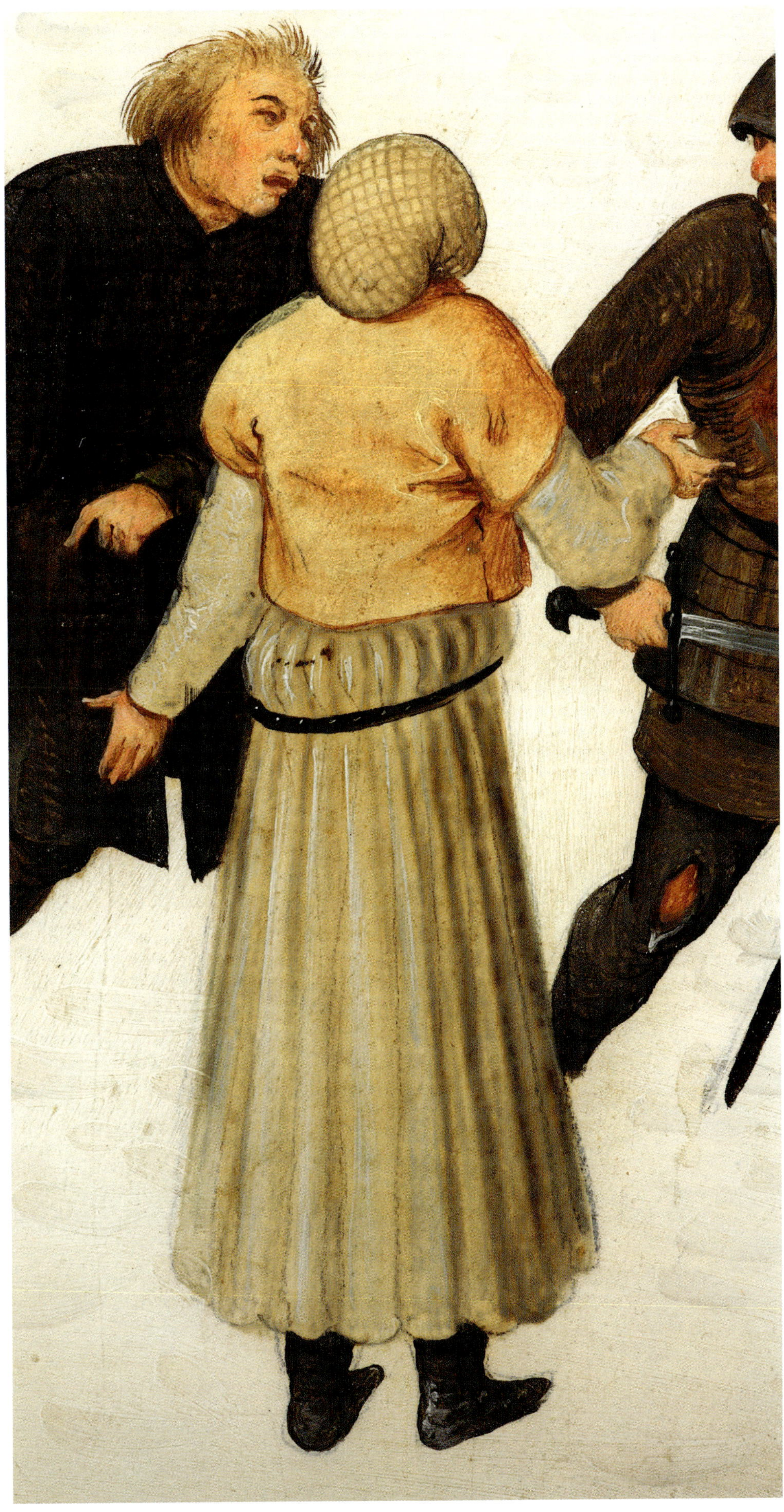

Fig. 8 Pieter Brueghel the Younger, *Massacre of the Innocents* (Fig. 3) detail: faded smalt in skirt and sleeves. (© KIK-IRPA, Brussels.)

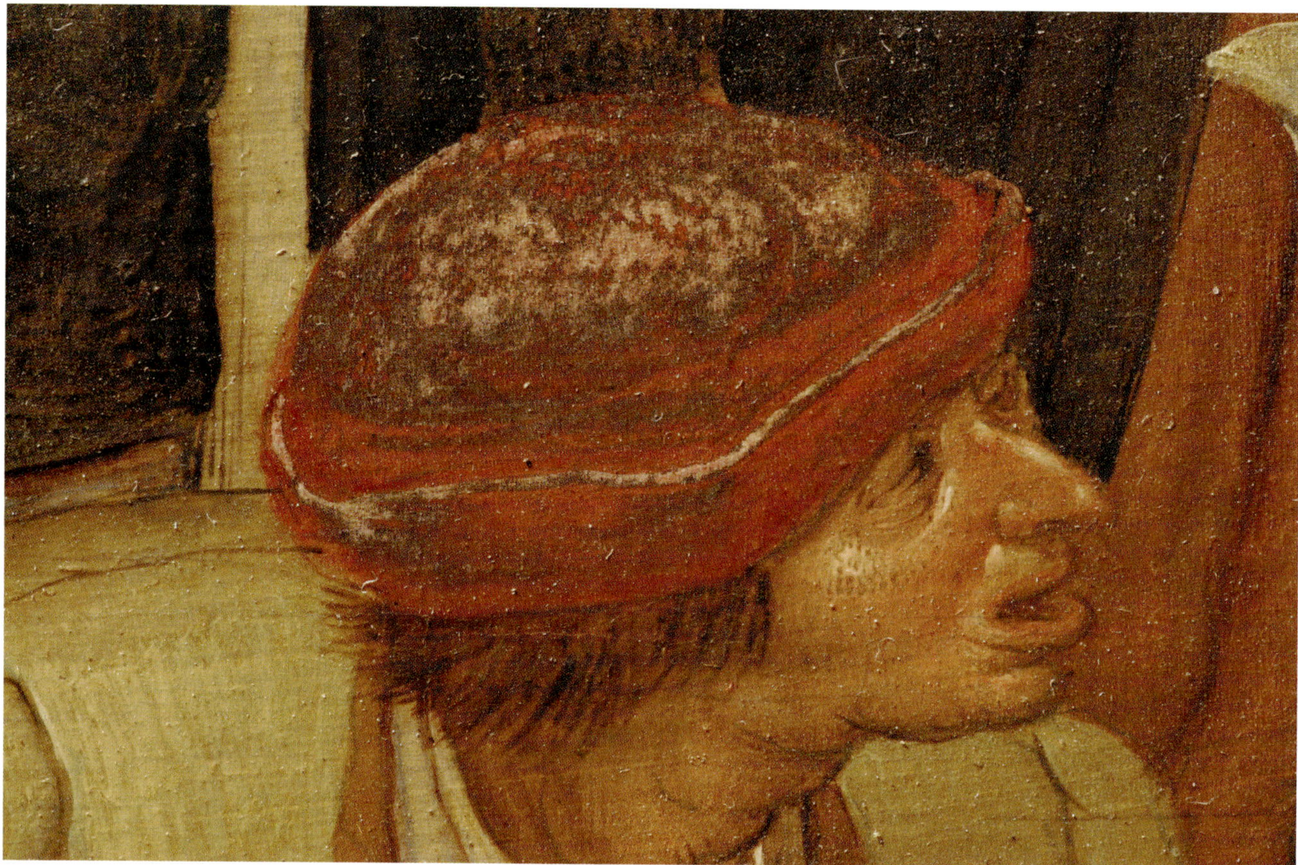

Fig. 9 Pieter Brueghel the Younger, *Wedding Dance in the Open Air*, oil on panel, 40 × 56 cm, signed and dated 1620, Narbonne, Musée des Beaux-Arts: detail of discoloration in the red cap. (© KIK-IRPA, Brussels.)

line in a snowy rooftop that was not covered by overlying paint.[12] The result was later confirmed through Raman analysis of a few minute drawing particles scraped off from this same zone. At odds with our expectations based on the previous findings, it was interesting to discover that black chalk was the underdrawing medium in this case. Brueghel therefore used both graphite and black chalk for underdrawing but further analyses would be needed on a wider range of paintings to determine whether one is more frequent than the other and if there is any correlation with a time period.

Paint layers

Brueghel the Younger followed the time-honoured method of leaving reserves in the paint layer for the forms to follow. But what is striking is that these reserves are identical in all versions of the same composition, suggesting that the master issued specific instructions as to the execution of his copies that his assistants were then expected to follow scrupulously.

A good example of this is the *Census at Bethlehem* series, of which 10 copies were examined with scientific imagery.[13] Several different hands could be identified on stylistic grounds, but all the copies follow the exact same placement of reserves. For instance, while painting the punt to the left, the copyists left a gap for the large tree, as manifest in infrared details from eight versions of the composition. Similarly, the legs of a figure carrying a tree stump are reserved in a wagon handle in all 10 copies examined (Fig. 7).[14] And a space was always left in one of the wagon wheels for Joseph's wide-brimmed hat.

To identify Brueghel's usual layer structure and palette, cross-sections were taken from numerous paintings, and X-ray fluorescence analysis was performed on certain works. In many paintings, two pigments used frequently were found to have changed in appearance over the years: smalt, which has faded in many draperies, as for example in the Sibiu *Massacre of the Innocents* (Fig. 8); and vermilion, which has developed dark grey patches with blanched areas in 25 of the paintings examined, representing just over a third of the works in the study (Fig. 9).[15]

Brueghel the Younger's copying practice

Research into Brueghel's method (or methods) of copying was one of the main thrusts of the study. This was tackled from several different angles, one of which was the physical tracing of several versions of the same composition. In practice, paintings were verified for flaking paint, a thick PVC sheet laid over them, and the outlines traced with a thin black permanent marker.

In the case of the *Wedding Dance*, for instance, five versions were examined and four traced.[16] When these tracings were superimposed, they all showed the same close match for the figural group, with no correspondence for background trees or

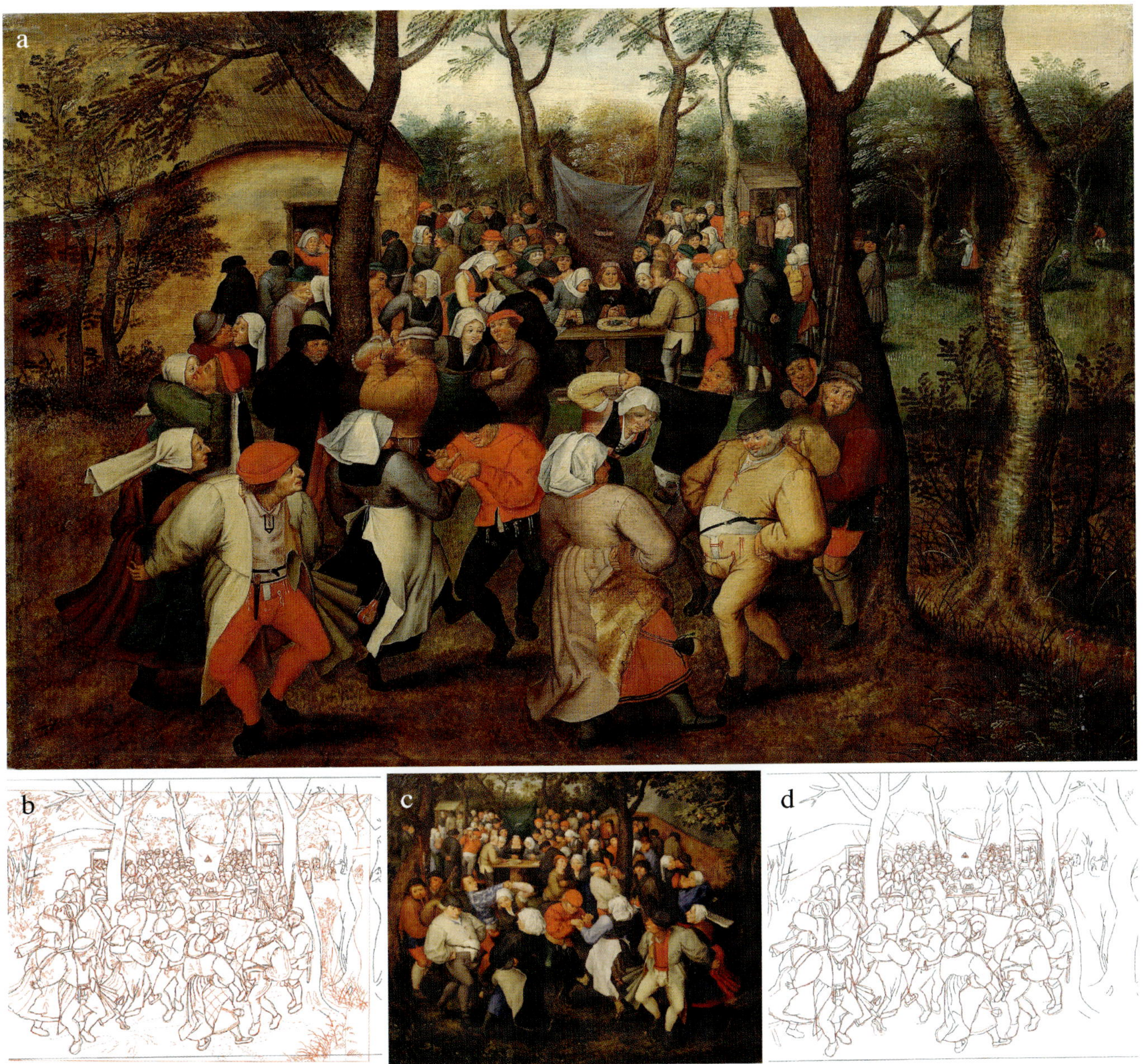

Fig. 10 (a) Pieter Brueghel the Younger, *Wedding Dance in the Open Air*, oil on panel, 41 × 61.4 cm, unsigned, private collection (Coppée-le Hodey collection); (b) overlay of tracings of two versions of Pieter Brueghel the Younger's *Wedding Dance in the Open Air*. (Coppée-le Hodey and Ghent, Museum voor Schone Kunsten); (c) Jan Brueghel the Elder, *Wedding Dance in the Open Air*, oil on copper, 40 × 50 cm, unsigned, Bordeaux, Musée des Beaux-Arts; (d) overlay of tracings of Coppée-le Hodey and Bordeaux versions with Jan's version flipped over. (© KIK-IRPA, Brussels.)

buildings (Fig. 10b).[17] This suggests the use of a common cartoon for the figures. It was also possible to examine and trace Jan Brueghel the Elder's version of this composition, which is painted on copper (Bordeaux, Musée des Beaux-Arts).[18] Although Jan inverted the composition, when the tracing was flipped over, the foreground figural group was found to fit well with that of Pieter's, suggesting the use of a common cartoon by the two brothers (Fig. 10d).[19]

But the *Wedding Dance* series, although showing that Brueghel the Younger had recourse to cartoons to transfer designs, did not reveal his actual method. The answer to this question was discovered in one of his copies of the *Battle between Carnival and Lent*. Brueghel the Younger made at least five copies of this composition after the original version by his father (Vienna, Kunsthistorisches Museum). But it is the version in the Musées royaux des Beaux-Arts de Belgique/ Koninklijke Musea voor Schone Kunsten van België in Brussels that gave the biggest clue as to Brueghel the Younger's transfer technique.[20]

The infrared reflectogram (IRR) of the Brussels *Battle between Carnival and Lent* reveals pouncing marks in many places running alongside the underdrawing lines, as in the guitar player in the lower left (Fig. 11). This confirms the use of a pricked cartoon or cartoons for the transfer of the image. Most of the remaining pouncing is confined to the lower left quadrant and the upper centre-right, with virtually none detectable elsewhere. There is no difference whatsoever in the underdrawing style or level of detail between areas with and without pouncing. The fact that any pouncing marks remain at all was probably totally unintentional on the part of the artist, as he would not have wanted the black powder to sully his paint in any way.

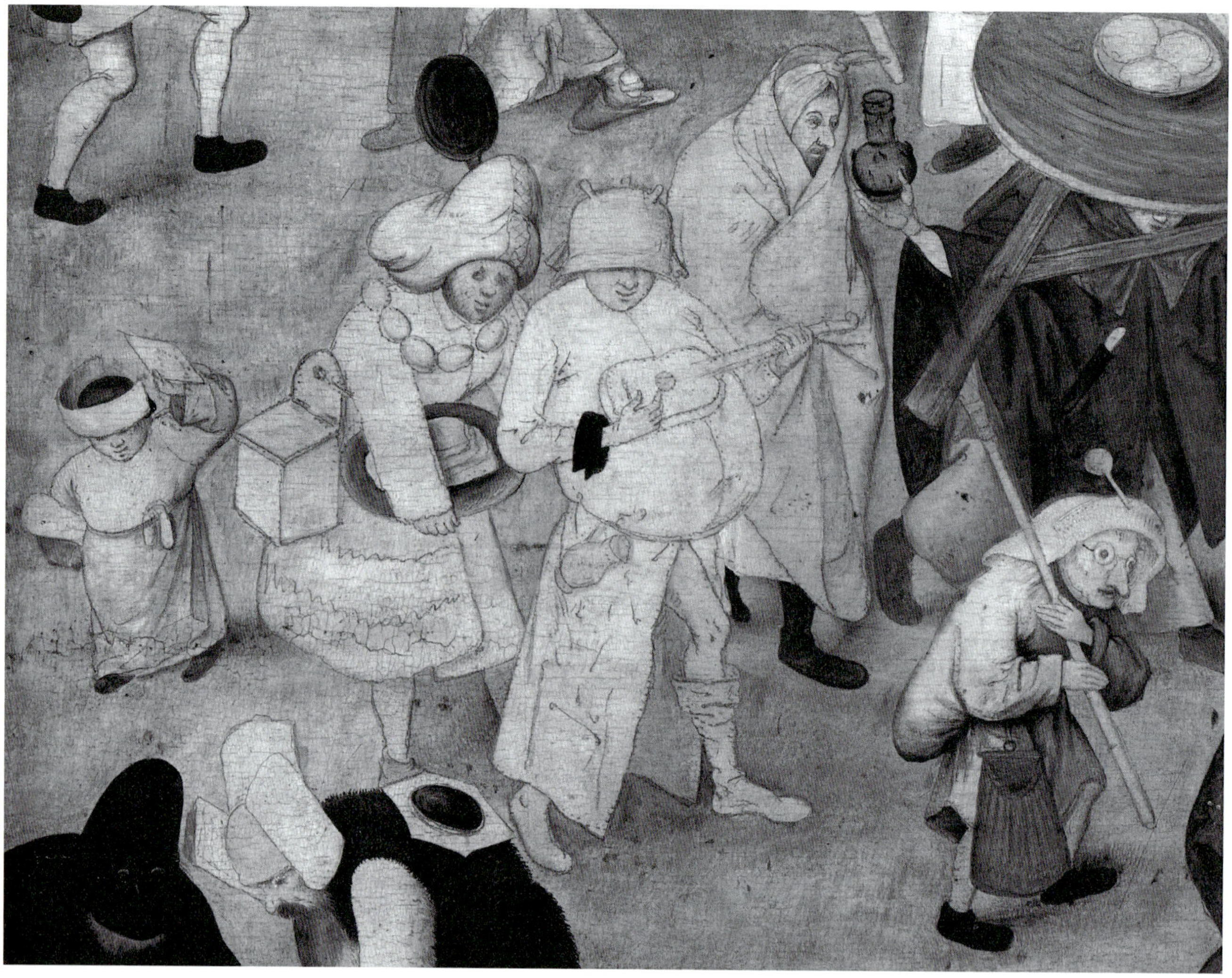

Fig. 11 Pieter Brueghel the Younger, *Battle between Carnival and Lent*, oil on panel, 121.1/ 121.4 × 171.3/ 171.9 cm, unsigned, Brussels, Musées royaux des Beaux-Arts de Belgique/ Koninklijke Musea voor Schone Kunsten van België: detail, IRR. (© KIK-IRPA, Brussels.)

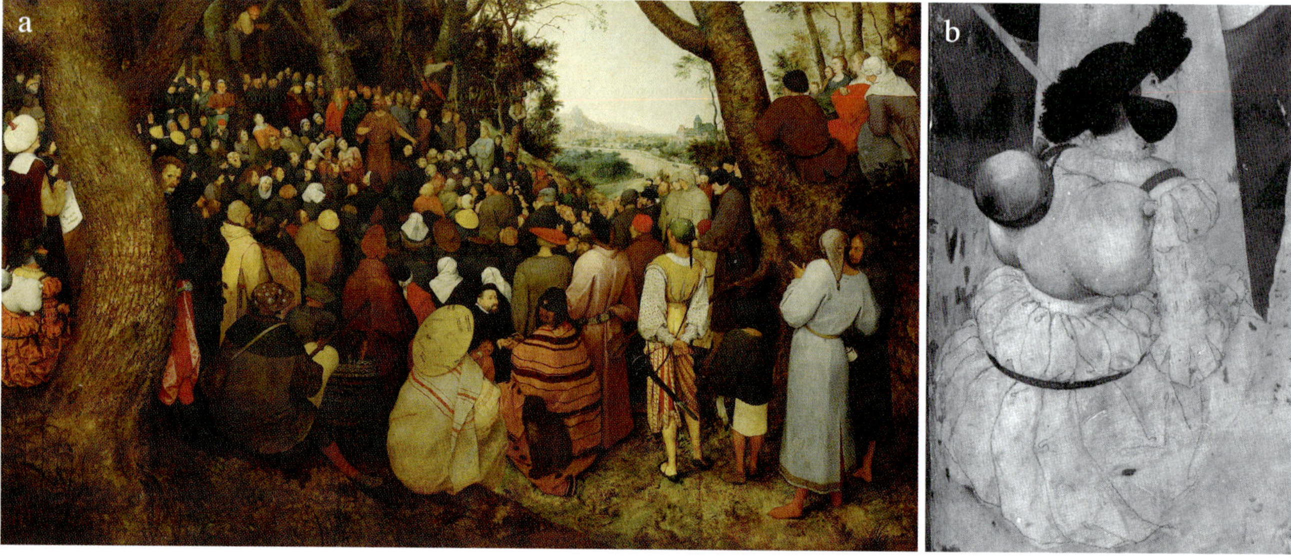

Fig. 12 (a) Pieter Bruegel the Elder, *Sermon of St John the Baptist*, oil on panel, 95.1/ 95.2 × 161.6/ 161.7 cm, signed and dated 1566, Budapest, Szépmüvészeti Múzeum; (b) detail, IRR. (© KIK-IRPA, Brussels.)

Reconstructions were carried out to test the feasibility of removing pouncing marks from a dried, oil-based *imprimatura* layer. It was found that the dots wipe off easily leaving no trace, but that if the layer is slightly tacky for any reason the pouncing marks become trapped, as probably happened in the Brussels *Battle between Carnival and Lent*.

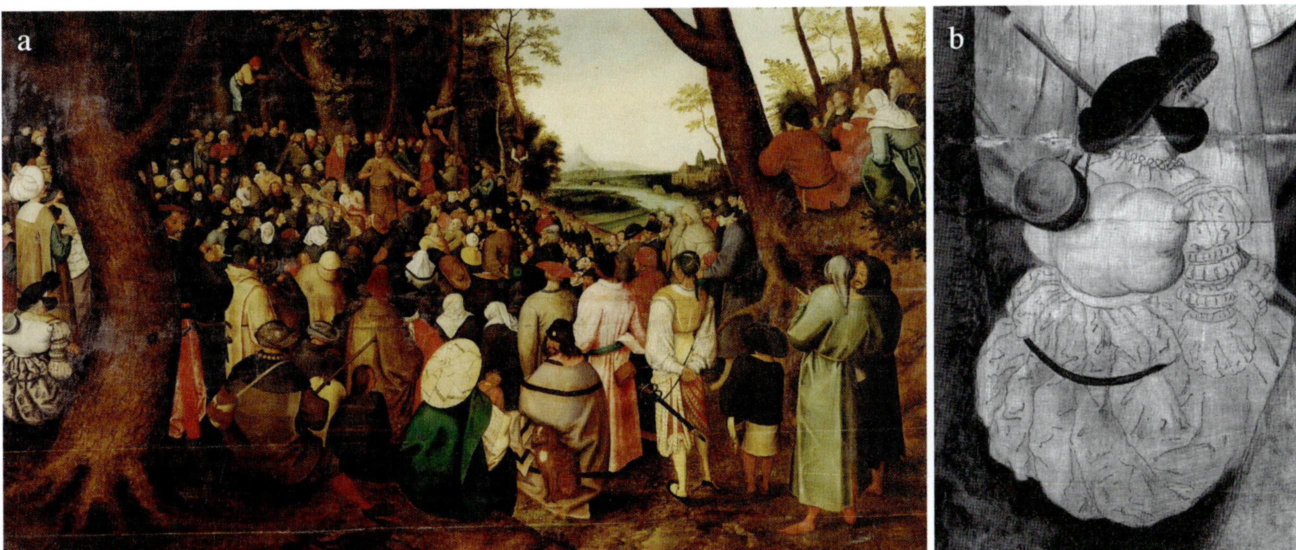

Fig. 13 (a) Pieter Brueghel the Younger, *Sermon of St John the Baptist*, oil on panel, 104.5/ 104.9 × 169.3/ 169.6 cm, signed and dated 1624, Lier, Stedelijk Museum Wuyts-Van Campen en Baron Caroly; (b) detail, IRR (© KIK-IRPA, Brussels.)

Comparing the manner of underdrawing in the Brussels *Carnival and Lent* with that in other paintings by Brueghel reveals many similarities. An example is the *Procession to Calvary* (Antwerp, Koninklijk Museum voor Schone Kunsten),[21] which shares an identical style of drawing for drapery folds, with small circles or hooks at the end of lines.

The evidence from IRR together with that of the tracings suggests that Brueghel the Younger employed pricked cartoons for design transfer in all his copying work. Furthermore, the tracing overlays indicate that cartoons were sometimes employed for whole compositions and sometimes for groups of motifs, depending on format.

The source of the cartoons

In the Brussels *Battle between Carnival and Lent*, several pounced motifs have been subsequently adjusted during underdrawing. An example is the figure of a woman dragging a cart, whose outstretched arm in the pouncing stage has been replaced by a bent arm during underdrawing. In Bruegel the Elder's original version, as in two faithful copies, the painted arm appears as it does in the Brussels underdrawing. In the case of two atypical copies, the motif appears in the same guise as that in the Brussels pouncing stage design, in other words, how it must have appeared on the pricked cartoon.[22] This suggests that the cartoon represents an earlier prototype of the composition by Bruegel the Elder that Brueghel the Younger inherited and used for design transfer. While underdrawing the Brussels version, he must have corrected certain details in line with their final appearance in his father's original painting.

The implications of the study of the *Battle between Carnival and Lent* shed light on a new aspect of Bruegel the Elder's working practice. It suggests that this great master himself might have used pricked cartoons as part of his preparatory work for painting. The question was also raised in relation to Bruegel the Elder's *Sermon of St John the Baptist* (Budapest, Szépmüvészeti Múzeum) (Fig. 12).[23] The original was traced, along with three of Brueghel the Younger's copies. When the tracing of the original version was overlaid with that of one of the copies and aligned on the figures to the far left, the motifs to the far left were found to match well, unlike the rest of the composition. Similar correlations were found with other groupings. This raises the possibility that Bruegel the Elder made a series of cartoons of motifs, which were inherited and reused by his elder son. Comparison of the underdrawings made by each of them also supports this hypothesis. In the pilgrim woman in the lower left, the underdrawing in both cases is a unwavering linear outline drawing carried out freehand in a dry medium (Figs 12 and 13). The style of the underdrawings suggests that they followed pounced guidelines, the dots themselves being wiped away as soon as the underdrawing was completed.

Brueghel the Younger's authorship within his production

Examination of over 60 works from Brueghel the Younger's workshop led to the conclusion that different hands were involved. This assessment was made on the basis of close comparisons of underdrawing and painting style. In the case of smaller format paintings though, discrimination was often impossible.

Underdrawings of two of Brueghel's versions of the *Census at Bethlehem*, one signed and dated 1604 (Galerie De Jonckheere), the other signed and dated 1610 (Brussels, Musées royaux des Beaux-Arts de Belgique/Koninklijke Musea voor Schone Kunsten van België) clearly show two different hands at work: the 1610 version reveals a draughtsman with a loose and confident touch and an ability to portray a sense of movement in his figures while the 1604 version reveals a studious and more applied hand.

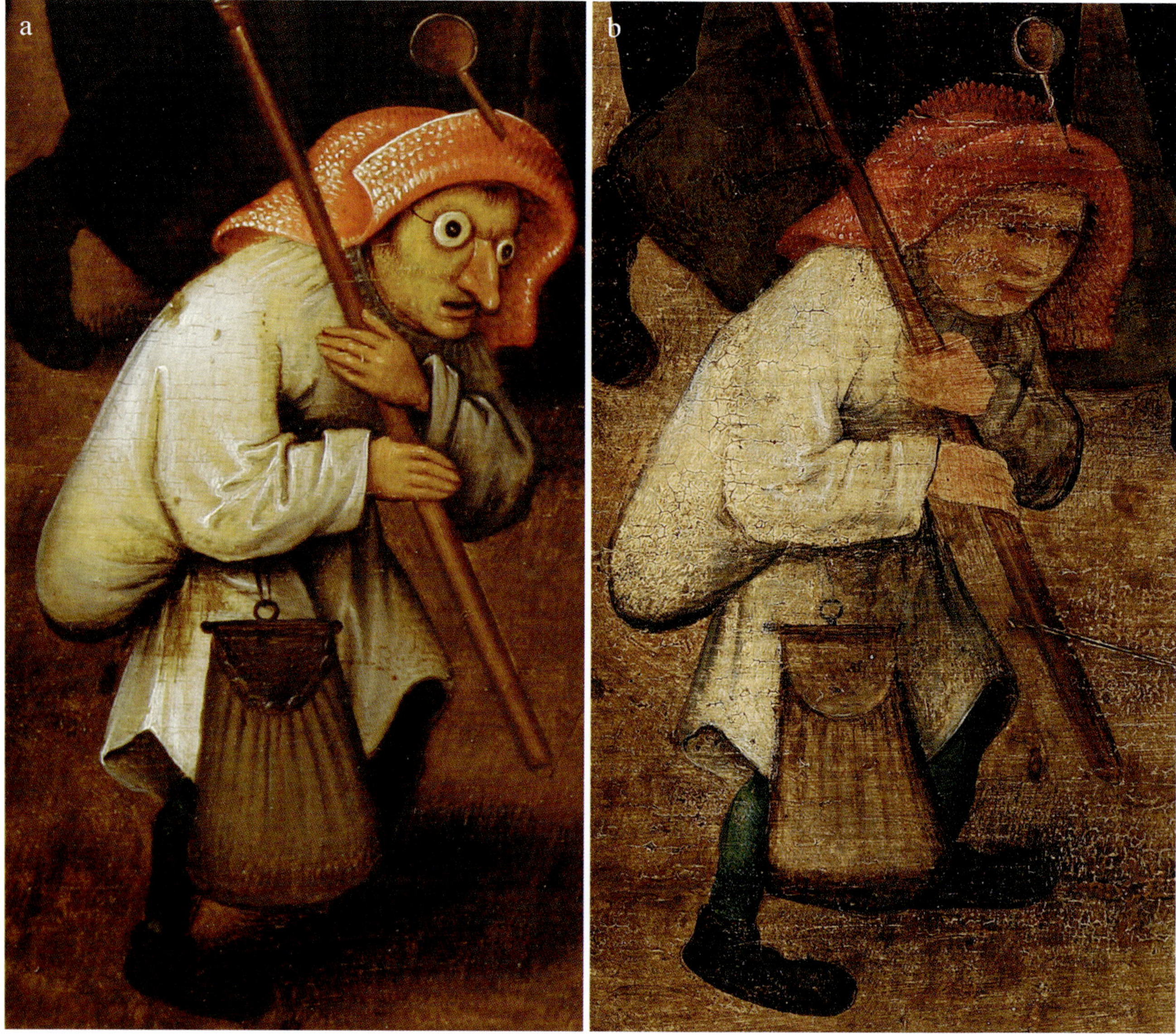

Fig. 14 (a) Pieter Brueghel the Younger, *Battle between Carnival and Lent* (Fig. 11): detail. (b) Pieter Brueghel the Younger, *Battle between Carnival and Lent*, oil on panel, 118.1 × 166.3 cm, unsigned (former Portland collection): detail. (© KIK-IRPA, Brussels.)

Considerable differences in painterly style can be seen in two versions of the *Carnival and Lent* (Brussels, Musées royaux des Beaux-Arts de Belgique/Koninklijke Musea voor Schone Kunsten van België and an example sold at Christie's London).[24] Even taking into account the poor condition of the latter, the Brussels painting reveals infinitely more skill in terms of gesture and movement (Fig. 14).

It was possible to distinguish two core groups amongst the paintings studied – one for underdrawings and one for paintings – that share similar stylistic features and a consistently higher quality of expression. These are attributed to Brueghel the Younger's own hand. For the most part, the core group of paintings corresponds to the core group of underdrawings, implying that Brueghel himself was solely responsible for this group from start to finish. Twenty-three out of the 28 core group paintings are signed, which suggests that the master generally signed his personal production. Occasionally, however, a signature is present on a painting that falls outside the core group, such as the above-mentioned 1604 version of the *Census at Bethlehem*. The presence of a signature on a painting can therefore be seen as the mark of a good-quality product from Pieter Brueghel the Younger's workshop, but is not an absolute guarantee of his hand.

Conclusions

Brueghel the Younger's workshop production shares a common technical fingerprint, enabling his works to be singled out from those of contemporary and later followers. This includes the use of pricked cartoons as part of his copying process, sometimes for whole compositions and sometimes for groups of motifs. The hand of Brueghel the Younger himself can sometimes be distinguished from those of his workshop, although certain cases will always remain ambiguous.

With regard to Bruegel the Elder's working practice, one of the most significant discoveries is that he also used cartoons on occasion as part of his preparatory design process.

Notes

1. On this fascinating phenomenon, see C. Currie and D. Allart, *The Brueg[H]el Phenomenon: Paintings by Pieter Bruegel the Elder and Pieter Brueghel the Younger with a Special Focus on Technique and Copying Practice*, 3 vols, Brussels, Royal Institute for Cultural Heritage (KIK-IRPA), 2012 (*Scientia Artis 8*). In volume 1, an overview on the historical and socio-economic background is also given, which cannot be discussed here. On Pieter Brueghel the Younger's life and work, see also G. Marlier, *Pierre Brueghel le Jeune*, posthumous edition by J. Folie, Brussels, Robert Finck, 1969, and K. Ertz, *Pieter Brueghel der Jüngere 1564–1637/8. Die Gemälde mit kritischem Oeuvrekatalog*, Luca Verlag Lingen, 1998–2000.
2. Pieter Brueghel the Younger, *Good Shepherd* (Fig. 2), oil on panel, 41.2/ 41.3 × 56.8/ 57 cm, signed and dated '[-] BREVGHEL·1616·' in the lower left, Brussels, Musées royaux des Beaux-Arts de Belgique/Koninklijke Musea voor Schone Kunsten van België, inv. 10830.
3. Pieter Brueghel the Younger, *Massacre of the Innocents* (Fig. 3), oil on panel, 115.2 × 163.7 cm, signed '·P·BRVEGEL·' in the lower right, Sibiu, Muzeul National Brukenthal, inv. 148. On this painting, see D. Allart, C. Currie and S. Saverwyns, 'Eine Kopie, die dem Original gerecht wird: Der *Bethlehemitische Kindermord* von Pieter Brueghel d. J.', in D. Dâmboiu, G. Thewes and D. Wagener (eds), *Brueghel, Cranach, Tizian, van Eyck. Meisterwerke aus der Sammlung Brukenthal*, Berlin/ Munich, Deutscher Kunstverlag, 2012, pp. 72–87 and D. Allart, C. Currie and S. Saverwyns, 'Une copie qui fait honneur à son modèle: le Massacre des Innocents de Pierre Brueghel le Jeune (Sibiu, Muzeul National Brukenthal)', *Bulletin de l'Institut royal du Patrimoine artistique* 33, 2012, pp. 133–151.
4. We thank Jørgen Wadum for kindly sending us an image of this mark.
5. On these new regulations, see J. Van Damme, 'De Antwerpse tafereelmakers en hun merken. Identificatie en betekenis', *Jaarboek Koninklijk Museum voor Schone Kunsten Antwerpen* 1990, pp. 235–236.
6. Currie and Allart 2012 (cited in note 1), vol. 3, Appendix V.
7. Pieter Brueghel the Younger, *Massacre of the Innocents* (Fig. 4), oil on panel, 73.3 × 105.1 cm, signed 'P·BREVGHEL·' in the lower right, Antwerp, Koninklijk Museum voor Schone Kunsten, inv. 832.
8. Pieter Brueghel the Younger, *Wedding Dance in the Open Air* (Fig. 5), oil on panel, 38.5 × 51.5 cm, signed and dated 'P·BRVEGHEL·1607·' in the lower right, Brussels, Musées royaux des Beaux-Arts de Belgique/ Koninklijke Musea voor Schone Kunsten van België, inv. 8725.
9. Pieter Brueghel the Younger, *Magpie on the Gallows* (Fig. 6), oil on panel, 66 × 76.8 cm, unsigned, Paris, private collection (Georges De Jonckheere collection).
10. Pieter Brueghel the Younger, *Crucifixion*, oil on panel, 81.5/ 81.6 × 123.4 cm, signed and dated '·P·BREVGHEL·1617·' in the lower left, Budapest, Szépmüvészeti Múzeum, inv. 1038.
11. SEM-EDX and MRS on the underdrawing carried out by Steven Saverwyns at the Royal Institute for Cultural Heritage (KIK-IRPA). For details of these analyses, see Currie and Allart 2012 (cited in note 1), vol. 3, Appendix IV.
12. The overlying varnish was first removed from the zone analysed with MRS. This was to minimise interference from the varnish layer, which often exhibits a strong fluorescence and masks the Raman signal.
13. Currie and Allart 2012 (cited in note 1), vol. 2, pp. 380–445.
14. Pieter Brueghel the Younger, *Census at Bethlehem* (Fig. 7a), oil on panel, 108.5 × 160.5 cm, unsigned, Caen, Musée des Beaux-Arts, inv. 22; Pieter Brueghel the Younger, *Census at Bethlehem* (Fig. 7b), oil on panel, 115.3 × 164.5 cm, signed and dated '·1610·/·P·BRVEGHEL·' on a barrel in the centre foreground, Brussels, Musées royaux des Beaux-Arts de Belgique/ Koninklijke Musea voor Schone Kunsten van België, inv. 2903.
15. Pieter Brueghel the Younger, *Wedding Dance in the Open Air* (Fig. 9), oil on panel, 40 × 56 cm, signed and dated 'P·BRVEGHEL 1620' (dots could not be verified) in the lower left, Narbonne, Musée des Beaux-Arts, inv. 597.
16. On the *Wedding Dance* series, see Currie and Allart 2012 (cited in note 1), vol. 2, pp. 572–614.
17. Pieter Brueghel the Younger, *Wedding Dance in the Open Air* (Fig. 10a and b), oil on panel, 41 × 61.4 cm, unsigned, Brussels, private collection (Coppée-le Hodey collection); Pieter Brueghel the Younger, *Wedding Dance in the Open Air* (Fig. 10b), oil on panel, 40.1/ 40.3 × 55.5/ 55.87 cm, unsigned, Ghent, Museum voor Schone Kunsten, inv. 1914 C-J.
18. Jan Brueghel the Elder, *Wedding Dance in the Open Air* (Fig. 10c), oil on copper, 40 × 50 cm, unsigned, Bordeaux, Musée des Beaux-Arts, inv. Bx E 103.
19. On the *Wedding Dance* series, see Currie and Allart 2012 (cited in note 1), vol. 2, pp. 572–613.
20. Pieter Brueghel the Younger, *Battle between Carnival and Lent* (Fig. 11), oil on panel, 121.1/ 121.4 × 171.3/ 171.9 cm, unsigned, Brussels, Musées royaux des Beaux-Arts de Belgique/ Koninklijke Musea voor Schone Kunsten van België, inv. 12045.
21. Pieter Brueghel the Younger, *Procession to Calvary*, oil on panel, 117.0/ 117.1 × 164.1/164.3 cm, signed and dated 'P·BRVEGHEL·/·1603·' in the lower left, Antwerp, Koninklijk Museum voor Schone Kunsten, inv. 5006.
22. The two atypical copies are the following: Pieter Brueghel the Younger, *Battle between Carnival and Lent* (see Fig. 12b), oil on panel, 118.1 × 166.3 cm, unsigned, private collection, sold at Christie's London, 7 December 2010, lot 15 (former Portland collection) and Pieter Brueghel the Younger, *Battle between Carnival and Lent*, oil on panel, 117 × 165 cm, unsigned, sold at Sotheby's London, 4 July 2012, lot 11 (previously sold at Christie's New York, 31 May 1989).
23. Pieter Bruegel the Elder, *Sermon of St John the Bapist* (Fig. 12), oil on panel, 95.1/ 95.2 × 161.6/ 161.7 cm, signed and dated ·BRVEGEL·/·M·D·LXVI·' in the lower right, Budapest, Szépmüvészeti Múzeum; Pieter Brueghel the Younger, *Sermon of St John the Baptist* (Fig. 13), oil on panel; 104.5/ 104.9 × 169.3/ 169.6 cm, signed and dated 'P·BREVGHEL·/·1624·' in the lower right, Lier, Stedelijk Museum Wuyts-Van Campen en Baron Caroly, inv. 44.
24. Pieter Brueghel the Younger, *Battle between Carnival and Lent* (Fig. 14b), oil on panel, 118.1 × 166.3 cm, unsigned, private collection, sold at Christie's London, 7 December 2010, lot 15 (former Portland collection).

Authors' addresses

- Christina Currie, Head of Scientific Imagery and Photography, KIK-IRPA (Koninklijk Instituut voor het Kunstpatrimonium/ Institut royal du Patrimoine artistique/Royal Institute for Cultural Heritage), Brussels, Belgium (christina.currie@kikirpa.be)
- Dominique Allart, Professor at the University of Liège, Head of 'Transitions. Department of Research on the Late Middle Ages and Early Modern Times', ULg, Belgium (D.Allart@ulg.ac.be)

COPIES OF PROTOTYPES BY QUENTIN MASSYS FROM THE WORKSHOP OF HIS SON JAN: THE CASE OF THE *BUTTER MADONNA*

Maria Clelia Galassi

ABSTRACT The so-called *Butter Madonna* in the Gemäldegalerie, Berlin, is one of the most important paintings of Quinten Massys' late production. This paper discusses the possibility that a copy derived from this prototype could have been executed by Jan, Quinten's son and workshop collaborator. Based on the results of technical investigations (examination of the underdrawing by infrared reflectography) and stylistic analysis, it is proposed that this work should be included amongst the paintings that the young Jan produced at the beginning of his career, following his father's prototypes. Technical and stylistic comparisons with a painting securely attributed to Jan's early career before the 1540s, the *Virgin and Child* in Sint-Jacobskerk (Antwerp), which strictly follows the composition of the Brussels *Madonna*, offer further evidence for attributing the latter to Jan. Finally, this paper traces its provenance history to examine collectors' specific interest in copies by Jan Massys derived from his father's repertory.

Introduction

The workshop of Quinten Massys (1467–1530) was a productive centre where the master's legacy of subjects and models was copied, replicated and emulated over a long period of time, probably lasting many years after Quinten's death. When Quinten died at the age of 63 in 1530, his son Jan had already been active in the workshop for several years. Since Jan was born around 1509, his training would have taken place during the 1520s. Therefore, the importance of his role as Quinten's primary assistant would have increased during the last years before his father's death.

Jan became a free master immediately after Quinten's death. The presence in his workshop of an apprentice in 1536, a certain Frans Van Tuylt, and of a second apprentice, Frans de Witte, in 1543, testifies that as a young autonomous master, Jan was able to maintain the respectable position in Antwerp's artistic milieu that he had inherited from his father. This brilliant career was suddenly interrupted one night in October 1544 when, as a result of his membership of the libertine sect of the Loists, Jan was captured in a raid along with the sect's founder Eligius Pruystinnck (called Loys de Schaliedecker) and other intellectuals and artists, including his brother Cornelis and the engraver Cornelis Bos. On 10 November, Jan and Cornelis were banished in absentia from Brabant, their property confiscated and sold publicly. Only after 11 years had elapsed, in 1555, was Jan able to return to Antwerp and to resume his role as a productive painter; his success greatly increased during the 1560s.[1]

If the years of his exile are not documented at all, the years before are almost equally obscure, since we can securely date only three paintings to this period: a *Saint Jerome* (Vienna, Kunsthistorisches Museum, dated 1437), the *Tax Collector* (Dresden, Gemäldegalerie Alte Meister, dated 1539) and a *Judith with the Head of Holofernes* (Boston, Museum of Fine Arts, dated 1543).[2] Therefore, the role played by the young Jan Massys in his father's workshop, first as his assistant, and later as his successor, is still not completely understood.

Authorship and collaboration

In past publications, Luìs Reis-Santos[3] and Villy Scaff[4] have discussed the possibility that some of Quinten's paintings were executed in collaboration with Jan, or were finished by Jan, or that copies of Quentin's prototypes were produced by Jan after 1530 in order to perpetuate his father's legacy. Using

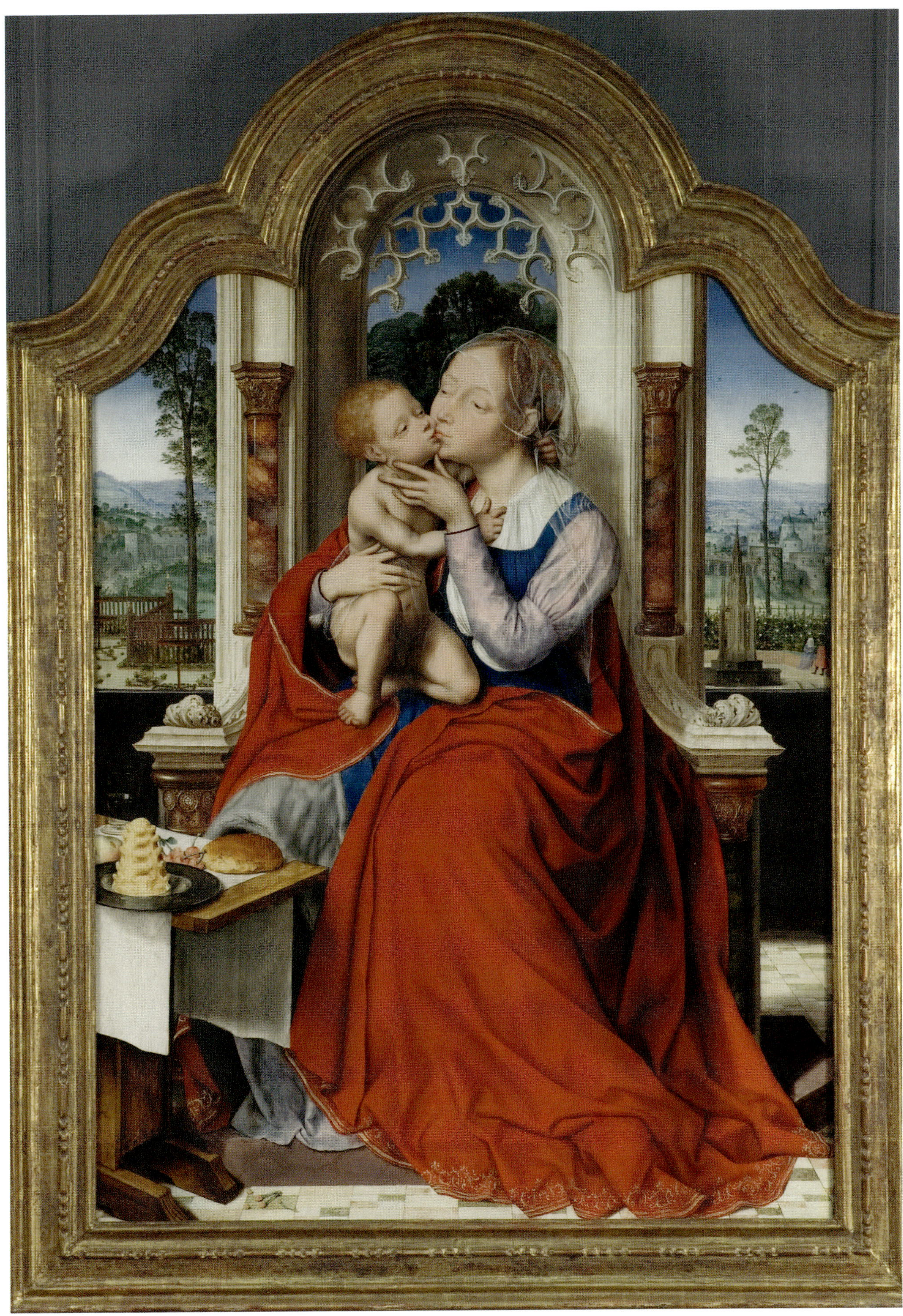

Fig. 1 Quinten Massys, *Virgin and Child* (*Butter Madonna*), oil on panel, 135 × 90 cm, Berlin, Gemäldegalerie. (© UGent, Gica&s.)

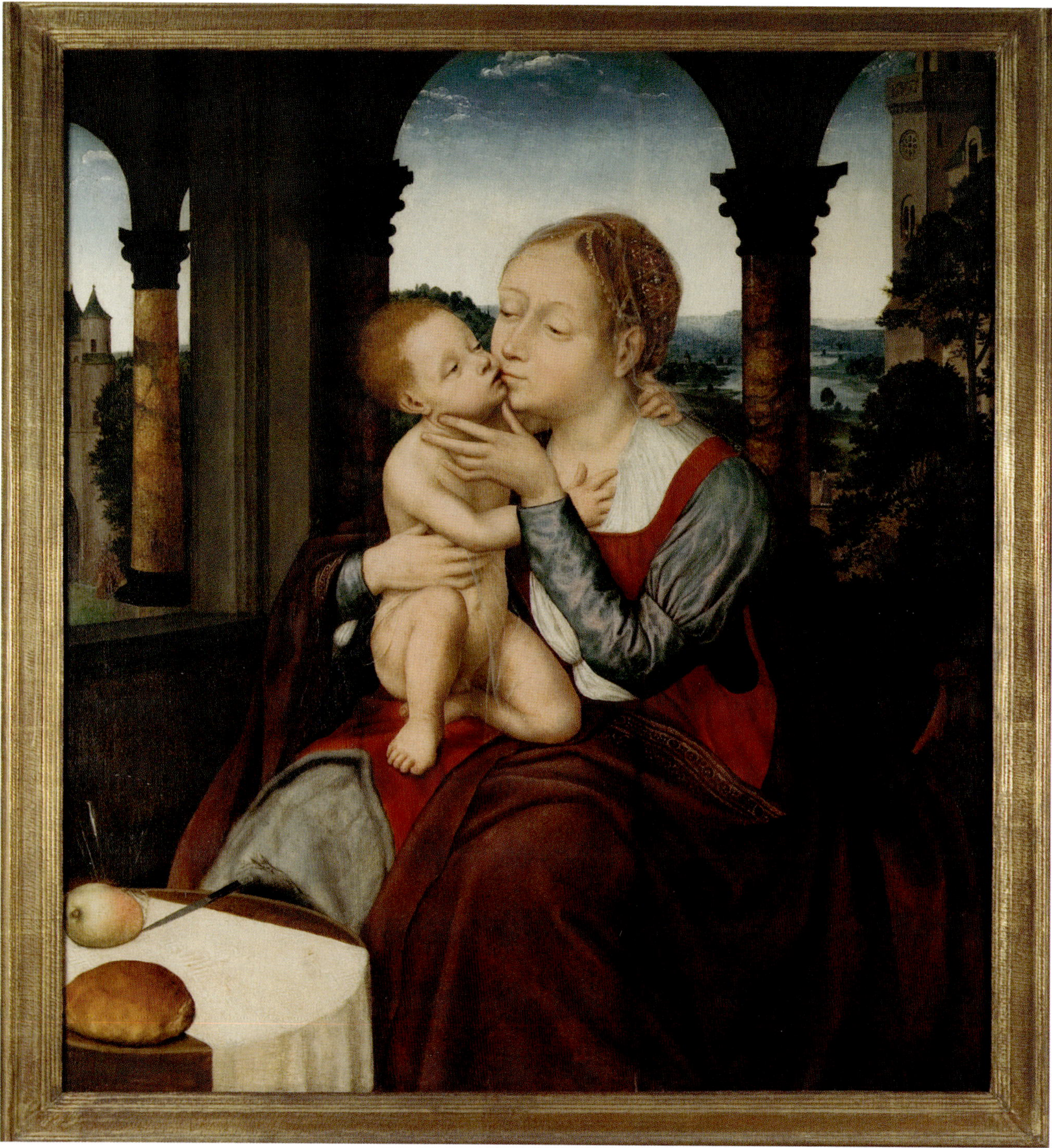

Fig. 2 Jan Massys (attr.), *Virgin and Child*, oil on panel, 84.5 × 74.5 cm, Brussels, Musées royaux des Beaux-Arts. (© UGent, Gica&s.)

methods of traditional connoisseurship, both scholars tried to distinguish Jan's authorship through the identification of stylistic elements, pinpointing formal features to characterise his style in comparison with his father's, such as a weaker way of rendering chiaroscuro, the tendency to expand the foreground of the composition in order to create a larger perspectival space and a propensity for depicting slightly anatomically impossible but very elegant figures, following the contemporary models of International Mannerism. Nevertheless, among the paintings and their several versions – often literal copies – that are currently connected to the late works of Quinten's oeuvre, it is not easy to identify those that could have been done by Jan, since it is very likely that the son, at the very beginning of his career, made a conscious effort to follow his father's production in terms of subjects and style in order to maintain the identity of the family workshop and to respond to specific requests of the market. The recent debate about the authorship of the diptych with the *Virgin at Prayer* and the *Christ as Saviour* (Madrid, Museo Nacional del Prado), most likely by Quentin with the presumed collaboration of his son, is one of the unresolved questions in this field.[5]

However, more recent technical and scientific examination can now offer new data for comparing the paintings in terms of underdrawing and painting techniques. These new perspectives for research have proved to be highly effective since, as we have discovered more about Jan's technique, we have found more clues for addressing questions of attribution. In a previous paper,[6] based on an analysis of technical data from dendrochronology and infrared reflectography (IRR), I proposed an attribution to the young Jan for a *St Jerome* (Vienna, Kunsthistorisches Museum). This painting has been described by Max Friedländer as being 'close to the master, possibly a work by Jan',[7] judged by Larry Silver to be a copy from a lost Quinten,[8] and Leontine Buijnsters-Smets, in her monograph on Jan Massys,[9] suggested it should be attributed to Quinten himself.

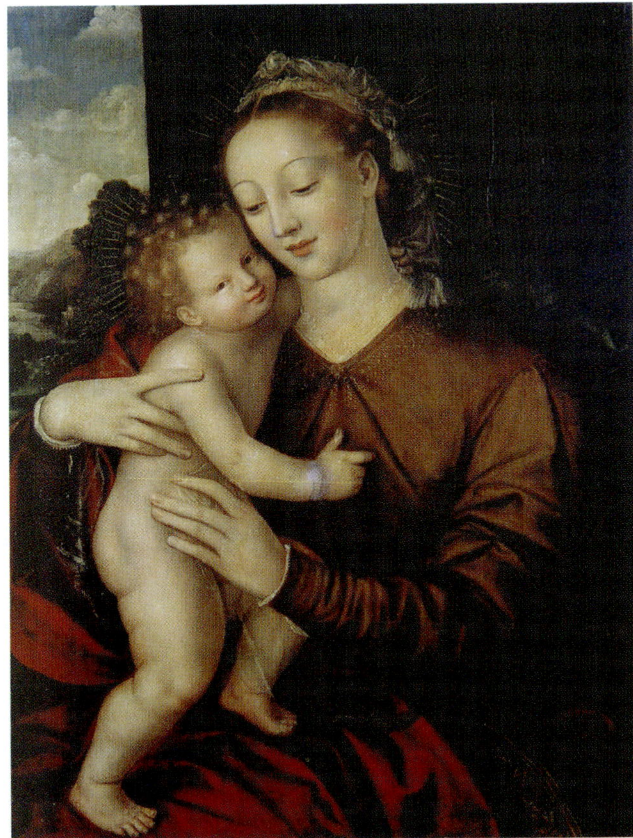

Fig. 3 Jan Massys, *Virgin and Child*, oil on panel, 78 × 60 cm, Genoa, Galleria di Palazzo Bianco, signed and dated 1552. (© Maria Clelia Galassi.)

Prototypes and the *Butter Madonna*

Quinten's late production is dominated by the subject of the *Kissing Virgin and Child*, which the artist developed following three prototypes. The first is the so-called *Madonna of the Cherries*, a painting now lost but preserved in numerous copies, the best of which is housed at the Mauritshuis, The Hague.[10] The second is the so-called *Butter Madonna* in the Gemäldegalerie, Berlin[11] (Fig. 1), which derives its title from the unusually large mound of butter on a plate in the foreground still life. In this paper, I will discuss a *Virgin and Child* in the Musées royaux des Beaux-Arts, Brussels, which is a copy of the *Butter Madonna*. The third is the so-called *Rattier Madonna*, in the Musée du Louvre, which Quinten signed and dated one year before he died, in 1529.[12]

As Larry Silver has pointed out, this iconographic type is a direct derivation from examples by Dieric Bouts, which in turn are derived from the Byzantine model of the *Cambrai Madonna* (Cambrai Cathedral). Following the American scholar, it is worth underscoring the innovations introduced by Quinten, namely, the 'intimacy between mother and Child, centred on the kiss that they exchange in a close embrace', and the introduction of an older Christ Child, no longer a mere infant, as in, for example, the Berlin *Butter Madonna*, who adds an erotic component to the scene in the way he firmly clasps the neck of his mother. Larry Silver noted in the two interlaced figures 'an echo of the amorous overtures of the *Ill-matched Pair*', a secular subject that Quinten painted at approximately the same time.[13]

The three prototypes by Quinten have a distinguished provenance that can be traced back to the early 17th century: both the *Butter Madonna* and the *Rattier Madonna* were listed in the 1639 inventory of the Coudenberg collection of the Archduke Albert and Isabella, while the *Cherries Madonna* was in the collection of Cornelis van der Geest of Antwerp in 1628. The great popularity of these subjects with collectors certainly encouraged Quinten and his workshop to produce numerous replicas. A replica of the *Rattier Madonna* that was sold by the Galerie Pardo in Paris in 1954 (present location unknown) has been attributed by Leontine Buijnsters-Smets to Jan himself.[14] Similarly, we cannot exclude that future investigations may allow us to recognise Jan's authorship among the extensive number of replicas derived from the lost *Cherries Madonna*.

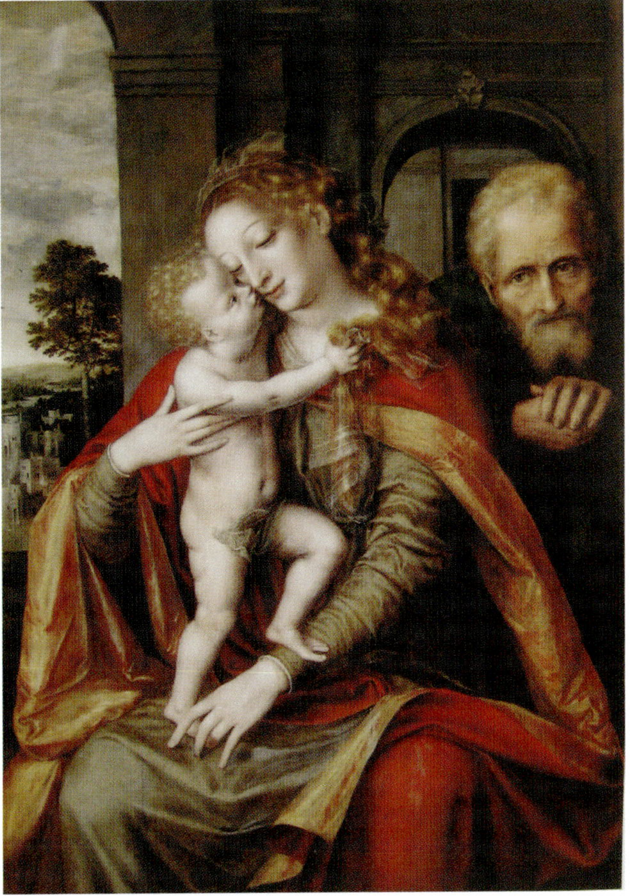

Fig. 4 Jan Massys, *Holy Family*, oil on panel, 101 × 73 cm, Antwerp, Koninklijk Museum voor Schone Kunsten, signed and dated 1563. (© Koninklijk Museum voor Schone Kunsten, Antwerp.)

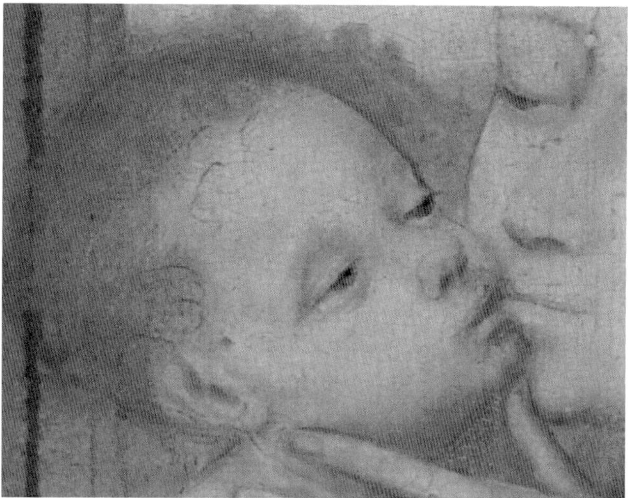

Fig. 5 Jan Massys (attr.), *Virgin and Child*, Brussels, Musées royaux des Beaux-Arts: IRR detail. (© UGent, Gica&s.)

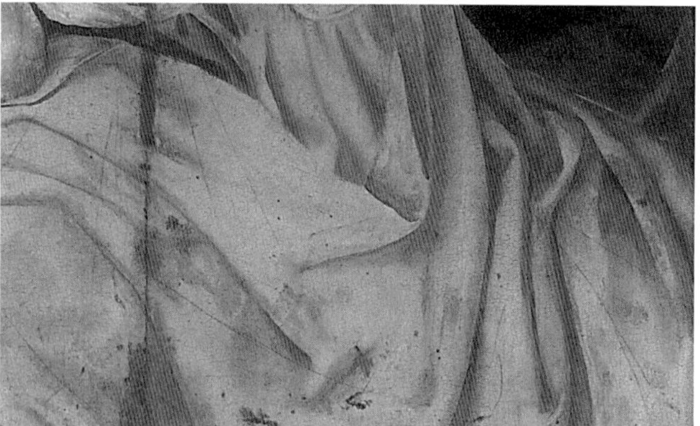

Fig. 6 Jan Massys (attr.), *Virgin and Child*, Brussels, Musées royaux des Beaux-Arts: IRR detail. (© UGent, Gica&s.)

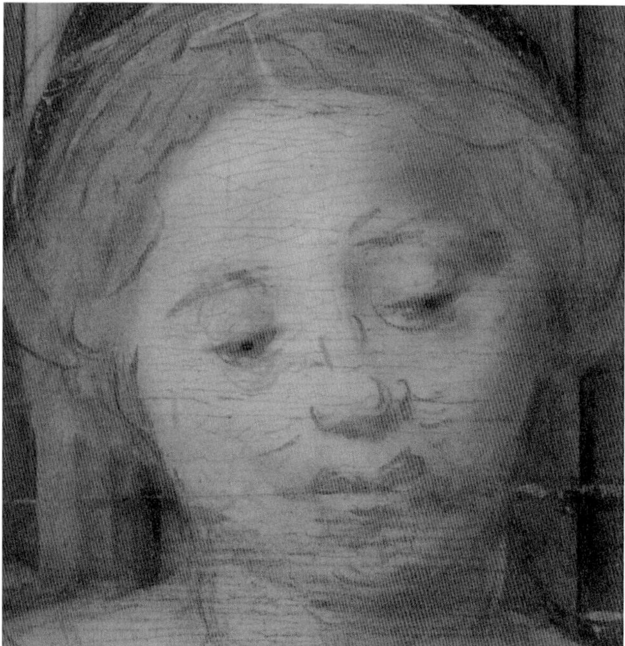

Fig. 7 Jan Massys, *The Tax Collector*, oil on panel, 85 × 115 cm, Dresden, Gemäldegalerie Alte Meister, dated 1539: IRR detail. (© Gemäldegalerie Alte Meister, Dresden.)

A *Virgin and Child* at the Musées royaux des Beaux-Arts, Brussels (Fig. 2), is clearly connected with Quinten's *Butter Madonna* in Berlin. The former was considered by Friedländer as a copy from Quinten,[15] by De Bosque as Quinten's own work,[16] and by Silver as a late variant.[17] Based on technical data and stylistic analysis, I propose that it should be included among the paintings that the young Jan produced at the beginning of his career, following one of Quinten's prototypes.

Technical investigation

The comparison of the two panels, which are of a different size and format but are quite close in the dimensions of the figures, exhibits numerous and relevant differences. First, the palette of the Brussels version is less brilliant but is enriched with new nuances in the brown and in the *changeant* colour of the Virgin's mantle and robe. The interior setting and the landscape reflect a different approach in rendering the space. The emphatic verticality of the throne, which isolates the figures by giving them a hieratic appearance, has been replaced with a new, more intimate environment that depicts the interior of a loggia, which opens beyond a line of columns onto a 'leonardesque style' landscape. It is worth noting that the horizon line of the Brussels version is much higher, thus strictly integrating the figures into the landscape of the background. These differences may indicate a later date, certainly after the Berlin version, and probably during the 1530s.

Features in the painting technique also suggest an attribution to Jan's hand. There is a new taste for a soft and sweet modelling of the flesh tones, in comparison with the more dynamic and sharper forms of the prototype as can be seen in a kind of passivity in the pose of the kissing lips that misses the animated tension in the original, and in the way the painter has placed the anatomical features such as the hands, adding one to the others, and following an intellectual – actually mannerist – method in composition. There is also a tendency to expand the drapery into the space, changing the fall of some of the folds. If the two paintings are superimposed, it is clear that they do not coincide perfectly, since the body of the Child is significantly more elongated in the Brussels version. This is consistent with Jan's tendency to change the proportion of the Child's body, which was increasingly enlarged into the space. This aspect of how he developed the theme of the *Kissing Virgin and Child* over the years can be seen in the sequence of paintings beginning with the Genoa *Virgin and Child* (Galleria di Palazzo Bianco, dated 1552) (Fig. 3) and continuing to the Antwerp *Holy Family* (Koninklijk Museum voor Schone Kunsten, dated 1563) (Fig. 4).

Analysis of the underdrawing style in the two paintings has distinguished two different hands at work, confirming the attribution of the Brussels version to Jan. Both of the Madonnas were examined with IRR by Maximiliaan Martens and Annick Born, University of Ghent, using an Osiris InGaAs camera. The Berlin prototype has an underdrawing that barely registers in the IRRs because of its thinness and its coincidence with the painted contours, as is typical of many autograph paintings by

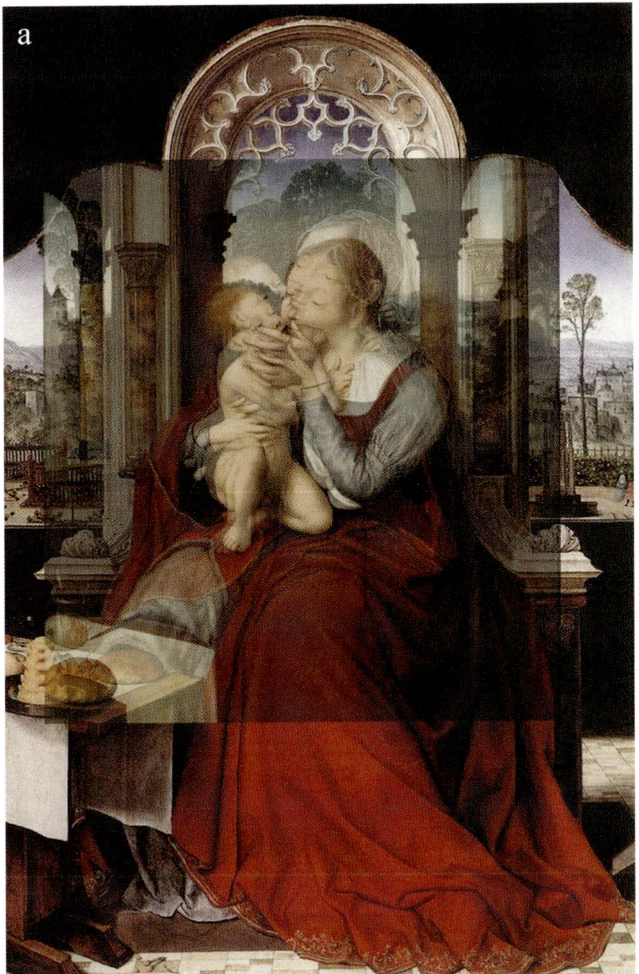

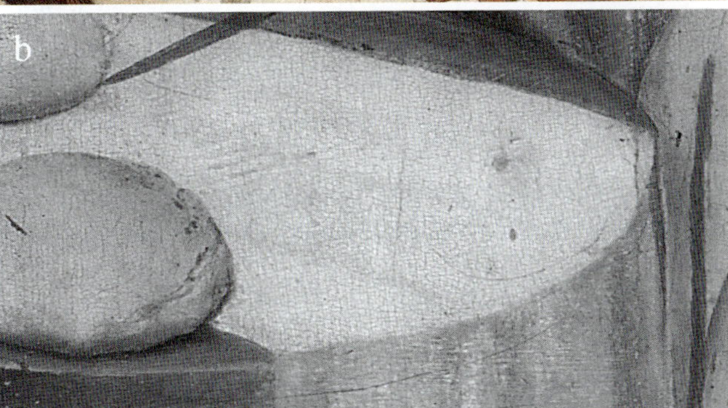

Fig. 8 (a) Superimposition of Figures 1 and 2. (b) Jan Massys (attr.), Virgin and Child, Brussels, Musées royaux des Beaux-Arts: IRR detail of bread showing the different position of the bread in the underdrawing. (© UGent, Gica&s.)

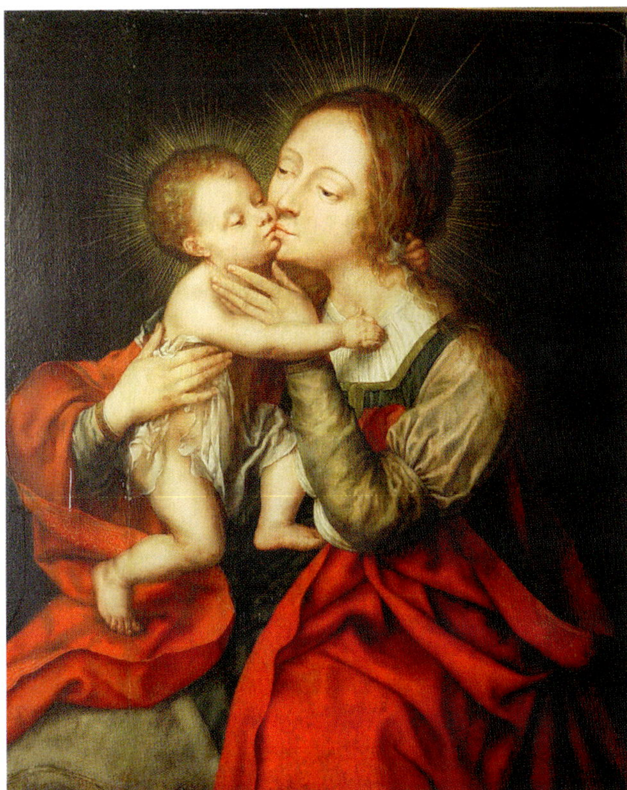

Fig. 9 Jan Massys, *Virgin and Child*, oil on panel, 65 × 53 cm, Antwerp, Sint-Jacobskerk. (© Maria Clelia Galassi.)

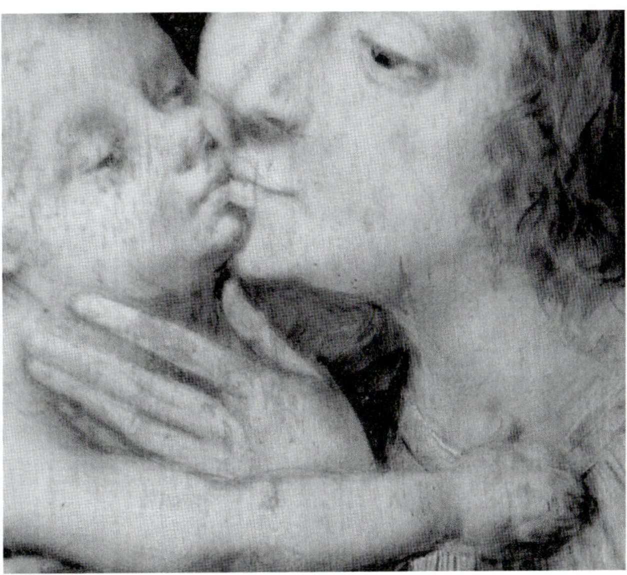

Fig. 10 Jan Massys, *Virgin and Child*, Antwerp, Sint-Jacobskerk: IRR detail. (Digital photo © Maria Clelia Galassi.)

Quinten.[18] On the other hand, the Brussels version exhibits a copious linear underdrawing, executed freehand with brush in a dark liquid medium, with many shifts in the contours of the figures (Fig. 5) and some radical changes in the folds of the Virgin's red mantle (Fig. 6). This underdrawing is consistent with that of the young Jan, in particular the 1539 *Tax Collector* (Dresden, Gemäldegalerie), which shows the same method of sketching the features of the figures with short and bold lines (Fig. 7).

Although the Brussels underdrawing exhibits the copiousness of a freehand drawing, it seems likely that the composition is based on a workshop cartoon, because the first step in underdrawing would have consisted in tracing the main outlines of the figures, which are notably bold and firm. It is interesting to note that if the two paintings are superimposed, using the children's legs as a fixed point (Fig. 8a), it can be seen that the painted bread in the foreground still life of the Berlin panel coincides with the first idea of the underdrawing of the bread in the Brussels version (Fig. 8b).

Based on these results, I suggest that the Brussels painting is one of Jan's earlier works. In his debut as a young painter, Jan showed a penchant for following the models inherited from his father, probably as requested by collectors and based on workshop cartoons, yet inescapably making some interesting changes and quickly revealing his own personality, a style not fully conceived but already making its presence known.

A painting securely attributed to Jan's early career, before the 1540s, is the *Virgin and Child* in Sint-Jacobskerk, Antwerp (Fig. 9),[19] which strictly follows the composition of the Brussels *Madonna* and thus offers further evidence for attributing the latter to Jan. The two paintings are different sizes but if they are superimposed, we see that the figures are the same size and partially overlap (the upper part of the Child and the proper left part of the Virgin). Thus, the two paintings originated from the same model cartoon, appropriately updated for the second version. In the Antwerp *Madonna* we find the same soft rendering of the flesh tones, the languid attitudes, and the tendency to flatten the volumes. The underdrawing is linear and very thin, with some shifting in the folds and the contours. Some *pentimenti* (changes in composition) were introduced during the paint stage, for example in the Child's proper right hand (Fig. 10).

If we compare the underdrawing of the red drapery in the Brussels *Madonna* (Fig. 6) with the red drapery in the Antwerp *Madonna*, we see that the first idea for arranging the folds in the Brussels version was replicated and developed in the Antwerp version, providing compelling evidence that the same artist conceived the two paintings.

Collectors

During the 1530s, who were the clients ordering and buying replicas based on the famous models of Quentin Massys? How did Jan target his audience? Some remarks about the provenance of the Brussels *Madonna* suggest that this kind of painting could have been produced, in particular, for foreign businessmen who might have requested copies made by Jan and derived from his father's repertory in order to possess an artistic memory of the celebrated Quentin's oeuvre.

Up until the end of the 19th century, the Brussels version belonged to the Genoese collection of the Pallavicini Grimaldi family; it was sold at auction in 1899.[20] Thanks to the auction catalogue, which was lavishly illustrated with photographs, we know that Alessandro Pallavicino's collection was rich in Flemish paintings, many of which were sold with an incorrect attribution. For instance, our *Madonna* was referred to as 'German School'; Rogier van der Weyden's *Deposition*, also now in the Musées royaux des Beaux-Art, Brussels, was sold with an attribution to Gossaert;[21] and a female portrait by Antonious Mor, now at the Art Institute of Chicago, was sold as 'Venetian School'.[22] With the information currently available, we do not know how or when Alessandro Pallavicino's great collection was amassed, but most likely it was gathered *ab antiquo*. Alessandro belonged to an important aristocratic family with close connections to the Netherlands in the 16th century. He was a direct descendant of Tobia Pallavincino, a banker and trader of alum in northern Europe, as well as a patron of the arts. Tobia himself is not recorded in Antwerp, but two of his brothers are recorded in Flanders. His older brother, Damiano, was the consul of the Nazione Genovese in Bruges in 1517[23] and he was still living in Antwerp in 1522.[24] A second brother, Agostino, was active in the Antwerp market as a trader of alum. Agostino's brother-in-law was Ambrogio Di Negro, most certainly a patron of Jan Massys, having commissioned from him the *Venus in the Garden with the View of Genoa*, now at the Nationalmuseum, Stockholm.[25]

Therefore, it seems very likely that the Brussels *Madonna* was commissioned by one of the members of the Pallavicino family. It also seems probable that there was a high demand for copies based on famous prototypes by Quinten, particularly from the communities of foreign businessmen working in Antwerp. These purchases, examples of the production of 'Maestro Quintino', the painter who enjoyed the reputation of being the greatest Flemish painter of his time, would have been brought back to the collectors' native countries. And finally, Jan, his son and follower, must have been equally regarded in order for Jan to perpetuate his father's legacy.

Conclusions

Understanding that the Brussels *Madonna* can probably be attributed to Jan Massys allows us to better comprehend the role and the activity of the young Jan at the beginning of his career, before and immediately after the death of his father. The possibility that copies of Quentin Massys' prototypes could have been produced by Jan in order to continue his father's legacy seems to be convincing, and in the future may be further verified through the examination of other copies, using not only traditional connoisseurship methods but also technical examination. In fact, the more we know of Jan's painting technique, the more it seems evident that he differs significantly from his father in both his use of underdrawing and colour handling. Also, particular attention should be paid to the copies that were present *ab antiquo* in Italian collections in order to verify the extent to which the production of copies by Jan was specifically addressed by foreign clients.

Acknowledgements

I am very grateful to the Flemish Academic Centre for the Science and the Arts (VLAC) for funding this research. For allowing me to investigate the paintings mentioned in this article, I would like to thank Véronique Bücken, Musées royaux des Beaux-Arts, Brussels; Stephen Kemperdink, Gemäldegalerie, Berlin; Uta Neidhardt; Gemäldegalerie, Dresden; Guy Wyffels, Sint-Jacobskerck, Antwerp. I am also grateful for the help of Annick Born, University of Ghent; Michel Ceuterick, Asper; Marc De Mey, Flemish Academic Centre for the Science and the Arts; and Sven Van Dorst, Antwerp. Special thanks to Max Martens, University of Ghent, for discussions on the topics of this paper and for allowing me to study the infrared reflectographs of the *Butter Madonna* of the Gemäldegalerie, Berlin, and the *Virgin and Child* of the Musées royaux des Beaux-Arts, Brussels. Last but not least, thank to Elizabeth Walmsley, National Gallery of Art, Washington, for reading the earlier version of this text.

Notes

1. L. Buijnsters-Smets, *Jan Massys een Antwerps schilder uit de zestiende eeuw*, Zwolle, Waanders Uitgevers, 1995, pp. 13–23.
2. Ibid.
3. L. Reis-Santos, 'Jan Quinten Massys discípulo e colaborador de seu pai Mestre Quinten Metsys', *Belasartes* 20, 1964, pp. 3–12.
4. V. Scarff, 'Joannes Quintini Massiis Pingebat', in *Mélanges d'Archéologie et d'Histoire de l'Art offerts au Professeur Jacques Lavalleye*, Louvain, Pubblications Universitaires, pp. 257–280.
5. J.O. Hand, C.A. Metzger and R. Spronk (eds), *Prayers and Portraits: Unfolding the Netherlandish Diptych*, exh. cat., New Haven/London, Yale University Press, 2006, pp. 104–105.
6. M.C. Galassi,'Application of dendrochronology and infrared reflectography for the study of Jan Massys' oeuvre', in H. Verougstraete and C. Janssens de Bisthoven (eds), *The Quest of the Original*, Leuven/Paris/Walpole, MA, Uitgeverij Peeters, 2009, pp. 55–63.
7. M.J. Friedländer, *Early Netherlandish Painting*, vol. 7, Leiden, A.W. Sijthoff/ Brussels, La Connaissance, 1971, p. 67, no. 70.
8. L. Silver, *The Painting of Quinten Massys with Catalogue Raisonné*, Oxford, Phaidon, 1984, pp. 218–219.
9. Buijnsters-Smets 1995 (cited in note 1), pp. 34–35
10. Silver 1984 (cited in note 8), pp. 230–231.
11. Ibid., pp. 224–225.
12. Ibid., pp. 229–230.
13. Ibid., pp. 78–79.
14. Buijnsters-Smets 1995 (cited in note 1), p. 158.
15. Friedländer 1971 (cited in note 7), p. 62, no. 18a.
16. A. De Bosque, *Quentin Metsys*, Brussels, Arcade, 1975, pp. 216–218.
17. Silver 1984 (cited in note 8), p. 224.
18. J. Dunkerton, 'The technique and restoration of the *Virgin and Child Enthroned, with four Angels* by Quinten Massys', *National Gallery Technical Bulletin* 29, 2008, pp. 60–75; A. Born and M.P. Martens, 'O políptico de Quinten Metsys para o convent da Madre de Deus: notas sobre a técnica' ('A poliptych by Quinten Metsys for the Convent of Madre de Deus: notes on technique') in A. Curvelo (ed.), *Casa Perfeitíssima: 500 anos da fundação do Mosteiro da Madre de Deus* (*Celebrating 500 Years of the Foundation of the Convent of Madre de Deus, 1509–2009*), Lisbon, Museu nacional do Azulejo, Ministério da Cultura, Instituto dos Museus e da Conservação, 2009, pp. 155–165, 373–377.
19. Buijnsters-Smets 1995 (cited in note 1), pp. 156–157.
20. *Catalogue de la vente de feu Monsieur Marquis Alexandre Pallavicino Des Ducs Grimaldi*, Rome, Galleria Sangiorgi, 1899, no. 293.
21. Ibid., no. 197.
22. Ibid., no. 276.
23. V. Vitale, 'Diplomatici e consoli della Repubblica di Genova', *Atti della Società Ligure di Storia Patria* LXIII, 1934, p. 302.
24. C. De Simoni and L.T. Belgrano, 'Documenti ed estratti enediti o poco noti riguardanti la storia del commercio e della marina ligure, Brabante, Fiandra, Borgogna', *Atti della Società Ligure di Storia Patria* V(1), 1867, p. 471.
25. M.C. Galassi, 'Jan Massys and artistic relationships between Antwerp and Genoa during the XVI century', in M. Faries (ed.), *Making and Marketing: Studies of the Painting Process in Fifteenth and Sixteenth-Century Netherlandish Workshops*, Turnhout, Brepols, 2006, pp. 179–200.

Author's address

Maria Clelia Galassi, Università degli Studi di Genova, Genova, Italy (mcgalassi@lettere.unige.it)

AN UNPUBLISHED COPY OF HIERONYMUS BOSCH'S *TEMPTATION OF SAINT ANTHONY*

Catheline Périer-D'Ieteren

ABSTRACT This paper focuses on an unknown version of the *Temptation of Saint Anthony* dated around 1567, which is part of a private collection and attributed to a follower of Hieronymus Bosch. The composition presents, on a single panel, that of the *Triptych of the Temptations of Saint Anthony*, one of the main autograph paintings of the master that belong to the Museu Nacional de Arte Antiga in Lisbon. Following analysis of the style and the painting technique, the phenomenon of copying the original triptych is discussed. Finally, the link is made between the known variants of this work, the theme of which was very popular.

Introduction

An as-yet unpublished late copy of the Lisbon *Temptation of Saint Anthony* (Fig. 1) belongs to a private collection in Brussels.[1] The work, dated by dendrochronology to around 1567,[2] unites in a single composition the iconographical theme and motifs that Bosch arranged over three panels in his autograph Lisbon triptych (Fig. 2).[3]

Scenes representing the torments suffered by Saint Anthony in the Egyptian desert unfold before the viewer's eyes within the blue-grey tones of the landscape, punctuated by the red accents of the fabrics.[4] In a tiny chapel within the ruined fortress that the saint has made his home, the figure of Christ gestures toward the redeeming Crucifix. The hermit kneels on the wide esplanade below, making the sign of benediction. He is surrounded by all manner of demons, which embody his fantasies and symbolise human vices. He is watched by a crippled magician, dressed in red and leaning against a wall. His amputated foot is displayed in front of him on a white cloth to attract alms. The demonic creatures that proliferate across the space and the sky above it are rooted in alchemical symbolism, mystical writings and heretical doctrines. The air, the fire that has set the sky ablaze, and the water covering the earth evoke the painting's cosmic dimension.

The left part of the panel shows the world at the mercy of demons of the kind described in the Life of Athanasius. Saint Anthony appears in the sky (Fig. 1), borne up to the heavens by devils, which torment him before dropping him back to earth. Back on the ground, he is supported by his companions, who help him limp home. In the lower corner, a bird perched on its egg swallows its own chick whole. The composition on the right shows Saint Anthony in contemplation, turning his face from the carnal pleasures offered to him: a naked woman hiding in a hollow tree and figures feasting at a table laid by demons. In the left foreground, strange figures emerge from a burst-open fruit shaped like a strawberry, while in the centre weird fishermen cast their nets from the backs of aquatic monsters.

We believe that, given the unusual and unpublished character of the Brussels composition, a close examination could add something to the 'group of *Temptations of Saint Anthony* after Bosch' and lead to conclusions that might be of use in subsequent comparisons.

The *Temptation of Saint Anthony* copy

The theme of the *Temptation of Saint Anthony* tormented by visions, treated by Bosch in his Lisbon triptych of 1503–4, inspired a series of copies from the 1520s to the latter part of the 16th century.[5] Frequently described as a 'painter of the demonic', Bosch is viewed as the inventor of this genre. The only surviving complete and full-sized copy of the Lisbon triptych is that in the Musées royaux des Beaux-Arts in Brussels (Fig. 3).[6] It was executed around 1514 – most likely in the master's own workshop – and is signed 'Hieronymus Bosch' in the lower left corner. The other versions are partial copies by Bosch's

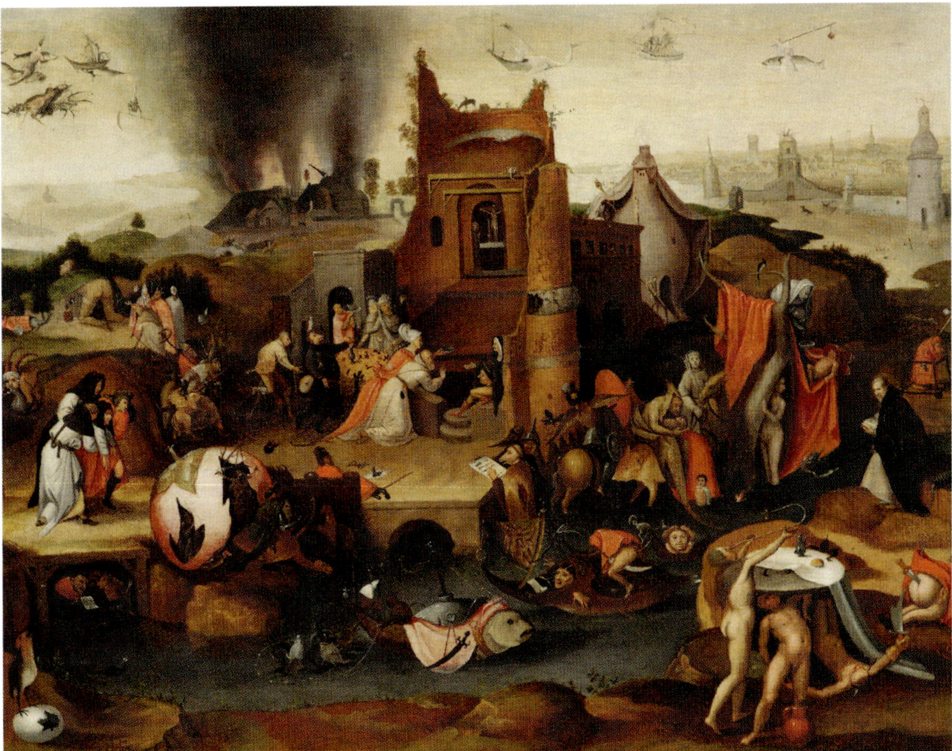

Fig. 1 *Temptation of Saint Anthony*, *c.*1567, oil on oak panel, 58 × 66.3 cm, Brussels, private collection. (© KIK-IRPA.)

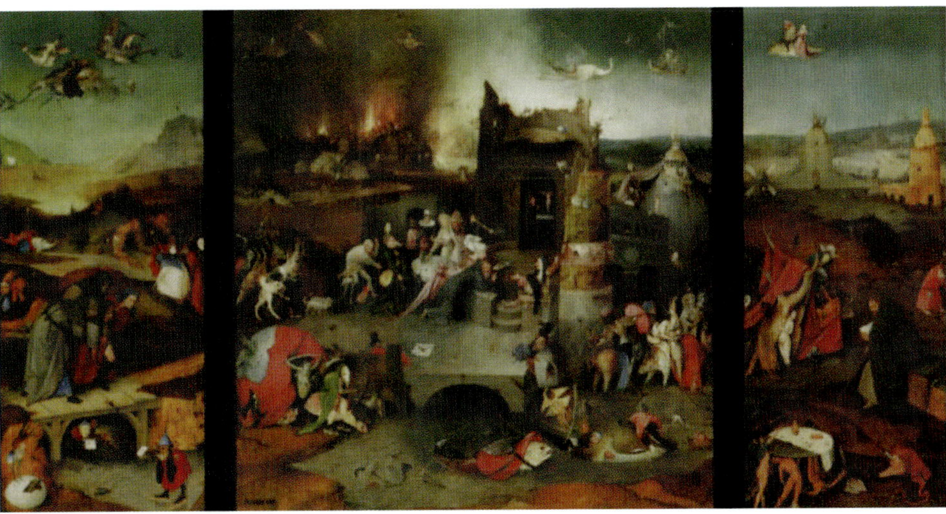

Fig. 2 Hieronymus Bosch, *Triptych of the Temptation of Saint Anthony* ,oil on oak panel, 131.5 × 119–53 cm, 1503–4, Lisbon, Museu Nacional de Arte Antiga. (© KIK-IRPA.)

workshop or his followers, which scale down and rework the central panel or individual scenes from the prototype.[7]

The painting (Fig. 1) in which we are interested offers yet a different formula, and one that is unique among the other known variations. It embraces the original composition in its entirety, but places it within a single panel. The work is signed in the same place as the Lisbon triptych and its copy in Brussels.

Bosch's paintings, which were much admired by the nobility for their intellectual and secular content, and in some cases their humour, enjoyed immense commercial success among the merchants of Antwerp.[8] The period following the artist's death in 1516 thus saw a steady flow onto the market of his most popular compositions, especially those featuring the *Temptation of Saint Anthony* (Figs 4 and 5), to satisfy the urban elite's desire to imitate princely tastes. The commercial success of the theme – copies of the Lisbon triptych in particular – peaked between 1550 and 1570.[9] The fashion for demonic imagery (*diableries*) then faded, though without entirely disappearing, as witnessed by the Dijon *Temptation* (Fig. 6), which was probably painted in the early 17th century. The iconography of the *Temptation* is intimately linked with the cult of Saint Anthony and the Antonine order reflecting an idea that haunted late medieval society, namely that of Satan's power over the world and the soul's struggle not to succumb.[10] The viewer therefore empathises with Saint Anthony as he is forced to choose between the devil and Christ.

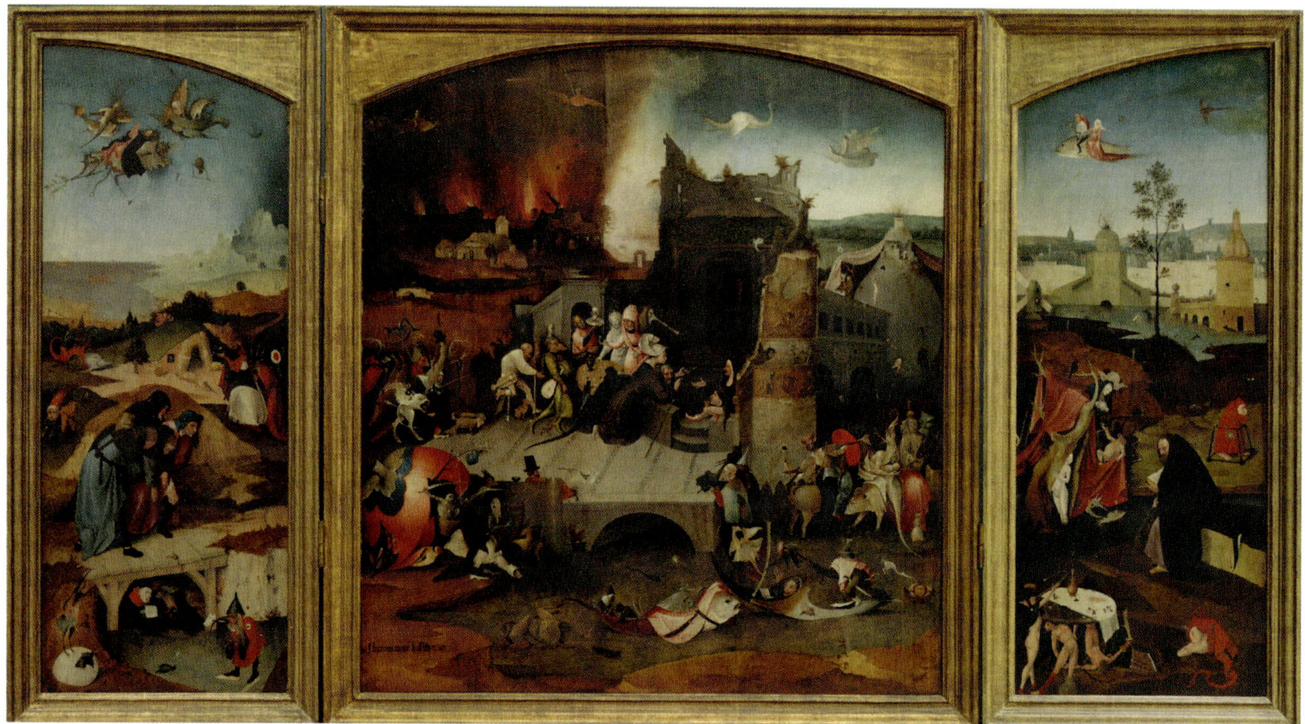

Fig. 3 *Triptych of the Temptation of Saint Anthony*, oil on oak panel,133.5 × 119.5 cm after Hieronymus Bosch, Brussels, Musée royaux des Beaux-Arts. (© MRBAB–KMSKB.)

The lack of archival evidence and documented copies renders futile any attempt to identify a particular hand among the many copies of the *Temptation of Saint Anthony*. We can, however, seek, as Frédéric Elsig suggested,[11] to group the paintings with shared stylistic and technical features into three categories: autograph works; workshop pieces, painted by artists trained by the master himself; and works done by followers.

The Brussels *Temptation of Saint Anthony* belongs to the latter, rather vague category of followers, consisting of masters – based mostly in Antwerp – who responded to art market demand by pastiching Bosch's iconography and even his style. The painting, which is almost half the size of the Lisbon triptych's central panel, is not an exact copy of the original, but is very close to it. It differs only in the limited addition and (more frequent) exclusion of certain figures and motifs. The most noteworthy omissions (Figs 1 and 2) are perhaps the bird which, in the original, approaches the little bridge brandishing in its beak a letter thought to be an indulgence, the two dogs in armour next to the crippled musicians and the panther under the table on the right wing. A technical investigation may add more insights into the genesis of this particular copy.

Technical investigation

The support

The panel (Fig. 7) on which the *Temptation of Saint Anthony* is painted consists of three boards of slow-growing oak from the Baltic region, radially cut and laid horizontally. Examination confirms that it was painted in an Antwerp workshop because the proportions and measurements used are customary for the panel-makers of that city in the 16th century.[12] The two sides are irregular and have been recut along the edge of the painted surface, the *barbe*. This is confirmed on the back by the original bevels still present on the sides. The panel therefore would originally have had four unpainted edges and might have been reduced in size by a few millimetres down the sides. This would not really have changed its original format, but would have allowed the panel to be placed in a new frame. The unpainted borders at the top and bottom of the panel as it exists today have been coated to a width of about 1 cm with a preparation containing lead white. The coating, displaying a network of fine cracks, is clearly visible in the X-radiograph (Fig. 8). The borders were then painted in a slightly lighter tone. The very smooth back of the panel was planed after the three horizontal boards were joined. The butt-jointed boards were glued together and reinforced by four tenons. Jean-Albert Glatigny, panel painting conservator in Brussels, noted during work on the panel the presence of an unusual feature in the way the panel is constructed. This is worth mentioning as it might also feature in other versions of the *Temptation of Saint Anthony* belonging to the group of copies painted in the 1560s. The positioning of the joints reveals that the widths of the three main boards differ significantly. The uppermost element is 11.5 cm wide, the middle one 22 cm and the lower board 19.5 cm. The latter, originally 16 cm wide but too thin, has been reinforced with two smaller oblique planks (8.5 cm and 11 cm) that stiffen and extend it to the lower edge of the panel. This unusual construction preceded the assembly of the panel. It suggests a possible shortage of oak at the time due to the wars being fought in the Baltic, obliging the workshop to recycle wood left over from the quartering.

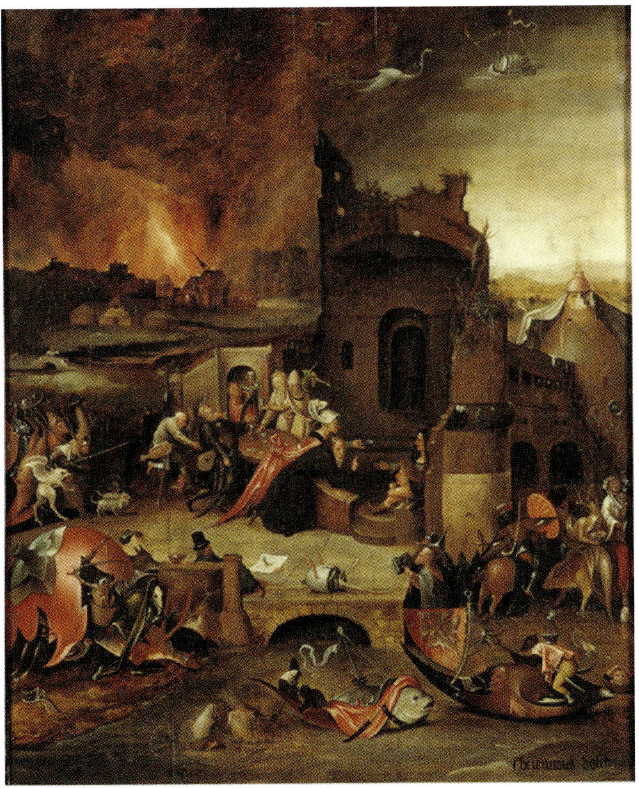

Fig. 4 *Temptation of Saint Anthony*, oil on oak panel, 88 × 71 cm, Antwerp, Koninklijk Museum voor Schone Kunsten. (© KMSK Antwerp.)

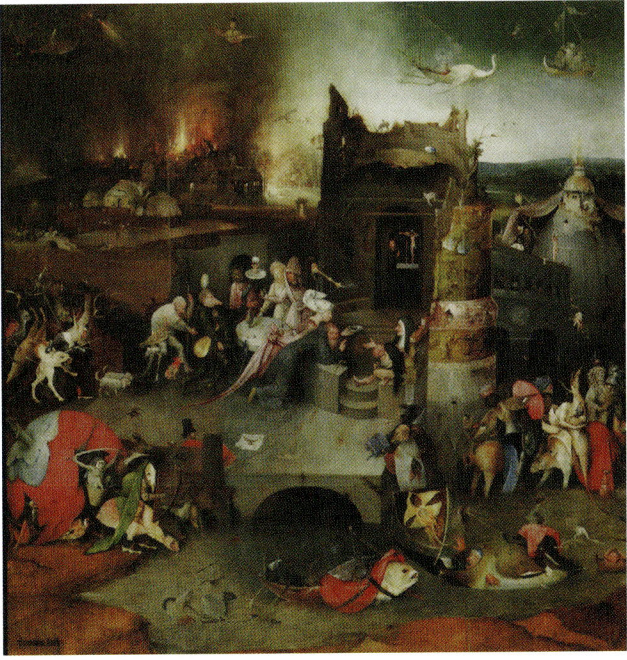

Fig. 5 *Triptych of the Temptation of Saint Anthony*, oil on oak panel, 50 × 39.5 cm, Rotterdam, Museum Boijmans Van Beuningen. (© Museum Boijmans Van Beuningen.)

Overpainting and the state of conservation

The picture as a whole features numerous areas of overpaint and retouching in the faces and clothing (Fig. 9), the naked bodies, the ruined tower, the sky, the ground and especially the water in the foreground. All these interventions, which have aged well, predate 1965 – the year in which the work was purchased. They are appropriately integrated in the composition with no significant adverse visual impact. The original chromatic effect, however, which would have been closer to that of the more vivid Lisbon triptych, has been substantially diminished by the generalised oxidation of the varnish. There ought to be a much greater contrast, for instance, between the colours of the sky, the fire and the castle.

The much abraded pictorial surface certainly justified the restorations. In the sky, for example, the fawn-coloured *imprimatura* is clearly visible between the retouchings on the thin layer of remaining original paint. Also noteworthy are the remains (Fig. 10) of a curious and extremely worn inscription on the front of the fortified city, of which only an 'A' can be made out.

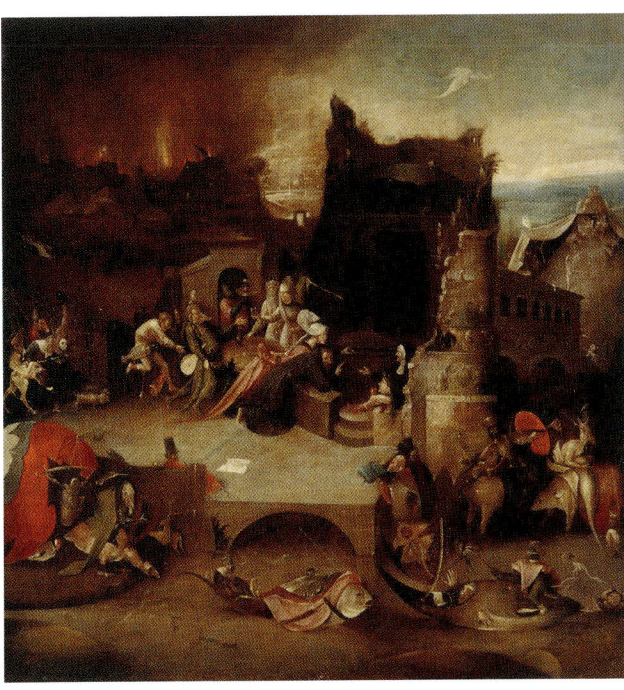

Fig. 6 *Temptation of Saint Anthony*, oil on canvas, late 16th/early 17th century, panel, 117.5 × 110.3 cm, Dijon, Musée des Beaux-Arts. (© Musée des Beaux-Arts de Dijon.)

Underdrawing

The scientific examination of the painting did not, unfortunately, produce any important data. Infrared reflectography (IRR) revealed little in the way of underdrawing. Although the artist has produced a faithful copy of the Lisbon *Temptation*, he did not resort to pouncing. That technique was used, however, in the closely related version in the Bonnefantenmuseum in Maastricht.[13] In the Bonnefantenmuseum copy, pouncing was employed to transfer the central group including the saint and the offertory of the holy vinegar. The Rotterdam version, meanwhile, shows no trace of underdrawing, as may be expected in the context of a copy.

The underdrawing of the Brussels painting was done freehand by brush and is rudimentary and lacking in assurance. It

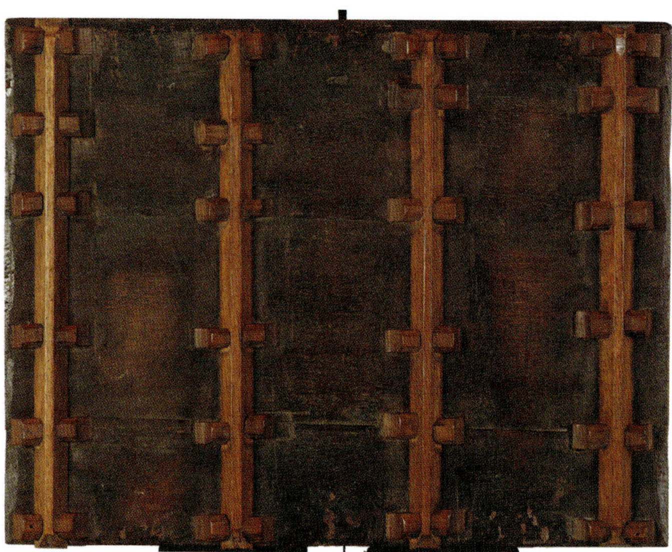

Fig. 7 *Temptation of Saint Anthony* (Fig. 1): reverse. (© KIK–IRPA.)

Fig. 8 *Temptation of Saint Anthony* (Fig. 1): X-radiograph. (© KIK–IRPA.)

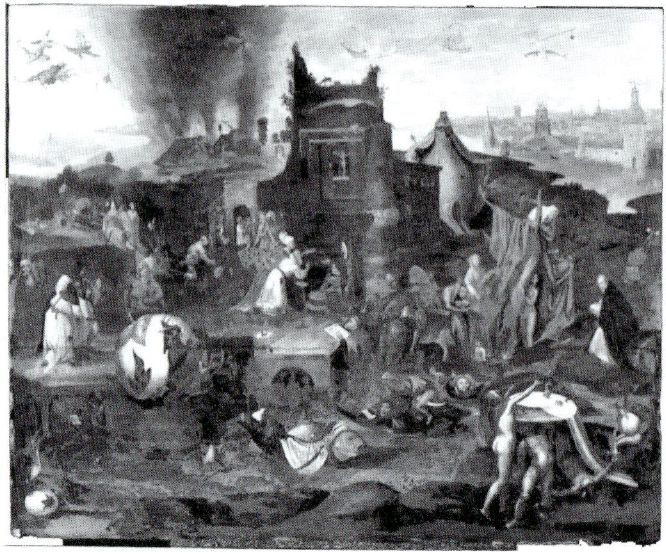

Fig. 9 *Temptation of Saint Anthony* (Fig. 1): ultraviolet photograph. (© KIK–IRPA.)

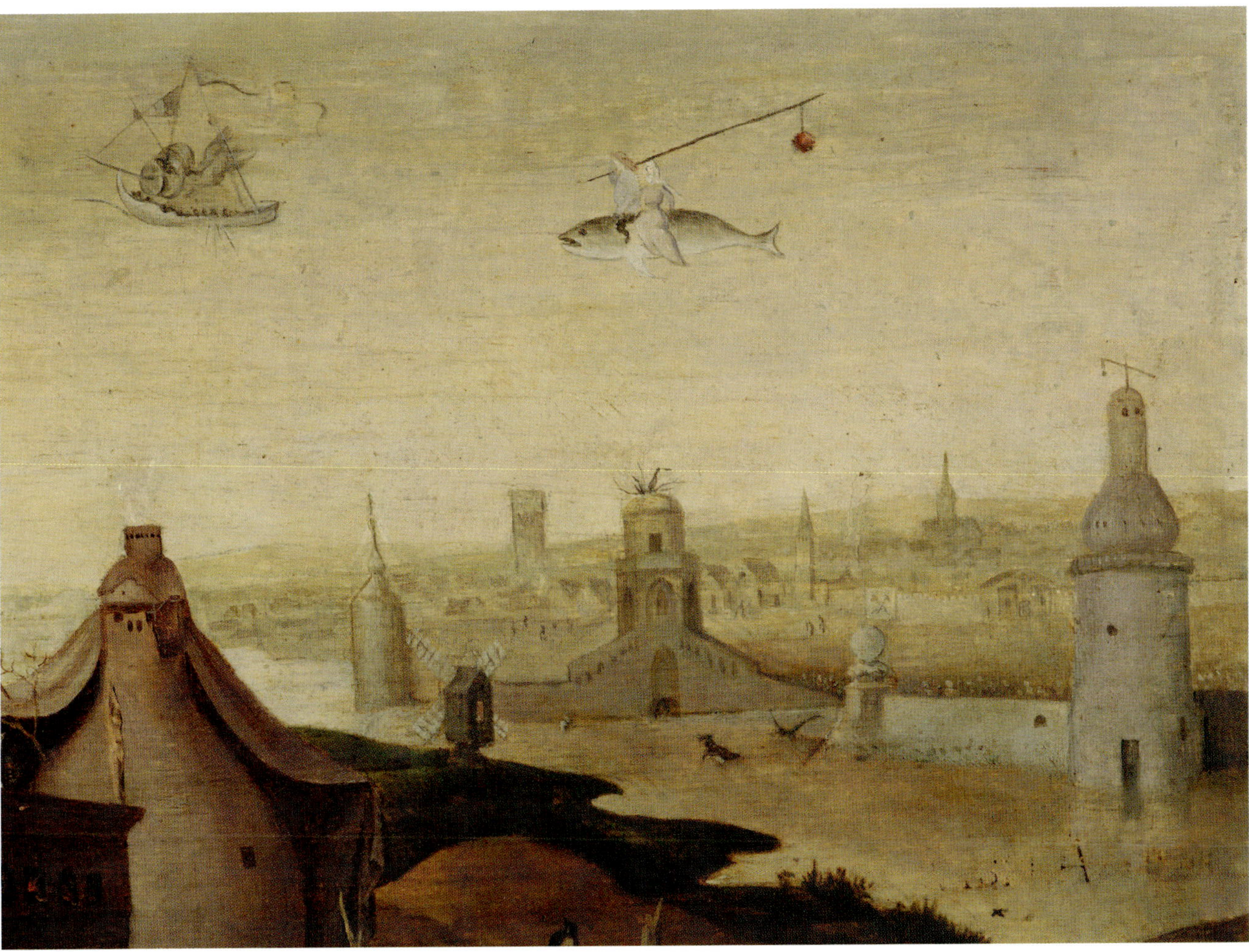

Fig. 10 *Temptation of Saint Anthony* (Fig. 1): detail of the inscription. (© KIK–IRPA.)

sets down certain volumes in rapid strokes, including that of the trees and hills in the landscape on the left. It also marks out shapes (Fig. 11) such as the little figure dressed in red below the fortified city. The drawing outlines several motifs such as those of the tower, the legs, and some folds in the clothes, most of which were shifted slightly during painting. There is no hatching of the shadow parts and hence no preparation for the modelling.

Examination of the X-radiograph (Fig. 8) shows that the majority of the alterations were superficial. The only deep and extensive lacuna is located on the wall of the fortress opposite the kneeling saint.

The panel appears to have been levelled in the upper left corner with a lead white-based filler before the ground layer was applied, which would explain the clearly visible light coloured patches in this area.[14] Use of an *imprimatura* can be detected throughout, giving the X-radiograph a uniform appearance. Most of the painted scenes are not very legible because of the thinness of the paint layer. Only a few motifs and figures display cursory highlights in relief to structure the forms or delineate a face. In the centre of the composition, space was reserved in the ground layer for the fortress and its outbuildings. The deer and the foliage at the top of the tower are painted over the sky, as are the zoomorphic vessels in grisaille that fly across it.

There was no trace of any underlying painted composition to suggest reuse of the panel, as we find with other copies after Bosch, including the Maastricht *Temptation* and that in Indianapolis.[15]

Style and painting technique of the Brussels version

The artist creates a sense of unity in the composition (Fig. 1) despite the mass of figures, fantastic creatures and the separate scenes of which it is comprised. There is a clear simplification in the details compared to the prototype, and this is seen in the faces, the architectural elements, the devastating fire that topples the church tower and in the treatment of the hybrid groups criss-crossing the sky. The figures are deftly integrated within the clear spatial arrangement of each scene. The fortress, by contrast, is awkwardly rendered.

One can clearly observe a lead white-based *imprimatura* (Figs 8–12) on the ground layer. This is applied in large brushstrokes and extends over the entire picture plane and across all the elements of the composition. Although the copyist borrowed this procedure from Bosch, who used it to brilliant effect, most of the colours laid on top of it lack the subtle modulation of the original, as the painter did not create

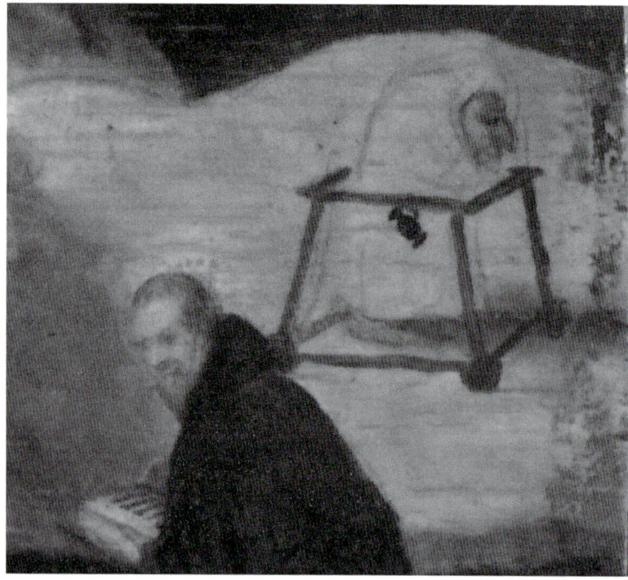

Fig. 11 *Temptation of Saint Anthony* (Fig. 1): detail of IRR. (© KIK–IRPA.)

Fig. 12 *Temptation of Saint Anthony* (Fig. 1): detail of X-radiograph of the fish. (© KIK–IRPA.)

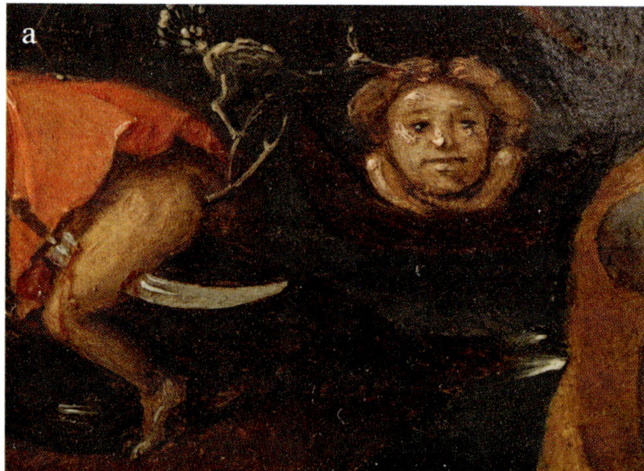

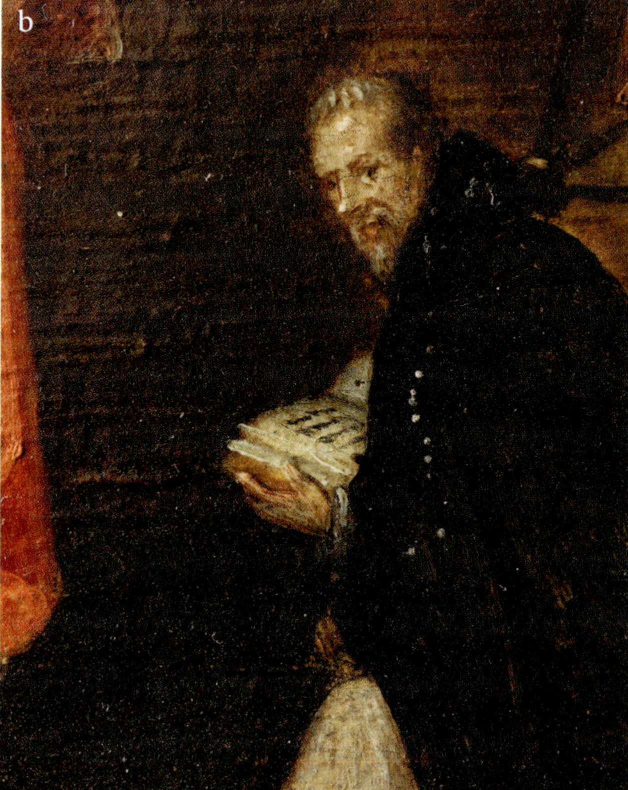

Fig. 13 *Temptation of Saint Anthony* (Fig. 1): details of the faces of (a) a male figure and (b) Saint Anthony.

varied lighting effects on the forms, the texture of the earth, the fabrics or the metal surfaces. The painting must have been executed extremely quickly. The handling of paint is thin and smooth, with only a few thicker strokes to structure a face or add highlights to clothing or objects. The head of the male figure with the curly hair (Fig. 13a), the feathers of the bird touching that hair with its beak, and the highlights on the sword of the man astride the fish are good examples. The face and hand (Fig. 13b) of Saint Anthony at prayer on the right of the composition are treated the same way. The other faces are merely sketched and have lost the individualised expressions that are so typical of Bosch's work.

The pictorial execution generally lacks sharpness, as can be seen in the contours of the fortress and its outbuildings, and in the scenes painted on the tower. The fish, by contrast, are rendered with great care. The lightness of the colours – particularly the white robes of the kneeling saint – contrast with the denser areas of white found on the giant fruit and the red fabric draped over the fish. The city, its defensive walls, the water in the upper right corner and the aerial scenes are painted in a blue-grey monochrome applied in fine transparent layers. Certain details are barely sketched, such as the form of the tiny figure perched on the back of the stork, the volume of which derives from a few sparse brushstrokes of white in slight relief.

Conclusions

We will conclude by returning to the comparison of the Brussels panel with the other versions cited above to recapitulate the key observations and to stimulate further reflection. Most of the versions deriving from the Lisbon prototype, including those from Antwerp, Rotterdam and Dijon used here for comparison (Figs 4–6), are copies of the triptych's central panel only.[16] The figure groups and the way they are distributed within the composition are virtually identical – only their scale varies according to the size of the work in question. Minor variations can be seen in the details, in the choice of colours (which, except in the Rotterdam version, are generally less vivid than the prototype) and in their modulation.

The landscape as well as the importance given to the burning buildings and the handling of the fiery lighting effects on the surroundings are the elements that change most frequently. In the Rotterdam variant, the fire's glowing intensity obliterates the details of the buildings which, in contrast, appear plunged into darkness. The adjacent landscape, on the other hand, is bathed in a yellow halo which gives it its depth. This effect is repeated in Dijon, where a stretch of yellow breaking through by the tower can be noticed. These fiery lighting effects are especially intense in the Antwerp version where the turbulent effect created by the artist's dynamic brushstrokes has an almost baroque feel.

The painting technique of most of these copies is considerably less polished than Bosch's. The handling is hurried and the faces are mostly just sketched. The hybrid vessels in the sky are not necessarily all included, apart from that shaped like a stork, which is always present. All these features appear in versions from the 1530s, including the Rotterdam version (*c.*1539) as well as those from the 1560s and 1570s, like the Brussels panel, and even in copies executed later still, such as that in Dijon (early 17th century). Comparative examination of the different versions did not allow a common hand to be identified, merely varying degrees of similarity in spirit or facture.

All the copies examined display their own style and painting technique. The brushwork of both versions discussed here and the Dijon copy is more rapid and swift than the technique of the Rotterdam version and the exact copy in the Musées royaux des Beaux-Arts in Brussels. The latter painting's technique is still close to Bosch's execution, yet without being as elaborate. What they all have in common, however, is the fact that they borrow several technical procedures introduced by Bosch, most importantly the *imprimatura*[17] and scumbling.

Some of the versions are signed 'Hieronymus Bosch' in Gothic script in the master's manner, regardless of their date of execution. Some, like the Brussels panel, are signed on the left of the composition; some, like those in Antwerp and Rotterdam, on the right. Others, including the Dijon *Temptation* are not signed at all. Consequently, the presence or otherwise of a signature cannot be used as a criterion for classification.

The privately owned Brussels *Temptation* (1567) stands out among this body of copies as the only one to combine the originally tripartite composition in a single panel. It is also the painting that most closely resembles the Lisbon triptych. With its focus on the demonic iconography and its somewhat cursory rendering, the work responds perfectly to the taste of collectors in the latter part of the 16th century – they were more interested in the strangeness of the motifs painted by Bosch than in the artistic quality of their execution.

The Brussels panel, painted around 1567, thus dates from a period in which, as Elsig has noted, Hieronymus Bosch was no longer viewed as the inventor of several different subgenres that were admired and avidly collected during the early part of the 16th century, but merely as the diverting painter of the demonic, whom Van Vaernewijck labelled the *duvelmakere* in 1566 ('because he was unparallelled as a painter of the demonic'). Felipe de Guevara, the great admirer and collector of the master's works, wrote in his *Comentarios de la pintura* that Bosch's paintings were widely misunderstood and that his genius had been unfairly reduced to a genre destined sooner or later to go out of fashion. And that is indeed what happened.

Acknowledgements

I would like to thank the staff of the Institut royal du Patrimoine artistique (IRPA), Brussels, and in particular its acting director Christina Ceulemans. For scientific imaging and making available laboratory reports I am also greatly indebted to Christina Currie, Catherine Fondaire and Sophie de Potter; for dendrochronology: Peter Klein; for research assistance: Valentine Henderiks. I also thank Ted Alkins and Paul van Calster for the English version of this contribution. And I would like to extend my gratitude to the museum curators who kindly allowed me to use digital photographs of their paintings for the publication of this paper.

Notes

1. The *Temptation of Saint Anthony*, oak panel, 58 × 66.3 cm, inv. 3032, signed lower left in Gothic characters: *jheronymus bosch*. Galerie Robert Finck, *Exposition de tableaux de maîtres flamands du XVe au XVIIe siècle*, s.l. 1965, no. 11, s.p.
2. I am grateful to Peter Klein for having agreed to perform the dendrochronological analysis of the Brussels panel. For the other Bosch panels see P. Klein, 'Dendrochronological analysis of works by Hieronymus Bosch and his followers', in *Hieronymus Bosch: New Insights into His Life and Work*, exh. cat., Rotterdam, Museum BoijmansVan Beuningen, 1994.
3. See G. Unverfehrt, *Hieronymus Bosch. Studien zur Rezeption seiner Kunst im frühen 16. Jahrhundert*, Berlin, Mann, 1980; J. Koldeweij, P. Vandenbroeck and B. Vermet, *Hieronymus Bosch: The Complete Paintings and Drawings*, Rotterdam, 2001; L. Silver, *Hieronymus Bosch*, New York and London, Abbeville Press, 2006.
4. An attempt will not be made to enter the ongoing debate about the painting's interpretation in view of its complexity and the many divergent views that continue to divide art historians.
5. F. Elsig, *Jheronimus Bosch. La question de la chronologie*, Geneva, Droz, 2004.
6. See *The Flemish Primitives: Catalogue of Early Netherlandish Paintings in the Royal Museums of Fine Arts of Belgium*, vol. III, Brussels, Brepols, 2001, pp. 85–117.

7. M.J. Friedländer, *Early Netherlandish Painting*, vol. 5, Leiden, A.W. Sijthoff/ Brussels, La Connaissance, 1969, pls 75–81.
8. Elsig 2004 (cited in note 5), pp. 133–134.
9. I have only taken account of the copies that are most closely related to the Brussels version. Several others are reproduced in Friedländer 1969 (cited in note 7).
10. J. Van Lennep, 'Feu Saint Antoine et Maudragore. A propos de la Tentation de Saint-Antoine par Jérôme Bosch', *Bulletin des Musées royaux des Beaux-Arts de Belgique*, 3–4, 1968, pp. 115–136.
11. Elsig 2004 (cited in note 5), pp. 133–134.
12. The panel is 66.5 cm wide – equal to 2⅓ Antwerp feet – and 53 cm high. I am grateful to Jean-Albert Glatigny for this information and for his help in examining the wooden support.
13. *Temptation of Saint Anthony*, 1550–70, oak panel, 68.7 × 86.9 cm, Maastricht, Bonnefantenmuseum (on loan from the Rijksmuseum), inv. SK–A–1795.
14. As kindly suggested by Christina Currie during the examination of the X-radiograph at the Institut royal du Patrimoine artistique (IRPA) in April 2012.
15. Van den Brink 2001, 'L'art de la copie. Le pourquoi et le comment de l'exécution de copies aux Pays-Bas aux XVIe et XVIIe siècles', in *L'Entreprise de Brueghel*, exh. cat., Gand, Ludion-Flammarion, 2001 , pp. 36–39.
16. Antwerp, Koninklijk Museum voor Schone Kunsten, panel, 88 × 71 cm, inv. 25; Rotterdam, Museum Boijmans Van Beuningen, panel (2 boards), 50 × 39.5 cm, inv. 2441 (*c.*1539); Dijon, Musée des Beaux-Arts, panel, 117.5 × 110.3 cm, inv. J.5 (late 16th–early 17th century).
17. C. Van Mander, 'Jérôme Bosch', in *Le livre des peintres*, Paris, 1884, pp. 169–175.

Author's address

Catheline Périer-D'Ieteren, 4 av. De L'Ecuyer, 1640 Rhode St. Genèse, Belgium

EMULATING VAN EYCK: THE SIGNIFICANCE OF GRISAILLE

Noëlle L.W. Streeton

ABSTRACT Scholars have devoted great efforts, especially over the past 30 years, to clarifying functional divisions within the workshops of late medieval painters. Arguments relevant to the workshop practices of Jan van Eyck, however, appear only to justify that he worked without the aid of assistants. This paper explores technical and visual aspects of van Eyck's surviving paintings, with particular attention to issues that surround regimentation and pictorial elements that are variously labelled as grisaille, monochrome, sandstone or reduced colour. Is it plausible that van Eyck designed an approach to producing pictorial space that would enable him to delegate specific, quantifiable tasks to members of his workshop? While this question will not be resolved here in any comprehensive way, it is argued that the physical make-up of the grisaille passages point to a formula and format that could be consistently laid in by an assistant rather than by the master.

Introduction

A recent publication to consider the workshop production of Jan van Eyck (*c*.1390–1441) reiterates a tenacious claim: that van Eyck had no commercial incentive to delegate tasks and that he worked unaided by the assistants who are known to have been present in the workshop.[1] This statement sits uncomfortably with what is known of workshop practices in the late medieval period – a period when emulating the master would have been a primary function of a workshop assistant or journeyman.

This paper aims to test the proposition that grisaille elements, which feature heavily in van Eyck's surviving paintings, point to a formula and format that could be consistently repeated, whether by the master or by an assistant. The objective is to demonstrate that there is no reason to insist that van Eyck's workshop assistants played no role in the painting process.

Replicating, copying and emulating

Over the past 30 years in particular, conservators together with art historians have established convincingly that van Eyck's paintings and selected motifs were replicated and copied - that is, replicated by assistants and followers probably in the painter's lifetime and in his Bruges studio, and copied after his death in 1441.[2] For example, Livia Depuydt and her team at the Royal Institute for Cultural Heritage in Brussels (KIK-IRPA) studied the two closely contemporary versions of *The Virgin at the Fountain*.[3] Through this they determined that the presumably principal version, which is signed and dated 1439 on the frame, is almost identical to the other version, which lacks its original frame. The technical similarities, beyond surface effects, indicate that these paintings were executed either simultaneously or in close succession. Likewise, two surviving versions of *Saint Francis Receiving the Stigmata* – and there were probably more – appear to have been faithfully replicated, although these two were painted on different scales, on different supports (panel versus parchment) and underdrawn with different drawing materials – one visible with infrared reflectography (IRR), the other not.[4] However, the faithful replication of minute details with directly comparable techniques, while also scaling up or down, indicates that the principal, or model, was in the same studio at the same time as that which was being replicated. In addition, studies of the Vera Icons and the *Woman at Her Toilet* have helped to demonstrate that these images were copied, probably from a principal version, between the late 15th and early 16th century.[5]

Interdisciplinary enquiries have also provided insights into the techniques of contemporary and later painters.[6] Moreover, it is generally acknowledged that elements from Eyckian paintings were widely admired and borrowed by other painters, who transmitted an oil technique and Eyckian motifs throughout Europe.[7] For example, Rogier van der Weyden paraphrased the pictorial recession over land and into the firmament from van Eyck's Rolin Madonna in multiple versions of *Saint Luke Drawing the Virgin*. Similar paraphrasing is evident in *The Adoration of the Kings* by Sandro Botticelli and Filippo Lippi (*c*.1470, London, National Gallery, NG592), who appear to have modelled the rocky panorama on a version of *Saint Francis Receiving the Stigmata*. Van Eyck's *Virgin in a Church* and *The Virgin at the Fountain* also provided points of reference, both for direct and explicit copies, such as *The Virgin in a Church* by the Master of 1499 (Antwerp, Koninklijk Museum voor Schone Kunsten) as well as for images based on model drawings, for example *The Virgin and Child in a Niche* (*c*.1500) in the Metropolitan Museum of Art in New York.[8]

These details are like pieces in a puzzle that have helped conservators and art historians to understand better how van Eyck and other late medieval painters worked. With the coupling of art-technical and art-historical studies, it is increasingly possible to support theories about the roles of workshop assistants beyond the grinding of pigments and beyond the use of pattern drawings. Having said this, the act of emulation, a core task of the apprentice, as well as ideas about the practical functions of a late medieval workshop have found little space in the literature devoted to van Eyck.

Contributions by assistants?

Reasons for opposition to a late medieval model for this painter are strongly associated with the positions of Giorgio Vasari and Karel van Mander, and later Gustav Friedrich Waagen and Erwin Panofsky, among many others, whose opinions eventually led to van Eyck's designation as a seminal figure in the western art-historical canon. Van Eyck is widely recognised as the esteemed court painter to Philip the Good, duke of Burgundy, a position that created a framework for fame in his own lifetime. However, opinions associated with van Eyck's singular artistic output continue to vary considerably because of a lack of evidence that could provide insight into the painter's intentions. There are no written sources that reflect in any way van Eyck's motivations. Equally, there are no documents that refer to contributions from other painters nor do underdrawings in signature works reveal evidence of other hands. Thus, the suggestion that studio assistants contributed to paintings attributed to van Eyck alone will undoubtedly be met with some resistance. Indeed, Susie Nash stated in her 2008 book *Northern Renaissance Art* that this artistic virtuoso had no commercial incentive to delegate tasks.[9] According to this logic, and because of his remarkable artistic abilities and status, van Eyck did not work like other late medieval artists. Rather, he produced his paintings, from the first marks drawn on top of ground layers all the way up to final glazes, unaided by the assistants who are known to have been present in his workshop.

It is of course perfectly possible that no other person contributed to the drawing or painting process after, for example, the chalk ground was applied to a panel and semi-integral frame – which in all likelihood was done by a craftsman outside van Eyck's studio. It should be borne in mind though that van Eyck had perhaps five assistants. The English medievalist James Weale, who worked in Bruges for nearly a quarter of a century from 1855, discovered references in city and ducal accounts that recorded two visits to the van Eyck studio(s). During the first visit in 1432, burgomasters and members of the Bruges council gave 5 *sous* to assistants and during a second visit in 1433, Philip the Good gave the assistants 25 *sous*.[10] Lorne Campbell suggested quite logically that because gratuities seem to have come in multiples of five, van Eyck might have had five assistants at the time.[11]

Van Mander

To documentary references to assistants should be added one more piece of information: in Karl van Mander's *Schilder-boeck*, first published in 1604, the author described van Eyck as a painter, whom he admired, and who used a *primuersel*.[12] This layer, which some identify with an *imprimatura*, others with a priming layer, might be described as a layer that is skin-toned, often based on lead white with small amounts of carbon black and red pigments.[13] According to van Mander this layer contributed to the overall tone of the picture, a comment that has also been discussed by Abbie Vandivere in relation to her research on Haarlem school painters. Such a layer is not generally considered to have great significance when looking at the ways in which van Eyck built up complex draperies on figures. However, this aspect of his technique is of consequence when considering the physical and iconographic significance of grisaille (or reduced-colour) elements in van Eyck's surviving works.

Naturally van Mander's descriptions of van Eyck's working methods should be taken with a pinch of salt because he did, after all, follow Vasari's lead in describing van Eyck as the inventor of oil painting. In addition, it could easily be argued that van Mander was relating his own use of a *primuersel* to examples of earlier, well-respected artists who worked in what he considered to be a similar fashion.[14] But there is something in his statement that is relevant here, both to a practice that later painters appreciated when considering van Eyck's paintings and a paint layer that was predictable enough to apply time after time. What seemed to matter to van Mander was its expedience or efficiency, and it is this specific form of expedience that has not been considered previously in relation to van Eyck.

The importance of lead white

Given the preoccupation of earlier studies with jewel tones in Eyckian paintings, especially on the interior panels of the Ghent Altarpiece, the uses and usefulness of lead white in van Eyck's workshop have been eclipsed by an appreciation for exotic and more expensive colours. Thus, for the purposes of this paper, it is instructive to examine the importance of lead white for van Eyck and for painters in general.

Lead white, or lead carbonate hydroxide ($2PbCO_3 \cdot Pb(OH)_2$), was well understood by painters working in both egg tempera and oil. It was widely available, comparatively

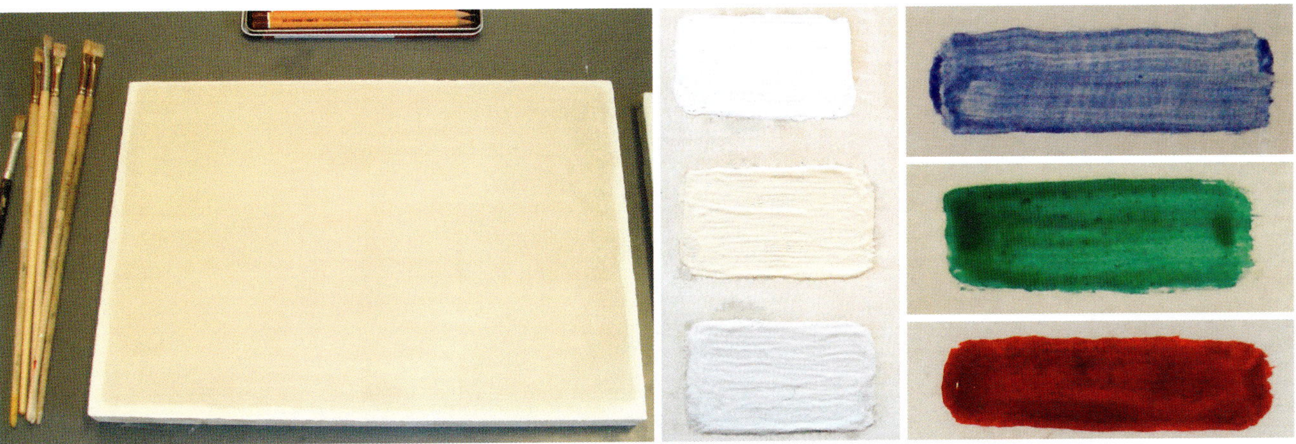

Fig. 1 Primed chalk ground on panel, with paint reconstructions, one layer each (clockwise from left): lead white (top), with varying amounts of ochres and ivory black; ultramarine in non-heat bodied linseed oil; madder lake in heat-bodied linseed oil; verdigris in heat-bodied linseed oil.

inexpensive and the only white pigment that could function in an oil medium.[15] Lead white was evidently valued for its handling properties, brightness and predictability, and consequently was employed extensively for underlayers and highlights. Furthermore, the reconstructions shown in Figure 1 reinforce the point that unlike coarse mineral blues, copper greens or red lakes, it could obscure a primed chalk ground and underdrawing, either partially or completely, in a smooth single layer. All aspects considered – such as hiding power, high refractive index relative to the oil medium and low oil-absorption index – the intrinsic properties of lead white pigment were surely a consideration for painters wishing to develop visually satisfying pictorial illusions that were also efficient and durable.

The properties of lead white pigment mixed with either an untreated or lead-treated linseed oil made this the ideal base material for expanses of panel – not just in isolation layers, but also for modelling with lightly toned mixtures over a primed chalk ground.[16] This could not be said of a thin layer of coarse ultramarine in oil, which is pale and gritty, or lake pigments, which lack sufficient body. A relatively quick-drying oil paint, based on lead white tinted with carbon black and finely ground red and yellow ochres – the mixture identified in the exterior Ghent wings and in the much smaller *Annunciation* in the Museo Thyssen-Bornemisza in Madrid – could effectively cover the white ground and underdrawing in a single layer.[17] Like the Thyssen Diptych, the tonality of the Ghent *Annunciation* and saints is subtle, and even if probably substantially more transparent today than originally, these images remain nevertheless rich and nuanced (Fig. 2).

Fig. 2 Jan and Hubert van Eyck, *The Adoration of the Lamb*, the Ghent Altarpiece (in closed position), dedicated 6 May 1432, oil on oak panel, 3.75 × 5.20 m (open); 137.7 cm × 242.3 cm (closed), Cathedral of Saint Bavo, Ghent. (Image: Saint Bavo Cathedral © Lukas-Art in Flanders vzw. Photo: Hugo Maertens.)

The wings of the Ghent Altarpiece

During the first Ghent Altarpiece project (1950–51), nine samples were taken from *The Annunciation*, *Saint John the Baptist* and *Saint John the Evangelist*, either from a highlight, shadow or mid-tone in areas that represent figures, their chamber or stone.[18] Another two were taken later. Despite sampling and the iconographic importance of the grisaille imagery, which covers approximately 90% of the exterior wings, the majority of the samples taken from the grisailles have not been addressed in published material. A single cross-section was referred to in *L'Agneau mystique au laboratoire* and a further two samples were analysed by Jean Thissen and again by Leopold Kockaert.[19] The information contained in these samples was therefore not integral to their descriptions of *la technique picturale eyckienne*. It is, however, pertinent here to look at the paint structure.

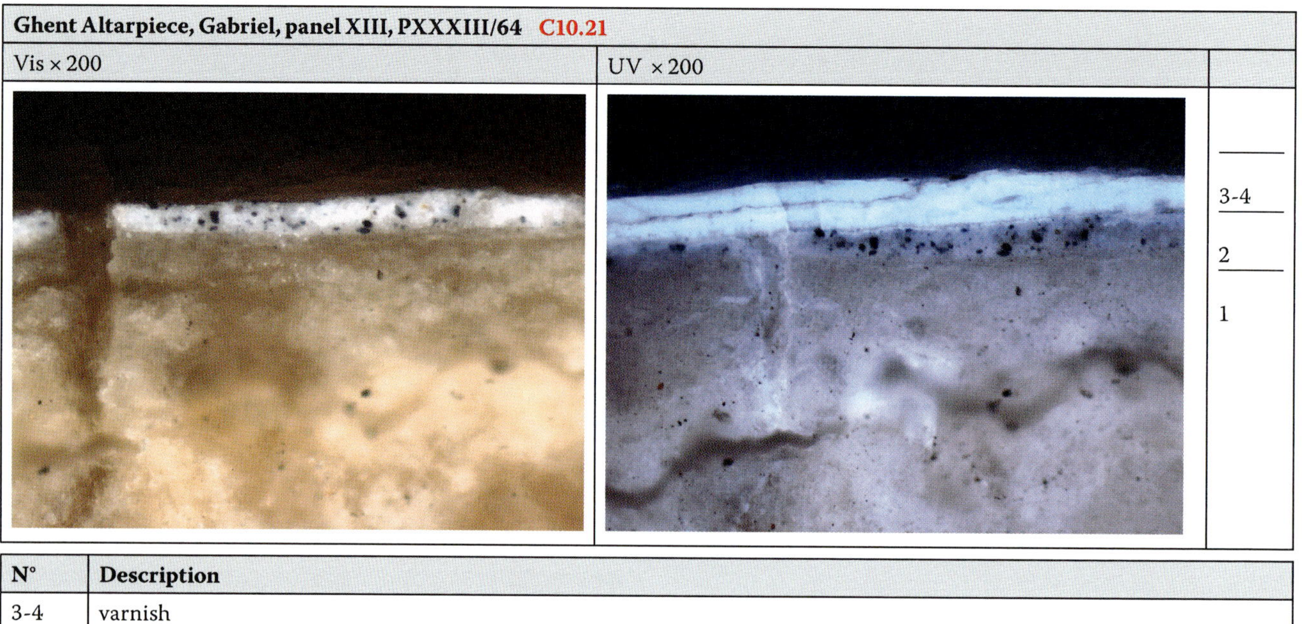

N°	Description
3-4	varnish
2	lead white with coarse grains of carbon black, particles of yellow ochre, a red pigment (probably red ochre) and a blue pigment (unidentified)
	(no isolation layer)
1	chalk ground, with a number of pigment particles

Fig. 3 Sample C10.21, derived from a mid-tone in the drapery of Gabriel's mantle, near the frame, lower left. Note: chemical analysis of this and other Ghent Altarpiece samples is in progress at KIK-IRPA as part of a project that commenced in 2012. (Images: the author and KIK-IRPA, Brussels.)

The stone statuary and niches in the Ghent *Annunciation* appear to have been produced with reasonably uniform mixtures of lead white with carbon black and finely ground red and yellow ochres (Fig. 3).[20] Similarly, the greyish paint that forms the draperies of both *Gabriel* and *Saint John the Evangelist* consists in many areas of a single layer, while two successive thin layers of similar composition form the highlights on the niche columns of both *Saint John* figures. Likewise the highlight over the mid-tone for the niche floors is formed of two layers. A light layer also sits on top of a somewhat darker one to intensify a highlight on the Evangelist's robe. Apart from the highlight employed to lighten a darker shade, this procedure appears little different from that used to prepare a surface for more intense shades of red and blue in the *Three Marys* and in the panels of the Ghent Altarpiece interior (which begin with the lightest tone).[21]

Samples from the mid-tones show that these were painted with a nearly identical mixture, with the predictable exception that more carbon black was added for a darker tone. Greyish paint was applied either in a single layer in the draperies in the Evangelist's sleeve or in two thin layers, judging from the edge of a highlight in another area of the sleeve.[22] Conversely, the shadow in the sleeve of the Evangelist is composed of a single layer of carbon black with brown (an ochre or sienna) under a thin resin- or varnish-like layer, which has been covered with successively lighter layers of paint.[23] The identification of a possibly modern blue indicates that at least some of the upper layers might derive from retouching.[24]

This description of the uniformity of paint layers forming *The Annunciation* and the Saint John statues is repetitive, but should serve to make the point that the figures represented in these panels pose a stark contrast to those on the interior of the altarpiece. Even more significant though is the observation that their thin and simple tones, often laid side-by-side in single layers, characterise the architectural settings of other paintings. In this way, van Eyck's methods for rendering grisaille effects and for tonal (under)modelling appear to correlate with those found in the much smaller Madrid *Annunciation*,[25] as well as with the architectural elements of interior scenes, such as in the Washington *Annunciation*, the Lucca Madonna, the Dresden Triptych and, on a far larger scale, the van der Paele Madonna.[26] Each features architectural elements that are formed of simple mixtures based on lead white. Of examples that survive, and the fabled *Woman at Her Toilet* is one example that has not, all paintings with significant reduced-colour elements have been assigned dates post-1432 – after the Ghent Altarpiece was dedicated.[27] The manner of painting found on the exterior of the Ghent Altarpiece might therefore be considered a step towards the iconography and formal elements that were developed for the Lucca Madonna, *The Virgin of Canon van der Paele*, the Dresden Triptych and other small, potentially portable images.

Regimentation

Is it plausible then that van Eyck designed an approach to producing pictorial space that would enable him to delegate specific, regimented, quantifiable tasks to members of his workshop? To be clear, I am not proposing that members of

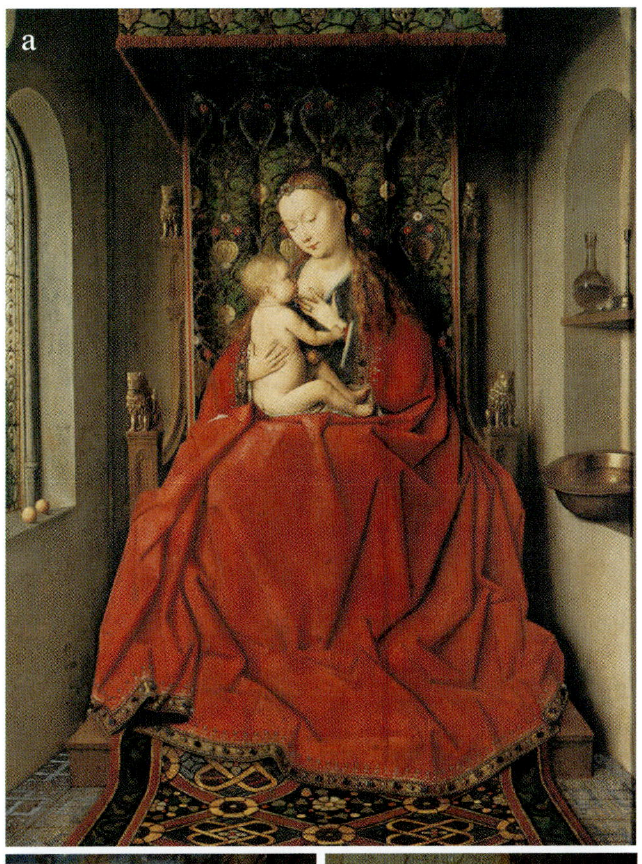

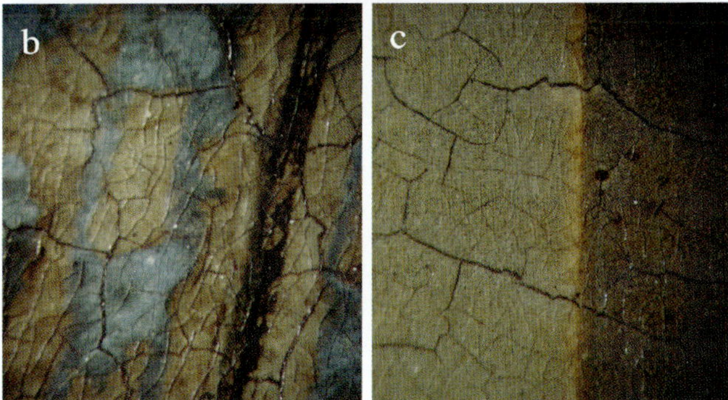

Fig. 4 (a) Lucca Madonna, *c*.1435, oil on oak panel, 65.7 × 49.6 cm, Städel Museum, Frankfurt (image: U. Edelmann, Städel Museum – Artothek). Macrophotographs showing a consistent, *primuersel*-like paint used for the floor (b) and wall (c) with a visible separation between passages. (Images: the author with permission of Jochen Sander.)

the workshop would only possess the requisite skill to lay in a backdrop. There seems to be general agreement that at least one member of the workshop also produced a small grisaille diptych of Saint John the Baptist and the Virgin and Child, which is now in Paris.[28] I am also not proposing that a formula was simple, or that formulaic practices were readily established. As discussed by Melanie Gifford, the continuous beige tone on the rear wall of the Washington *Annunciation* conceals an earlier scheme, which initially incorporated a narrow red line around the three arches,[29] a possible *pentimento* that points to experimentation before arriving at a viable solution. What I am proposing is that, given the nature of van Eyck's interior scenes, there is no reason to insist that van Eyck alone was capable of executing all elements of paintings that are attributed to him – especially passages that behave most predictably. Here too one might consider underlayers in landscape and some red and blue passages, which were also built up in regimented ways. Nevertheless, at this point at least some must be asking: What role could a predictable, even formulaic structure play in the work of a virtuoso court painter?

A response to this question must consider that for van Eyck this was a period of rapid production, the beginning of which coincided with the dedication of the Ghent Altarpiece in May 1432. The prolific court painter had recently set up his Bruges workshop in what is now the Gouden-handstraat. He was well rewarded for his work by the duke, from whom he received a substantial increase in salary in 1434 after his marriage, a raise calculated by Lorne Campbell to be some 720%.[30] The painter travelled extensively to attend to ducal business, probably to the negotiations at Arras over two months in the summer of 1435 and abroad in 1436.[31] During this period van Eyck made a name for himself, producing a sort of surrogate splendour in the form of paintings on panel, which were valued across social divides: by merchants, who lived all around him, a canon (Joris van der Paele) and a goldsmith (Jan de Leeuw). His services were also sought for civic monuments. There was a commission for polychromed and gilded statues and their tabernacles for the façade of the town hall in Bruges, of which the workshop finished six and for which van Eyck was paid in 1434/35.[32]

The paintings that survive from these years are diverse in size and function, but if a common feature between *The Arnolfini Portrait* (1434), the Lucca Madonna (*c*.1435), the Washington *Annunciation* (*c*.1434–36), the Van der Paele Madonna (1436), the Dresden Triptych (1437) and the *The Virgin and Child in a Church* (*c*.1437–38) were to be identified, it would be the nature of their setting. In each, the backdrop appears to consist of a greyish base tone onto which highlights and shadows were applied (Fig. 4). The consistency of this approach might therefore be considered a sort of formula that arguably could have been applied by any number of hands, time after time, in much the same way. It required a regimented range of opaque tones, which could be thinly and consistently applied, often in a single layer.

Workshop organisation

Once the structure of the chamber or church was set out in neutral tones and largely complete, the interior could then be balanced with human forms clothed in jewel-encrusted scarlets and brocades, painted mainly with imported colours. The visual impact of a shock of colour in a reduced-colour chamber was evidently viewed as a success. For van Eyck himself, one measure of the painter's perception of its efficacy is that the formulaic construction of isolated colour, either over or in tandem with monochromatic architectural elements, was employed in roughly one-third of the surviving paintings produced before the master's death in 1441.

The effect (if not the structure) was evidently appreciated by later painters for whom workshop organisation was a key to commercial success. For example, Bernart van Orley used a similar device in an Italianate *Annunciation* (Cambridge,

Fitzwilliam Museum);[33] and van Mander relied on flesh-coloured and sandstone tones to produce the grotto in his *Adoration of the Shepherds* (Haarlem, Frans Hals Museum), which incidentally appears to embody what he himself described as a *primuersel*.[34] Van Mander valued this lightly pigmented flesh-coloured paint because it expedited the painting process by acting as a base tone that could also be left exposed and thus finished in one layer. Furthermore, it is interesting that van Mander should imply that van Eyck was among the earlier painters, whom he admired, who employed a *primuersel*.

Conclusions

The question of whether or not van Eyck designed an approach to produce pictorial space that would enable him to delegate specific, quantifiable tasks will not be resolved here. However, it is noteworthy that the physical make-up of the grisaille and reduced-colour passages point to a formula and format that could be consistently laid in by an assistant instead of by the master. Given that assistants were trained to emulate the master, this potentially allowed van Eyck to meet the demands of his role as servant to the duke of Burgundy, while still completing commissions for merchants and courtiers. Furthermore, pictorial elements that could be considered complete in a single layer point to a significant function of the reduced-colour passages in Eyckian paintings, which were also valued by later artists who were attempting to emulate them.

Whether or not those with a stake in van Eyck studies agree with this proposal, it should be borne in mind that scientific and technical art-historical studies addressing the works of this painter have hitherto been defined by the study of colour. For this reason, the physicality of these passages has not been examined by conservators to the same extent as multilayered jewel tones – arguably because the paradigmatic description of van Eyck's use of colour, as identified on the interior panels of the Ghent Altarpiece, cannot be applied to them. Observations such as those presented here might therefore be given greater consideration in approaches to van Eyck studies in the future, with the potential to offer a more balanced assessment of this painter's methods and motivations. Nevertheless, the possibility of acknowledging contributions from unknown assistants in paintings assigned to a great master will clearly continue to be problematic, not least because such suggestions inevitably struggle under the weight of the pre-existing literature. Thus, for now, identifying whether or how others contributed to works attributed to van Eyck alone must remain grounded in larger studies that ultimately aim to situate van Eyck and his painting practices in a broader context, both inside and outside of his workshop.

Acknowledgements

I am grateful to Libby Sheldon (University College London), Jana Sanyova (KIK-IRPA) and Abbie Vandivere (University of Amsterdam) for their help and inspiration while developing this paper. Thanks also to Jørgen Wadum (SMK/CATS, Copenhagen), the Arts and Humanities Research Council of Great Britain, Members of the Objects and Beliefs research group, University of Oslo (UiO), and the Humanities Faculty, Institute of Archaeology, Conservation and History, UiO.

Notes

1. W.H.J. Weale, *Hubert and John van Eyck: Their Life and Work*, London, John Lane, 1908, pp. xxxviii–xxxix; S. Nash, *Northern Renaissance Art*, Oxford and New York, Oxford University Press, 2008, pp. 194–195.
2. The language used to describe the acts of replicating (in the studio), emulating (the technique of the master) or copying (usually later by followers or admirers) requires some clarification. I would consider a replicated work to be one that was reproduced in its entirety, probably by assistants and, in this instance, in van Eyck's studio. However, 'to emulate' refers to a core task of an apprentice: to emulate the master's technique and be capable of contributing to a kind of corporate style associated with a particular workshop. Both of these terms stand in contrast to the term 'copy', which here might be associated with later productions, usually by followers or admirers, or at the request of a patron.
3. L. Depuydt-Elbaum, '*The Madonna at the Fountain* by Jan van Eyck', in P. Vandenbroeck and L. Depuydt-Elbaum, *Jan van Eyck: Madonna at the Fountain. Restoration*, tr. G. Ball, Antwerp, Koninklijk Museum voor Schone Kunsten, 2002, pp. 8–20; L. Depuydt-Elbaum, 'La Technique picturale de la *Vierge à la fontaine* de Jan van Eyck. Étude sous binoculaire stéréoscopique/ De schildertechniek van de *Madonna bij de fontein* van Jan van Eyck. Onderzoek onder de binoculaire stereomicroscoop', *Bulletin KIK/IRPA* 30, 2003/04, pp. 165–172.
4. M.H. Butler, 'An investigation of the Philadelphia "Saint Francis Receiving the Stigmata"', in J.R.J. van Asperen de Boer, K. Bé, M.H. Bulter, P. Klein, K.C. Luber, J.J. Rishel, M. Smeyers, J. Snyder and C. Spantigati, *Jan van Eyck: Two Paintings of* Saint Francis Receiving the Stigmata, Philadelphia, Philadelphia Museum of Art, 1997, pp. 29–46, esp. pp. 38–39.
5. Copies of Vera Icons are held in the Groeningemuseum, Bruges, the Gemäldegalerie, Berlin, the British Royal Collection, Alte Pinakothek, Munich and at least two private collections; *Woman at Her Toilet* (after 1511, oil on panel, 27.5 × 16.5 cm) is in the collection of the Fogg Art Museum, Harvard University, Cambridge, MA. See T. Hensick, 'The Fogg's copy after a lost van Eyck: conservation history, recent treatment and technical examination of the *Woman at Her Toilet*', in M. Faries and R. Spronk (eds), *Recent Developments in the Technical Examination of Early Netherlandish Painting: Methodology, Limitations and Perspectives*, Cambridge, MA and Turnhout, Harvard University Art Museums and Brepols, 2003, pp. 83–95, esp. p. 90.
6. P. Coremans, A. de Schryver, L. Hauman, R. Lefeve, L. Loose, R. Marijnissen, A. Philippot, P. Philippot, R. Sneyers and J. Thissen, *Les Primitifs flamands, III. Contributions à l'étude des Primitifs flamands, 2. L'Agneau mystique au laboratoire: Examen et traitement*, Antwerp, De Sikkel, 1953, p. 76; M. Broekman-Bokstijn, J.R.J. van Asperen de Boer, E.H. van 't Hul-Ehrnreich and C.M. Verduyn-Groen, 'The scientific examination of the polychromed sculpture in the Herlin Altarpiece', *Studies in Conservation* 15, 1970, pp. 370–400; C.A. Metzger and B.H. Berrie, 'Gerard David's *St. Anne Altarpiece*: evidence for workshop participation', in

A. Wallert, E. Hermens and M. Peek (eds), *Historical Painting Techniques, Materials, and Studio Practice*, Los Angeles, Getty Conservation Institute, 1995, pp. 127–134, esp. pp. 131–132.
7. M. Sellink, 'A new look on the world: the invention of landscape', in T.-H. Borchert, *The Age of Van Eyck: The Mediterranean World and Early Netherlandish Painting 1430–1530*, London, Thames & Hudson, 2002, pp. 213–215, esp. p. 214.
8. M.W. Ainsworth, 'A meeting of sacred and secular worlds', in M.W. Ainsworth and K. Christiansen (eds), *From Van Eyck to Bruegel: Early Netherlandish Painting in the Metropolitan Museum of Art*, New York, Metropolitan Museum of Art, 1998, pp. 220–223; Y. Yiu, 'Hinging past and present: diptych variants of Jan van Eyck's *Virgin in a Church*', in J.O. Hand and R. Spronk (eds), *Essays in Context: Unfolding the Netherlandish Diptych*, Cambridge, MA, New Haven, CT and London, Harvard University Art Museums and Yale University Press, 2006, pp. 110–123.
9. Nash 2008 (cited in note 1), pp. 194–195.
10. Weale 1908 (cited in note 1), pp. xxxviii–xxxix.
11. L. Campbell, *The Fifteenth Century Netherlandish Schools*, London, National Gallery, 1998, p. 23.
12. H. Miedema (ed.), *Karel van Mander: De grondt der edel vry schilder-const*, Utrecht, Haentjens Dekker and Gumbert, 1973, fol. 48r; P. Brinkman, *Het geheim van Van Eyck: aantekeningen bij de uitvinding van het olieverven*, Zwolle, Uitgeverij Waanders, 1993, pp. 211–213; A. Vandivere, 'In search of van Mander's *primuersel*: intermediate layers in Early Netherlandish Paintings', in J. Bridgland (ed.), *Preprints of ICOM-CC 16th Triennial Conference, Lisbon, 19–23 September 2011*, Almada, Critério, 2011, pp. 1-8, esp. pp. 5–6.
13. Vandivere 2011 (cited in note 12), pp. 5–6.
14. Ibid., p. 6.
15. R.J. Gettens, H. Kühn and W.T. Chase, 'Lead white', in A. Roy (ed.), *Artists' Pigments: A Handbook of their History and Characteristics*, vol. 2, Washington, DC and Oxford, National Gallery of Art and Oxford University Press, 1993, pp. 67–81, esp. pp. 70–72; N. Eastaugh, V. Walsh, T. Chaplin and R. Siddall, *Pigment Compendium: A Dictionary of Historical Pigments*, vol. 1, Oxford, Elsevier Butterworth-Heinemann, 2004, p. 234; C.S. Tumosa and M.F. Mecklenburg, 'The influence of lead ions on the drying of oils', *Reviews in Conservation* 6, 2005, pp. 39–47, esp. pp. 41–42.
16. The function of the isolation layer was to seal the ground, fix the underdrawing and prevent the leaching of medium from the paint, thus weakening it. Also, the oil type used in the Ghent Altarpiece *Annunciation* has hitherto been classified as untreated linseed oil; see Coremans *et al.* 1953 (cited in note 6), pp. 119–120.
17. Ibid.; E. Bosshard, 'The examination of the Thyssen-Bornemisza Annunciation', *Apollo* July 1992, pp. 4–11, esp. pp. 6–7.
18. Sample sites for the 1950–51 campaign are designated in sample maps made by van Asperen de Boer from Coremans' files. Maps: J.R.J. van Asperen de Boer archive, RKD, The Hague.
19. Coremans *et al.* 1953 (cited in note 6), p. 119, pl. LXII; J. Thissen, undated/unpublished report for samples PXXXIII/61, C10/18 and PXXXIII/64 C10/21 from Panel XIII, Angel Gabriel (*The Annunciation*), Brussels, KIK-IRPA, *c.*1965; P.W.F. Brinkman, L. Kockaert, L. Maes, L. Masschelein-Kleiner, F. Robaszynski and E. Thielen, 'Het Lam Godsretabel van van Eyck: een heronderzoek naar de materialen en schildermethoden. 1. De plamuur, de isolatielaag, de tekening en de grondtonen', *Bulletin KIK/IRPA* 20, 1984/85, pp. 137–166, esp. pp. 163–164.
20. Cross-sections were examined at the KIK-IRPA in May 2008. Highlights were formed in either one layer (samples C10.18, C10.21, C10.32) or two layers (samples C10.30, C10.31, C10.35, C10.36). For a detailed discussion of these samples see N.L.W. Streeton, *Perspectives on the Painting Technique of Jan van Eyck: Beyond the Ghent Altarpiece*, London: Archetype Publications, 2013, pp. 89–97.
21. The structure of specific colours and motifs are described in cross-section reports on the 17 samples from the Rotterdam *Three Marys at the Tomb*, J.R.J. van Asperen de Boer archive, RKD, The Hague.
22. Samples C10.33 and C10.35.
23. Sample C10.34.
24. Raman spectra for the blue did not offer a sufficient basis for interpretation. Steven Saverwyns, KIK-IRPA, May 2008.
25. Bosshard 1992 (cited in note 17), pp. 6–7.
26. Streeton 2013 (cited in note 20), pp. 97–102.
27. I am aware of Hugo van der Velden's assertion (in 'The quatrain of *The Ghent altarpiece*', *Simiolus* 35(1/2), 2011, pp. 5–39) that portions of the Ghent Altarpiece, most notably the upper register and the exterior wings, were completed later. While potentially significant for this argument, van der Velden's claims will not be pursued here.
28. J.O. Hand, C.A. Metzger and R. Spronk, *Prayers and Portraits: Unfolding the Netherlandish Diptych*, Washington, DC, New Haven, CT and London: National Gallery of Art and Yale University Press, 2006, pp. 78–79.
29. E.M. Gifford, 'Van Eyck's Washington *Annunciation*: technical evidence for iconographic development', *The Art Bulletin* 81, 1999, pp. 108–116, esp. pp. 111–112.
30. Weale 1908 (cited in note 1), pp. xl–xlii, nos. 23 and 24; Campbell 1998 (cited in note 11), p. 174.
31. Weale 1908 (cited in note 1), pp. xliv–xlv, no. 27.
32. Ibid., p. xxxvii, no. 25; Stadsarchief, Bruges, Stadsrekening, 2 September 1434–2 September 1435, f. 61.
33. Bernart van Orley, *The Annunciation*, 1517, oil on panel, 68 × 54 cm, Fitzwilliam Museum, Cambridge University, inv. 98.
34. Karel van Mander, *The Adoration of the Shepherds*, *c.*1598, oil on panel, 36 × 46.5 cm, Frans Hals Museum, Haarlem; see Vandivere 2011 (cited in note 12), pp. 1–2 and table 1.

Author's address

Noëlle L.W. Streeton, Conservation Studies, Department of Archaeology, Conservation and History (IAKH), University of Oslo, Norway (n.l.w.streeton@iakh.uio.no)

TWO VERSIONS OF A BOUTSIAN *VIRGIN AND CHILD* PAINTING: QUESTIONS OF ATTRIBUTION, CHRONOLOGY AND FUNCTION

Eva de la Fuente Pedersen and Troels Filtenborg

ABSTRACT A small painting of the *Virgin and Child with a Rosary* in the collection of Statens Museum for Kunst (SMK), the national gallery of Denmark, was re-examined and restored in 2010–11. Removal of discoloured layers of varnish and overpaint, revealing the high quality of the painting, prompted a reassessment of its attribution and date. In addressing these issues, comparison with another, closely related version of the same composition played a significant role.

Provenance and historiography

The *Virgin and Child with a Rosary* (Fig. 1) entered the collection of Statens Museum for Kunst (SMK), the national gallery of Denmark, in 1922 as a long-term deposit from the Ny Carlsberg Glyptotek.[1] The brewing magnate and founder of the Glyptotek, Carl Jacobsen (1842–1914), acquired it in 1878 at an auction held by J.M. Heberle in Cologne, from the collection of Simon Emil Moritz Oppenheim, a banker from Frankfurt am Main, who had died a year earlier.[2] Simon Oppenheim purchased paintings at well-renowned German art dealers such as Gsell, Finger, Zu Rhein, von Peucker, Lyversberg, and others. His collection of 101 artworks contained 77 old master paintings, and of these more than half were from Dutch and Flemish schools from the 16th and especially the 17th century. The collection also included some Italian masters and a few French and Spanish Renaissance and baroque masters. Just two paintings in the Oppenheim collection represented the Early Netherlandish School: a *Virgin and Child* attributed to the workshop of Jan van Eyck and *Virgin and Child with a Rosary*. In the auction catalogue from J.M. Heberle, this panel was attributed to Rogier van der Weyden and described as 'A fine and worthy painting on golden ground, in best condition.'[3]

Once the painting had entered the collection, Carl Jacobsen began to doubt the attribution to Rogier van der Weyden. In the Ny Carlsberg Glyptotek summary catalogues from 1885 and 1887 the painting was catalogued as 'Old Flemish School'.[4] In the catalogues from 1900, 1902 and 1905 the Glyptotek reverted to the attribution to Rogier van der Weyden.[5]

In an article from 1903 in the Danish art magazine *Tilskueren*, the director of SMK, Karl Madsen, discusses the attribution to Rogier van der Weyden and suggests that the panel is more likely to be an early work by Dieric Bouts the Elder.[6] This attribution was adopted for the Glyptotek's summary catalogue from 1916.[7] In 1924–25, Madsen again published the painting as a work by Dieric Bouts the Elder in an article on Early Netherlandish paintings in the Copenhagen museum.[8] Madsen compares the painting to two other known versions of the composition: one, very closely related, in a private collection[9] and a second, more removed in design and dimensions and with a landscape background, but obviously derived from the same source (present whereabouts unknown)[10] (Figs 2 and 3). The first was then owned by the art dealer Goudstikker in Amsterdam, who exhibited it in The Hague in November 1920. The version with a landscape was sold in 1911 with the rest of Henri Haro's collection in Paris,[11] and in 1927 it was in the Achilito Chiesa collection, New York.[12] In Madsen's view the Copenhagen painting is of a better artistic quality than the privately owned version, although it was marred by an 'insensitive restoration on the Virgin's right sleeve'. He notes that the underdrawing, visible to the naked eye, follows the privately owned version's composition in which the rosary 'in a clumsy way' overlaps the arm, stating that the altered position of the rosary in the Copenhagen version is a change for the better. On the subject of the third version he suggests that a pupil or follower copied the Copenhagen composition and added the landscape.

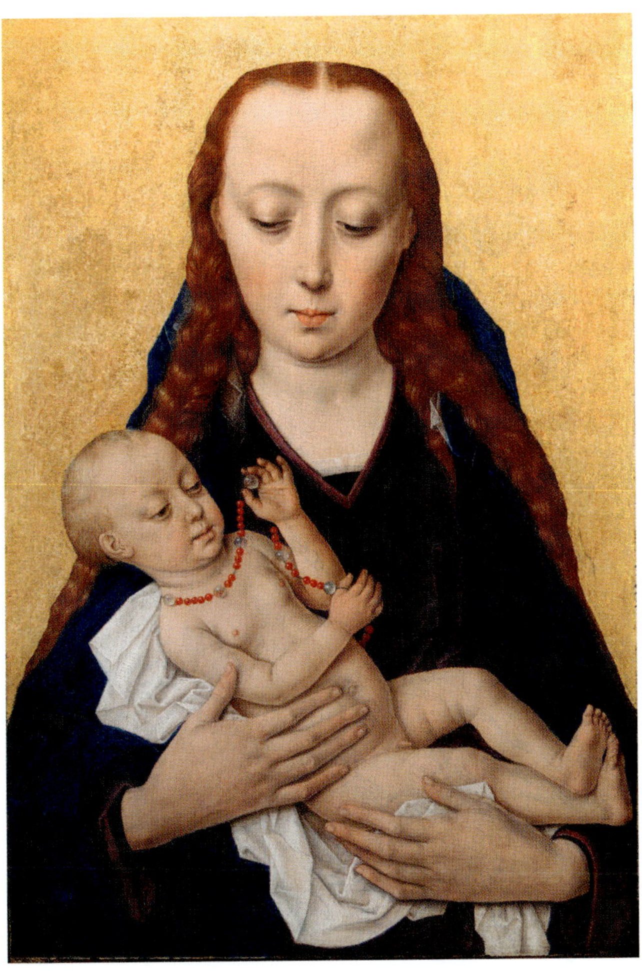

Fig. 1 Dieric Bouts workshop, *Virgin and Child with a Rosary*, after *c.*1459, oil on panel, 42.5 × 27.5 cm, Copenhagen, Statens Museum for Kunst, inv. DEP2. (© SMK.)

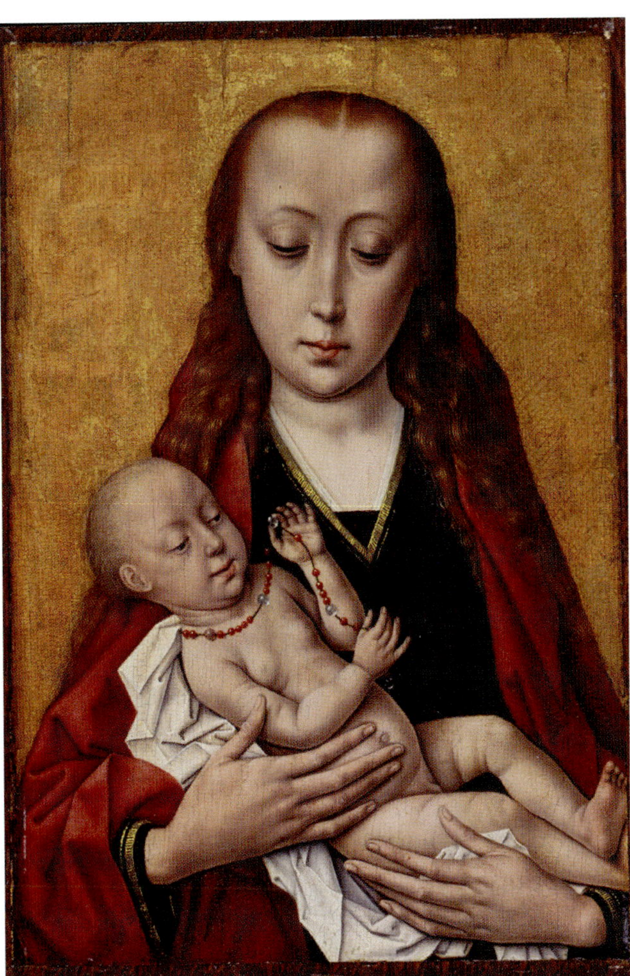

Fig. 2 Dieric Bouts workshop, *Virgin and Child with a Rosary*, after *c.*1471, oil on panel, 35.9 × 24.2 cm, private collection.

Madsen may have been in contact with J. Friedländer in Berlin as in 1925, Friedländer also attributed the Copenhagen panel to a follower of Dieric Bouts in his *Die Altniederländische Malerei*.[13] Friedländer does mention the two other versions of the composition, also attributing them to followers of Dieric Bouts.[14] In Wolfgang Schöne's monograph, *Dieric Bouts und seine Schule* from 1938, the privately owned panel was attributed to Albrecht Bouts.[15] Schöne catalogued the Copenhagen version as an exact repetition with the exception, he explained, that the Virgin's face is softer. Perhaps as a result of this attribution, a label with Albrecht Bouts' name was applied to the panel's frame. Although the painting was exhibited in Brussels in 1931, Wolfgang Schöne did not have an opportunity to view it with his own eyes (indicated by a star attached to the catalogue number). In SMK's *Catalogue of Old Foreign Paintings* from 1951, the painting was catalogued as 'Flemish artist, latter half of the 1400's'.[16] At some point after this the panel went into storage and vanished from art history.[17]

Technical notes

During examination of the Copenhagen painting, comparison with the privately owned version proved rewarding and led to the establishing of a tentative relationship between the two paintings. Both had been examined by dendrochronology, X-radiography and infrared reflectography (IRR).[18] In addition, cross-section analysis and micro-Raman spectroscopy (MRS) were carried out on the Copenhagen version. Despite the obvious affinity of the two paintings the examination did uncover some discrepancies in their techniques.

Each panel consists of a single plank of oak with the grain running vertically. While the privately owned panel has unpainted borders on all four sides, the image itself shows the obvious marks of having been trimmed along the right-hand and bottom edges, meaning that paint was removed at a later date to create these borders. In addition, the panel has been thinned and cradled.

In the Copenhagen panel, a 5–6 mm border of unpainted wood has survived along the bottom edge, whereas the border has been removed on the other three sides of the panel. No clear *barbe* has been indentified on the trimmed sides. However, remnants of an incised line along the top and left-hand edges indicate that the original dimensions of the image itself most likely are intact. The reverse of the panel has what appear to be its original tool marks as well as some bevelling remaining on all sides, which again corroborates the assumption that nothing more than the unpainted border was removed on the three sides.

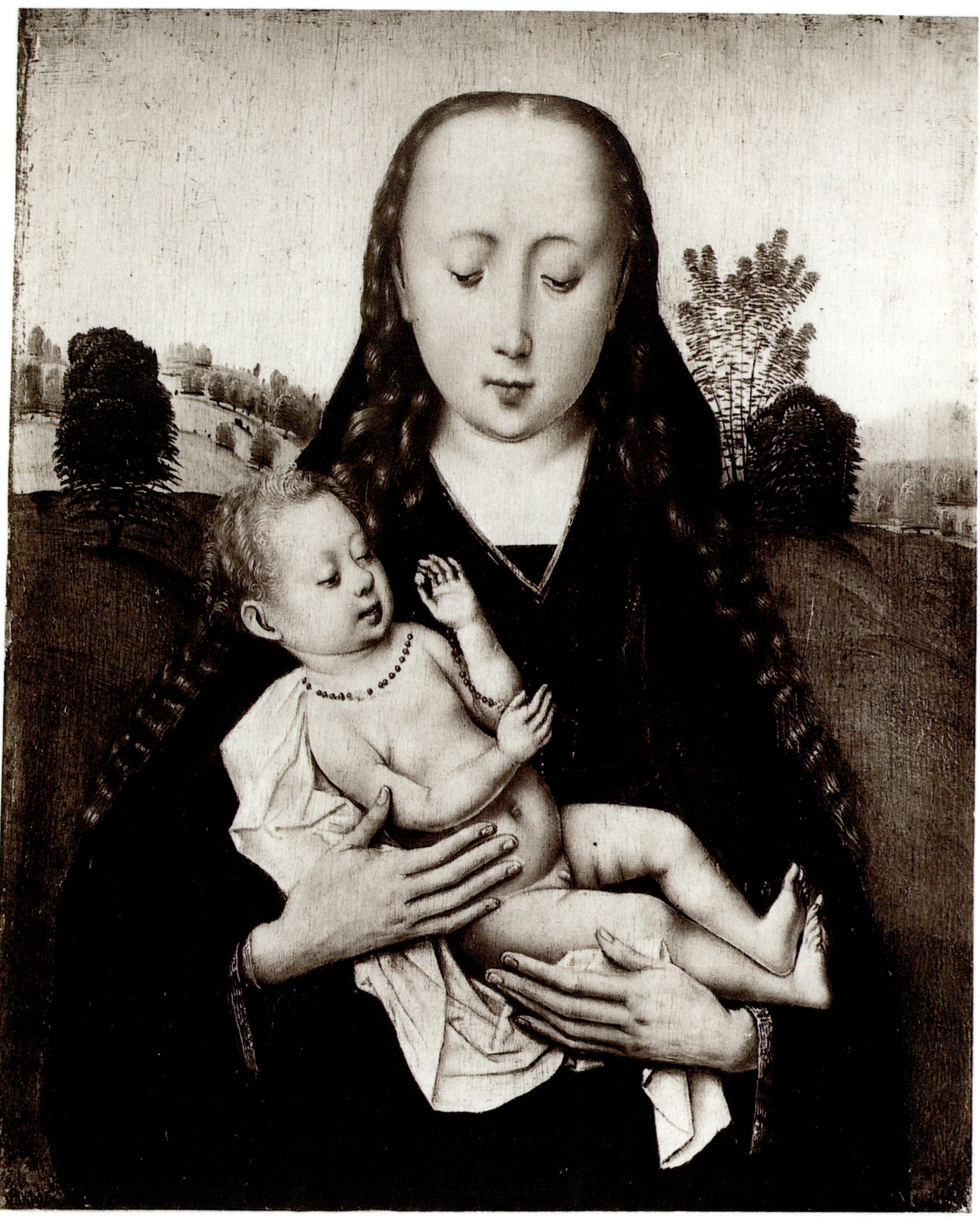

Fig. 3 Follower of Dieric Bouts, *Virgin and Child with a Rosary in a Landscape*, oil on panel, second half of the 15th century, 33 × 27 cm, present location unknown. (© RKD, The Hague.)

The result of the dendrochronological analysis of the Copenhagen painting, based on analysis of the trimmed panel, indicates that the panel is made of Baltic oak with a plausible production date from 1454 on.[19] Assuming, with reference to the surviving border, that at least 6 mm has been removed from each of the vertical sides, a minimum of five growth rings would have to be added to the upper as well as lower end of the date profile, resulting in a probable production date from 1459 on.[20] For the privately owned panel the corresponding data also indicate a Baltic origin, in this case with a production date from 1471 on.[21] However, bearing in mind that this panel too has been trimmed, at least along the right-hand

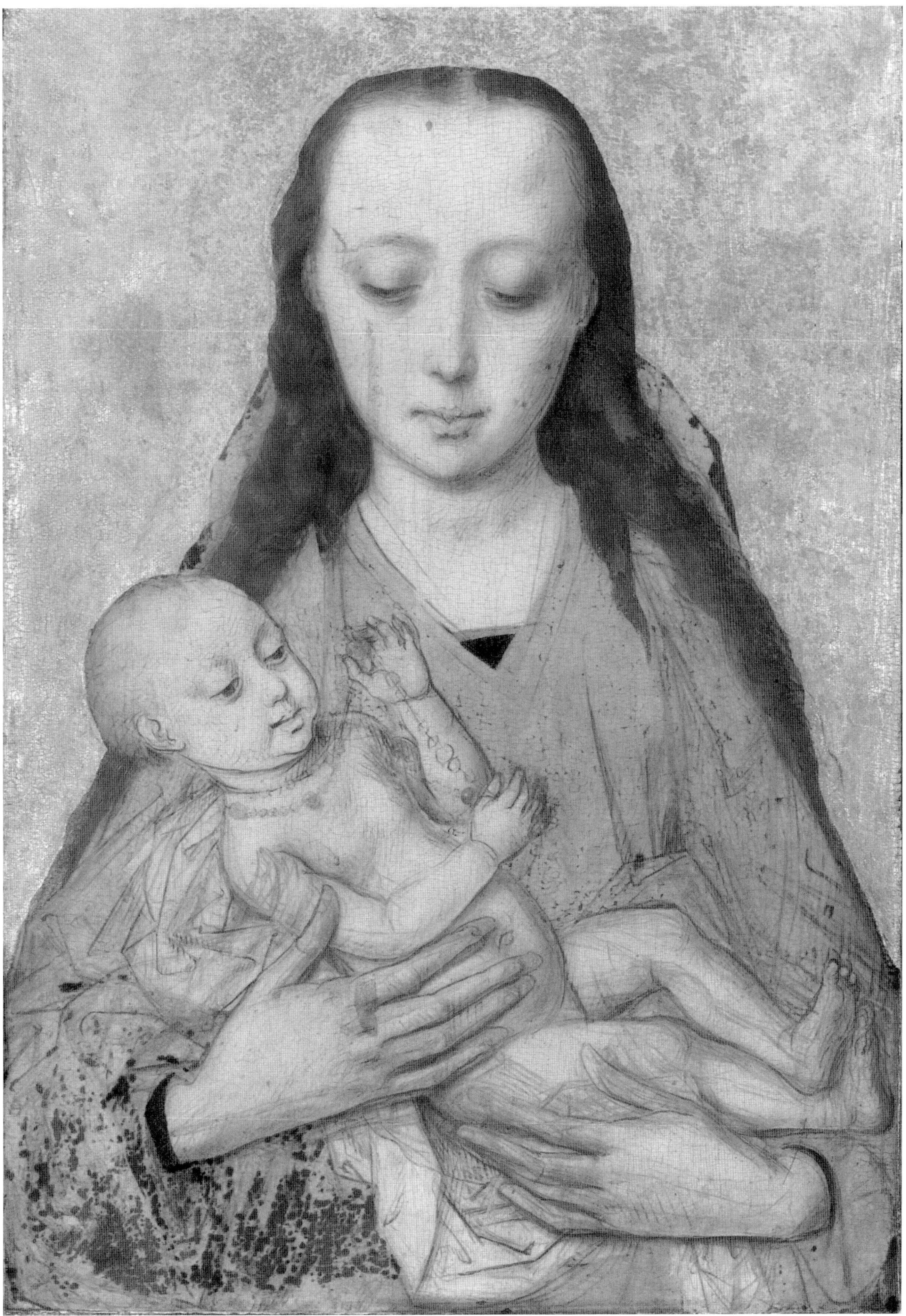

Fig. 4 *Virgin and Child with a Rosary* (Fig. 1): infrared image. (© SMK.)

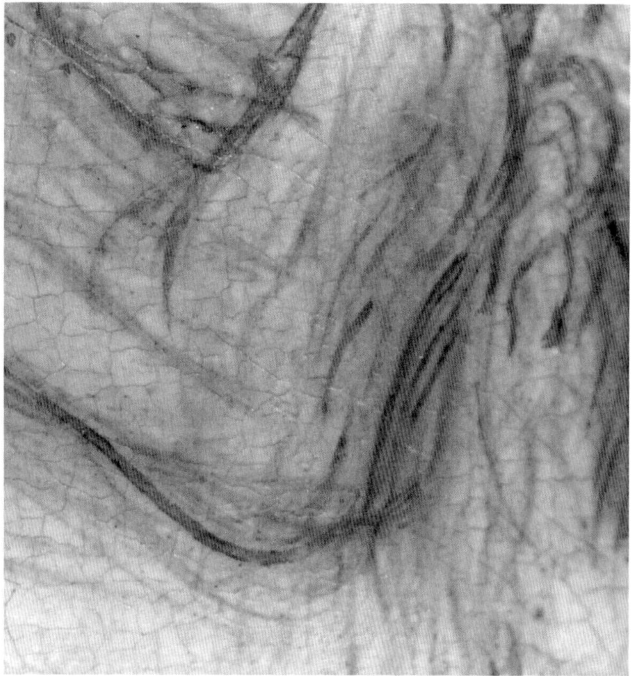

Fig. 5 *Virgin and Child with a Rosary* (Fig. 1): infrared image – close-up of the Child's feet. (© SMK.)

and bottom edges, the actual production date would appear to be somewhat later.

Examination by IRR of the two paintings produced quite dissimilar results. The reflectogram of the privately owned painting did not reveal any underdrawing,[22] so any existing drawing would have been made in a medium that cannot be identified with this technique. By comparison, the reflectogram of the Copenhagen painting shows a distinct and rather complex underdrawing, indicating a more convoluted genesis of this painting (Fig. 4).[23] The design, initially identical to that of the private version, has subsequently been subjected to significant changes and revisions.

The drawing in this case has clearly been carried out in two stages: the first, in soft-looking, pale lines, has many modifications, such as the length of the fingers, and some quite significant changes, particularly related to the positioning of the thumb on the left that was shifted at least four times. Other noticeable alterations can be found in the hands of the Virgin and the legs of the Child that were initially drawn higher up. The second stage of the underdrawing consists of darker reinforcing lines, made in order to clarify and strengthen the composition and establish what was meant to be the final design in the profusion of lines in the initial, searching drawing of the first stage.

There is parallel hatching, in many places fairly cursory, but very little cross-hatching. The scarce rendering of shade and volume in the underdrawing suggests the existence of a preliminary drawing or another model used at least in the later stages of the production, if not for mechanical transfer onto the panel.

Close-up imaging shows that both stages of the drawing were executed in a liquid medium, most recognisable however in the lines of the second stage with their tendency to pooling of the medium along the edges of the lines and in some places towards the ends (Fig. 5).

The draperies, especially the blue mantle of the Virgin, received little attention in the underdrawing in terms of modelling. The folds of the drapery were defined by little more than fairly straight contour lines, some of them with a small hook at the end. What there is of hatching appears rather hasty and casual. However, this may simply be an example of the painter's rational approach, as the stratigraphy of the blue paint would to some degree have obscured the drawing: an underpaint layer, composed of blue and white and most likely quite opaque, would result in the painter not gaining much benefit from a very detailed underdrawing after the application of that first paint layer (as opposed to other parts of the composition where a thinner or more transparent first layer would leave the drawing more visible). Finally, the large number of diversions in the painting stage from the underdrawing demonstrates a certain disregard of the guidelines of the drawing.

The hatching in the underdrawing is more developed and structured in the modelling of the upper body of the Child and the heads of the figures. But minor adjustments or modifications are evident also in these areas, for instance in the outer contours of the faces. Likewise, the neckline of the Virgin's robe was altered and the edges of an inner garment indicated, a detail also found in the final edition of the privately owned version, but in the end not followed in the painting stage of the Copenhagen panel. Last but not least, the position of the rosary was altered, and in this case the change was probably introduced only in the painting stage as there is no sign of an adaptation in the underdrawing corresponding to the rosary in its changed position. Strikingly, the abandoned design of the rosary in the underdrawing of the Copenhagen panel is identical to the painted rosary of the privately owned panel, indicating either that the latter is after all the earliest version or that a pre-existing drawing or painting was the model for both compositions. Likewise, the white edges of an inner garment at the neckline of the Virgin in the private version are depicted in the underdrawing of the Copenhagen version but were ignored in the painting stage. Other changes, introduced late in the process, are modifications to the Virgin's hands, for example the length and position of some of the fingers where the X-radiograph, as well as the crack pattern on the surface, shows that paint had already been applied to the fingers in their initial, longer form before they were shortened (Fig. 6).[24] At this early stage of the execution they corresponded to the more elongated design of the Virgin's hands in the private version. In comparison, the X-radiograph of the latter shows that no changes were apparently made in the execution of this painting (Fig. 7).[25]

It is debatable whether the underdrawing of the Copenhagen painting is supplemented by any incised lines such as those often found in works by Dieric Bouts and his workshop.[26] Some lines in the X-radiograph along the outer contour of the Child, and a few lines in other places, might possibly be interpreted as such. However, their jagged appearance suggests that they are more likely to be results

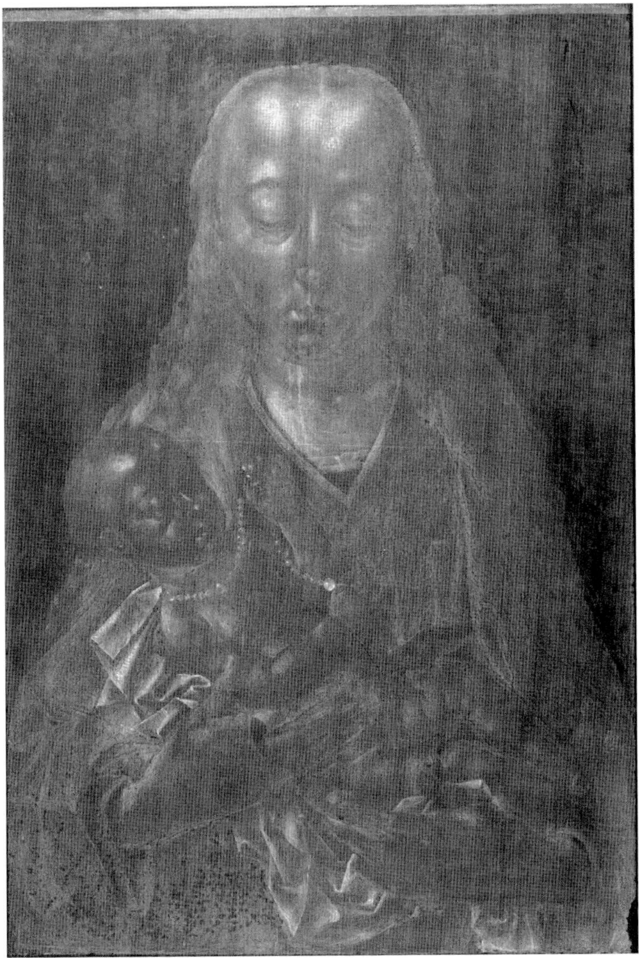

Fig. 6 *Virgin and Child with a Rosary* (Fig. 1): X-radiograph. (© SMK.)

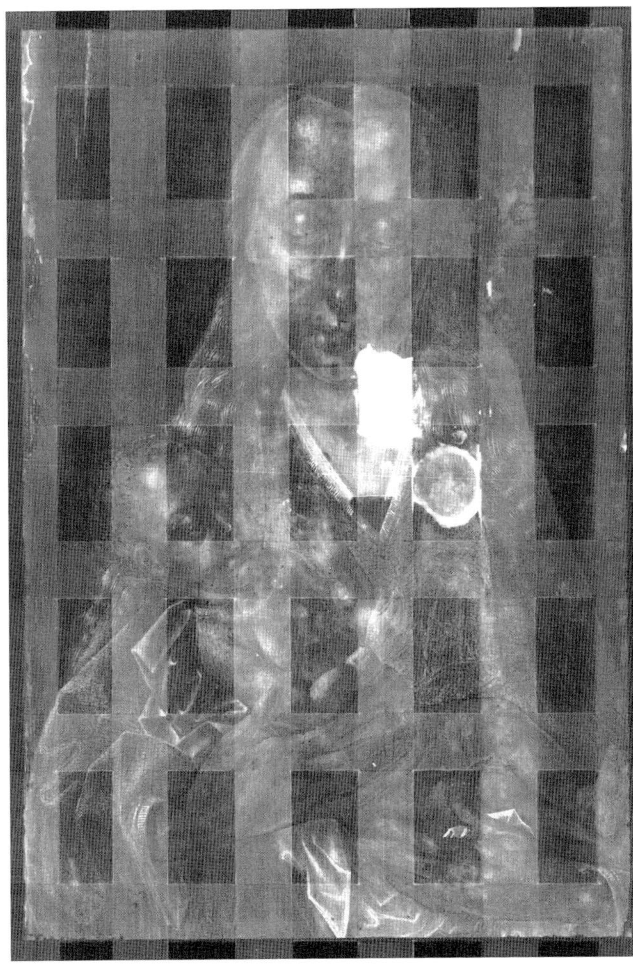

Fig. 7 *Virgin and Child with a Rosary* (Fig. 2): X-radiograph. (Rhona MacBeth, Museum of Fine Arts, Boston.)

of the particular crack pattern in areas where different fields of colour adjoin.

In the white cloth to the left of the Child in the Copenhagen panel the underdrawing was entirely disregarded in the painting stage and is not recognisable in the final design of the modelling. However, the painted cloth is again quite similar to that in the other version. As a further change the blue sleeve was painted over the lower part of the cloth.

The sequence of manufacture of the image was found to be the traditional method of applying the gilding before the painting. The paint itself was mainly applied very thinly with a slight impasto visible in the blue of the Virgin's mantle, in the highlights of the white cloth and to a small degree in a few highlights of the flesh paint. In one area scratching in the wet paint was used as a method of texturing the surface, an effect also found occasionally in paintings by Dieric Bouts or his workshop.[27]

The method of modelling the flesh tones by the addition of varying amounts of lead white to the paint, complemented with glazes in the shadow areas, is seen with increased clarity in the X-radiograph. It is rather distinctive with concentrations of dense pigment (lead white) in areas on the forehead of the Virgin, above the eyebrows, particularly the left-hand brow, underneath the eyes, on the ridge of the nose, on the upper lip and on the lower parts of the corners of the mouth. The distribution of lead white is very similar to that seen in the privately owned version, although differences in the contrasts between the two X-radiographs suggest higher concentrations of the lead white pigment in the flesh paint modelling of the latter.[28] This characteristic treatment of the modelling has been found in a number of other *Virgin and Child* compositions from the Bouts group – by Dieric Bouts himself and also largely adopted by his workshop.[29]

Another characteristic paint technique is found in the Virgin's hair which was created by applying a layer of golden brown paint followed by a form of 'modelling', with strands of hair in two or three shades, an approach obviously identical to that applied in the hair of the other version.

While only the paint layers of the Copenhagen *Virgin and Child* have been investigated by cross-section analysis, both versions of the composition have the appearance characteristic of Early Netherlandish painting, the result of a stratified paint structure and consistent also with the painting technique found in works by Dieric Bouts and his circle.

The investigation of the Copenhagen painting showed a structure with two to four, even occasionally five layers,[30] as exemplified by two examples: a sample from the mantle of the Virgin showed a classic method of constructing a blue paint layer with a first layer of azurite with some lead white, followed by a layer with lapis lazuli as the main component on top.[31] In areas of a deeper blue the lapis is used almost pure as a glaze, whereas it is mixed with a little lead white in the more light coloured zones.

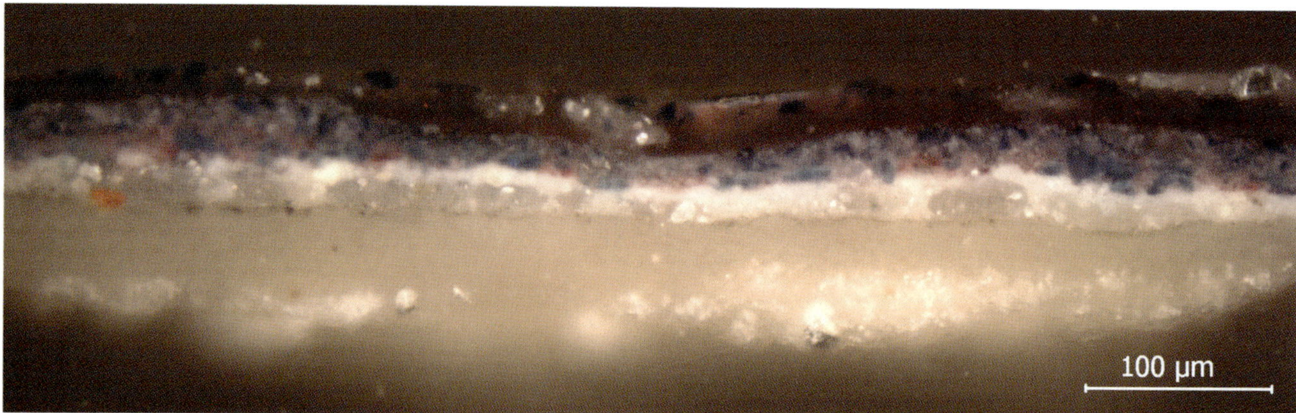

Figure 8 *Virgin and Child with a Rosary* (Fig. 1): cross-section of ground and paint layers in the Virgin's purple gown. (© CATS – SMK.)

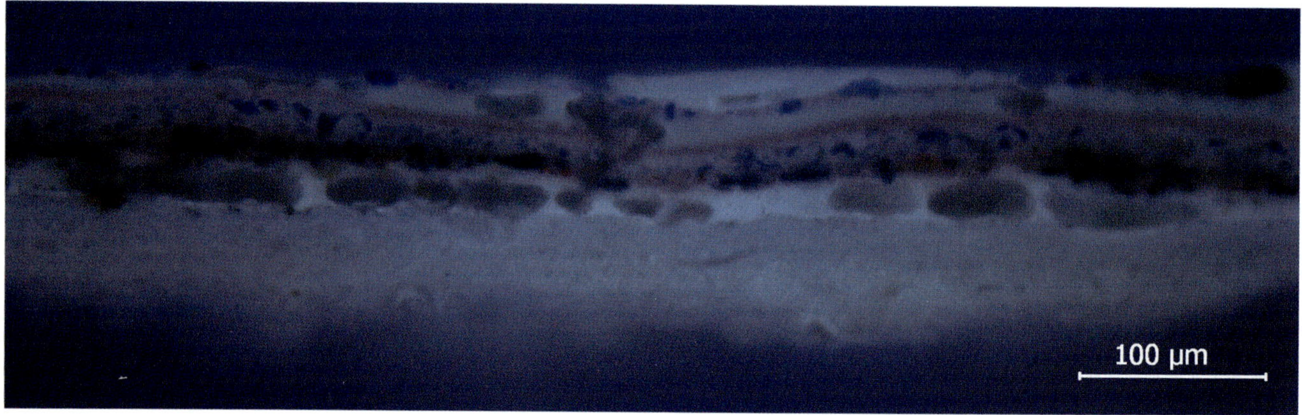

Fig. 9 *Virgin and Child with a Rosary* (Fig. 1): cross-section in UV light of ground and paint layers in the Virgin's purple gown. (© CATS – SMK.)

A characteristic stratigraphy is also demonstrated by the purple gown of the Virgin in which a white priming layer on top of the ground is followed by two to three layers of red lake mixed with different proportions of blue pigment, respectively azurite and lapis lazuli (Figs 8 and 9).

The white priming layer on top of the ground, a typical feature of Early Netherlandish painting technique, has been found in a number of works by Dieric Bouts and his workshop. This particular layer was difficult to distinguish with certainty in some of the samples from the Copenhagen painting, perhaps due to variations in thickness related to an uneven method of application. However, a priming layer that was applied only locally has been found occasionally in paintings of the period.[32]

Tiny black particles on top of the ground in several of the samples presumably relate to the underdrawing and show that the drawing was executed before the application of the priming, a usual practice of the period.[33] In contrast to the paint of the draperies, samples from the flesh paint and hair showed a more simple stratigraphy with generally no more than two layers.

Medium analysis by MRS of various samples from the blue mantle and the white cloth revealed linseed oil as the medium used in both cases.[34] Binding medium analyses were not carried out on other paint areas. Different media have been identified in blue paint layers of works by Dieric Bouts and his workshop, for instance oil-protein mixtures, sometimes reserved for underpaint layers but also occasionally found in the top paint layers.[35]

Style, iconography and function

No halo, no jewels, no gold embroidered garments: nothing but the golden background identifies the Virgin as Queen of Heaven. Mother and Child appear tightly framed within the pictorial space. The viewer is invited to share the intimacy of the scene in which the Virgin envelops her child in a white cloth as she contemplates him. This sense of closeness and accessibility was in demand for devotional panels, helping the viewer to enter into the spirit of inner life.[36] For private prayer, rosaries such as that in the painting were used as a mnemonic device to count the prayers to Christ and the Virgin. In the era of *Devotio Moderna*, the rosary was a popular object, often seen in portraits and in still lifes that form part of religious scenes in Early Netherlandish painting, the *Ars Nova*.[37] However, representations of the Child with a rosary are not very common in Early Netherlandish depictions of the Virgin.[38] One of the earliest extant examples of the rosary iconography is a small panel *Madonna and Child by a Fountain* (1439) attributed to Jan van Eyck by Friedländer.[39] Here the Virgin is represented in full figure in a garden, the *Hortus Conclusus*. The Child's rosary is a single string of beads to which he does not pay any attention. In other representations the Child is playing with the rosary as if it was a toy, and in one example he grasps the rosary of the donatrix as if teasing her.[40]

The Copenhagen painting shows a novel approach to the iconography of the *Virgin and Child with a Rosary*. The close-up, half-length composition and the position of the

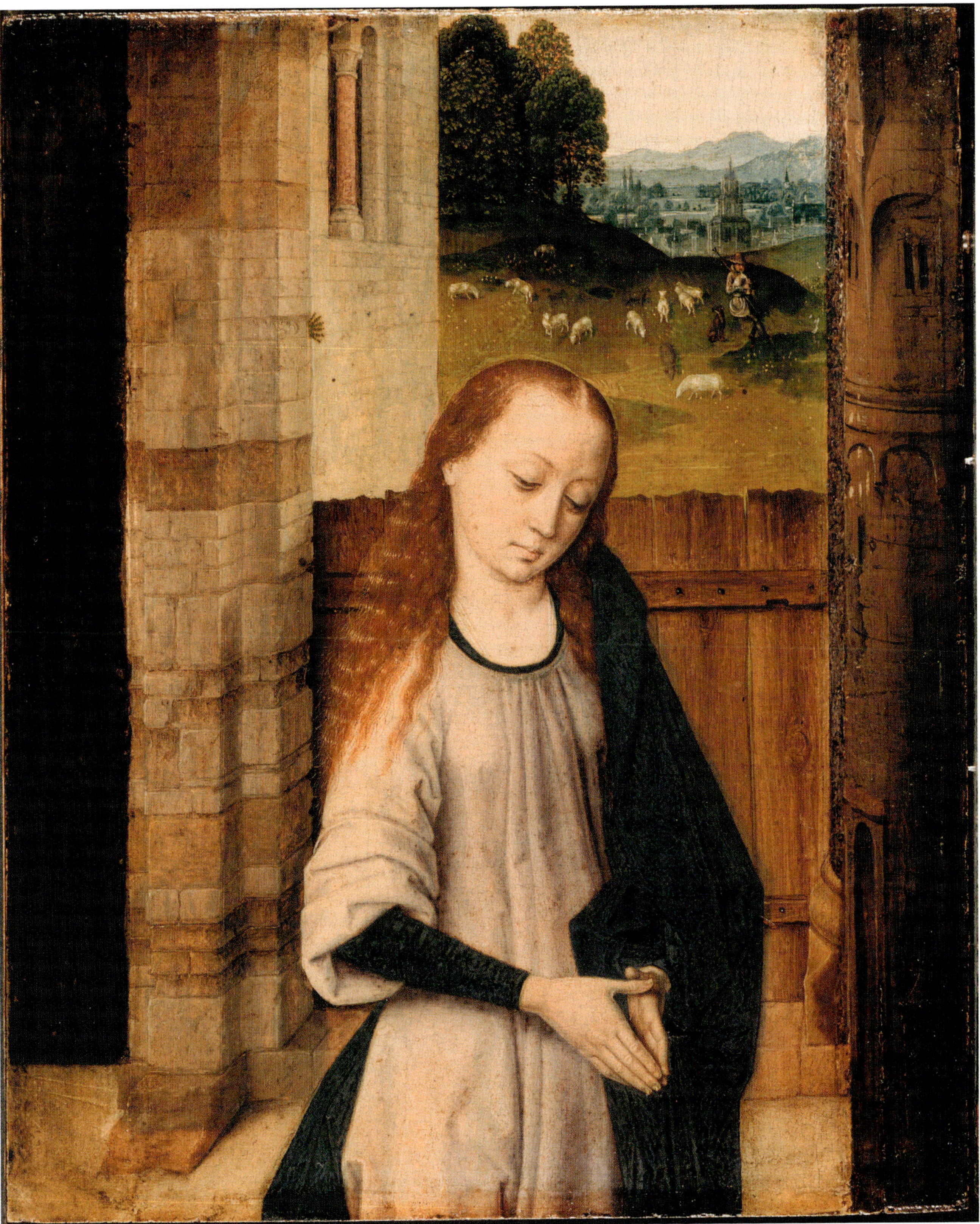

Fig. 10 Dieric Bouts workshop, *Virgin at Prayer* (fragment of a *Nativity*), *c.*1475–1500, oil on panel, 25 × 19.6 cm, Gemäldegalerie, Staatliche Museen zu Berlin, inv. 545B. (© bpk Berlin. Photo: Jörg P. Anders.)

rosary impart a new emphasis to the *Pater Noster* bead. In this design the artist decided to isolate the *Pater Noster* bead in the Child's hand, making it a protagonist in the composition, not only as a result of the formal change, but also through the Child's absorbed contemplation and through the meticulousness with which it has been painted. It is larger than the other glass beads, its lights and colours reflected from the near surroundings are carefully rendered and added what appears to be an immanent light. The same care in the execution is evident in the other glass *Pater Noster* beads.

The emphasis on the prayer to Our Lord is also implicit in the number of beads, as rosaries at this time normally had one *Pater Noster* bead per 10 *Ave Maria* beads.[41]

The emphasis on the human character of the Virgin and Child is common in Netherlandish 15th-century paintings. With the innovative rosary motif and the emphasis on the *Pater Noster* bead the Boutsian panel has become a foretelling of Christ's prayers during the Passion and the Virgin's Sorrows.[42] The implicit focus on the Passion of Christ, and not least the Seven Sorrows of the Virgin, is perhaps due to a general focus on the Passion in epical as well as devotional painting towards the end of the 15th century. The function of the Boutsian devotional Madonna was to help the pious owner to enter an inner space of contemplation and prayers that took part in the sorrows of the Mother of God over her son's agonies.

Compared to the privately owned panel, the Copenhagen panel is more modern in terms of style with its less elongated proportions and clearer in terms of composition, as well as more costly due to the lavish use of lapis lazuli. We may conclude that the Copenhagen *Virgin and Child with a Rosary* was made on commission, whereas the privately owned version was probably created for the art market. Both panels were most likely intended for private devotional use. As a commissioned artwork the Copenhagen panel may have formed the left wing in a diptych with the portrait of the commissioner or commissioners on the right wing. The frontal symmetrical pose of the Virgin does not rule out this possibility as is evident from Hans Memling's *Diptych with Virgin and Child and Maarten van Nieuwenhove* dated 1487 or Rogier van der Weyden's *Diptych with Virgin and Child and Jean de Froimont*.[43] The Boutsian Rosary Madonna is an example of one of the new types of Virgin and Child iconographies developed in the 15th century to satisfy an ever more demanding market for non-epical, devotional paintings.

The Copenhagen panel's innovative approach to the iconography is in contrast with archaic features such as the gilded background and the hieratic frontal pose of the Virgin. Both elements were out of fashion and not common in the Boutsian oeuvre, where the extant examples exhibit different solutions for the backgrounds, such as a dark or green plain one (New York, The Metropolitan Museum of Art; Frankfurt, Städel and Cambridge, MA, Harvard University Art Museums, Fogg Art Museum), a green and gold brocade cloth of honour (San Francisco, Fine Arts Museum), or a cloth of honour combined with a window with a view (London, National Gallery), and the Madonnas in three-quarter profile.[44] However, both these atypical elements of the Copenhagen panel could be the results of special requests by the commissioner.

The Virgin's characteristic physiognomy with the high forehead also appears in a fragment of a *Nativity* in the Gemäldegalerie in Berlin attributed to Dieric Bouts the Elder (Fig. 10).[45] The Virgin's simple hairstyle and the beautiful juxtaposition of ultramarine and rich purple is also present in the Berlin panel. The Copenhagen panel and the Berlin fragment share a number of similarities as to how paint is handled and the way in which the candid expression of the Virgin with downcast eyes is rendered. In both panels the soft expression is obtained by the lack of sharp contours and a certain blurring of the iris. In the Copenhagen panel an ultramarine (lapis lazuli) glaze was applied to the white of the eye, and the fact that the long eyelashes turn white when overlapping the iris also adds to the soft expression.

Dieric Bouts the Elder received two official commissions: the altarpiece of the *Holy Sacrament* for Saint Peter's Church (commissioned 15 March 1464 and finished after 9 February 1468) and the four *Justice* panels for the town hall of Louvain (commissioned 1468). Of the last-mentioned series only one panel was finished before the death of the master: *The Justice of Emperor Otto III. Ordeal by Fire* (delivered 1473) (Fig. 11). A second panel, *The Justice of Emperor Otto III. Beheading of the Innocent Count* was completed by the workshop.[46] The workshop of Dieric Bouts the Elder employed, in addition to assistants whose identities remain unknown, his two sons Dieric Bouts the Younger (*c.* 1448–1490/9) and Albrecht (1451/55–1549) who, according to his will, were to inherit all the tools and equipment of painting and all unfinished paintings.[47] From Dieric Bouts the Younger's hand no autograph work is known. From Albrecht's hand only one extant work is documented – an 'A' for Albrecht is visible in the painter's guild shield on the right wing of the altarpiece *The Assumption of the Virgin* (*c.*1495–1500) in the Musées royaux des Beaux-Arts, Brussels, originally a documented gift from the artist to the chapel Notre-Dame-hors-les-murs, Louvain, where he was sacristan until 1508.[48]

There seem to be general affinities in the style of the Copenhagen *Virgin and Child* to *The Ordeal by Fire* such as the angular rhythm of the folds in the draperies and the advanced skills in rendering different surface textures. One particular element can be mentioned as a typical example: in the Copenhagen panel the painter added a thin transparent veil between the Virgin's mantle and dress, a detail absent in the privately owned version. The structure of the paint layer in the veil consists of a transparent glaze upon which carefully drawn parallel hatching and reinforced lines along the contours depict the texture in the organza linen (Fig. 12). This characteristic method used for the rendering of transparent veils is also found in *The Ordeal by Fire* in the countess's veil that falls from her hat and is used by her to envelope the head of the innocent count in much the same way as the Virgin envelops the Child with the cloth in the two Madonna panels. The veil in the second *Justice* panel, *Beheading of the Innocent Count*, finished after the death of Dieric Bouts, is handled in a very different way. Here the transparent fabric is rendered as a plain surface without any rendering of the texture of the organza.

In her recently published monograph on Albrecht Bouts, Valentine Henderiks has shown that within the context of Boutsian devotional painting, prototypes by Dieric Bouts the Elder were transferred mechanically with calque and cartoon by his sons who reused and developed the designs.[49] Within the workshop of Albrecht this practice of copying and replicating devotional paintings for the open market as well as on commission was organised as a workshop within the workshop. One of the most popular devotional images were the pendants with *Christ Crowned with Thorns* and *Mater Dolorosa* after

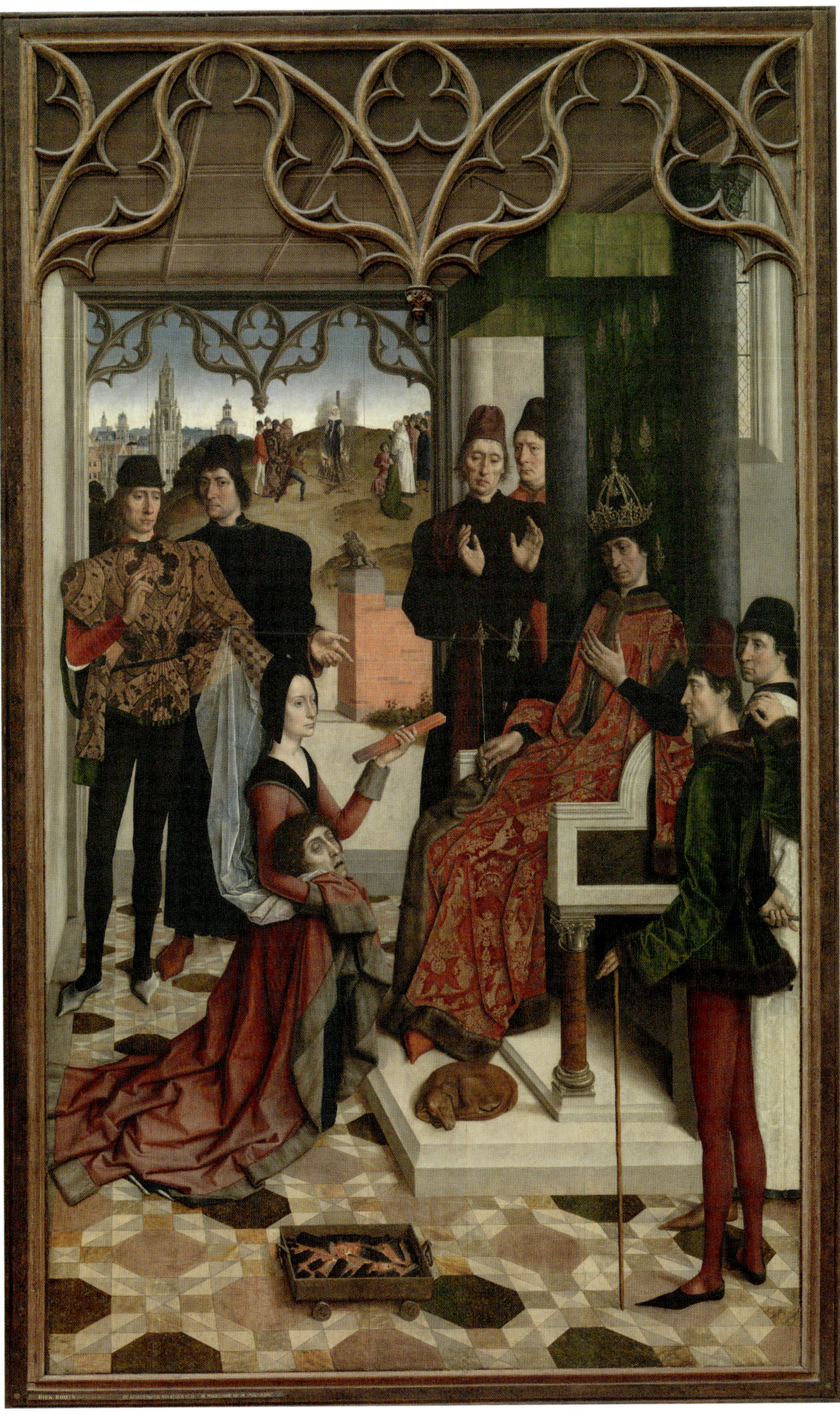

Fig. 11 Dieric Bouts, *The Justice of Emperor Otto III. The Ordeal by Fire*, *c.*1471–73, oil on panel, 323.5 × 181.5 cm, Brussels, Musées royaux des Beaux-Arts de Belgique, inv. 1448. (© Musées Royaux des Beaux-Arts de Belgique, Brussels. Photo: J. Geleyns.)

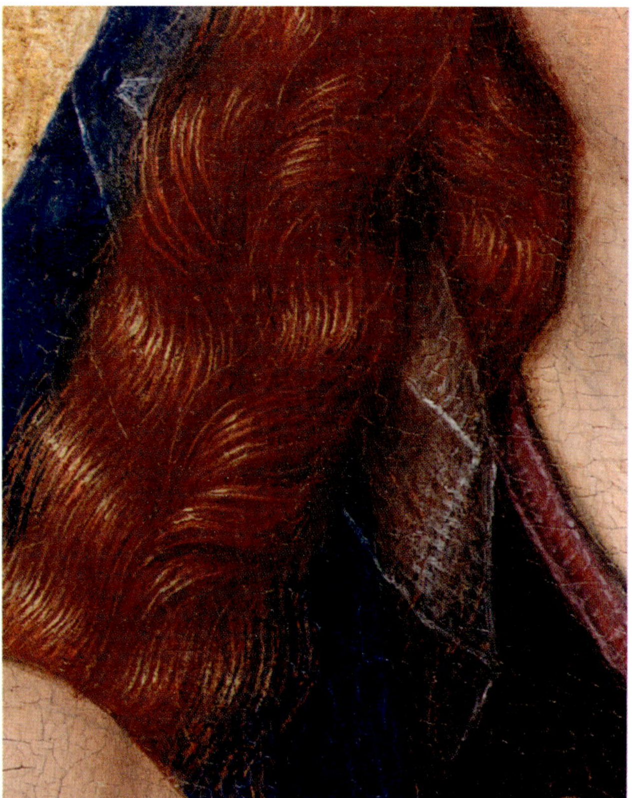

Fig. 12 *Virgin and Child with a Rosary* (Fig. 1): detail. (© SMK.)

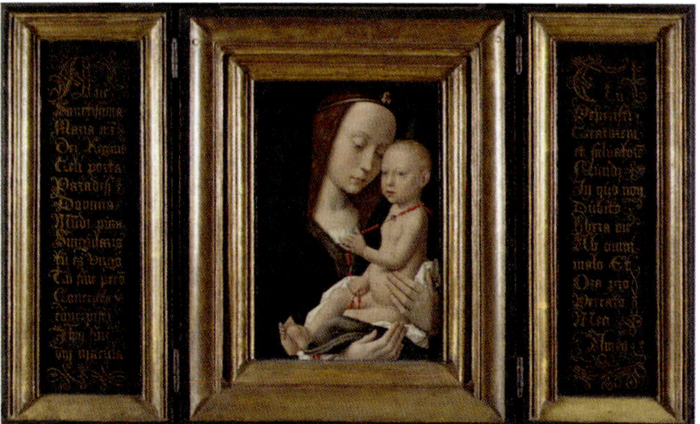

Fig. 13 Follower of Hugo van der Goes, *Virgin and Child*, *c.*1485, oil on panel, 32.3 × 21.4 cm, London, The National Gallery, inv. NG3066. (© The National Gallery, London.)

a lost prototype by Dieric Bouts.[50] Albrecht Bouts also created his own prototypes for some of the images. He painted no less than four extant variations of *Christ Crowned with Thorns*: in Dijon, in a private collection, in Luxembourg and in Kansas City.[51] This is also the case for *Saint John's Head on a Plate*. A lost prototype by Dieric Bouts the Elder served as a model, but Albrecht himself also created a prototype, the one in Oldenburg, that served as a model for further workshop replicas.[52]

The versions of the *Virgin and Child with a Rosary* in Copenhagen and in a private collection should be added to the examples of the copying and replicating practice of the Boutsian workshop. Perhaps both paintings derive from a now lost prototype. The version with a landscape background more remote in composition and dimensions could be an example of how a Boutsian design was used outside the workshop. Another example of this is a small devotional panel in the National Gallery, London, attributed to a follower of Hugo van der Goes and dated *c.*1485.[53] We see a Rosary Madonna very similar to our panels with identical positions of the Child's legs, feet and left arm (Fig. 13). While the Child has been reversed and raised to a sitting position, and his attention is not focused on the beads, all other aspects of the pose and physiognomy are strikingly similar to the Child of the Copenhagen and privately owned panels.

Conclusions

Although the dendrochronological analyses at first glance might indicate the Copenhagen painting to be the earliest of the two versions, the reservations linked to the evaluation of the results as well as the style of the privately owned version suggest that this painting may well be close in date, or indeed the older of the two. In both cases the date falls within the range (though at the late end) of dendrochronological findings in panels attributed to Dieric Bouts and his workshop.[54]

From a technical point of view, both paintings appear to be typical products of Flemish painting practice in the late 15th century, and within that framework consistent with what has been found in works from the Bouts group. The differences in method and quality of the underdrawings do not seem to conflict with both paintings originating in the same workshop, though obviously by different hands. There appears to be no particular consistency in the amount of underdrawing on panels attributed to Bouts or his workshop. The nature of the underdrawing of the Copenhagen painting with its numerous revisions and changes does suggest a degree of autonomy or independence in the creation of this work, as does the partial disregard in the painting stage of the guidelines of the drawing. The close similarity of the abandoned edition of the underdrawing to the (completed) privately owned version indicates either that this other version does indeed predate the Copenhagen panel or that a pre-existing model was the prototype for both paintings.

The mind of the Copenhagen panel artist was focused on the search for new paths to follow, whereas the master of the privately owned version closely followed the design of a potential, now lost Boutsian workshop prototype. The Copenhagen artist was more forward-looking in his search for less elongated proportions of the bodies and an enhanced realism that rendered each bead, each fabric, each surface structure with great pictorial ambition and skill. The artist, probably a member of Dieric Bouts' workshop, could be identical to the originator of the Berlin *Nativity* fragment. In accord with his time, he was capable of developing the pictorial idiom and iconography of the Rosary Virgin in order to meet the demands of the *Devotio Moderna*. That this happened in Louvain is hardly surprising, as at the time the city was one of the most important intellectual, ecclesiastical and cultural centres of Europe.

Acknowledgements

We wish to thank Peter van den Brink, Catheline Périer-D'Ieteren, Valentine Henderiks and Molly Faries for their valuable comments and observations, many of which were made during fruitful discussions at a Scholars' study day at the National Gallery on 23 May 2012. Catheline Périer-D'Ieteren is thanked for a comprehensive review of the Copenhagen painting during its restoration in 2010. This was supplemented by Valentine Henderiks with observations on possible links to Albrecht Bouts. Rhona MacBeth and Peter van den Brink generously shared a wealth of information and data on the privately owned version, and Molly Faries contributed much appreciated reflections on the interpretation of the dendrochronological analyses. Finally, thanks are due to Ole Faurskov Nielsen for carrying out micro-Raman analysis on the Copenhagen painting.

Notes

1. V. Villadsen, *Statens Museum for Kunst 1827–1952*, Copenhagen, Gyldendalske Boghandel, Nordisk Forlag A.S., 1998, p. 228; M. Moltesen, C. Fischer and T. Thunoe, *Buddha, Barok & Bryggeren. Carl Jacobsens ukendte samlinger*, Meddelelser fra Ny Carlsberg Glyptotek, no. 14, 2012, p. 33.
2. J.M. Heberle, *Katalog der Gemälde-Sammlung des zu Frankfurt am Main gestorbene Herrn Simon Emil Moritz Oppenheim*, Cologne, 1878. Heberle auction catalogue, introduction with biographical notes on Simon Emil Moritz Oppenheim; for the Bouts panel see no. 75, 20.
3. Ibid.
4. *Fortegnelse over Ny Carlsberg Malerisamling. Udstillet i Kunstforeningen i Februar og Marts*, Copenhagen, Thieles Bogtrykkeri, 1885, p. 8; *Fortegnelse over Ny Carlsberg Malerisamling. Udstillet i Kunstforeningen i Februar og Marts*, Copenhagen, Thieles Bogtrykkeri, 1887, p. 79.
5. *Ny Carlsberg Glyptotek. Fortegnelse over kunstværkerne*, Copenhagen, Thieles Bogtrykkeri, 1900, p. 42; *Ny Carlsberg Glyptotek. Fortegnelse over kunstværkerne*, Copenhagen, F.E. Bording, 1902, p. 74; *Fortegnelse over billedhuggerarbejder fra den nyere tid og renaissancen samt medailler malerier og tegninger*, Copenhagen, F.E. Bording, 1905, p. 84.
6. K. Madsen, 'Brügge-udstillingens udbytte. II Nederlandsk og fransk malerkunst fra det 15. Aarh.', *Tilskueren*, Copenhagen, 1903, p. 683.
7. *Fortegnelse over kunstværkerne i den moderne afdeling*, 7th edn, Copenhagen, J. Cohens bogtrykkerier (Georg A. Back), 1916, p. 79.
8. K. Madsen, 'Billeder af gammel-nederlandsk Malerkunst I Kunstmuseet', *Kunstmuseets Aarsskrift* 1924–25, pp. 1–16, pp. 2–4.
9. Private collection, oil on panel. Conflicting data exist on the dimensions of this painting: Friedländer (1968, p. 76, no. 96) and the RKD database give the dimensions 34 × 22.5 cm, while in Sotheby's auction catalogue (Sale no. 8321, 8 June 2008, Lot 233) the dimensions are reported as 35.9 × 24.2 cm. Both sizes are somewhat smaller than the 42.5 × 27.5 cm of the Copenhagen panel; M.J. Friedländer, *Early Netherlandish Painting. Volume 3: Dieric Bouts and Joos van Gent*, Leiden, La Connaissance, 1968.
10. Present location unknown. Formerly in the Haro collection and the Achillito Chiesa collection. According to the RKD database the dimensions are 33 × 27 cm.
11. Henri Haro's collection in Paris (auction catalogue no. 117).
12. Friedländer 1968 (cited in note 9), pl. 99, fig. 96b.
13. Ibid., pl. 99, fig. 96a. The SMK archives does not hold any correspondence between Friedländer and Madsen on this matter.
14. Ibid., pl. 99, figs 96, 96b.
15. W. Schöne, *Dieric Bouts und seine Schule*, Berlin/Leipzig, Verlag für Kunstwissenschaft, 1938, p. 203, no. 116.
16. L. Swane, *Royal Museum of Fine Arts: Catalogue of Old Foreign Paintings*, Copenhagen, Langkjærs Bogtrykkeri, 1951, p. 376, no. 858.
17. The painting is not mentioned in M. Smeyers (ed.), *Dirk Bouts (ca. 1410–1475). Een Vlaams primitief te Leuven*, Leuven, Isd. (Sint-Pieterskerk en Predikherenkerk), 1998, nor was it mentioned at any of the scholars' talks in an international colloquium held in conjunction with the exhibition (*Bouts Studies 2001*). As a natural consequence the painting was not included in the monograph on Dieric Bouts by Catheline Périer-D'Ieteren; see C. Périer-D'Ieteren, *Dieric Bouts: The Complete Works* (with the assistance of Valentine Henderiks), Antwerp, Mercatorfonds, 2006. It is not included either in the monograph on Albrecht Bouts by Valentine Henderiks; see V. Henderiks, *Albrecht Bouts (1451/55–1549)*, Brussels, Brepols, 2011. It has not appeared in any of the prestigious exhibitions celebrated on Early Netherlandish masters over the years.
18. Extensive research on the privately owned version has been carried out by Peter van den Brink. We are grateful to him for sharing his views and observations. The technical investigation of the painting was carried out by Rhona MacBeth at the Museum of Fine Arts, Boston who is also thanked for sharing the images.
19. Dendrochronological analysis was carried out by Peter Klein. The report states that the wood originates from the Baltic region. The 200 growth rings ranged from 1238 to 1437. The youngest heartwood ring was formed in the year 1437. Regarding the sapwood statistics for Eastern Europe, an earliest felling date can be derived for the year 1446, but more plausible is a felling date of 1450–1456+. With a minimum of two years required for seasoning, an earliest creation of the painting is possible from 1448 on. Assuming a median of 15 sapwood rings and two years for seasoning, a creation date is plausible from 1454 on.
20. According to Molly Faries the panel could have been trimmed by at least 1 cm on each vertical side. Supporting this view is research on prevalent formats in the period, carried out by Sytske Weidema (unpublished), suggesting the panel to have been somewhat wider. Also, if the panel had been taken from one board, there is no reason to assume it would need to be centred and trimmed equally on both sides. Time might have been saved by trimming just one side, i.e. all older or younger year rings (personal communication from Molly Faries).
21. The information was kindly provided by Peter van den Brink. Dendrochronological analysis was carried out by Peter Klein 2008. The wood was confirmed as being of Baltic origin with 149 growth rings, 1306–1454, and the youngest heartwood being formed in 1454. Regarding the sapwood statistics of Eastern Europe, an earliest felling date can be derived for the year 1464, but a felling date of 1467–1473+ is more likely. Assuming a minimum of two years for seasoning an earliest date for the creation of the painting would be 1448 on. Assuming a median of 15 sapwood rings and two years for seasoning, a creation date of 1471 on is plausible.
22. IRR was carried out at the Museum of Fine Arts, Boston, by Rhona MacBeth.
23. IRR was carried out with an Osiris Camera at 1700 nm by Riccardo Buccarella in the Photographic Department, SMK.
24. X-radiography of the Copenhagen panel was carried out with an Andrex BW85 X-ray tube at 28 kV, 5 mA, 120 sec on AGFA Structurix D7 DW ETE film.
25. X-radiography was carried out at the Museum of Fine Arts, Boston, by Rhona MacBeth.

26. Among several occurences: in the *Virgin and Child* in the National Gallery, London, the *Virgin and Child* in Städel, Frankfurt and the *Virgin and Child* in the Fogg Art Museum, Cambridge, MA.
27. See for instance Périer-D'Ieteren 2006 (cited in note 17), p. 149.
28. Interpretation and comparison of X-ray images such as these should be approached with some caution as variations in contrast and brightness of the images can to some extent be a result of different parameters of the X-ray exposures as much as by dissimilarities in materials and painting technique.
29. See D. Bomford, R. Ashok and A. Smith, 'The techniques of Dieric Bouts: two paintings contrasted', *National Gallery Technical Bulletin* 10, 1986, pp. 39–57, p. 53; J. Sander, *Niederländische Gemälde im Städel 1400–1550*, Frankfurt, Städelsches Kunstinstitut, 1993, p. 53; G. Pocobene and R. Spronk, 'The Fogg Art Museum's *Virgin and Child* from the workshop of Dirk Bouts: findings from technical examinations and recent conservation treatment', in M. Faries and R. Spronk (eds), *Recent Developments in the Technical Examination of Early Netherlandish Painting: Methodology, Limitations and Perspectives*, Cambridge, MA, Harvard University Art Museums 2003, pp. 97–107, p. 100; Pèrier-D'Ieteren 2006 (cited in note 17), pp. 131–132, 148–149, 160, 380.
30. Cross-sections were examined in a Leica DM4000M microscope.
31. Lapis lazuli was identified by MRS by Ole Faurskov Nielsen at the Chemical Institute, Copenhagen University; see O. Faurskov Nielsen and T. Filtenborg, 'A microRaman spectroscopic investigation of a Flemish painting from the late 15th century', *Asian Chemistry Letters* 15(4), 2011, pp. 247–254. Identification of the pigments in the underpaint layer was based on visual examination in the microscope.
32. See L. Depuydt-Elbaum, R. Guislain-Wittermann *et al.*, 'De restauratie van het Laatste Avondmaal. Technologisch onderzoek en behandeling', in A. Bergmans (ed.), *Dirk Bouts. Het Laatste Avondmaal*, Brussels, Ministerie van de Vlaamse Gemeenschap, Department Monumenten an Landschappen, Lannoo nv, Tielt, 1998, pp. 208–238, pp. 236–237; Périer-D'Ieteren 2006 (cited in note 17), p. 101.
33. R. Billinge, L. Campbell, J. Dunkerton *et al.*, 'Methods and materials of Northern European painting in the National Gallery, 1400–1550', *National Gallery Technical Bulletin* 18, 1997, pp. 6–55, p. 25; L. Kockaert, 'Onderzoek van de schilderstechniek', in A. Bergmans (ed.), *Dirk Bouts. Het Laatste Avondmaal*, Brussels, Ministerie van de Vlaamse Gemeenschap, Department Monumenten an Landschappen, Lannoo nv, Tielt, 1998, p. 237; R. Billinge, L. Campbell, J. Dunkerton *et al.*, 'The materials of underdrawing', in D. Bomford (ed.), *Underdrawings in Renaissance Paintings*, London, National Gallery Company, 2010, p. 28.
34. See Faurskov and Filtenborg 2011 (cited in note 31), pp. 251–252.
35. Billinge *et al.* 1997 (cited in note 33), pp. 34, 41; Kockaert 1998 (cited in note 33), pp. 237–238; Pocobene and Spronk 2003 (cited in note 29), p. 102.
36. For a classical study of the close-up half-length Madonna in Early Netherlandish painting see: S. Ringbom, *Icon to Narrative: The Rise of the Dramatic Close-up in Fifteenth-century Devotional Painting, Acta Academiae Aboensis*, ser. A, 31(2), 1965, pp. 93–106. On the close-up half-length Madonnas by Dieric Bouts and his workshop, see Périer-D'Ieteren 2006 (cited in note 17), pp. 126–133. On the production of devotional panels within the workshop of Albrecht Bouts, see V. Henderiks, 'L'atelier d'Albrecht Bouts et la production en série d'oeuvres de dévotion privée', *Revue Belge d'Archéologie et d'Histoire de l'Art / Belgisch Tijfschrift voor Oudheidkunde en Kunstgeschiedenis* 78, 2009, pp. 15–28, and Henderiks 2011 (cited in note 17), pp. 207–210 (with a discussion of the German term *Andachtsbild*).
37. On the style concept *Ars Nova*, see S. Kemperdick and J. Sander (eds), *Der Meister von Flémalle und Rogier van der Weyden*, exh. cat., Gemäldegalerie Staatliche Museen zu Berlin, Städel Museum, Hatje Cantz Verlag, Ostfildern, 2008, pp. 31–38.
38. On the rosary iconography in general, see G. Schiller, *Ikonographie der Christlichen Kunst. Maria*, vol. 4.2, Gütersloh, Gütersloher Verlagshaus Gerd Mohn, 1980, pp. 199–205.
39. M.J. Friedländer, *Early Netherlandish Painting. Volume 1: The van Eycks – Petrus Christus*, Leiden, La Connaissance, 1967, pl. 27.
40. L. Campbell and J. Van der Stock, *Rogier van der Weyden 1400–1464: Master of Passions*, Zwolle and Leuven, Waanders Publishers and Davidsfonds, 2009, p. 213, fig. 113 Colijn de Coeter, *St Luke Painting the Virgin*, late 15th century, Vieure, Church of Vieure; 413, no. 46, Master of the View of St Gudule, *Virgin and Child adored by a Female Donor accompanied by Mary Magdalen*, *c.*1475, Liége, Le Grand Curtius. For examples of full-length Rosary Madonnas attributed to Albrecht Bouts relying on Jan van Eyck's full-length type set in a garden, see Friedländer 1968 (cited in note 9), pl. 79, figs 64 and 65.
41. Schiller 1980 (cited in note 38), p. 200.
42. Luke 22–24.
43. J.O. Hand, C.A. Metzger and R. Spronk, *Prayers and Portraits: Unfolding the Netherlandish Diptych*, New Haven/London, Yale University Press, 2006, pp. 178–185, cat. 26; pp. 258–263, cat. 39. For an example with a frontally posed Madonna Lactans and two donors see pp. 206–209, cat. 30.
44. Périer-D'Ieteren 2006 (cited in note 17), p. 251, cat. 7, p. 288, cat. 19, p. 257, cat. 10, p. 267, cat. 12. A small panel in the Músée du Louvre, Paris, with a Madonna in full length and gold background is an exception: *op. cit.*, pp. 153–155, fig. 146, p. 289, cat. 20. For the attribution of the *Virgin and Child* in Cambridge, MA, Harvard University Art Museums, Fogg Art Museum to Albrecht Bouts see Henderiks 2011 (cited in note 17), pp. 105–108, p. 344, cat. 7.
45. Most scholars attribute the fragment in Berlin and another fragment of the same composition in the Musée du Louvre (Périer-D'Ieteren 2006 (cited in note 17), pp. 363–365, B4-B5) to Dieric Bouts the Elder, others to his workshop. For an overview, see *op. cit.*, pp. 364–365.
46. Périer-D'Ieteren 2006 (cited in note 17), p. 46, fig. 22. For the history, problems of attribution and iconography of the justice panels, see *op. cit.*, pp. 45–57, p. 298, cat. 24; C. Stroo, P. Syfer-d'Olne, A. Dubois and R. Slachmuylders, *The Flemish Primitives: Catalogue of Early Netherlandish Painting in the Royal Museums of Fine Arts of Belgium*, vol. II, Brussels, Brepols, 1999, pp. 56–104.
47. On 30 April 1475, Dieric Bouts the Elder changed his will making his sons heirs to 'toutes les créances qu'il posséde à charge de la ville de Louvain ainsi que de toutes les objets servant à l'art de peindre et de tous les tableaux (*tabulae*) et portraits (*imagines*) restés inachevés et incompletes'; Henderiks 2011 (cited in note 17), p. 20.
48. Ibid., pp. 27, 45–71, 348–349, cat. 12. Valentine Henderiks lists a total of 16 autograph works by Albrecht Bouts based on thorough analyses of style and technique, pp. 339–352.
49. Ibid., chapter V : 'La production en série d'oeuvres de devotion privée: un "atelier dans l'atelier"', pp. 207–338, for Virgin and Child motifs see pp. 304–307. See also: Henderiks 2009 (cited in note 36).
50. Henderiks 2011 (cited in note 17), pp. 373–377, cat. 51–66.
51. Ibid., Dijon: 345, cat. 9, replicas: pp. 386–388, cat. 121–131; private collection: p. 347, cat. 11, replicas: pp. 389–390, cat. 138-144;

Luxembourg: p. 346, cat. 10, replicas: pp. 395–398, cat.168–187; Kansas City: p. 351, cat. 15, replicas: pp. 400–402, cat. 199–214. In addition to the workshop replicas numerous variants of each design are known.

52. Ibid., pp. 407–409, cat. 236–253; Oldenburg: p. 351f., cat. 16, replicas: pp. 409–410, cat. 255–257.
53. L. Campbell, *National Gallery Catalogues: The Fifteenth Century Netherlandish Schools*, London, National Gallery, 1998, pp. 240–247.
54. See P. Klein, 'Dendrochronological findings of the Bouts group', in B. Cardon, K. Smeyers, R. Van Schoute and H. Verougstraete (eds), *Bouts Studies: Proceedings of the International Colloquium, Leuven, 26–28 November 1998*, Leuven/Paris/Sterling, VA, Uitgeverij Peeters, 2001, pp. 411–422, and Périer-D'Ieteren 2006 (cited in note 17), pp. 370–371.

Authors' addresses

- Eva de la Fuente Pedersen, Senior Research Curator, Statens Museum for Kunst, Copenhagen, Denmark (eva.pedersen@smk.dk)
- Troels Filtenborg, Senior Paintings Conservator, Statens Museum for Kunst, Copenhagen, Denmark (troels.filtenborg@smk.dk)

COPIES AND VERSIONS: DISCUSSING HOLBEIN'S LEGACY IN ENGLAND. TECHNICAL EXAMINATION OF COPIES OF HOLBEIN PORTRAITS AT THE NATIONAL PORTRAIT GALLERY

Sophie Plender and Polly Saltmarsh

ABSTRACT This paper presents findings from the technical analysis of a selection of portraits copied after works by Hans Holbein the Younger. The research was carried out as part of the *Making Art in Tudor Britain* (MATB) project at the National Portrait Gallery (NPG).[1] A range of analytical techniques was used, including dendrochronology, X-radiography, infrared reflectography and paint sample analysis. The paint handling methods were examined and compared using microscopy. While the visual aesthetic of the versions is superficially similar to Holbein's work, closer examination revealed that the handling and management of the paint could not be compared with the sophisticated and subtle technique of Holbein. The analysis undertaken and the interpretation of the results have furthered our understanding both of the methods of transfer and of the workshop production of copies and versions of portraits in the late 16th and early 17th century.

Introduction

Holbein worked in England for two extended periods from 1526 to 1528 and 1532 until his death in 1543. He enjoyed great success in England, painting portraits of significant individuals and nobility at the court of Henry VIII. Despite this demand Holbein had no real successors and few imitators in England after his death. The question of whether Holbein had assistants or followers has been widely debated and, although there is no documentary evidence to confirm the existence of a studio, it is generally agreed that he must have had assistance in producing such a large volume of portraits.[2] Elizabethan artists and collectors knew his name and valued his work, for example John, Lord Lumley (1533–1609) who possessed works by Holbein in his collection.

Copies of portraits by Holbein form a group of paintings that has often been dismissed having been established that they are not autograph works. Certainly many of the copies do not match the high quality of artistic skill and paint handling seen as characteristic of Holbein's technique. However, in many instances the versions show a close correlation in composition and dimensions to the originals, which demands further investigation into when, how and why they were produced.

Seven skilfully executed copies of portraits by Holbein in the NPG collection were examined and used as the basis of this research: *Sir William Butts* (NPG 210); *Sir Richard Southwell* (NPG 4912); *Nicholas Kratzer* (NPG 5245); *Thomas Cromwell, Earl of Essex* (NPG 1727); *Sir Nicholas Poyntz* (NPG 5583); *Sir Thomas More* (NPG 4358); and *Archbishop William Warham* (NPG 2094). Each painting in the survey was examined with microscopy, infrared reflectography (IRR), X-radiography, dendrochronology and paint sample analysis.[3] A second version of the portrait of William Warham, archbishop of Canterbury was generously loaned by Lambeth Palace for the purposes of the project. The results of this research identified two notable outcomes: first that dendrochronology showed that the wood used for the panels dates from the late 16th and early 17th century, long after Holbein's lifetime; and secondly,

Table 1 The results of dendrochronology for the NPG copies and comparison of the dimensions of the Holbein originals and the copies.

	Holbein original		Versions		
Sitter	Date	Dimensions	NPG number	Date range from dendrochronology	Panel dimensions
Sir Thomas More	1527	749 × 603 mm	4358	–	749 × 584 mm
Archbishop Warham	1527	820 × 660 mm	2094	1605–1621	822 × 663 mm
Archbishop Warham	1527	820 × 660 mm	Lambeth Loan	1575–1600	826 × 662 mm
Nicholas Kratzer	1528	830 × 670 mm	5245	1585–1617	819 × 648 mm
Thomas Cromwell	1533–1534	784 × 645 mm	1727	1596–1627	781 × 619 mm
Sir Richard Southwell	1536	475 × 380 mm	4912	After 1588	457 × 356 mm
Sir William Butts	1540–1543	460 × 360 mm	210	1571–1603	470 × 375 mm
Sir Nicholas Poyntz	Drawing 1532–1543	283 × 183 mm	5583	After 1580 – date of panel onto which the paper is mounted	415 × 292 mm

that the underdrawing and paint handling methods cannot be compared very closely with each other, or with Holbein's technique, suggesting that they were made in several different workshops.

Dendrochronology

All the paintings were executed on wooden panels with the exception of Nicholas Poyntz, which is painted on paper mounted onto panel. Dendrochronological analysis was carried out to establish the type of wood employed and a possible usage date for the panels. Three of the panels were found to be constructed from oak grown in the eastern Baltic region. The panel used for Nicholas Kratzer is composed of three boards, two of which are eastern Baltic oak and one of which is English oak. A single board of English oak has been used for the panel of Richard Southwell, which matches reference data from London and the South East. The support used for the portrait of Thomas More is made from limewood and as a result it was not possible to date the panel using dendrochronology as currently there is no reference data for this wood.

All the NPG copies to which a conjectural usage date could be given were found to be painted 60–80 years after the Holbein originals. Table 1 also shows the sizes of the original panels compared to the copies. None of the NPG panels showed evidence of being trimmed or reduced in size. The dimensions of the originals and copies are very close, often differing by just a few millimetres, with the largest discrepancy being 26 mm. This close correlation in size would suggest that either the painters of the copies had information regarding the measurements of the Holbein panels, or possibly they had access to the originals.

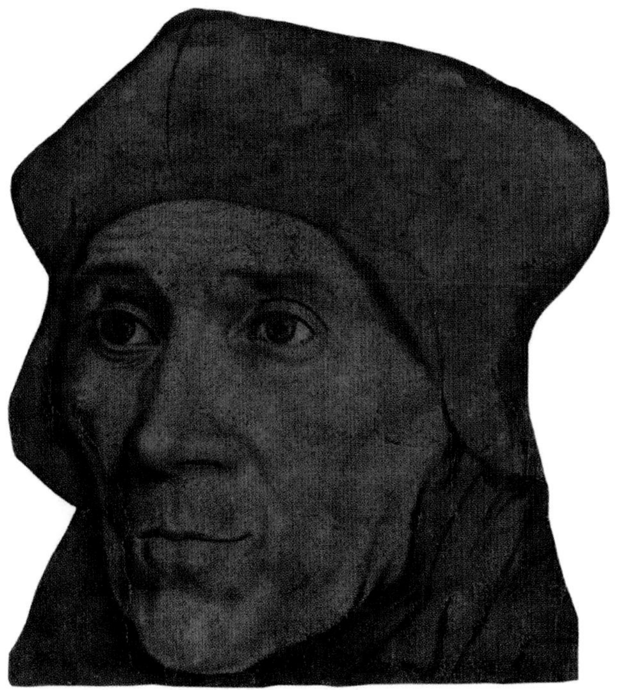

Fig. 1 After Hans Holbein the Younger, *Bishop John Fisher*, 16th century, oil on paper, 210 × 191 mm, National Portrait Gallery, London (NPG 2821). (© National Portrait Gallery, London.)

Underdrawing and evidence of transfer

Following Holbein's death in 1543, a group of 85 drawings passed from his studio into the possession of Henry VIII.[4] The fact that these preparatory studies were acquired by the king illustrates how much Holbein's work was appreciated at this time. This surviving body of drawings is now in the Royal Collection and provides useful information for technical analysis. Many of the drawings show evidence of transfer, indicating that they had been used as patterns to create other works or paintings.[5] Four drawings in the collection can be compared to the paintings included in this study: *Archbishop Warham* (RCIN 912272), *Sir Thomas More* (RCIN 912268), *Sir Nicholas Poyntz* (RCIN 912234) and *Sir Richard Southwell* (RCIN 912242).[6]

Preparatory sketches were used in studios and workshops to transfer a design onto the prepared panel or canvas ready for painting by the artist or studio assistants. A drawing could be prepared for transfer in a number of ways. One method,

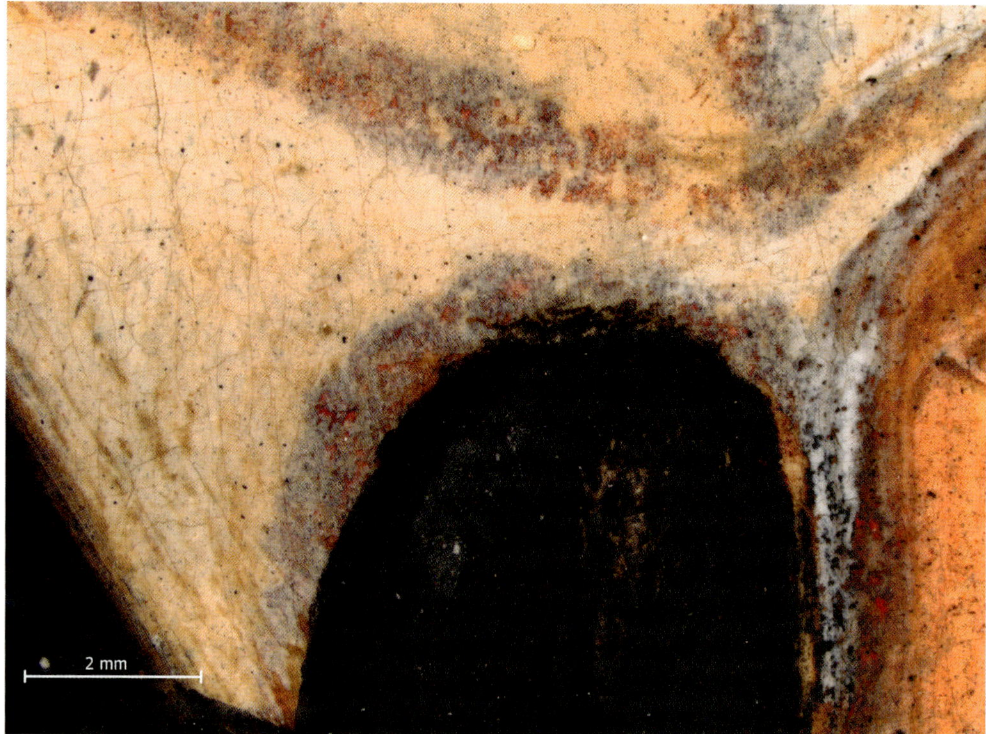

Fig. 2 Photomicrograph detail of *Sir Richard Southwell* (NPG 4912) showing red lake paint used to reinforce the outlines of the composition at the underdrawing stage. (© National Portrait Gallery, London.)

known as pouncing, involves pricking the outlines of a drawing to create small holes. The pattern is dusted with chalk or loose charcoal, leaving a series of dots that can then be reinforced to produce the underdrawing. This is a technique known to have been used by Holbein to transfer designs ready for painting, although of the 85 studies in the Royal Collection, only the drawing of Sir Thomas More has been pricked for transfer.[7] The NPG collection includes an interesting example of a pattern for Bishop Fisher (NPG 2821) after a drawing by Holbein (Fig. 1). This cut-out pattern is on paper which has been subsequently painted with oil paint. Around the features and outlines of the drawing, small regular dots are visible that are the result of transfer by pouncing. This suggests that patterns could also be utilised to create further patterns of popular sitters.

On many of the original Holbein drawings the outlines have been reinforced with metalpoint lines, and it is agreed that this is evidence of transfer using a method similar to modern carbon paper.[8] The technique involves laying a sheet of paper between the drawing required to be transferred and the prepared panel or other painting support. The side of the sheet of paper lying against the panel is covered with a layer of black chalk. A sharp instrument such as a metalpoint is then used to trace over the outlines of the original drawing. It is thought that this technique would have resulted in faint lines on the prepared support which would then be reinforced before painting.[9] The lines resulting from this method of transfer are characteristically mechanical. Examination using IRR has revealed underdrawing on the NPG painting of Nicholas Poyntz that is typical of this type of transfer. The features have been carefully outlined with a black (carbon-based) material using a consistent line. We can assume that that they are the result of a transfer technique in which the artist reinforced the key features rather than drawing the design in freehand, which would produce a sketchier, looser quality of line.

Only faint traces of a carbon-based underdrawing could be detected on the NPG portrait of Richard Southwell (Fig. 2). Under magnification, however, it is clear that the outlines of the composition have been painted with red lake. This is likely to be the result of a pattern being transferred using the carbon paper method. In this instance, the artist has reinforced the resulting faint lines with red lake paint prior to painting. When a tracing of the Holbein drawing was laid over this painting, the outline of the sitter was found to be a very close match.

Although it is unlikely that the original Holbein drawing was used to create this painting, a pattern has been employed that is not too far removed from Holbein's original design. Interestingly, the Holbein drawing in the Royal Collection has very definite metalpoint lines over the chalk lines of the drawing, presumably made following a transfer process to create a copy or pattern.

The underdrawing detected in the NPG portrait of Nicholas Kratzer illustrates how patterns often existed just for the face and hands of a sitter rather than for the whole painting (Fig. 3). The underdrawing in the face is very fine and carefully drawn, again indicating that the lines are reinforcing a transferred design. These lines are visible around the nose, and around the sitter's eyes there are short hatched strokes indicating areas of shadow. Kratzer, a mathematician and astronomer, is shown in the portrait surrounded by the instruments and tools of his profession. The underdrawing for the document on the table and the instruments is also drawn very finely but the handling is more loose and varied, suggesting the artist searching for a line rather than carefully reinforcing a transferred line. The

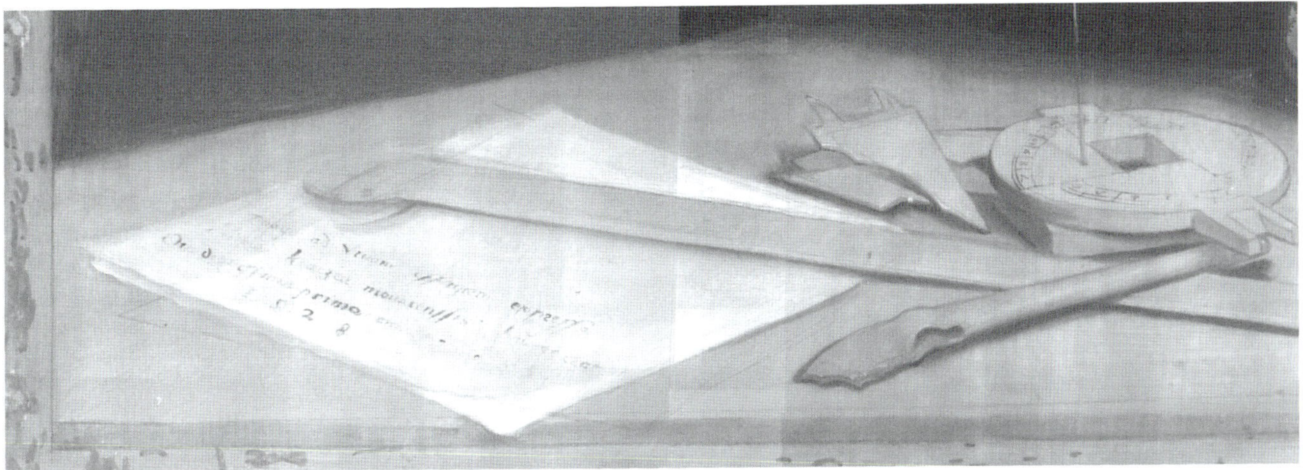

Fig. 3 IRR mosaic detail of *Nicholas Kratzer* (NPG 5245). (Image courtesy of Tager Stoner Richardson.)

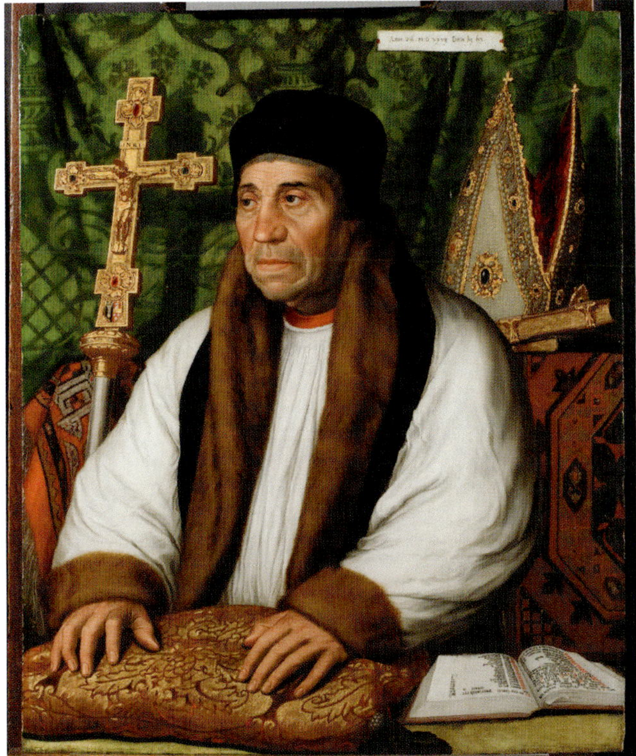

Fig. 4 After Hans Holbein the Younger, *Archbishop Warham*, early 17th century, oil on panel, 822 × 663 mm, National Portrait Gallery, London (NPG 2094). (© National Portrait Gallery, London.)

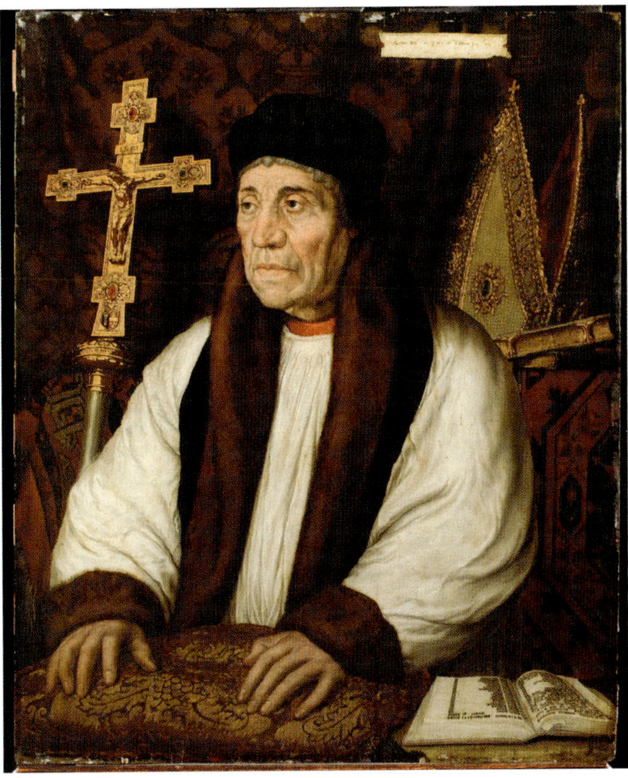

Fig. 5 After Hans Holbein the Younger, *Archbishop Warham*, late 16th century, oil on panel, 823 × 662 mm, Lambeth Palace Collection. (© National Portrait Gallery, London.)

artist has changed the position of the letter at the painting stage, moving it closer to the position seen in the original portrait by Holbein.

The Warham copies

The scope of the MATB project provided the opportunity to carry out a detailed examination and comparison of two copies of the portrait of Archbishop Warham: a version in the NPG collection and one from the collection of Lambeth Palace (Figs 4 and 5). Archbishop Warham was one of Holbein's first sitters during the artist's initial visit to England in 1526; the preparatory study for his portrait survives in the Royal Collection. Two portraits of Warham were produced at this time – one for the archbishop's residence at Lambeth, which is believed to be the version now in the Musée du Louvre in Paris, and another version that was sent to the Dutch humanist Desiderius Erasmus and is now lost.[10] Roy Strong suggested that the portrait of Warham now in the Lambeth Palace collection was commissioned when the original portrait by Holbein was sold later in the 16th century.[11] Although no documentary evidence survives to confirm this, it would support the idea that the Lambeth version was a copy made from the original. Dendrochronology also supports this theory with a conjectural usage date that places the Lambeth Palace painting to the last quarter of the 16th century. The NPG version is later and dates to the beginning of the 17th century.[12] The painting in the Louvre and the two copies have the same panel construction, being formed of three boards in vertical alignment, which is typical of panels of this date. The measurements of the three panels are surprisingly close, differing by just a few millimetres.

Both copies of the Warham portrait have extensive underdrawing that was detected using IRR. In the NPG version, all the elements of the composition have been underdrawn. The outline of the face and the features, as well as the hands, has been carefully drawn with bold, definite lines that are likely to reinforce a tracing. Other elements of the composition, such as the costume, are drawn more freely with loose zigzag lines indicating areas of shadow. The underdrawing detected in the Lambeth Palace version is extensive in the sitter's face and hands. The lines are very thick and have been strongly applied, again indicating that a pattern has been used for the composition.

Tracings were made of the two Warham copies by placing a thick sheet of polyester film over each painting and copying the outlines of the composition. When the two tracings are laid over one another, they match very closely. The tracings also closely matched the original Holbein drawing. The alignment of the face and hands was slightly different, however, and the tracings had to be moved in order to line up the hands. This would suggest that patterns may have existed in different parts with one pattern for the face of a sitter and a separate pattern for the hands. A detailed study for a hand survives in the Musée du Louvre collection.[13] Susan Foister has suggested that this drawing was used as the pattern for the hand in the painting of Erasmus by Holbein which is now in a private collection.[14] Unlike the numerous studies of faces, this is the only known example where a drawing of a sitter's hand can be directly related to a portrait by Holbein.

Painting technique

Primings

All the panel supports used for the copies examined in this study were prepared with a chalk ground and all except one have a grey priming layer applied over the ground. This is the usual priming, with some variations in tone, found in the majority of the paintings examined as part of the MATB project. The copy of Sir Thomas More has a reddish priming as used in Germany in the late 15th and 16th century by artists such as Albrecht Dürer and Lucas Cranach the Elder.[15] Holbein often used a grey priming, but use of a salmon pink priming has been noted on some of his English paintings.[16]

Paint handling

The combination of a limewood support and a reddish priming indicates that the painting of Sir Thomas More was not made

Fig. 6 Photomicrograph detail of *Archbishop Warham* (NPG 2094) showing the simple paint handling used for the sitter's fingernail. (© National Portrait Gallery, London.)

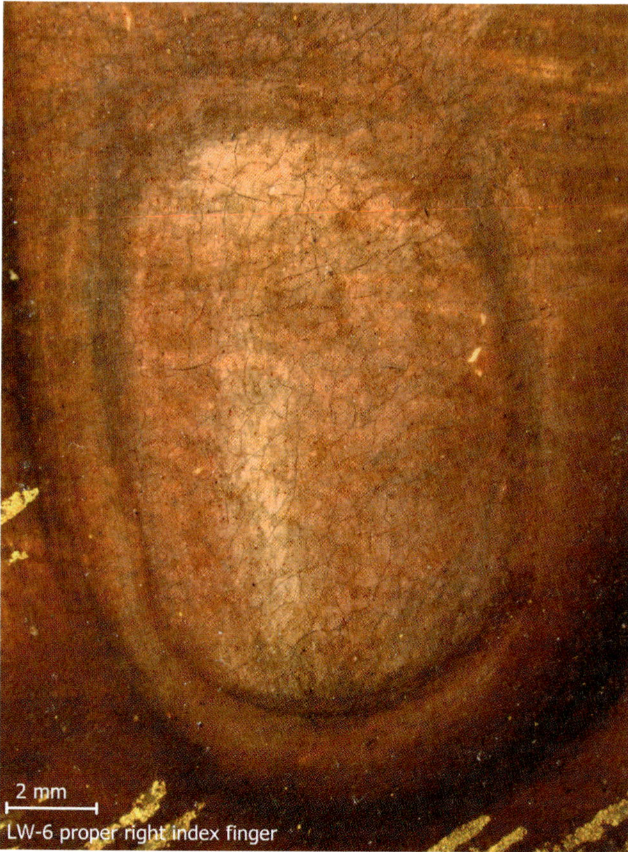

Fig. 7 Photomicrograph detail of *Archbishop Warham*, Lambeth Palace Collection. (© National Portrait Gallery, London.)

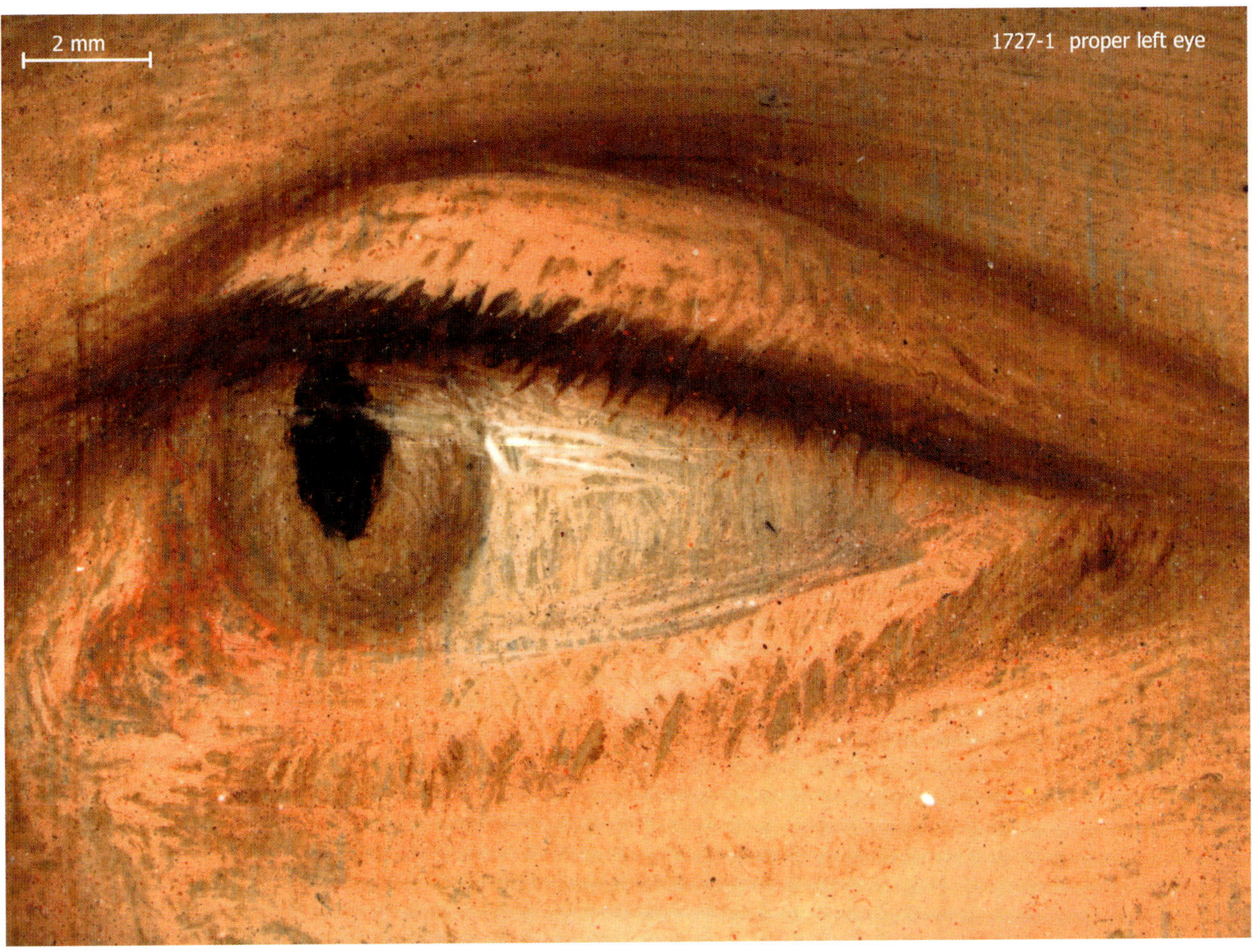

Fig. 8 Photomicrograph detail of *Thomas Cromwell, Earl of Essex* (NPG 1727) showing the careful attention paid to depicting the sitter's eyelashes. (© National Portrait Gallery, London.)

in England. Strong suggested that it may have been produced in Austria or Italy and Foister has suggested Switzerland.[17] It is interesting to note that the original portrait by Holbein, now in the Frick Collection, New York, is known to have travelled to Italy. The paint handling of the NPG portrait differs from the rest of the copies that were examined. The fluid paint seems closer to the consistency of Holbein's work than the other paintings, but the brushstrokes lack the subtlety of handling typical of his technique. Holbein's skills as a painter can be seen in the fine brushwork of his portraits, the use of wet-in-wet blending and the attention to detail.

In contrast, most of the other NPG copies have been created using thicker layers of paint. The portrait of Thomas Cromwell is notable for the pasty application of the paint layers; the paint has a raised texture in many areas and has been thickly laid on, creating hard edges along the sitter's forehead and the decoration of the book on the table. In the portraits of Nicholas Kratzer and Sir Nicholas Poyntz, the lead-tin yellow paint mixtures used for highlights contain similar, large pigment particles and have been piled up to create areas of impasto. The paint handling used in the copies varies, but none makes use of fine blending of the paint layers to create subtle effects as seen in Holbein's original technique. Instead, the paint is laid on rather deliberately, which could be argued to be the result of systematic copying of another painting.

The paint layers on the NPG portrait of Warham have been thickly applied across the entire surface, with no ground or priming showing through. The large pigment particles give the paint a somewhat gritty texture. The work is highly decorative, with the use of gilding in the same areas as the portrait in the Louvre. The Lambeth Palace copy of the portrait of Archbishop Warham is painted with more fluid paint and using finer brushwork than the NPG version. The flesh paint has been thinly applied with soft blending around the features. There is a fine use of gilding and details, such as the small coat of arms on the bottom of the crucifix, have been handled with delicacy and care. The thumbnails are painted with delicate parallel lines for the highlight, which is closer to Holbein's style than the systematic and simple single white line seen on the other versions (Fig. 6 and 7).

In his drawings, miniatures and oil paintings, Holbein defines the sitter's eyelashes using fine detail that adds character to the individual face. It is notable that in most of the Holbein copies particular care has been taken with painting the eyelashes (Fig. 8). This differs from the technique seen in the vast majority of the other portraits examined as part of the MATB project in which the eyelashes are indicated with simple lines around the eyes and the individual hairs of the eyelashes are not painted. This seems to indicate an awareness of the notably fine execution of the eyes in Holbein's works.

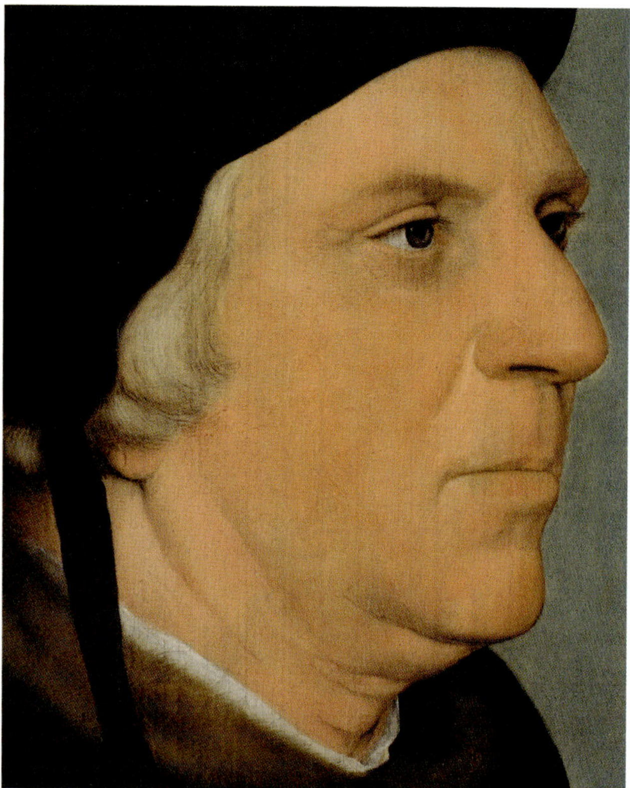

Fig. 9 Detail of *Sir William Butts* (NPG 210). (© National Portrait Gallery, London.)

The unusual paint technique employed in the portrait of William Butts differs from the other Holbein copies in the NPG collection (Fig. 9). The pale grey priming has been applied with thick-ridged brushstrokes which are very evident in the texture of the paint surface. The paint layers were laid on thinly and the features were painted in black and brown with fine brushstrokes. The features have been finished with very dry paint that looks almost like a drawn line.

Backgrounds

Intense blue-green backgrounds can be seen in many of Holbein's portraits including *Lady with a Squirrel and a Starling*, where the background is very well preserved; Holbein used the pigment natural (mineral) azurite in two layers mixed with lead white.[18] The blue pigment smalt has also been identified in the backgrounds of Holbein's portraits.[19] Natural azurite was one of the more expensive blue pigments available to artists, and by the late 16th century indigo was widely available and offered a cheaper, although less stable, alternative to azurite. The blue background of the portrait of Sir William Butts has been painted with indigo, which has faded considerably in most parts, except where the paint has been protected from light by the shadow of the frame. In the portrait of Thomas Cromwell, indigo was identified in the paint mixtures used for the brocade cloth background and the green elements of the carpet. Azurite is used on the NPG copy of the portrait of Richard Southwell but is only found on the jewel of the sitter's ring. The blue background on this painting has been extensively restored but the original pigment has been identified as blue verditer, an artificial azurite that is not known to have been used by Holbein. Azurite was also found on the NPG version of Archbishop Warham in small details painted with blue.

The green background on the NPG version of Archbishop Warham is painted with a complex layer structure and the damask pattern has a raised surface texture. The copper green pigment used in the background fabric of the Lambeth Palace version has discoloured and become brown but the original colour has survived at the edge of the panel where it has been protected by the frame. The damask pattern does not have the raised texture seen in the NPG version.

Conclusions

Examination of the range of techniques used in these paintings indicates that there must have been a number of workshops producing copies of Holbein's portraits in the later 16th and early 17th century, showing that there was a still great demand for copies after Holbein of well-known sitters. By the later 16th century, collecting portraits had become increasingly fashionable in European court circles. John, Lord Lumley was notable in England for putting together an unprecedented portrait collection.[20] Lumley's collection included the group of Holbein's drawings which he had inherited from his father-in-law, the 12th earl of Arundel, also known as a great collector. Lumley also owned a number of paintings by Holbein and his followers, including eight half-length male portraits. These eight portraits are clearly listed in the 1590 Lumley inventory followed by the inscription 'all this eight drawne by Haunce Holbein'.[21] At a later date an alteration to the text reduced this number to just three. Susan Foister has convincingly argued that this alteration shows an awareness of the difference between autograph works and reproductions, which indicates that original Holbeins were still highly prized objects.[22]

Portrait sets of monarchs and the nobility were being collected in the late 16th century by the gentry and the elite to display on the walls of their great houses. Often, these portrait sets were simply painted and the versions of Holbein's portraits discussed here show a significantly higher level of skill and execution than the sets. However, the copies reflect a trend for images of notable men and women for which there was clearly a high demand. Holbein's images of these famous sitters would often have been the only example of a likeness of them.[23]

There appear to be a number of ways that these copies were produced. It is possible that Holbein's original drawings were still in use as patterns in a workshop some time after his death. Copies of his patterns are likely to have been in circulation between artists' studios and it is also possible that patterns and tracings could have been made by tracing the original painted portraits. The question concerning whether a Holbein workshop existed has not been resolved, but detailed examination of these versions shows that there was a demand and a market for good quality copies of portraits after Holbein.

Notes

1. Images of all of the National Portrait Gallery paintings discussed in the text as well as further information about the technical analysis is available at: www.npg.org.uk/research/programmes/making-art-in-tudor-britain.php. *Making Art in Tudor Britain* is a major research project carried out by the NPG over the last five years, forming a technical survey of the portraits from 1500 to 1620.
2. For example see S. Foister, *Holbein in England*, London, Tate Gallery, 2006, pp. 113–123; S. Foister, *Holbein and England*, New Haven, CT, Yale University Press, 2004, pp. 65–71; S. Foister, 'The production and reproduction of Holbein's portraits', in K. Hearn (ed.), *Dynasties: Painting in Tudor and Jacobean England 1530–1630*, London, Tate Gallery, 1995, pp. 21–29; S. Foister, 'Workshop or followers? Underdrawing in some portraits associated with Hans Holbein the Younger', in *Le Dessin sous-jacent dans la Peinture: Colloque IX, Louvain-la-Neuve*, Louvain-la-Neuve, Collège Erasme, 1991, pp. 113–124.
3. Technical analysis, including photomicroscopy, ultraviolet examination and X-radiography was carried out by the authors with Helen Dowding and Sally Marriott at the National Portrait Gallery. Pigment analysis was carried out by Libby Sheldon, Painting Analysis Unit (UCL); dendrochronology by Dr Ian Tyers, Dendrochronological Consultancy Ltd.; and IRR by Tager Stonor Richardson using a Hamamatsu High Performance 'super infrared' Vidicon Camera C2741-03.
4. For a history of the drawings see J. Roberts, *Holbein and the Court of Henry VIII*, Edinburgh, National Galleries of Scotland, 1993, pp. 20–23.
5. For detailed technical analysis and discussion of the transfer marks found on the drawings see Foister 1991 (cited in note 1) and M. Ainsworth, '"Paternes for Phiosioneamyes": Holbein's portraiture reconsidered', *The Burlington Magazine* 132, 1990, pp. 173–186.
6. We are grateful to Michael Clayton, senior curator of prints and drawings at the Royal Collection, who traced the Holbein drawings allowing comparison with the paintings examined.
7. Another example of Holbein preparing drawings for transfer using the pouncing method can be seen on the Whitehall Palace cartoon of Henry VIII, NPG 4027. For further information see Foister 2004 (cited in note 1), p. 190.
8. See Foister 2004 (cited in note 1) and Ainsworth 1990 (cited in note 5).
9. This method of transfer is discussed in artists' treatises, for example see G. Vasari, *Vasari on Technique*, New York, Dover Publications, p. 231.
10. Matthew Parker, archbishop of Canterbury from 1559 to 1575, recorded in his biography of Archbishop Warham that Holbein made two portraits at this time.
11. R. Strong, *Tudor and Jacobean Portraits*, London, HMSO, 1969, pp. 323–324.
12. Dendrochronology of the two Warham copies was carried out by Dr Ian Tyers. Both panels are made from eastern Baltic oak. Two of the three boards in the NPG Warham panel were suitable for analysis and the dates of the last tree rings were identified as 1597 and 1600. Adding the minimum and maximum expected number of sapwood rings to this suggested that the tree used for this board was felled between 1605 and 1621. These results indicate that the panel can be no earlier than 1605 and is likely to predate 1621. The last tree ring identified on the Warham version in the Lambeth Palace collection was dated 1568, which gives a conjectural usage date for the panel from 1575 to 1600.
13. Foister 2006 (cited in note 1), p. 103.
14. Ibid., p. 24.
15. See G. Heydenreich, '"... that you paint with wonderful speed": virtuosity and efficiency in the artistic practice of Lucas Cranach', in B. Brinkmann (ed.), *Cranach*, Frankfurt, Stadel Museum and London, Royal Academy of Art, 2007, pp. 29–47, p. 29; G. Heydenreich, 'Adam and Eve in the making', in C. Campbell (ed.), *Temptation in Eden*, London, Courtauld Institute of Art, 2007, pp. 18–33, p. 20.
16. For example a pink priming has been observed on the portrait of Edward, Prince of Wales, National Gallery of Art, Washington: R. Jones, 'The methods and materials of three Tudor artists: Bettes, Hilliard and Kettel', in K. Hearn (ed.), *Dynasties: Painting in Tudor and Jacobean England 1530–1630*, London, Tate Gallery, 1995, p. 234; and also on the portrait of Jane Seymour, Kunsthistorisches Museum, Vienna: Foister 2004 (cited in note 1), p. 99.
17. Strong 1969 (cited in note 11), p. 229; S. Foister, pers. comm.
18. S. Foister, M. Wyld and A. Roy, 'Hans Holbein's *A Lady with a Squirrel and a Starling*', *National Gallery Technical Bulletin* 15, 1994, pp. 6–19, p. 9.
19. For example see Jones 1995 (cited in note 16), p. 234.
20. C. Macleod and T. Cooper, 'The portraits', in M. Evans (ed.), *The Lumley Inventory and Pedigree: Art Collecting and Lineage in the Elizabethan Age*, Roxburghe Club, 2010, p. 62.
21. Foister 2004 (cited in note 2), pp. 266–267.
22. Ibid.
23. Foister 1995 (cited in note 2).

Authors' addresses

- Sophie Plender, Senior Research Conservator – Tudor Project, National Portrait Gallery, London, UK (splender@npg.org.uk)
- Polly Saltmarsh, Assistant Research Conservator – Tudor Project, National Portrait Gallery, London, UK (psaltmarsh@npg.org.uk)

A TECHNICAL STUDY OF PORTRAITS OF KING JAMES VI AND I ATTRIBUTED TO JOHN DE CRITZ THE ELDER (D.1642): ARTIST, WORKSHOP AND COPIES

Caroline Rae and Aviva Burnstock

ABSTRACT This paper examines the materials and techniques used for a number of portraits of James VI of Scotland and I of England that have been attributed to the Antwerp-born émigré artist working in England, John de Critz (*c.*1552–1642). De Critz was Serjeant Painter to the king from 1605 until his death in 1642 and was a celebrated artist of his era. However de Critz's oeuvre is hard to define. Unlike many of his contemporaries, neither de Critz nor artists employed in his workshop signed or inscribed their works. Surviving documentary evidence and the many extant portraits and later copies attributed to his name suggest that he was in great demand and ran a sizable business. The study illuminates de Critz's workshop practice by examining comprehensively his painting technique including pigments and binding media, brushwork, the use of painting tools, face patterns and underdrawing techniques. Interpretation of the technical evidence is used to define different hands in the works, the methods of transfer and evolution of techniques for making the images of the monarch and evidence for the production of copies. This research will be contextualised by findings from current technical research into Anglo-Netherlandish workshop practice in the Tudor and Jacobean era at the National Portrait Gallery, London (NPG) and elsewhere.

Introduction

John de Critz the Elder was born in Antwerp and brought to England by his parents as a child in 1568. He trained with the accomplished Ghent-born painter Lucas de Heere (1534–1584) during his exile in England. De Critz worked in Walsingham's spy network in the 1580s, travelling to France and possibly Italy at his behest, and was patronised by his successor Robert Cecil, 1st earl of Salisbury. De Critz found favour at the court of King James VI of Scotland and I of England and became his Serjeant Painter, responsible for the extensive decorative works associated with the Crown, from his accession in 1603 until his death in 1642.[1]

However, despite his renowned position, de Critz's oeuvre remains an unsolved mystery. In common with many paintings made at the time, no signed or inscribed works are associated with his hand. Documentary evidence exists to link de Critz with the production of portraits of Cecil and the king in the early years of his reign.[2] However, few existing paintings can be linked directly to these references.[3] This lack of a definable style has led to huge numbers of paintings of varying quality being attributed to de Critz.

Some comparisons are provided by recent technical study carried out during the *Making Art in Tudor Britain* (MATB)[4] project at the National Portrait Gallery (NPG) of paintings in its collection associated with de Critz that has highlighted the problems inherent in studies of his oeuvre.[5] Within this group no consistent similarities in technique were found that might point to the works being substantially by the same hand or workshop. However, only circumstantial evidence links three of these works to de Critz, and the provenance of the Cecil portrait only goes back to the 19th century when it entered the NPG's collection.

This paper discusses the findings of a recent technical examination of seven portraits of King James VI and I attributed to de Critz. Study focused on the comparative examination of close details, with the aim of investigating whether it is possible to use technical/stylistic evidence to identify elements in these paintings that are consistent with the same hand/workshop.[6] Three portraits within this group that share common elements are described in detail with context provided by comparison with the other paintings examined to illustrate the idiosyncratic nature of the techniques used for the portraits. The implications for their production and other contemporary images of the king provide context for workshop practice at the time.

Methodology

Critical to the interpretation of the technical evidence generated as part of the present study was to identify a painting that could with confidence be linked with the de Critz workshop and could provide a focus for comparison with other portraits of the same sitter. The accounts of the Treasurer of the Chamber in 1608 describe a portrait of the king painted by de Critz and sent to the grand duke of Florence, Ferdinando I de Medici.[7] This reference has a credible link to an existing portrait in the Palazzo Pitti[8] (Fig. 1). Six other portraits of King James VI and I attributed to de Critz were chosen as comparative examples because they were accessible and because they were considered good examples of the 'de Critz type': from the National Trust at Montacute House in Somerset; Dulwich Picture Gallery in London; a private collection (the 'Sutherland' portrait); the Government Art Collection (GAC); the former Tyninghame collection in Scotland; and the collection of Lord Rosebery (Dalmeny House, Scotland).

Technical investigation and examination of the Pitti, Dulwich, Sutherland, GAC, Tyninghame and Dalmeny portraits were performed *in situ*. In-depth and thorough technical investigation of the Montacute painting was carried out at the Courtauld Institute of Art, London. Elemental analysis of samples taken from the Montacute, Pitti and GAC paintings was carried out using scanning electron microscopy with energy dispersive X-ray spectroscopy (SEM-EDX) in order to study the painting materials and techniques. Limiting factors to the research were differing levels of access to the paintings and the variation in the conditions of the works.

Due to the high demand for portraits of the reigning monarch, this face pattern would have circulated between many contemporary workshops. However, these portraits must be considered particularly in relation to Marcus Gheeraerts the Younger (1561/2–1636),[9] who was related to de Critz by marriage and who received payments for portraits of the king in 1611 and 1618.[10] Technical research into paintings by Gheeraerts at Tate performed by Rica Jones in 1999 and 2002[11] and at the NPG in 2011–2012[12] was considered comparatively, as was recent technical research into contemporary workshop practice carried out during the MATB project at the NPG and other institutions.[13]

Iconography

King James is depicted in all seven paintings wearing the accoutrements of the Order of the Garter, the highest order of chivalry in England. He is shown wearing a hat adorned with one of two jewels, the 'Feather' and the 'Mirror of Great Britain' (constructed in 1604 to commemorate the union of England and

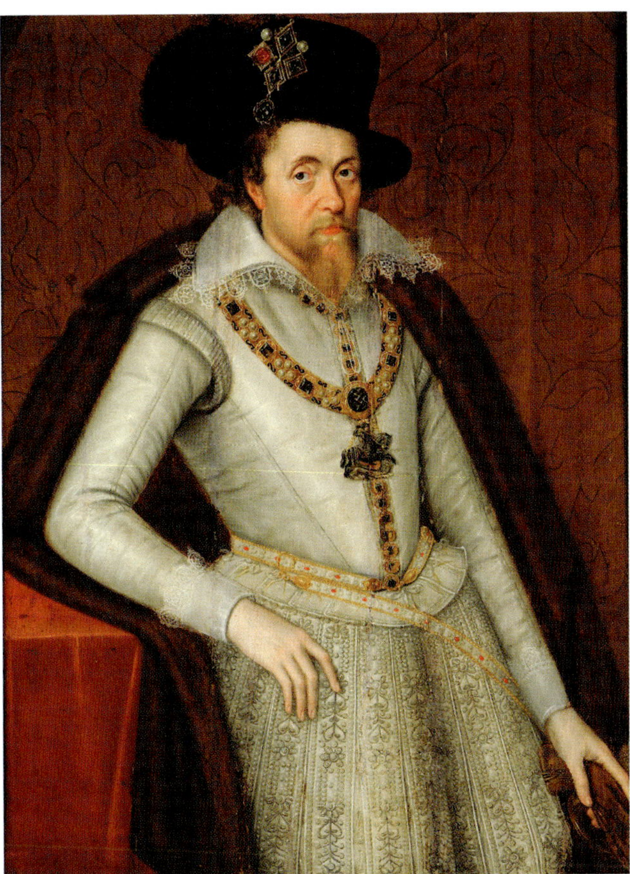

Fig. 1 John de Critz the Elder, *King James VI of Scotland and I of England*, oil on panel, 113.5 × 83.2 cm, 1608, Palazzo Pitti, Florence. (Image courtesy of SSPSAE and the Polo Museale della città di Firenze - Gabinetto Fotografico.)

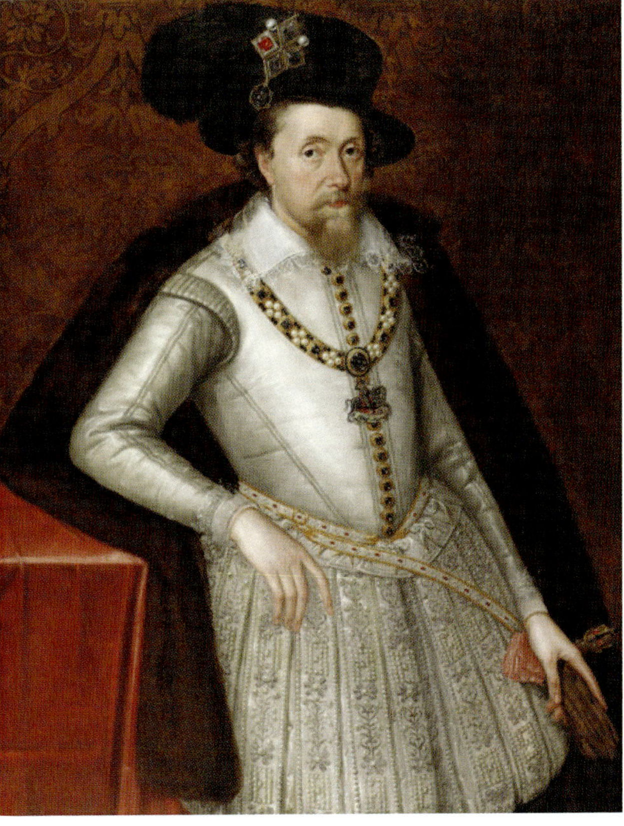

Fig. 2 John de Critz the Elder, *King James VI of Scotland and I of England*, oil on panel, 113.4 × 87.5 cm, *c.*1605. (Courtesy of Montacute House, the National Trust.)

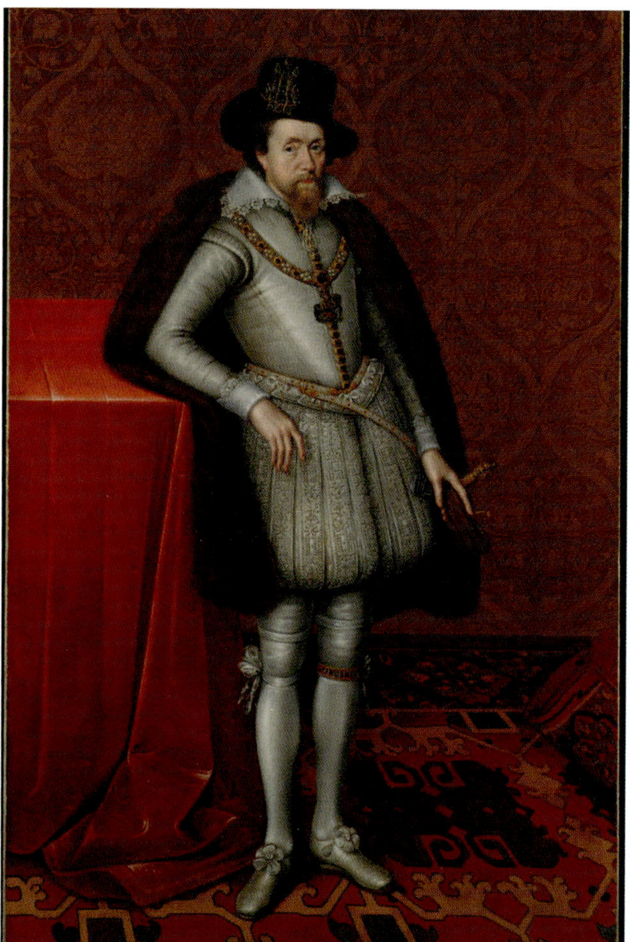

Fig. 3 John de Critz the Elder, *King James VI of Scotland and I of England*, oil on canvas, 223 × 150 cm, *c.*1606. (Courtesy of Dulwich Picture Gallery.)

Scotland at the time of James's accession).[14] The lavish jewels, garter insignia and rich surroundings of the highly decorated background, Anatolian carpet and embellished chair (which in this context operates as a throne), place these paintings in a direct visual continuity with works such as the *Hampden Portrait of Elizabeth I*[15] or *The Allegory of the Tudor Succession*[16] thus asserting James's place in the English dynastic succession and also in a wider context of Renaissance princely portraiture.

The paintings can be split stylistically into two groups. Four of the paintings – Montacute (Fig. 2), Pitti and Dulwich (Fig. 3) and Tyninghame[17] – depict the king wearing a fur cape and leaning on a table. These portraits are similar in composition, however, the hat jewels and positioning of the gloves vary across the four paintings.

The Dalmeny,[18] Sutherland (Fig. 4) and GAC[19] paintings show James wearing a jewelled cape and darker breeches. In the 'fur cape' paintings, the king is depicted more naturalistically, leaning backwards in a relaxed pose. In the Dulwich painting his head is in more natural proportion to his body length than in the Sutherland portrait. In the 'jewelled cape' portraits, the king has a more upright stance and a more militant pose, with his proper left hand resting on his sword hilt. This pose, the positioning of the legs and the more exaggerated proportions of the figure (including far wider shoulders) are stylistically closer to the mannerist distortions of paintings associated with the Gheeraerts workshop[20] than to the fur cape group.[21]

Technical examination and discussion

Supports

Five of the portraits are on panel and two on canvas supports. It was possible to examine the verso of the Dalmeny, Montacute and Pitti panel paintings. Each consists of three vertical good quality oak boards[22] bevelled at the top and bottom. The four three-quarter length panel paintings are close in size.[23] The use of similarly sized panels in conjunction with generic face patterns could have greatly increased workshop efficiency in the production of large volumes of portraits of the same sitter.[24] The extensive use of panels of the same size could also suggest the speculative production of portraits without a specific commission.[25] Several other works attributed to the Gheeraerts and de Critz workshops are close in dimensions,[26] suggesting the use of standard sizes by English panel-makers.[27]

Preparatory layers and underdrawings

The five panels have a white ground layer. This was more thinly applied on the GAC painting as the wood grain is visible throughout the painted surface. Samples taken from the Pitti, Montacute and GAC paintings, which were mounted as cross-sections, show that the panels are prepared in a similar manner typical of contemporary Northern paintings, with a thin pale priming layer comprised of finely ground red lead, lead white and black pigments above a chalk ground layer.[28]

Samples taken from the Montacute painting (Fig. 5) reveal that on this painting the priming layer lies above charcoal underdrawing, carried out in a fluid medium, suggesting that the priming layer was applied in the workshop rather than by a panel-maker. Underdrawing was visible using infrared (IR) on all the panel paintings. It was evident that although drawn by different hands, a roughly similar pattern was used to transfer the design of the face on each.

In the Sutherland portrait no underdrawing is visible in IR or ordinary light, however in this and in the Dulwich painting[29] (both on canvas) the artist has utilised a grey layer beneath the flesh tones which is instrumental in structuring the form of the face. Marcus Gheeraerts also utilises a dark grey layer beneath the flesh tones on some of his full-length canvas portraits.[30] However, Gheeraerts's superimposition of thin layers of pale, cool flesh paint to create a pearly lustre[31] contrasts with the use of warm opaque flesh tones for the Dulwich and Sutherland portraits.

Paint layers

In examining the technique used to paint the seven portraits, it was apparent that the GAC and Tyninghame portraits were less finely painted. The Tyninghame painting is comparatively crudely and quickly painted, and in some areas appears half-finished. In contrast, the GAC painting has a polished but wooden appearance, and the flesh paint is relatively opaque, with a greater use of earth pigments for the shadows. This artist uses the less sophisticated technique of applying paint layers only once the underlying layers had dried. The remaining five portraits have a similar level of finish. Some similarities in approach were noted between the Sutherland and Dalmeny paintings, however comparison was hampered by the poorer condition of the Dalmeny portrait.

A closely comparable approach to painting can be seen in the Montacute, Dulwich and Pitti paintings, which indicates that they may have been created in the same workshop environment. A striking similarity between the three latter paintings is the technique used to paint the eyes. This can be seen in the almost identical sequence of colours and brushstrokes used to create the proper right eyes (Figs 6–8). A bluish stroke of paint is used in each to create the shadow on the eyeball (this is azurite on the Pitti and Montacute paintings and a greyish-blue in the Dulwich painting, perhaps indicating the use of a black pigment mixed with lead white). This shadow appears to have been painted in at the same stage as the black pupil and the iris – a translucent, greenish glaze with either daubs (Pitti and Montacute) or a line (Dulwich) of an ochre colour on top. The white of the eyeball has then been painted in followed by a thin curved line of white paint of a thick consistency below the iris, adding to the bulging appearance of the eye. The three paintings have similar double or triple dot white highlights in the eye, a generic feature that is seen in other contemporary portraits.

The modelling of the flesh around the eyeball in the three paintings is also very similar. Underdrawing is visible in each in ordinary light and appears to have been used by the artist to define the bags below the eye. This may be more visible than originally intended due to the increasing transparency of the oil paint layer over time. Underdrawing is clearly intended to be left visible and is used to outline the form of the inner eye on the Pitti painting. Similar bright pinkish red shapes, although not outlined with underdrawing, are seen in the corner of the inner eyes of the Dulwich and Montacute paintings. A line of the same colour is used beneath the bulge of the eye socket at the outer edge to suggest the inner lower eyelid on the Montacute and Pitti paintings. This is less prominent on the Dulwich work, however this may be due to its condition (note the application of lines of this colour on the proper left eyes are identical among the three).

A dark reddish line of paint has been used to delineate the eye socket on all three paintings (this is a lighter, pinker red in the Montacute painting) with a pale pink line painted directly beneath. The upper edge of the eyelid is defined in a similar manner using a reddish brown stroke with, directly above it, a thick pale pink stroke of paint. A pale pink line of paint is used to delineate the edge of the lower lid. In the Pitti and Montacute paintings this line has a thick, stiff appearance that may indicate the use of a heat-bodied medium. Strokes of paint of a similar consistency can be seen on the earlobes of both paintings. It is again possible that the Dulwich painting, which has a more abraded surface than the other two works, originally had these additional details.

In comparison with the remaining portraits of James attributed to de Critz examined during this study, portraits by Gheeraerts and also with two of their contemporaries, Englishman Robert Peake,[32] and Netherlandish artist Michiel van Mierevelt,[33] none has a closely related approach to the painting of the eyes or the surrounding flesh. This comparison further emphasises the similarity and idiosyncrasy of technique in the three paintings. The overall handling of the flesh

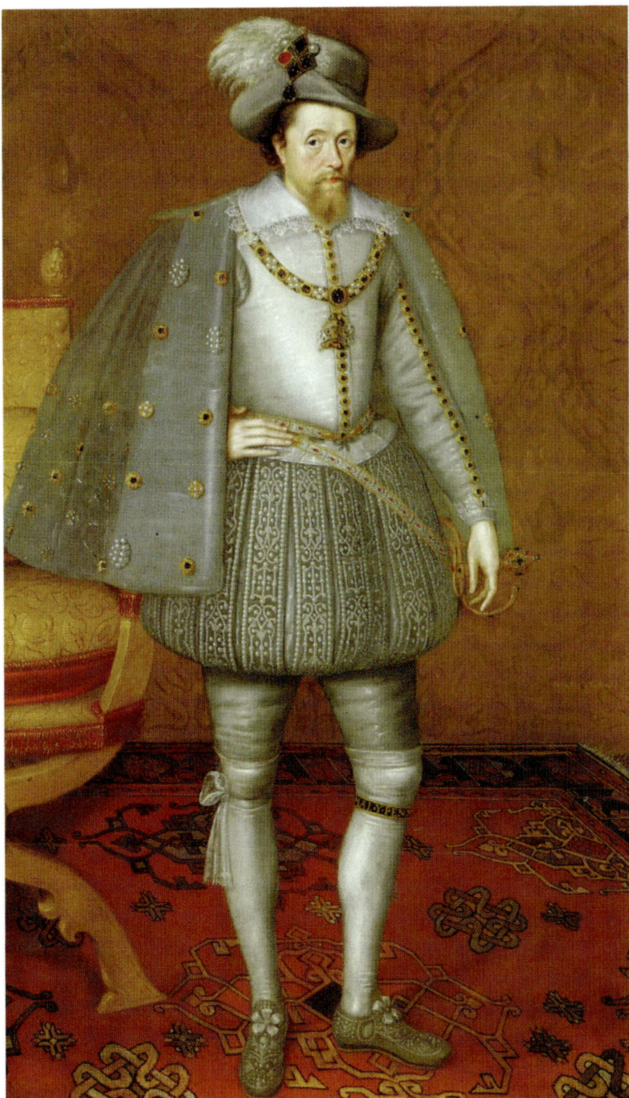

Fig. 4 John de Critz the Elder, *King James VI of Scotland and I of England*, oil on canvas, 203 x 116 cm, *c.*1608, private collection. (Image courtesy of the Witt Library, Courtauld Institute of Art, London.)

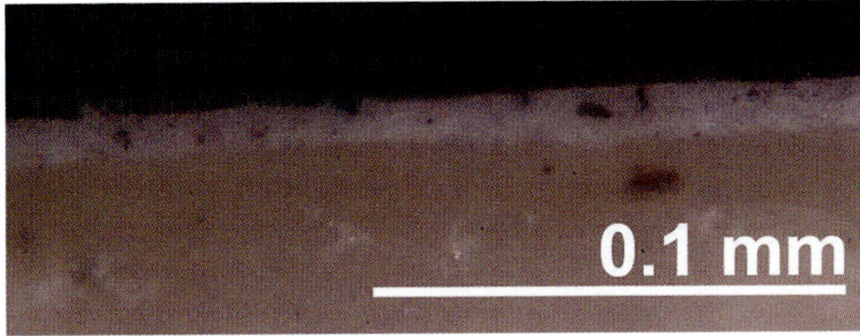

Fig. 5 John de Critz the Elder, *King James VI of Scotland and I of England* (Fig. 2): cross-section taken from blue paint on a pearl on the breeches (photographed in visible light). The image shows charcoal underdrawing in a fluid medium lying above the ground layer and below the *primuersel* layer, and (at the top edge of the sample) an azurite particle strewn into the underlying paint layer. (Courtesy of Montacute House, the National Trust.)

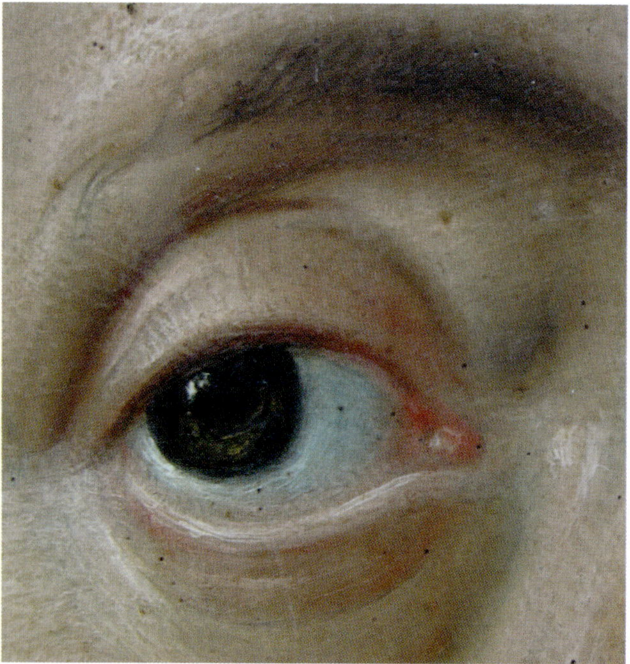

Fig. 6 John de Critz the Elder, *King James VI of Scotland and I of England* (Fig. 1): detail showing the technique used to paint the proper right eye. (Image courtesy of SSPSAE and the Polo Museale della città di Firenze - Gabinetto Fotografico.)

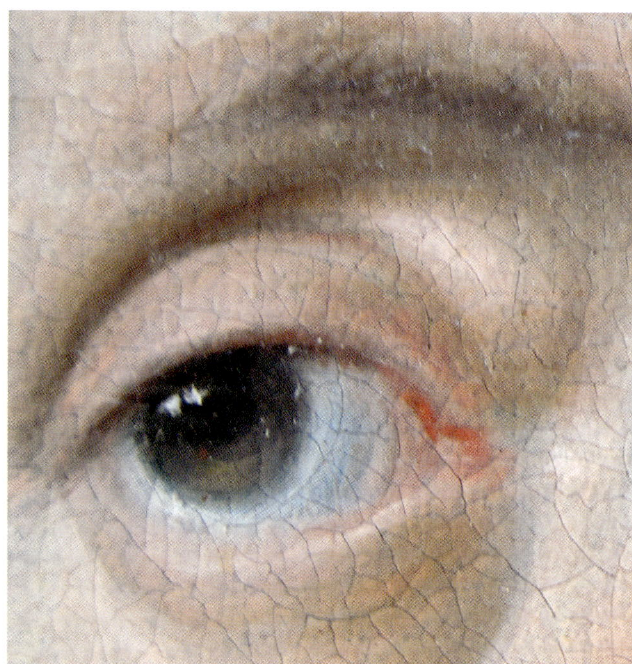

Fig. 8 John de Critz the Elder, *King James VI of Scotland and I of England* (Fig. 3): detail showing the technique used to paint the proper right eye. (Courtesy of Dulwich Picture Gallery.)

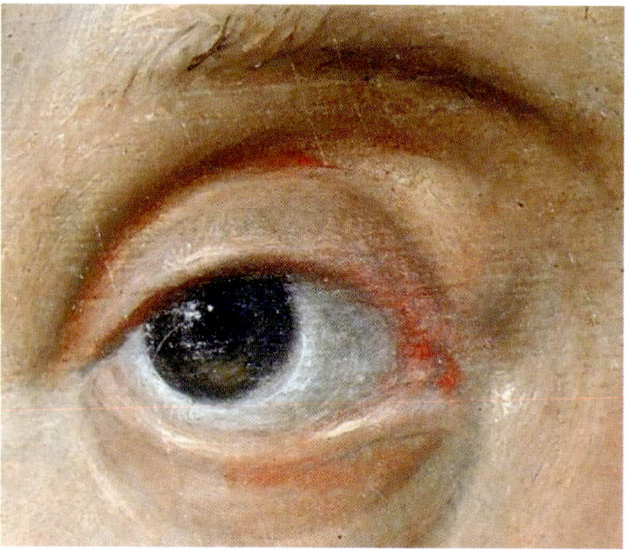

Fig. 7 John de Critz the Elder, *King James VI of Scotland and I of England* (Fig. 2): detail showing the technique used to paint the proper right eye. (Courtesy of Montacute House, the National Trust.)

paint in these three paintings differs, however, suggesting that although they may have originated in the same workshop, they are not necessarily painted by the same hand.[34] This finding is in line with recent scholarship and technical study into contemporary artists' workshops.[35]

The background elements of the portraits from Montacute, Dulwich and Pitti were also painted using a similar approach. Evidence of blotting of red lake using fabric could be seen in microscopy of the tablecloths. However this was a widespread practice at the time, described in contemporary artists' treatises.[36] The Dulwich and Montacute portraits share a distinctive wall decoration, which is a pattern of alternate pomegranate and floral forms, encased within a curved geometric framework. The Pitti painting has a simplified design. The Dalmeny and Sutherland paintings, in the 'jewelled cape' group, retain the curved framework but have greatly simplified interiors. The pomegranate design is also depicted in several paintings of Anne of Denmark, also attributed to de Critz, perhaps pendant portraits.[37] These backgrounds may depict stamped and gilded leather, a highly fashionable luxury item at European courts in the 16th and early 17th century.[38] Such a decorative brown background is relatively unusual in paintings attributed to de Critz, Gheeraerts and their contemporaries.[39]

The technique used to paint the background of the Montacute, Dulwich and Pitti paintings is strikingly similar. Comparison shown here, between the Pitti and Dulwich pictures (Figs 9 and 10) illustrates the technique used in all three, with the application of a tan base layer that once dry was overlaid with patterns painted in brown or dark red paint, with ochre highlights. These patterns were then filled in methodically using a fine brush with small curved strokes of bright orange-coloured paint. The technique used for the background of the Dulwich and Pitti paintings is compellingly close and must surely have been painted by the same hand.

The technique used to paint the pearl decoration on the king's breeches in the Dulwich, Pitti and Montacute paintings is also similar in approach. In these works a pale grey underlayer was painted first, then yellow and dark grey curved brushstrokes were applied, followed by circles made of pale blue azurite and lead white paint, and finally lead white highlights. Although the handling of the Pitti and Montacute pearls is not precisely identical, the approach taken is so close that it is perhaps arguable that they originated in the same workshop.[40] In a sample (Fig. 5) taken from a blue circle on a pearl on the Montacute painting it appears that the azurite was applied

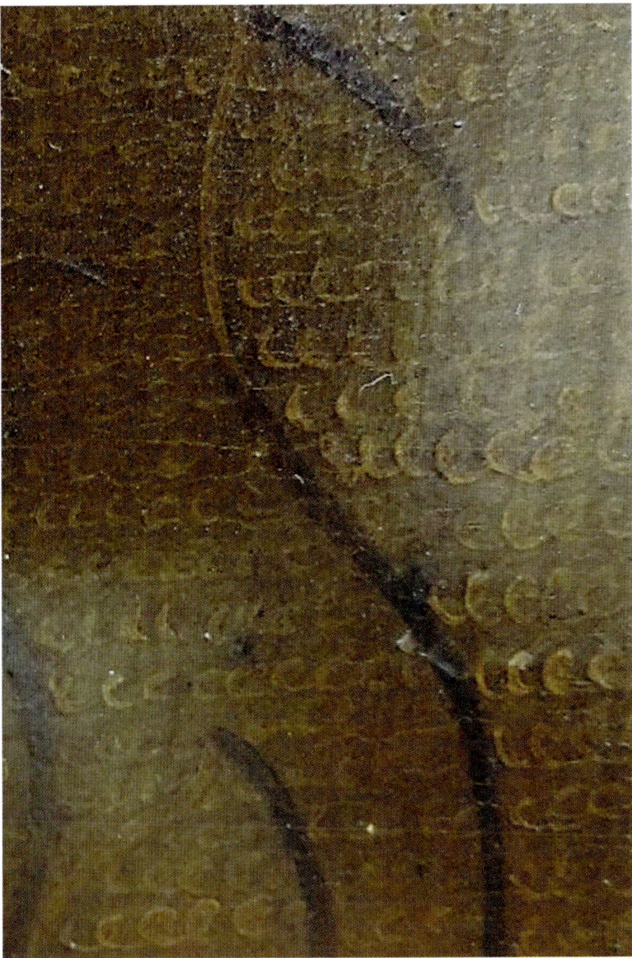

Fig. 9 John de Critz the Elder, *King James VI of Scotland and I of England* (Fig. 1): detail showing the technique used to paint the background decoration. (Image courtesy of SSPSAE and the Polo Museale della città di Firenze - Gabinetto Fotografico.)

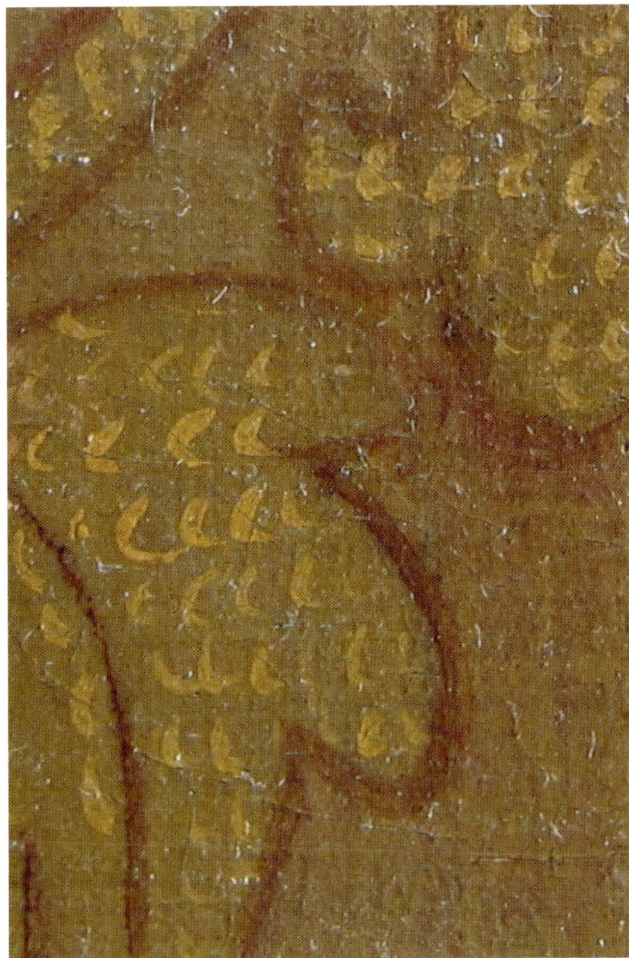

Fig. 10 John de Critz the Elder, *King James VI of Scotland and I of England* (Fig. 3): detail showing the technique used to paint the background decoration. (Courtesy of Dulwich Picture Gallery.)

using a strewing technique, while the underlying paint layer was still tacky. Such a method of application has previously been associated with smalt,[41] a pigment known in the 17th century to quickly discolour in oil.[42]

It has been argued that contemporary artists were aware of the potential for discoloration in oil of both azurite and smalt and that they experimented with different techniques and media in an effort to counteract this.[43] The strewing method of application is interesting because it is potentially an identifiable trait. It also suggests knowledge of the deteriorative properties of pigments within the oil medium on the part of the artist, and that it was a concern of the artist that this painting should stand the test of time. Pearls on the *Ditchley Portrait* (NPG) and *Unknown Lady* (*c.*1595 at Tate) by Gheeraerts are also painted in a broadly similar manner, however it must be noted that this was a known contemporary technique, close to a description given by Nicholas Hilliard in his treatise, *The Arte of Limning*.[44]

A strikingly similar technique is also used to paint the 'Mirror of Great Britain' hat jewels on the Montacute and Pitti portraits. The overall outline of the jewel is identical, with small loops of gold added to the setting of each stone. The area surrounding the ruby has been painted in a closely similar fashion, using thick, viscous white paint. In the Dalmeny and Sutherland paintings, by contrast, the setting of the jewel is simpler, the ruby is more rectangular and its setting is golden and far more smoothly painted.

Conclusions

The de Critz workshop

Striking similarities in technique in the painting of the eyes and surrounding flesh, the background and the pearls on the breeches suggest that the Dulwich, Pitti and Montacute paintings originated in the same workshop environment. The detailed handling of brushwork used for the wall decoration in the background of the Pitti and Dulwich paintings is so similar that these may have been painted by the same hand. Similarly, the technique of painting the 'Mirror of Great Britain' hat jewel on the Montacute and Pitti paintings is extremely similar, and may be the work of one artist. Differences in flesh painting between the three paintings suggest the presence of more than one studio hand.

The Sutherland and Dalmeny portraits are compositionally similar and display some similarities in painting technique.

However, this is not as visually convincing as the link between the above three paintings. Comparison of technique between the two is hampered by the poorer condition of the Dalmeny painting. Stylistically these two paintings are compositionally closest to portraits attributed to Gheeraerts, who is also documented to have produced portraits of the king. However, there are no striking similarities in technique when compared to extant research into paintings attributed to his workshop. Technical examination of two further works that are closely linked compositionally – at Loseley Park in Surrey and in the Museo Nacional del Prado in Madrid – may shed further light on these paintings. There is a significantly different level of finish and approach to technique taken in the GAC and Tyninghame paintings, which suggests that they were created in entirely different workshop environments.

There are no significant technical similarities between the paintings examined and extant research on paintings attributed to de Critz or Gheeraerts. However, as the Pitti painting can be more credibly linked through documentary evidence to the de Critz workshop than those examined at the NPG, it is tentatively argued that the significant shared characteristics identified between this, the Montacute and the Dulwich paintings may assist in forming an initial comparative framework that can be used to identify other works linked to the same workshop.

Workshop practice in general

The portraits examined were painted by competent artists trained and working in the Northern tradition, skilled in the use of materials and techniques and well versed in contemporary approaches. Shared characteristics include the use of good quality oak panels, chalk grounds and a pale priming layer, and the use of grey grounds (or localised grey underlayers) on the two full-length canvas portraits.

The use of generic patterns and panels of a closely similar size for these portraits, which do not clearly appear to have all been painted in the same workshop, suggests the wider use between workshops of standard sized panels, which would have facilitated the efficient creation of portraits of the same sitter using shared patterns. Elements of the technique of the paintings in general (with the exception of the Tyninghame painting, which is significantly cruder than the other works) suggest that priority in the workshops was given to speed of execution in combination with an overall high level of finish. This emphasis on workshop efficiency is also suggested by what appears to be the presence of more than one hand in several of the paintings.

The examination of samples mounted in cross-section revealed sophistries of technique such as the knowledge of the deterioration of pigments in the oil medium. Stiff and creamy paint, which holds the form of the brushstrokes, used on the Dulwich and Montacute paintings may be heat-bodied paint. Comparative analysis of the media used in these paintings using attenuated total reflectance-Fourier transform infrared spectroscopy (ATR-FTIR) would be of great interest for future study, as would dendochronology, which would date the panels and aid in identifying later copies from earlier versions. Consideration of the canvas paintings in the context of wider knowledge of the use of different contemporary canvas supports would also be illuminating. Further archival research into the provenance of the Dulwich and Montacute paintings may prove fruitful in exploring their relationships to the Pitti painting and the de Critz workshop.[45] Dendrochronology and ATR-FTIR are outside the bounds of this study, which is a limitation. However it is hoped that applying the methodology and findings of this study to other attributed paintings will further illuminate understanding of the workshop of John de Critz as well as workshop practice at the time.

Notes

1. For an outline of de Critz's biography see M. Edmond, 'John de Critz, the Elder (d.1642). Serjeant Painter', in L. Goldman (ed.), *Oxford Dictionary of National Biography: 2001–2004*, vol. 14, Oxford, Oxford University Press, 2009, pp. 225–227.
2. See E. Town, '"Whilst he had his perfect sight" – new light on the life and career of John de Critz the Elder', *The Burlington Magazine* 154(1312), 2012, pp. 482–486, and D. Piper, 'Some portraits by Marcus Gheeraerts II and John de Critz reconsidered', *Proceedings of the Huguenot Society of London* XX(2), 1960, pp. 210–229.
3. See R. Tittler, 'Three portraits by John de Critz for the Merchant Taylors' Company', *The Burlington Magazine* 147(1228), 2005, pp. 491–493.
4. Material from the MATB project database, NPG. It includes X-radiographs and surface examination observations carried out using a stereo microscope by S. Plender, S Marriott and P. Saltmarsh, microscopic examination and analysis of paint samples by S. Sheldon, dendrochronology carried out by I. Tyers and infrared reflectography carried out by Tager Stonor Richardson. This information will be available at the end of the project in the Registered Packets for each painting in the NPG library.
5. The paintings examined were: *Robert Cecil, 1st Earl of Salisbury* (NPG 107) 1602; *Francis Walsingham* (NPG 1807) *c.*1585; *Thomas Sackville, Earl of Dorset* (NPG 4024) *c.*1601; *Henry Wriothesley, 3rd Earl of Southampton* (L114) 1600.
6. It is argued that paintings that show similarities in construction and technique such as the support, preparatory layers, underdrawing and method of painting may have originated in the same workshop. Idiosyncratic characteristics such as distinctive and identifiable brushwork that appear closely similar in different paintings are argued to be the work of the same hand.
7. The National Archives E 351/543 f.199 (reference given in Town 2012 (cited in note 2), p. 483).
8. Like the Uffizi, the Palazzo Pitti collection was formed from the Medici collections.
9. For a biography of Gheeraerts, see K. Hearn and R. Jones, *Marcus Gheeraerts II: Elizabethan Artist*, London, Tate Publishing, 2002, pp. 8–15.
10. E. Auerbach, *Tudor Artists: A Study of Painters in the Royal Service and of Portraiture on Illuminated Documents from the Accession of Henry VIII to the Death of Elizabeth I*, London, Athlone Press, 1954, p. 165
11. R. Jones, 'Marcus Gheeraerts the Younger (1561–1635/6): portrait of Captain Thomas Lee 1594', in J.M. Townsend and S. Hackney (eds), *Paint and Purpose: A Study of Technique in British Art*, London, Tate Gallery, 1999, pp. 26–31, 203; R. Jones,

'A note on the techniques of painting found in Gheeraerts's portraits in the Tate collection', in K. Hearn and R. Jones, *Marcus Gheeraerts II: Elizabethan Artist*, London, Tate Publishing, 2002, pp. 53–61.

12. The portraits examined were: *Mary, Lady Scudamore* (NPG 64) 1619; *Elizabeth I* ('The Ditchley Portrait', NPG 2561) 1592; *Robert Devereux* (NPG 4985) 1597; *Henry, Prince of Wales* (NPG 2562) 1603.
13. For example recent research into the studio of Michiel van Mierevelt (1566–1641), *Portrait Factory Van Mierevelt: Discover the Hand of the Master*, exhibition held at Het Prinsenhof Museum, Delft, 24 September 2011–4 March 2012.
14. R. Strong, 'Three royal jewels: the Three Brothers, the Mirror of Great Britain and the Feather', *The Burlington Magazine* 108(760), 1966, pp. 350–353.
15. For a reproduction see B. Grosvenor, 'The identity of "the Famous Paynter Steven" not Steven Van Der Meulen but Steven Van Herwijk', *British Art Journal* IX(3), 2009, pp. 12–17.
16. Reproduced in R. Strong, *Gloriana: The Portraits of Queen Elizabeth I*, London, Thames & Hudson, 1987, p. 73.
17. R. Strong, *The English Icon: Elizabethan & Jacobean Portraiture*, Studies in British Art, London, Paul Mellon Foundation for British Art/Routledge & Kegan Paul, 1969, p. 264.
18. Image filed in the 'de Critz' folder, Witt Library, Courtauld Institute of Art, London.
19. www.gac.culture.gov.uk/artist.aspx?id=136796.
20. A good comparative image is Gheeraerts's portrait of *Robert Devereux, 2nd Earl of Essex*, *c*.1596; Strong 1969 (cited in note 17), p. 297.
21. Edmond 2009 (cited in note 1) also discusses the possible attribution of the Sutherland portrait to Gheeraerts, however her argument is based on her assessment of de Critz's 'patent' as Serjeant Painter, omitting discussion of receipts from the Crown to de Critz, evidence of his production of portraits of the king.
22. Untested. Medullary rays are visible on the verso of all three panels indicating the use of radially or tangentially cut planks; J. Wadum, 'Historical overview of panel-making techniques in the Northern Countries', in K. Dardes and A. Rothe (eds), *The Structural Conservation of Panel Paintings: Proceedings of a Symposium at the J. Paul Getty Museum 24–28 April 1995*, Los Angeles, The Getty Conservation Institute, 1995, pp. 149–177, p. 151.
23. 113 × 85 cm (Dalmeny), 113.4 × 87.5 cm (Montacute), 113.5 × 83.2 cm (Pitti), 114.3 × 82.8 cm (Tyninghame). The Dulwich canvas painting is 223 × 150 cm (dimensions taken from *Loan condition report for 'King James VI and I' after John de Critz the Elder (DPG384)*, Conservation file, Dulwich Picture Gallery, 1999, p. 1) and the Sutherland painting is 203 × 116 cm (K. Hearn (ed.), *Dynasties: Painting in Tudor and Jacobean England 1530–1630*, London, Tate Gallery, 1995, p. 184). Note that it has been extended at the top edge by 9–10 cm.
24. G. Heydenreich, *Lucas Cranach the Elder: Painting Materials, Techniques and Workshop Practice*, Amsterdam, Amsterdam University Press, 2006, pp. 45–46.
25. Ibid., p. 46. Heydenreich makes this suggestion in relation to production methods in the Cranach workshop. It is not known whether there was such an open art market in England. However, inventories demonstrate that there was a high demand for portraits of the reigning monarch in Tudor and Stuart England; S. Foister, 'Paintings and other works of art in sixteenth-century English inventories', *The Burlington Magazine* 123(938), 1981, pp. 273–282, p. 277.
26. Within Gheeraerts's attributed oeuvre: *Lady Scudamore* (panel, 1615, NPG 64) is 115.1 × 82.8 cm; *Richard Tomlins* (panel, 1628, Oxford, Bodleian Library) is 111.8 × 83.9 cm; *Anne Hale, Mrs Hoskins* (panel, 1629, private collection) is 111.8 × 82.7 cm, *Robert Devereux* (panel, 1595–1600, Cambridge, Trinity College) is 118 × 81.4 cm. Panel portraits of Lord and Lady Petre (1599) at Ingatestone Hall, Essex, are 111.8 × 90.2 cm. Of paintings attributed to de Critz, several portraits of Anne of Denmark are of close dimensions, such as the portrait formerly in the Tyninghame collection (114.3 × 83.9 cm).
27. On standard panel sizes in Antwerp see J. Kirby, 'The painter's trade in the seventeenth century: theory and practice', *National Gallery Technical Bulletin* 20, 1999, pp. 5–49, pp. 18–19. Comparatively very little is known of the use of standard sizes by English panel makers. For a pioneering study of this subject, see I. Tyers, 'Panel making, sources of wood, construction "trademarks" and conclusions on the making and trade in the UK', in A. Burnstock, T. Cooper and M. Howard (eds), *Painting in Britain 1500–1630: Production, Influences and Patronage*, London, British Academy, 2014. All four panels comprise three vertical planks of standard board widths for Baltic oak panels: I. Tyers, *The Tree-ring Analysis of Panel Paintings from the National Portrait Gallery: Group 5.3*, 2011 (see note 4). It is possible that these dimensions arose out of a desire to use the proportion 3:4 in conjunction with the most efficient use of the wood.
28. Wadum 1995 (cited in note 22), p. 167.
29. See *Loan condition report* (cited in note 23). This is not visible in surface examination of the painting.
30. For example *Robert Devereux, 2nd Earl of Essex*, *c*.1597, NPG 4985. S. Plender and P. Saltmarsh, accessed 13 March 2012, *Surface examination observations on 'Robert Devereux, 2nd Earl of Essex' by Marcus Gheeraerts the Younger, NPG 4985* (see note 4).
31. Jones 2002 (cited in note 11), p. 55.
32. Reports on *Henry, Prince of Wales* (NPG 4515), *Elizabeth of Bohemia* (NPG 6113) and *Charles Cornwallis* (NPG 4867), accessed 13 March 2012 (see note 4).
33. Museum Het Prinsenhof, *More Van Mierevelt. Exhibition Guide: Portrait Factory Van Mierevelt; Discover the Hand of the Master. Guide to Accompany the Exhibition Held at the Museum Het Prinsenhof, Delft, 24 September 2011– 4 March 2012*, Delft, Museum Het Prinsenhof, 2011, p. 29.
34. The Montacute portrait is painted more fluidly, has elongated fingertips and relatively warmer flesh tones. The Pitti portrait employs more visible, directional brushwork. Abrasion to the flesh paint limits close comparison with the Dulwich painting.
35. It has been argued that Mierevelt painted the faces of portraits while assistants painted costumes and backgrounds (Museum Het Prinsenhof 2011 (cited in note 33), p. 34) and that portraits attributed to Peake appear to be the products of more than one hand, with the quality of flesh painting varying between paintings; C. Macleod, 'Robert Peake: technical evidence and patronage', paper presented at the National Portrait Gallery and Courtauld Institute of Art *Conference on Tudor and Jacobean Painting: Production, Influences and Patronage*, 3 December 2010.
36. This method of application is suggested by circular shapes on the Montacute painting and dots visible on the Pitti painting and the (abraded) Dulwich painting. See H.P. De Melo, J. Sanyova and A.J. Cruz, 'An unusual glazing technique on a Portuguese panel painting from the second half of the 16th century: materials, technique and reconstructions', in J. Bridgland, C. Antomarchi, M.C. Corbeil, M.C. Eshøj, F. Hannsen-Bower, L. Pilosi *et al.* (eds). *Preprints of the ICOM-CC 16th Triennial Conference*, Lisbon, September 2011 (CD copy).
37. For example in the collection of the National Trust at Blickling Hall in Norfolk (NT 355475) and in the National Maritime Museum, Greenwich (BHC4251).
38. J.W. Warterer, *Spanish Leather: A History of its Use from 800 to*

1800 for Mural Hangings, Screens, Upholstery, Altar Frontals, Ecclesiastical Vestments, Footwear, Gloves, Pouches and Caskets, London, Faber and Faber, 1971.

39. Two portraits of *Henry, Prince of Wales* attributed to Peake also have similar backgrounds (Strong 1969 (cited in note 17), pp. 250–251).
40. The technique is harder to read on the Dulwich painting due to abrasion and overpaint, however the approach taken appears similar.
41. M.H. Van Eikema Hommes, *Discolouration in Renaissance and Baroque Oil Paintings: Instructions for Painters, Theoretical Concepts, and Scientific Data*, PhD dissertation, University of Amsterdam, 2002, p. 25.
42. Ibid.
43. Ibid., pp. 18–20, 25–26.
44. N. Hilliard, *The Arte of Limning*, R.K.R. Thornton and T.G.S. Cain (eds), Manchester, Carcanet Press, p. 79.
45. The provenance of the Dulwich painting can be traced back to 1716 when it was in the collection at Holland House, London. The painting entered the Dulwich collection as a gift from Henry Yates Thomson in 1917 (email correspondence with Lucy Findley, Dulwich Picture Gallery, 15 May 2012). The Montacute painting has traditionally thought to have been a gift to Sir Edward Phelips (1555–1614), who built Montacute, from the king, however there is no documentary evidence to support this. The Crown records relating to payments to de Critz have been examined thoroughly by Edmond and also by Town (cited in notes 1and 2). Neither author has uncovered a specific commission for a portrait to be painted by de Critz, however it is possible that this would not have been mentioned in the receipts. Seventeenth-century records at Montacute only exist from 1632 onwards; see Phelips MSS, Somerset Archive and Record Service, overview available at www.nationalarchives.gov.uk/a2a/records.aspx?cat=168-ddph&cid=0#0 (accessed 14 February 2012).

Authors' addresses

- Caroline Rae, Department of Conservation and Technology, Courtauld Institute of Art, London, UK (Caroline.Rae@courtauld.ac.uk)
- Aviva Burnstock, Department of Conservation and Technology, Courtauld Institute of Art, London UK (Aviva.Burnstock@courtauld .ac.uk)

MICHIEL VAN MIEREVELT, COPY MASTER: EXPLORING THE OEUVRE OF THE VAN MIEREVELT WORKSHOP

Anita Jansen and Johanneke Verhave

ABSTRACT The portrait market in the northern Netherlands was dominated by the studio of the Delft painter Michiel van Mierevelt in the first half of the 17th century. He portrayed the prominent Dutch and members of the rich upper class, as well as a smaller number of foreign royalty and noblemen. Recent research by Museum Het Prinsenhof in Delft focused on the painting techniques of Van Mierevelt with an emphasis on his methods of copying his own originals. Evidence from some of the paintings studied suggests that these were used as models for copying in Van Mierevelt's studio. This research sheds new light on the interpretation of the inventory of Van Mierevelt's possessions, drawn up after his death in 1641, and on the hypothesis that Van Mierevelt kept one painted version of his popular portraits to serve as a model for further replication.

Introduction

In the first half of the 17th century the portrait studio of Michiel van Mierevelt (1566–1641) dominated the market for portraits in the northern Netherlands (Fig. 1). Museum Het Prinsenhof in Delft hosted a four-year research project working towards the first exhibition of Van Mierevelt's work (Museum Het Prinsenhof, Delft, September 2011–March 2012) accompanied by the first monograph dedicated to the painter and his work since 1894.[1] The project combined art historical, archival and material technical research to reconstruct and explore Van Mierevelt's vast oeuvre.

Over a period of 50 years his workshop produced thousands of portraits and Van Mierevelt died an extremely wealthy man. It is no exaggeration to claim that the extent of Van Mierevelt's copying of portraits did not find its equal in the 17th century. In fact, his compositions, choice of materials and painting technique all served the purpose of replication. This article focuses on the new hypothesis concerning the models Van Mierevelt used for the production of these replicas.

Mass production through copying

Michiel van Mierevelt boasted that he had produced 10,000 portraits.[2] With a career of at least 50 productive years this

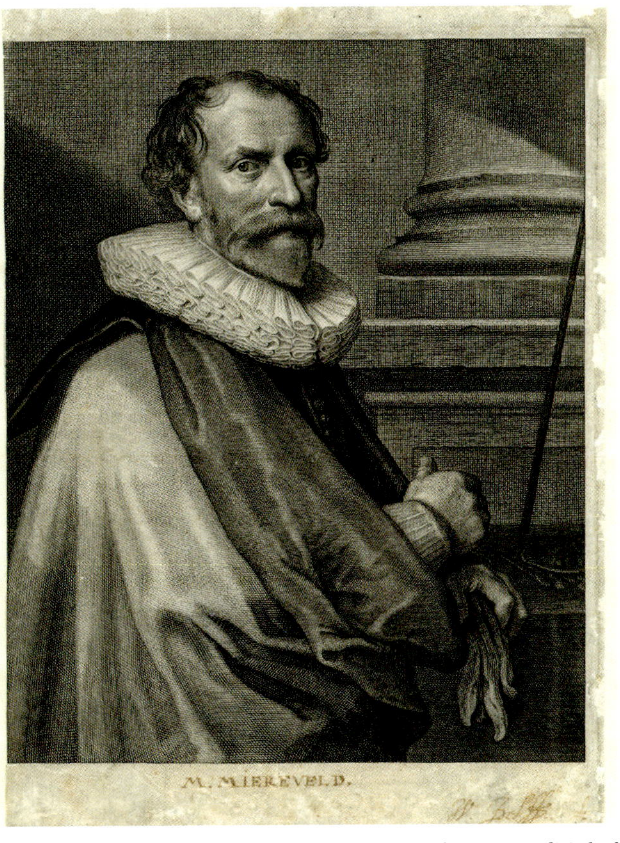

Fig. 1 Willem Jacobsz. Delff, after Anthonie van Dijck, *Portrait of Michiel van Mierevelt*, *c.*1635, engraving. Delft, Delft Archives, inv. 67963.

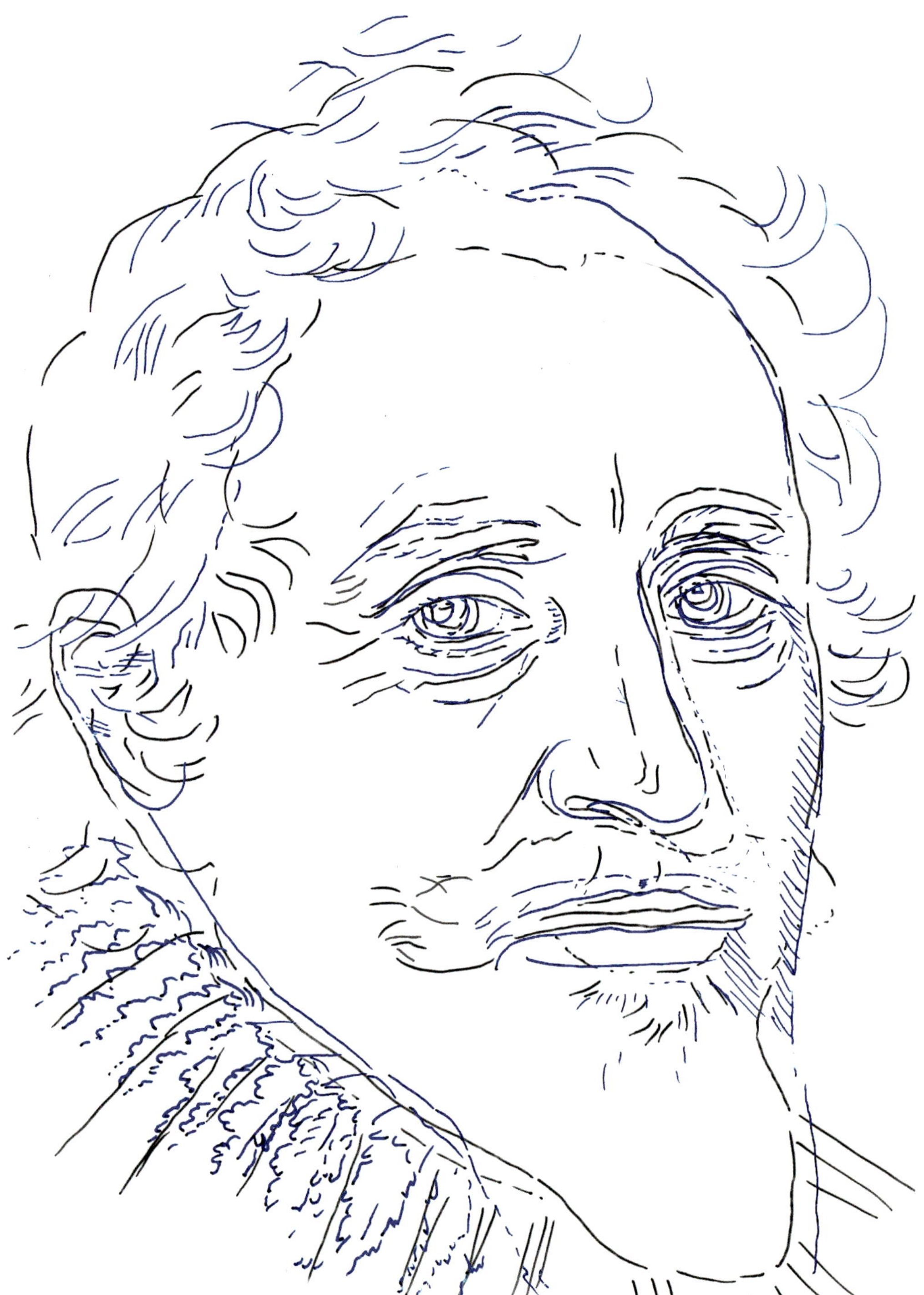

Fig. 2 Overlay of two tracings: the portrait of Maurits (Museum Het Prinsenhof, inv. PDS 68b) in blue and the portrait of Hugo de Groot (Museum Het Prinsenhof, inv. PDS 71) in black. The outlines of the faces are largely the same, in spite of the different sitters, painted in different years (1607 versus 1631).

would equate to an average of 200 portraits per year, an accomplishment of which the painter was obviously very proud. We have no proof of the validity of Van Mierevelt's statement, but after the study of his oeuvre we believe that the actual production was at least half this quantity: 5000 paintings. Regardless, these are considerable numbers that would seem to belong more to a modern Chinese art copy studio than to the painting practice of the 17th century. And therein lies a crucial point: a substantial part of the oeuvre consists of copies, and a copy can be created much faster than an original. Certainly part of the mass production in Van Mierevelt's studio was in the hands of assistants and pupils, but their contributions were considered as part of Van Mierevelt's work, as can be deduced from the presence of a signature on the portraits: 20% of the oeuvre is signed, whereas about half is dated. The signed paintings are generally portraits of higher quality and/or made for more prestigious clients.[3] The research on his paintings revealed that Van Mierevelt's signature is not restricted to works solely by the hand of the master. In addition, portraits that are considered to have been (partly) painted by Van Mierevelt alone do not necessarily bear a signature.

Table 1 Ten of most often reproduced portraits in the workshop of Van Mierevelt within the core group of 629 extant portraits related to the workshop.

1	Prince Maurits	43
2	Prince Frederik Hendrik	36
3	Johan van Oldenbarneveldt	18
4	Prince Willem van Oranje	17
5	Elizabeth Stuart, Queen of Bohemia	16
6	Amalia van Solms	15
7	Frederik V , King of Bohemia	15
8	Stadholder Willem Lodewijk	14
9	Prince Philips Willem	13
10	Edward Cecil	12
	Total	**199 portraits**

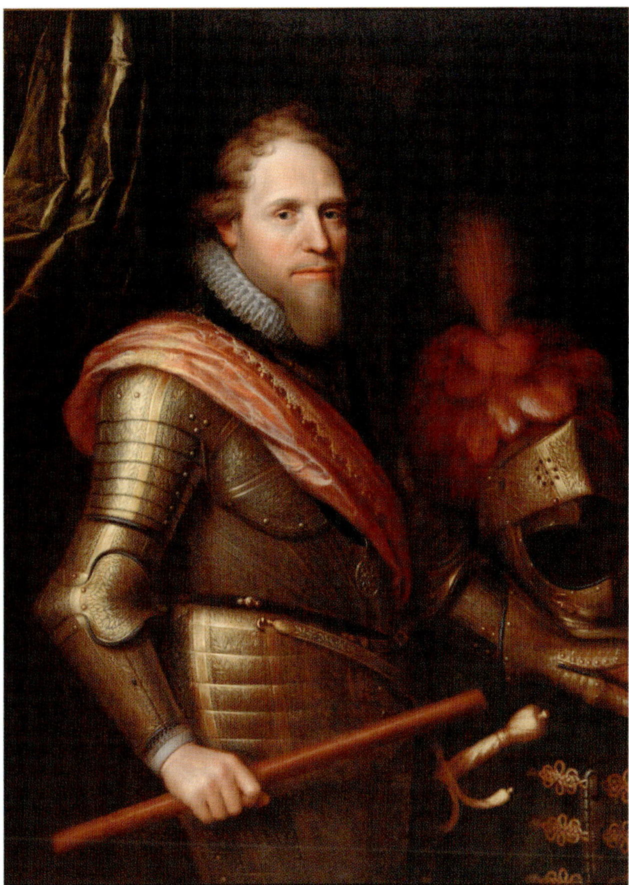

Fig. 3 Michiel van Mierevelt, *Portrait of Maurits*, 1607, oil on panel, 111.2 × 84 cm, Delft, Museum Het Prinsenhof, inv. PDS 68b.

Copying versus inventing

Why is producing a copy faster than painting an original? The obvious answer is that the creative process involved in conceiving the painting is bypassed. The conception of a portrait involves client sittings and the translation of the sketches into a portrait. However, even the creative process for the unique portraits produced in the Delft studio was limited. Van Mierevelt's portraits have largely the same parameters, consisting of a support of standard material and size and a predetermined composition, which only varied in relation to the attire of his sitters.[4] This set composition even extends to the faces of the clients, as was discovered in the comparison of tracings of different portraits. The overall likeness in scale and position of different faces is too close to be explained as the steady hand of a practised painter, but rather seems the result of using a template for the outlines of the face, which would be adjusted to fit the features and hair of the sitter (Fig. 2). There seems to have been one template for men and one for women.[5] In a sense Van Mierevelt developed a method for copying the *concept* of a Van Mierevelt portrait.

Replicating

Besides this high level of standardisation in the production of unique portraits, the studio had an equally extensive output of replicas. Portraits of popular figures were copied dozens of times, whereas some burghers had their portraits copied only once or twice for their children (Table 1). As far as we know, the earliest replicas date from 1607, the year when Van Mierevelt was given the commission to paint a portrait of Stadholder Maurits (1576–1625), the eldest son of William of Orange (1533–1584).[6] Van Mierevelt was not the first to paint Maurits – he was preceded by Daniel van den Queeborn (1552–1602). In 1607 there was no specific court painter active at the The Hague court and the ambitious Van Mierevelt saw an opportunity and seized it. Instead of just painting the commissioned portrait, he painted at least six replicas, four knee pieces and two busts, in the same year. Two of these remaining portraits

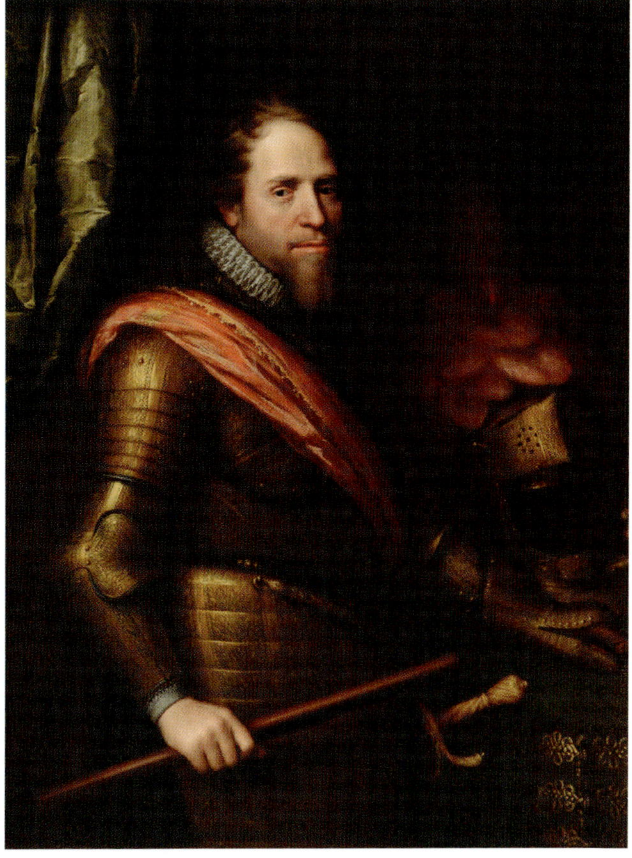

Fig. 4 Michiel van Mierevelt, *Portrait of Maurits*, oil on canvas, 111.4 × 88 cm, Delft, Museum Het Prinsenhof, inv. PDS 70.

were for a known destination: the portrait for the Delft City Hall and the portrait that Van Mierevelt presented to the States General in The Hague (Fig. 3). The other four are without a complete provenance. It can be assumed that one portrait was intended for Maurits himself. Of the remaining portraits, the portrait in the Rijksmuseum collection is the most likely version painted for the prince.[7] A fourth remaining portrait is still in Delft, in the Museum het Prinsenhof (Fig. 4). Curiously, this version is executed on canvas, whereas Van Mierevelt worked almost exclusively on oak panels. Is it possible that this painting had a special function in the workshop? In 1607–8 it was this version that was used by Jan Muller (1571–1628) to convert the portrait into an engraving.[8] This seems to indicate that the painting remained in the studio for some time after execution.[9] As the studio continued to produce portraits of Maurits after 1608 we have considered whether this version on canvas was left in the studio to act as a model for further copying. The idea is intriguing and leads to many more questions, which will be addressed in the following section.

Van Mierevelt's copies: materials and models

Stylistically and in their use of materials there are no major differences between the unique portraits and their replicas, although the quality of the master's hand is more apparent in the first category. The general build-up of a portrait by Van Mierevelt, whether an original or a copy, can be described as follows.[10] The support is an oak panel consisting of three vertical planks joined with a tongue and groove joint. The middle plank is the widest in order to ensure the face can be painted clear of a joint. The standard sizes of these panels vary according to the type of portrait: for example, the bust portraits measure approximately 64 × 59 cm, whereas the knee pieces are approximately 114 × 86 cm.[11] The preparation of the support is minimal: first a chalk glue ground is applied, which is scraped down to the point where it barely covers more than the deeper wood grain and irregularities of the oak. A thin layer of *imprimatura* is then applied, rich in oil and with pigments that combine into a warm grey to red colour (a combination of lead white, chalk, black, red lead and earth pigments).[12] In the paintings containing an *imprimatura* of a red tone rather than a warm grey, it is often seen that a local white underpaint is applied in the area of the face. The subsequent paint layers are thin and rich in oil, with a minimum number of layers in the background and clothing, but a refined finish due to different superimposed tones in the faces.

As Van Mierevelt copied some portraits many times, spread over a period of decades, it was initially assumed that he must have kept an archive of drawings or sketches that he used and reused for later copies of a particular portrait. Nevertheless not a single drawing by Van Mierevelt is known nor does the extensive inventory of Van Mierevelt's possessions at his death in 1641 mention any drawings or cartoons. Our curiosity was aroused by a piece of paper lying on the floor in a portrait of the Van Mierevelt family, painted by Michiel's oldest son Pieter, in which he is working on a portrait of one of his sisters. Close inspection of the painting showed the piece of paper to be blank and as Pieter is painting his sister from life it does not seem to have a function as a model for copying.[13]

Underdrawing

In light of the extensive copying practices in Van Mierevelt's studio, the presence of underdrawings was expected, which might have enabled us to distinguish between originals and replicas. This was not the case: although underdrawing has been found, its presence somewhat complicates our interpretations of the portraits. One technique of underdrawing commonly employed for copying – especially on a larger scale – using a pounced cartoon has been found in the face of the earliest versions of the portrait of Prince Maurits.[14] Infrared reflectography (IRR), tracings and observations with the naked eye revealed that the same cartoon was used for different versions of the portrait.[15] The choice of the use of a pounced cartoon is logical in light of Van Mierevelt's clear aspirations to paint the same portrait several times – it could be reused many times without significant wear. It is curious, however, that even the traditionally presumed 'prototype' of the Maurits portrait, the version painted for the Delft City Hall, was prepared using the cartoon. Therefore it can hardly be defined as more original than the other versions.

Almost 40 other portraits were studied with IRR with very little result. The use of pounced cartoons has not been found in any other portrait and only some slight indications of an underdrawing in a carbon-containing material were visible with IRR.[16] Studying the faces with a microscope did reveal the use of an underdrawing in a transparent red paint in several portraits. Traces of these red lines were usually found in the eyes of the sitter and along the contour lines of their faces and collars, but for the larger part they were covered with paint. The colour of this underdrawing was neither helpful nor disadvantageous to the appearance of the portrait, which made it more puzzling as it was found relatively often. A study of Van Dyck's copies of portraits suggests that he used red paint to follow the outlines of a finished portrait, which he could subsequently rub off on a different support, most likely paper or vellum.[17] This image would then be transferred onto the support of the copy, a technique called counterproof. Could the appearance of red underdrawing indicate that Van Mierevelt used paintings to replicate them in the same manner? Most of the red lines do not reveal that they were rubbed off, as they are relatively fine lines (*c*.2 mm wide) with a slightly bulky character. Reconstructions have indicated that counterproof lines tend to be wide, spotty and irregular.[18]

Only one painting by Van Mierevelt included in the research project, namely that of Edward Cecil in the National Portrait Gallery in London, was found to have an underdrawing in red lines with precisely these characteristics showing through in the final paint layers of the face (Fig. 5). Another version of this portrait, in the National Army Museum in London, was found to have exactly the same reddish lines showing through.[19] The version of Cecil's portrait used as a model for these two replicas was outlined with the red paint,

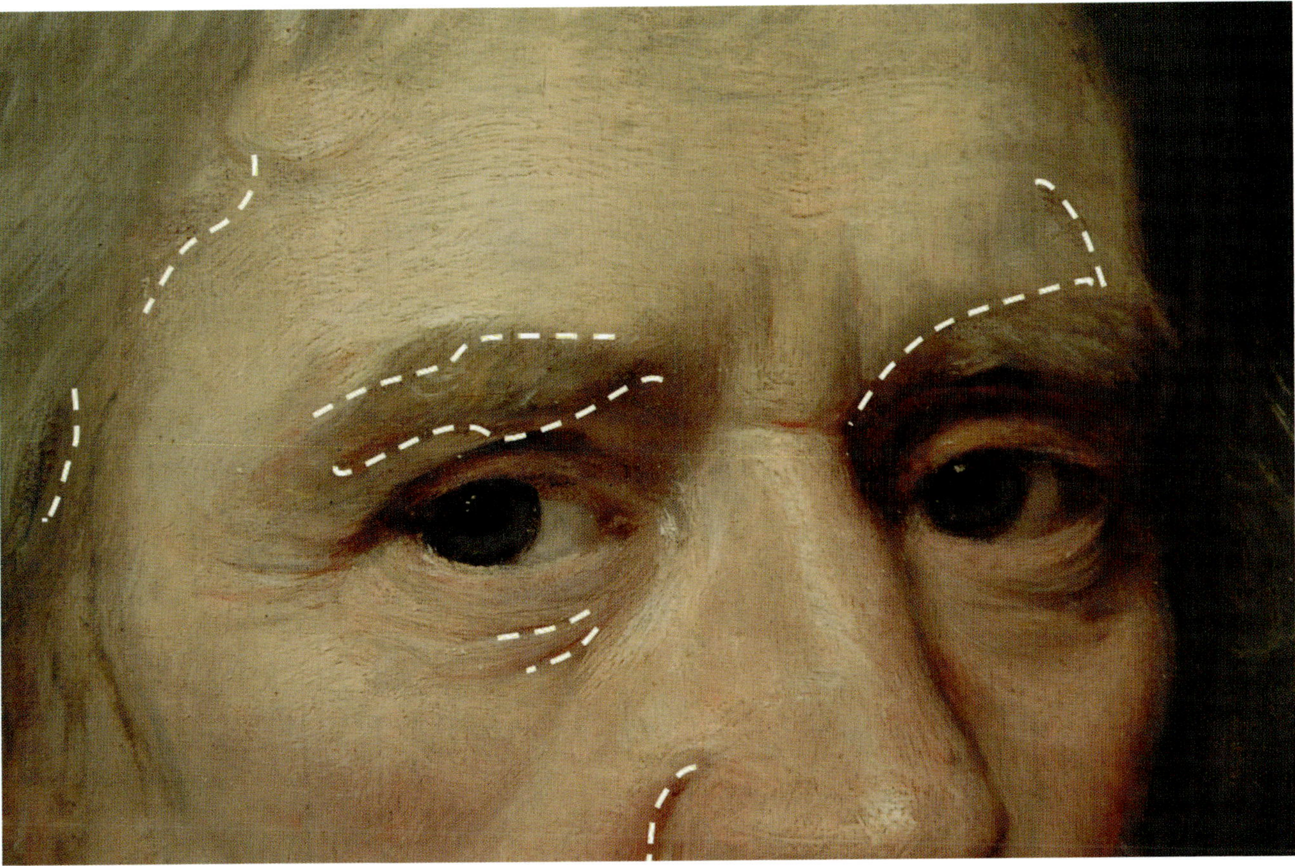

Fig. 5 Detail of the portrait of Edward Cecil, London, National Portrait Gallery, inv. NPG 4541. Red dotted lines are visible, a result of the use of a counterproof, here indicated by dotted lines.

seemingly in a rather abundant manner; it was then blotted off onto a secondary support that was then rubbed off on the new support, or possibly two new supports, for the replicas. The portrait of Edward Cecil shows that in some cases Van Mierevelt used the technique of a counterproof for the production of his replicas, probably using a painted portrait as a model rather than a (paper) cartoon.

The painted portrait as a model

With this convincing case in mind of the use of a painting as a model for a copy, we examined Van Mierevelt's oeuvre to find more evidence of this practice. One example is the portrait of Frederik V, the Winter King, painted as part of a series of Orange portraits for the Delft City Hall (Fig. 6).[20] During the recent restoration of the painting it was revealed that it had been used to produce a replica using another technique.[21] Thin horizontal lines became visible after varnish removal where the paint layer seemed to have lost its colour, especially in the dark red lake areas of the painting (Fig. 7). The horizontal lines cover the whole surface with a standard distance between them of about 11 cm. Although no vertical lines were found, it seems that a grid was placed on the surface of the portrait to facilitate copying, possibly using (moist) strings. This seems to have been done soon after its execution before the red lake paint had fully dried, causing the paint to blanch. The outlines of the composition in particular would have been easier to copy using a grid.

Another painting from the same series of Orange portraits also supports the idea that paintings were used as models for new replicas. In the portrait of Stadholder Lodewijk some adjustments were made in the last stage of the painting (Delft, Museum Het Prinsenhof, 1620–24, oil on panel, 113 × 87.3 cm, inv. PDS 68e). Using a wide brush with blackish paint, Van Mierevelt made the orange sash smaller and created a separation in the front of the white lace collar. From a distance these adjustments are not obvious, though they are done quite roughly – the folds of the sash are cut abruptly halfway through. But despite their clumsiness these alterations were copied faithfully in subsequent versions.

Updating the models

Looking at the most popular portraits of, for example, Stadholder Maurits or his brother Frederik Hendrik, we see indications that the model for the copies changed over the years, as small changes in the composition of the portraits were introduced that were consequently continued in all later portraits. For Maurits these changes were small adjustments to the armour (even though the actual guild armour of course did not change): from a round to a more rectangular pauldron, and the addition of a strap at the shoulder. The lace collar continues at the right side of the beard in all portraits painted after *c.*1613, whereas it ends at the beard in the earlier versions. And indeed, Maurits gradually grows older. To be able to repeat the right

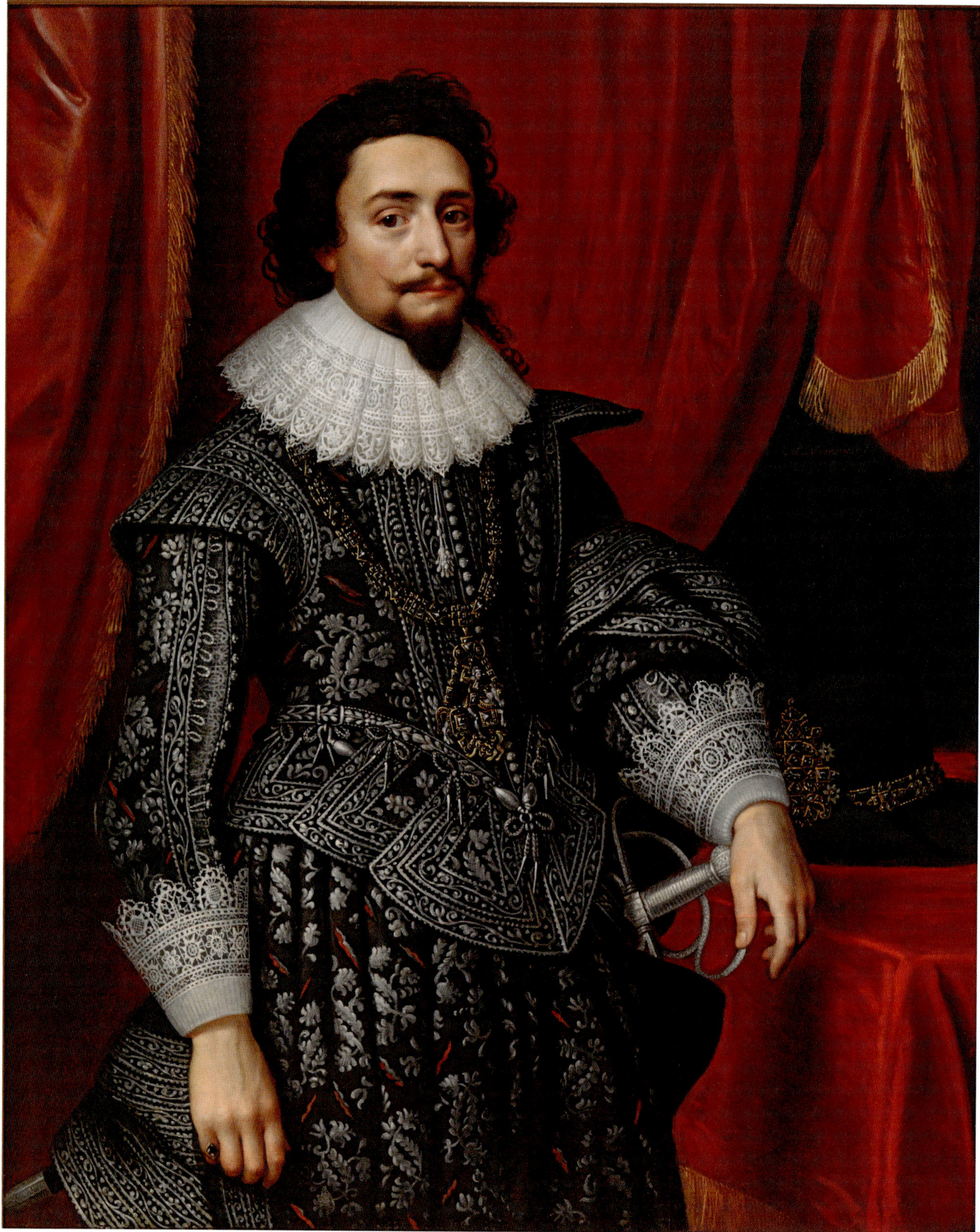

Fig. 6 Michiel van Mierevelt, *Portrait of Frederik V*, oil on panel, 113.4 × 89.3 cm, Delft, Museum Het Prinsenhof, inv. PDS 68g.

type there must have been an updated model in the studio, which was again replaced after a couple of years.

That this model was not a worked-out drawing on paper, replaced as the need or desire for changes in the composition arose, is a possible conclusion that can be drawn from the portrait of Frederik Hendrik painted for the Delft City Hall (Delft, Museum Het Prinsenhof, 1620–24, oil on panel, 111.7 × 84.9 cm, inv. PDS 68c). The study of this portrait with X-radiography and IRR revealed that the painting was originally executed with a shorter collar, known from other early

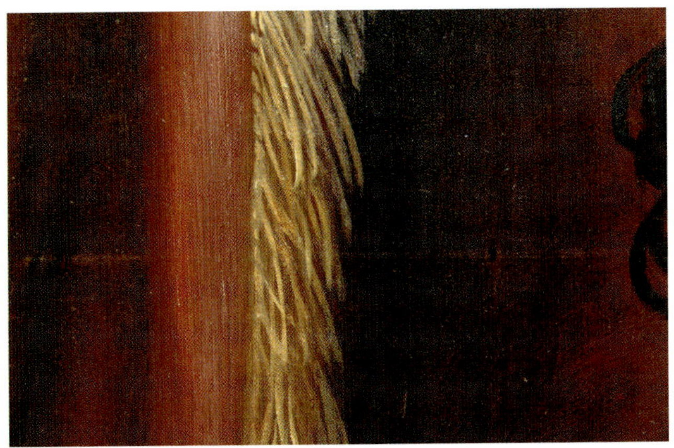

Fig. 7 Detail of a horizontal mark in the dark red paint layers on the portrait of Frederik V (Museum Het Prinsenhof, inv. PDS 68g). Photo taken during treatment (before retouching), Atelier Boersma, Rotterdam.

versions of Frederik's portraits. This shorter collar was finished in great detail, as highlights in lead white are present on the elegant lace edge, as is shown on the X-radiograph; shadow edges were applied in a carbon-containing black paint, visible with IRR. The new version of the collar was simply painted over the earlier one. Later copies repeat this new version of the collar until it was again replaced with a more fashionable flat version around 1632.

Van Mierevelt's copies: archival documents

The technical evidence described above led to the current hypothesis that Van Mierevelt might have used his own paintings as models for his replicas. With this in mind the existing archival documents concerning the Van Mierevelt workshop were considered once more to see if they could support or counter this theory. Is it likely that Van Mierevelt kept some kind of archive of painted prototypes, especially for the purpose of copying?

Original versus copy

From the contemporary documents it becomes clear that the painter himself made a distinction between originals and copies produced in his studio – both in importance and price. In an invoice, drawn up by Van Mierevelt in 1624, he states that the English ambassador, Dudley Carleton, owes him 596 guilders for nine portraits ordered and delivered between 1620 and 1624.[22] It concerned two original portraits (*'conterfeitsel nae het leven gedaen'*: portrait made from life) and seven copies (*'copie'*). Two portraits of Lord Goring mentioned in this bill show that Van Mierevelt charged different prices for an original or a copy: while the bust-sized copy cost *'vier pondt vlaems'* (=24 guilders), the sum charged for the original was more than twice that price at 50 guilders.

In some cases the inscriptions on portraits refer to Van Mierevelt's distinction between copies and originals. On five of the seven knee-length portraits of the stadholders, in the series of Orange portraits commissioned by the city of Delft, a Latin text reads: *'Michaël a Miereveld ad sui // ipsius principale depinxit'* (Painted by Michiel van Mierevelt after his own original).[23]

A short list of popular portraits

Analysis of the extant oeuvre of Van Mierevelt and his studio showed that 50% of the core group of 629 portraits consists of copies. The list of sitters for the portraits comprises 323 different individuals but only 75 persons were painted more than once. Within this group a far smaller cluster of famous, public individuals can be identified, whose portraits were replicated many times. This small group of 35 sitters is responsible for a relatively high percentage of the total production of portraits in the workshop.[24]

The short list of 35 most popular sitters was cross-referenced with the inventory drawn up after Van Mierevelt's death.[25] This inventory, compiled by his son-in law, a notary, not only gives a detailed account of the personal belongings of the Van Mierevelt household, but also provides an intriguing list of the contents of the painter's studio. When Van Mierevelt died, there were still 175 (finished and unfinished) portraits in his workshop. All the portraits are described: the name of the sitter, the value of the portrait and whether or not it is finished. The portraits are divided into two categories. The first category, consisting of 66 paintings, is described as: *'die desen Boedel in eijgendomme sijn toebehoorende alle wesende copie behalve daer anders bijstaet'* (all these portraits belong to the inventory [of Van Mierevelt] and are all copies, unless otherwise specified). The second category of 109 paintings is characterised as: *'Conterfeitsels gemaeckt voor perticuliere persoonen, daer van t'schilderloon noch resteert'* (portraits painted for private clients, for which the 'painter's wages' had not yet been paid).[26] The inventory cites the stages for each of these paintings, for example describing paintings in their dead colouring stage (*gedootverwt*) or specifically stating which parts still needed to be finished (the hands or the clothing). It is clear that the portraits from this second category were ordered by private clients and were waiting either to be finished or to be paid for and delivered.

But what was the function of the first category? These were all copies, and until now it has been assumed that they were made as stock for the free market to be sold in Van Mierevelt's studio or 'winckel', as first suggested by Abraham Bredius in his description of the inventory in 1908.[27] A closer look at the list of names of the individual sitters within this group of 66 portraits and a comparison with the total clientele leads to new conclusions. The list shows that Van Mierevelt kept copies of the most frequently reproduced famous clients he painted during his career. Portraits of rich burghers are lacking in the register, while the portraits of famous clergymen, the Dutch court members, stadholders and their relatives are well represented. The majority of these are only represented with a single portrait – they were clearly painted with no commercial intent in mind. Where more than one version of an individual exists, these versions differ in size, form or composition. The notary describes the differences by adding 'the old' or 'the new' or mentioning a different size, for example 'small' or 'round'.[28]

Portraits as an archive

The overlap of the 35 most popular individuals and the portraits belonging to Van Mierevelt personally (*'desen Boedel in eigendomme'*) seems to confirm the special function of these portraits within the workshop as a kind of archive of painted portraits to be used for the making of replicas.

The portraits could also have been used as a kind of catalogue for visiting customers – illustrating the products that were available in the studio from which to make their choice. Will it be a portrait of Maurits or of Hugo de Groot? Should it be a small or large portrait, round or rectangular, bust or full length? The archive/catalogue must have been a dynamic collection in which old versions would be replaced with the latest version. This could explain the consistent implementation of small changes in the portraits, such as the changes in collars and visual aging of the sitters.

Conclusions

The technique of painting and copying in the Van Mierevelt workshop will continue to be the focus of further research in the coming years. The current knowledge of his methods of copying, combining technical evidence and examination of archival documents seems to support the theory that actual paintings were used for reproductions. Using the counterproof, a grid and/or possible other transfer techniques made it relatively easy to reproduce portraits of the same scale. This way of copying, rather than working after a monochrome drawing or sketch, was fast and precise, producing copies that are often difficult to differentiate from their prototype. The working method, in combination with firmly set parameters in painting technique, enabled Van Mierevelt and his workshop to paint portraits at a high rate of production. Although copying was widespread and fairly common in the northern Netherlands of the 17th century, Van Mierevelt used it unabashedly to fulfil his commercial aspirations. Michiel van Mierevelt – copy master!

Notes

1. A. Jansen, R. Ekkart and J. Verhave, *De Portretfabriek Van Mierevelt* (1566–1641), exh. cat., Zwolle, Wbooks, 2011.
2. Contemporary art historian and colleague Joachim von Sandrart states that Van Mierevelt himself had often thought that he might have painted 10,000 portraits: J. von Sandrart, *Teutsche Academie der Bau-, Bild- und Mahlerey-Künste*, Neurenberg, 1675–1680, part 3, p. 302.
3. For more details on the trends in signatures on Van Mierevelt's portraits see Jansen *et al.* 2011 (cited in note 1), pp. 47–50.
4. The portraits can be divided into five types; small busts, large busts, half-figures, knee pieces and full figures. The sizes of the supports deviate very little per type, in particular the busts, the half-figures and the knee pieces. For more detailed information see Jansen *et al.* 2011 (cited in note 1), pp. 87–93.
5. Interestingly the small bust portraits that were produced in the studio in limited numbers do not have a comparable standard format. The differences between the scales of these faces are more distinct, suggesting that a template was not available for this portrait type as it was less common.
6. The production of replicas of Maurits' portrait continued up to the stadholders' death in 1625 and possibly even after. Almost 50 versions from the studio of Van Mierevelt are still known, which seems to imply that more than 100 were made. See Jansen *et al.* 2011 (cited in note 1), ch. 6 for a discussion on the portraits of Maurits.
7. The provenance of the painting includes the Dutch Ministry of Justice as the owner before 1875; no earlier data are available. See the entry by Jonathan Bicker in *Dutch Paintings of the Seventeenth Century in the Rijksmuseum Amsterdam. Volume 1: Artists born between 1570–1600*, Amsterdam, Rijksmuseum, 2007, p. 267. The portrait is unique among the 1607–8 paintings on two counts: it has a red drapery and tablecloth whereas all other versions are painted in a green colour scheme. Also Maurits' coat of arms has been added to the top right corner of the painting. Whether this coat of arms is original to the portrait has not been analysed.
8. No other painting fits the composition of the engraving as the portrait on canvas (Prinsenhof, inv. PDS70). The folds in the drapery of the curtain and the orange sash are similar and compared to other early versions these compositions have a gauntlet lying to the right of the helmet. A difference between the painting and the print in the height of the feathers of the plume on the helmet was found to be an adjustment by an earlier restorer and was removed during the recent restoration of the painting.
9. This argumentation is based on the assumption that Muller came to Van Mierevelts' studio to copy the portrait into his engraving.
10. For more detailed information see Jansen *et al.* 2011 (cited in note 1), pp. 85–107.
11. These sizes represent the averages of 25 (large bust) and 24 (knee piece) portraits that have been studied and measured as part of the research project. These averages only deviate by a couple of centimetres; Jansen *et al.* 2011 (cited in note 1), pp. 89–90.
12. All 38 portraits by Van Mierevelt in the Museum Het Prinsenhof collection have been sampled in light of the research project. These samples have been studied by Johanneke Verhave, with further technical analysis by Annelies van Loon and Katrien Keune; Jansen *et al.* 2011 (cited in note 1), pp. 93–94.
13. Pieter Michielsz. van Mierevelt, *Portrait of the Family of Michiel van Mierevelt*, *c.*1617–23 (Delft 1596–Delft 1623), oil on canvas, 191 × 282 cm, Château de Jehay, Jehay-Huy (Province of Luik).
14. The use of the cartoon was found on the portraits of Maurits painted between 1607 and 1609. For images and more information see Jansen *et al.* 2011 (cited in note 1), pp. 97–98.
15. The IRR research was carried out by Margreet Wolters, RKD Den Haag, using a Hamamatsu C 2400-07 with a N2606 IR vidicon, a Nikon Micro-Nikkor 1:2.8/55 mm lens and Heliopan RG 850 (of RG 1000) filter, using a Lucius & Baer VM 1710 monitor (625 lines). For the digital documentation the Meteor RCB framegrabber was used; 768 × 574 pixels, colorvision toolkit (Visualbasic).
16. Research into underdrawings in the paintings has been extended to reconstructions of the possible methods used by Van Mierevelt. The reconstructions have been studied with IRR, revealing that the difficulty of finding the underdrawing is

related to Van Mierevelt's painting technique. This study is the subject of the article by C. Caspers, J. Verhave and M. Wolters, 'Reconstructing towards a better understanding: a study of missing underdrawings in Van Mierevelt's portraits', in L. Wrapson, J. Rose, R. Miller and S. Bucklow (eds), *In Artists' Footsteps: The Reconstruction of Pigments and Paintings*, London, Archetype Publications, 2012, pp. 95–108.

17. See L. Bauer, 'Van Dyck, replicas and tracings', *The Burlington Magazine* 149(1247), 2007, pp. 99–100. Another method used for copying faces of portraits is mentioned by Richard Symonds, a collector of painters' recipes and techniques, among which can be found a recipe for the preparation of vermilion by Van Mierevelt. In his volume, published by the Walpole Society (vol. XVIII), he writes about the technique of making paper transparent with oil to trace the original painting. A counterproof could be made using this method, but it would create a mirror-image copy.
18. The technique was tested in a reconstruction workshop at the University of Amsterdam Conservation Training given by Charlotte Caspers in 2010.
19. National Army Museum, inv. NAM 1973-05-44-1.
20. This painting is part of the series of Orange portraits, which was started in 1607 with the portrait of Maurits and expanded in two commissions to a total of nine paintings, of which seven currently reside in the Museum Het Prinsenhof. See Jansen *et al.* 2011 (cited in note 1), pp. 139–153, entry 5.
21. The painting was restored in the studio of Annetje Boersma in Rotterdam as part of a restoration programme of the beautiful series of seven portraits of Dutch stadholders painted by Van Mierevelt for the Delft City Hall.
22. *Cedule van enighe schilderijen*, London National Archives, inv. PRO SP 84/121/247.
23. Jansen *et al.* 2011 (cited in note 1), p. 139.
24. See Jansen *et al.* 2011 (cited in note 1), pp. 51–53 for a discussion on the production and reproduction in Van Mierevelt's workshop.
25. The inventory is kept in the archives of the city of Delft in two different versions: Boedelinventaris 30-8-1641, AD, Archiefnr 161 Oud Notarieel Archief Delft, inv. 1670, fol.75–104v and boedelinventaris 3-9-1641, AD, Archiefnr. 72 Weeskamer Delft, inv. 3945 (- 3953).
26. In this second category copies of portraits of famous public persons are also mentioned, but these were apparently made for specific private clients. The notary differentiated between copies belonging to the workshop and those commissioned by clients.
27. The studio is called 'winckel' in the inventory ('shop' in modern Dutch): A. Bredius, 'Michiel Jansz van Mierevelt. Eene nalezing', *Oud Holland* 26, 1908, pp. 1–17.
28. For example, mentioned are two versions of the portrait of Reverend Johannes Uyttenbogaart: an old version valued at 8 guilders and a new one valued at 14 guilders. Three versions of the portrait of the king of Bohemia, Fredric V, vary in size and price: a large one at 36 guilders and two smaller ones at 12 guilders.

Authors' addresses

- Anita Jansen, Curator, Museum Het Prisenhof, Delft, The Netherlands (ajansen@delft.nl)
- Johanneke Verhave, Paintings Conservator, Rotterdam, The Netherlands (jhverhave@hotmail.com.)

THE ASSUMPTION OF THE VIRGIN BY THE STUDIO OF PETER PAUL RUBENS FROM THE NATIONAL GALLERY OF ART IN WASHINGTON: BETWEEN MASTER'S PIECE AND STUDENT'S COPY

Julia Burdajewicz

ABSTRACT The panel painting, *The Assumption of the Virgin* by the studio of Sir Peter Paul Rubens from the National Gallery of Art (NGA) in Washington, is one of several works linked to Rubens' altarpiece of *The Assumption of the Virgin* for the Cathedral of Our Lady in Antwerp. This paper attempts to establish the relationship of the NGA painting to other existing versions. Strong similarities between the overall composition and specific details suggest that the NGA's *Assumption* was based on the *modello* for the altarpiece at the Mauritshuis in The Hague. X-radiographs, infrared reflectograms, cross-sections and microscopic observations of the NGA painting revealed new evidence on the creation process. Noticeable differences in artistic quality of particular motifs of the scene indicate that at least three hands could have been involved in its creation and provide insights in Rubens' studio practice and the making of copies.

Introduction

The Assumption of the Virgin (Fig. 1), a panel painting attributed to the studio of Sir Peter Paul Rubens, was acquired by the Samuel Kress Foundation in 1952 and was soon after donated to the National Gallery of Art (NGA) in Washington, DC.[1] In the fall of 2011, the painting underwent the first major conservation treatment since its acquisition.[2] This offered an excellent opportunity for careful examination and technical study that has allowed us to re-evaluate the current state of knowledge of the history of the artwork, the process of execution and the attribution.

The authorship and the dating of *The Assumption of the Virgin* has long been a subject of discussion among scholars. Furthermore, the relationship of *The Assumption* to three very similar versions of the composition by Rubens – an oil sketch from around 1622, now at the Mauritshuis in The Hague (Fig. 2), an altarpiece from the Cathedral of Our Lady in Antwerp from 1627 and an engraving by Schelte à Bolswert made between 1635 and 1640 (Fig. 3) – has been investigated previously but has not yet been entirely resolved.[3] This paper presents new evidence addressing these questions.

Technique of execution

The Assumption of the Virgin is executed on an oak panel made of five vertical planks of roughly the same width.[4] A previous conservation treatment took place in 1953, immediately following the arrival of the painting from Europe to join the Samuel H. Kress collection. The panel was then thinned and a mahogany cradle was attached to its back. Wooden strips that were firmly attached to all sides of the panel at that time now prevent dendrochronological investigation. X-radiographs made before cradling cover only the central part of the composition, therefore they provide only limited information on the construction of the panel.

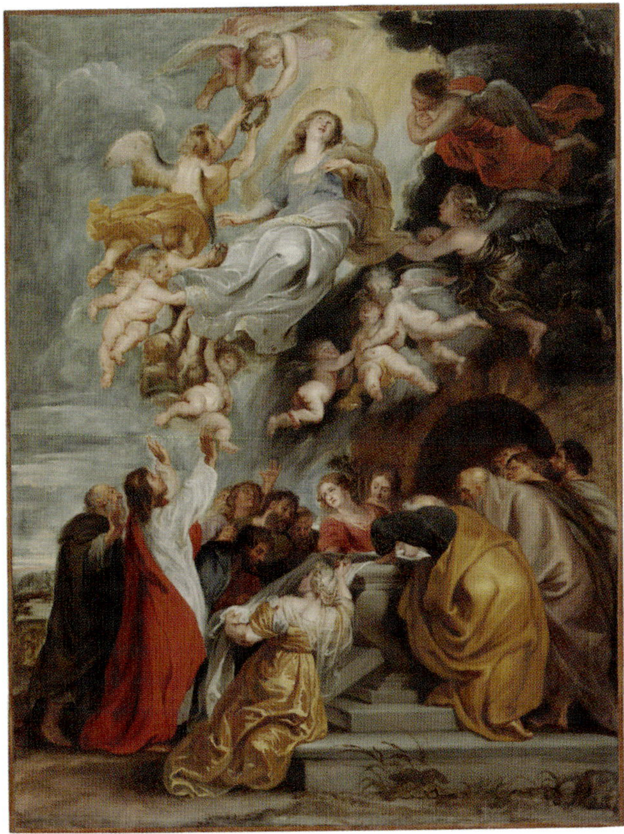

Fig. 1 Studio of Sir Peter Paul Rubens, *The Assumption of the Virgin*, late 1620s, oil (?) on panel, 123.5 × 92 cm, Washington, DC, National Gallery of Art, Samuel H. Kress Collection: after the conservation treatment. (Photo: Gregory Williams, National Gallery of Art.)

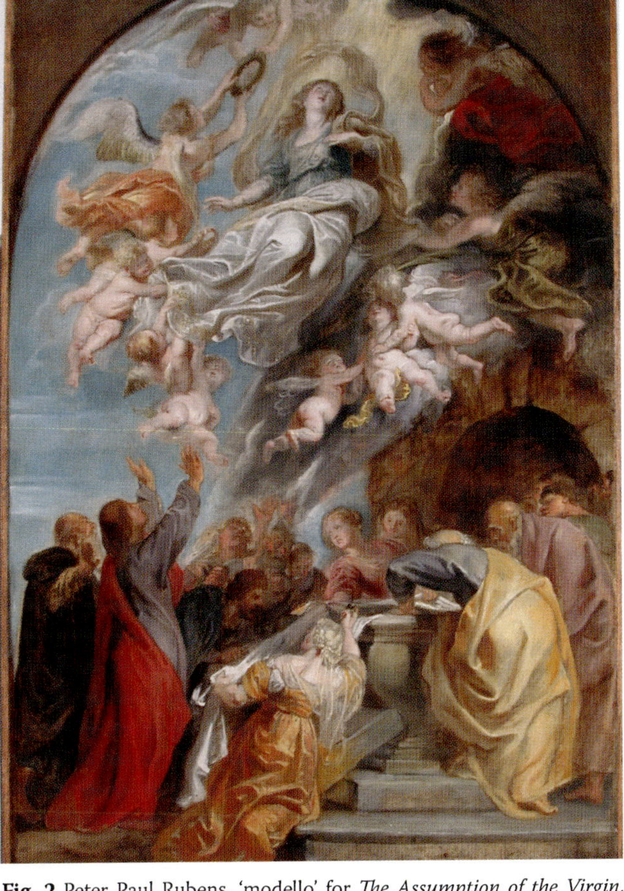

Fig. 2 Peter Paul Rubens, 'modello' for *The Assumption of the Virgin*, *c.*1622–1625, panel, 87.8 × 59.1 cm. (Courtesy of the Royal Picture Gallery Mauritshuis, The Hague.)

Macroscopic observations and paint cross-sections indicate that the panel was prepared with a smooth, white-coloured ground. The cross-sections also reveal that the ground was most likely applied in two layers, the upper one about three times as thickly as the lower (Fig. 4a).

A streaky brown *imprimatura* shows through certain passages of the paint and is clearly visible in the infrared reflectogram (IRR) (Fig. 5). The IRR does not show evidence of an underdrawing executed with a dry medium such as charcoal; instead the design seems to be sketched with a fluid paint medium. Judging by examination of the paint layers with a microscope, this paint seems to be of a brownish colour. The sketch appears to be executed with fast, short brushstrokes marking the forms and the disposition of the figures rather roughly. Just a few minor corrections in the same medium to the motifs of the scene can be noticed. This type of sketched design was also observed in IRR images of other paintings by Rubens and, together with the presence of the streaky *imprimatura*, seems to be characteristic of his working method.[5]

The application of the paint layer – as well as its consistency, transparency, thickness and texture – varies throughout the painting. In some areas, such as the sky, the landscape, but also the Madonna's brown mantle, the paint film consists of just one or two very thin layers. In others however, such as garments of the figures or their flesh tones, it is built up in several layers. There are passages painted *alla prima* with small impastos that mark details such as the embroidery of the

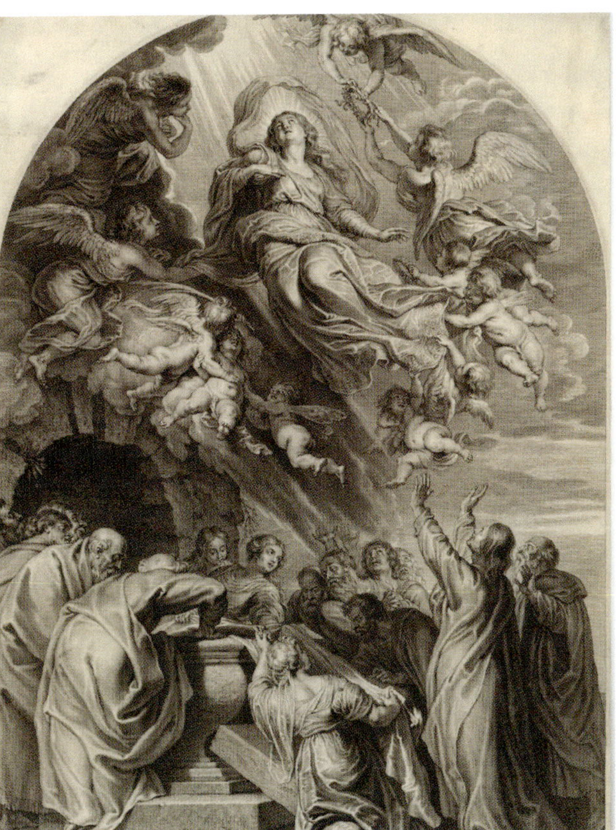

Fig. 3 *The Assumption of the Virgin*, engraving by Schelte à Bolswert, 1630–1645, 620 × 430 mm, London, The British Museum. (© Trustees of the British Museum.)

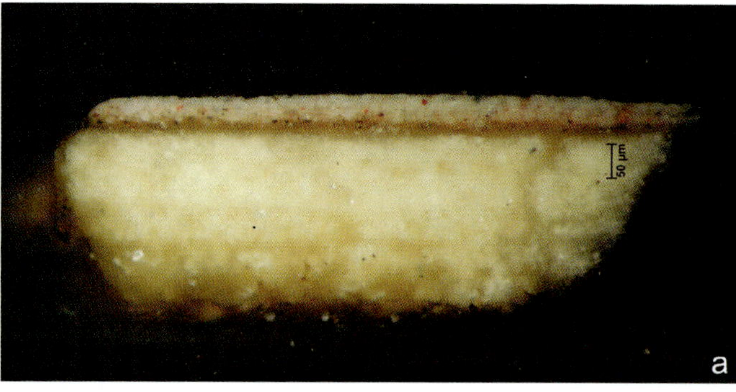

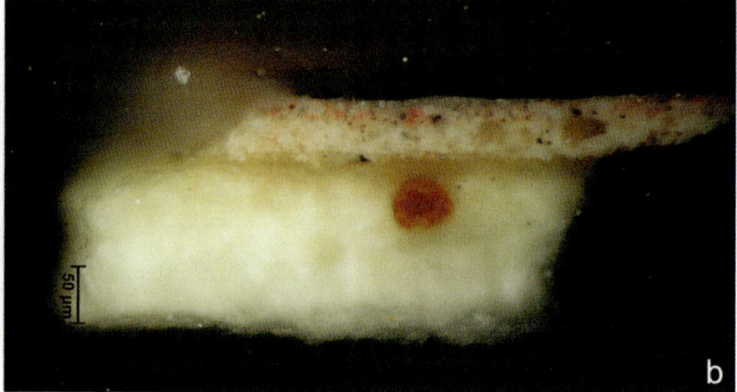

Fig. 4 *The Assumption of the Virgin* (Fig. 1): two cross-sections from the pink cloak of the bearded man standing on the far right. (a) The sample shows two layers of ground layer. (b) The sample, taken from within the right margin of the painting, shows no apparent differences from the sample taken from within the main field of the composition (a).

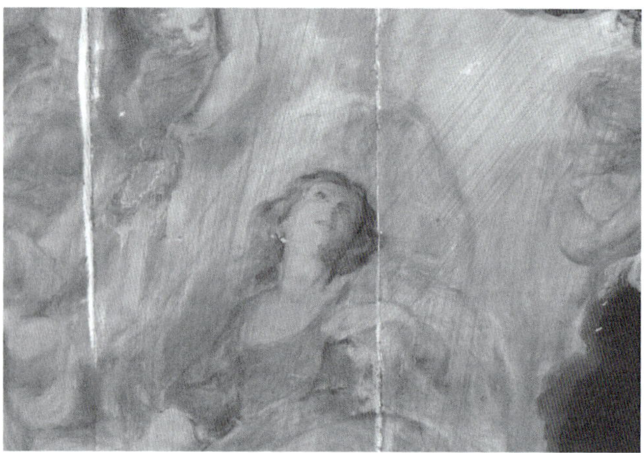

Fig. 5 *The Assumption of the Virgin* (Fig. 1): IRR detail showing the Madonna and diagonally striped *imprimatura*.

Madonna's gown, while other areas are finished with glazes applied over the opaque paint.

The quality of painting varies throughout the composition. Some elements seem to be executed by a very skilful hand; others look more like the work of a novice studio apprentice. There are some minor changes to the composition that seem to have been painted over an almost complete image. The evidence discussed below suggests that this was while the painting was still in the artist's studio.

Various versions of the *Assumption of the Virgin*

The NGA's *Assumption of the Virgin* seems to be directly linked to one of Rubens' most important religious commissions of the mid-1620s – the altarpiece of *The Assumption of the Virgin* for the Cathedral of Our Lady in Antwerp.[6] The commission had a long and complex history spanning 16 years, and involved several projects and versions of *The Assumption*.[7] One of the major questions concerns the relation of the NGA painting to the Antwerp altarpiece and its place in the chronology of execution of the successive versions.

The history of the commission began when the cathedral authorities decided to order a new altarpiece for the high altar.[8] It was intended to replace a triptych by Frans Floris (1517–1570), which had been damaged by the iconoclasts. In 1611 two artists submitted their projects to the chapter: the painter Otto van Veen (1556–1629) and his former pupil Rubens, who proposed two designs representing *The Assumption* and *The Coronation of the Virgin*. Those two projects were not executed but two preliminary designs survive: a sketch from the same year, which gives an idea of the design (St Petersburg, Hermitage Museum), and a larger version of this initial composition, now in the Kunsthistorisches Museum in Vienna, probably executed around 1613. It appears that Rubens' projects won the approval of the cathedral authorities, but no commission was awarded at that time.

Nothing seems to have happened with this undertaking until 1618 when two brothers from Utrecht – Robrecht (1570–1636) and Jan de Nole (1570–1624) – presented a design for a portico-like altar to the cathedral authorities. The general appearance of this monumental sculpted frame is now known only through an engraving by Adriaan Lommelin (1637–1673) because the altar itself was destroyed during the French Revolution. It is known that in 1618 Rubens again submitted two projects to the cathedral authorities, but it seems that they were related to the design for the altar rather than to the altarpiece. Finally, in November 1619 a contract was signed between Rubens and the dean of the cathedral, Johannes del Rio. The painter agreed to an honorarium of 1,500 guilders for the execution of the new altarpiece.[9] About three years later, probably in 1622, Rubens prepared a *modello* for *The Assumption of the Virgin*, the small oil sketch that is now in the Mauritshuis in The Hague.[10] However, the execution of the altarpiece could not begin until 1626 when the portico altar was finally completed about two years after the scheduled date of delivery. The dates on the surviving receipts for the final payments point to the time of the completion of the painting, which was probably the spring of 1627. The fact that the *modello* predated the final execution of the altarpiece by a number of years may explain certain compositional differences that exist between the two works.[11]

The last chapter of the history of the various versions of *The Assumption of the Virgin* falls in the years between 1635 and 1640 when Schelte à Bolswert (1586–1659), an engraver who cooperated with Rubens to make numerous reproductions of his paintings,[12] made an engraving after the small

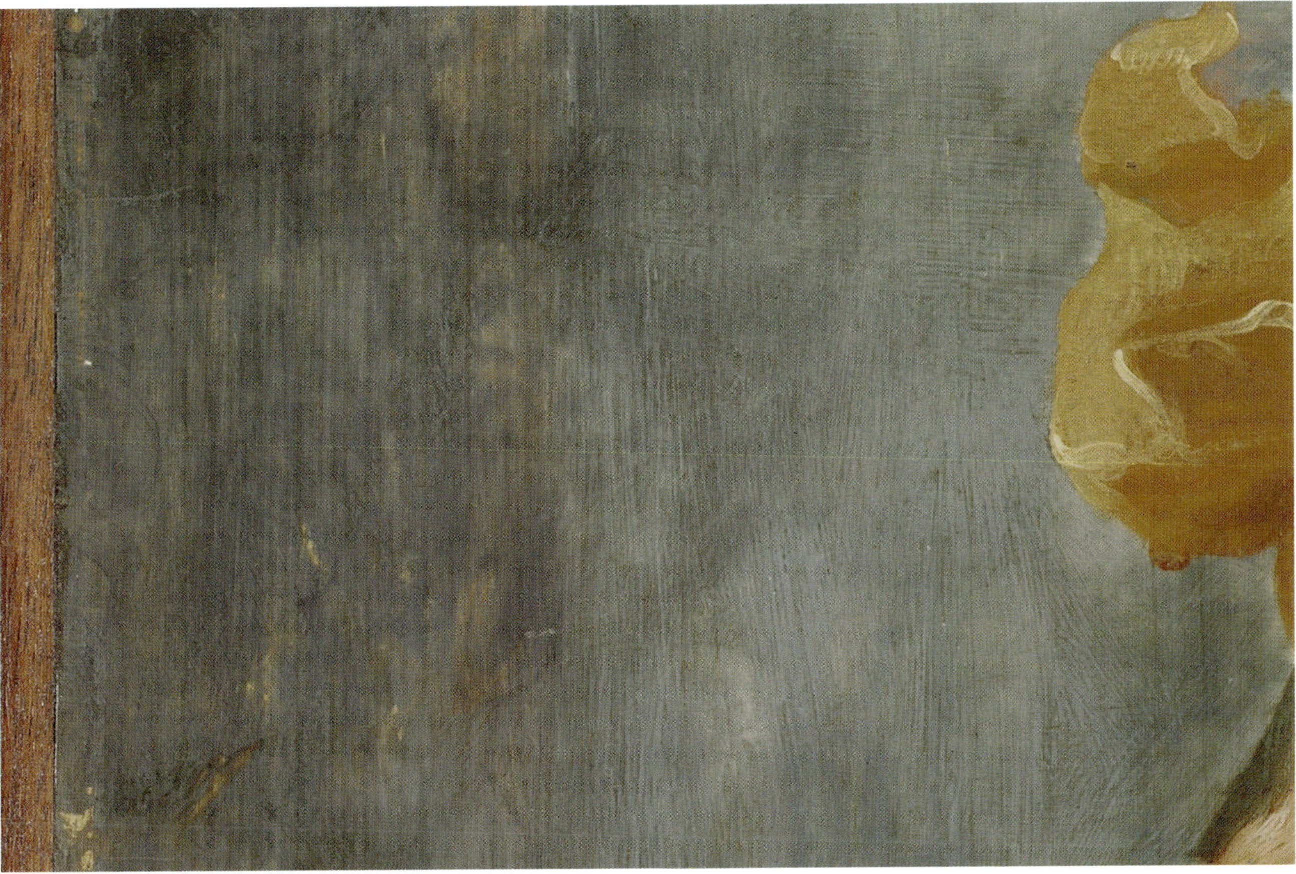

Fig. 6 *The Assumption of the Virgin* (Fig. 1): detail showing the left side of the painting (upper sky area), where two areas of paint of different appearance meet.

modello (Fig. 3). It is interesting that even though the altarpiece was then long completed, Rubens preferred the engraving to be produced after the *modello*, not after the altarpiece itself.

In considering the place of the NGA's *Assumption* in this history it is striking that the Washington composition has the least in common with the Antwerp altarpiece. Instead it is almost identical with the *modello* in the Mauritshuis and the Bolswert engraving. The question is: which of these two works served as the model?

The main difference between these three works is that both the Mauritshuis painting and the engraving have arched tops, while the NGA's *Assumption* has a rectangular format and a slightly expanded composition. Otherwise there are only a few minor discrepancies. One small difference is that in the *modello* and the engraving two outstretched hands are visible at the rear of the figure group, whereas only one hand appears in the NGA painting. On the other hand, the foot of the man in the yellow cloak standing to the right of the tomb is covered by drapery in both the Mauritshuis piece and the NGA painting, while it is visible in the engraving. A curious shadow occurs around the drapery of the angel at the very top in both of the paintings, but not in the engraving. Instead, the engraver added more rays of heavenly light on the upper left side of the sky. Another small difference between the engraving and the two paintings is that in the engraving the *putto* below and to the left of the Madonna has a long, extended wing.

Based on these distinguishing elements, it appears that the NGA painting is more closely linked to the Mauritshuis *modello* than to the engraving. Moreover, the fact that the colours are practically identical in the two paintings seems to undermine Broos's hypothesis that the NGA painting is a copy of the engraving (although, one cannot rule out a possibility that the design could have been made after the engraving, whereas the colours were copied from the altarpiece).[13] The fact that the NGA's *Assumption* is placed in a rectangular field with expanded edges instead of an arched format does not have to come as a surprise. Slight modifications of the composition when rendering different versions of a painting, and especially extensions to the design, are not uncommon in Rubens' practice.[14]

Technical evidence

The paint layer along the edges of the NGA's *Assumption* shows some curious features that may cast additional light on the history of this work.

The paint film along the left edge of the painting appears much thinner than that of the rest of the composition. Approximately 6 cm from the edge two different areas of paint meet, creating the appearance of a relatively straight, vertical line (Fig. 6). The paint layer to the left of this 'line' is so thinly painted that the creamy white tone of the ground shows through. On the right side, the paint appears thick and opaque. Brushstrokes visible in the sky appear to end to the right of this apparent border,

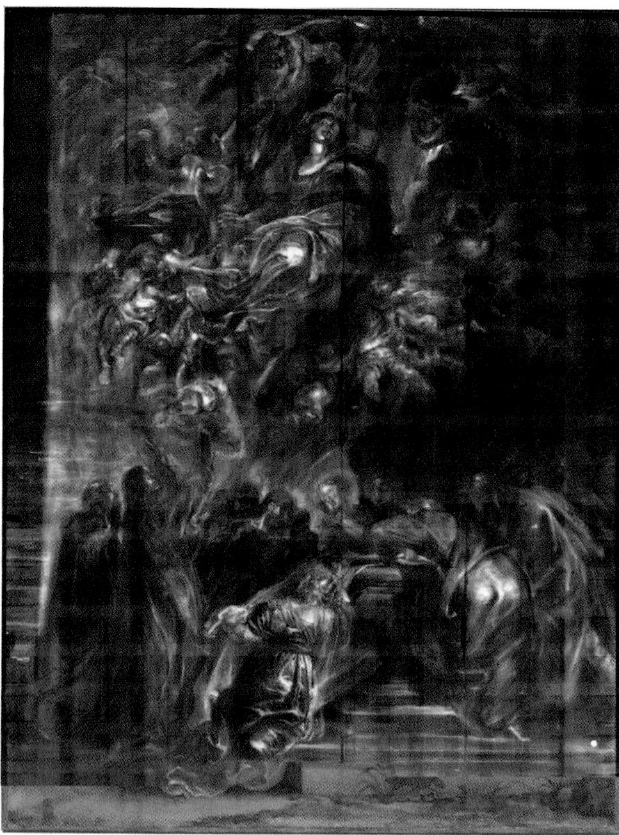

Fig. 7 *The Assumption of the Virgin* (Fig. 1): the composite X-radiograph (which does not cover the area along the bottom edge), shows a curious margin along the left edge of the composition.

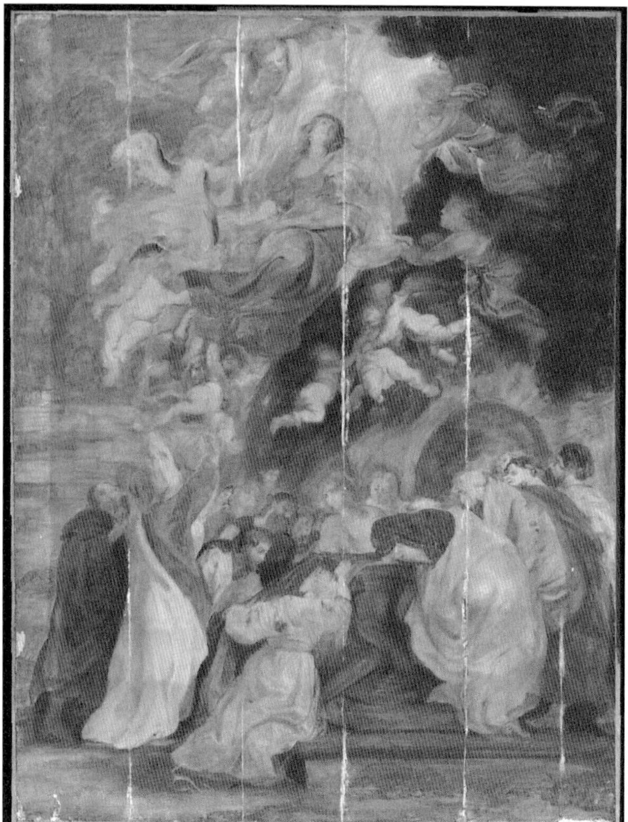

Fig. 8 *The Assumption of the Virgin* (Fig. 1): besides minor changes to the compositional sketch visible in the IRR, brighter 'bands' are visible along both side edges. (Photo: Douglas Lachance, National Gallery of Art.)

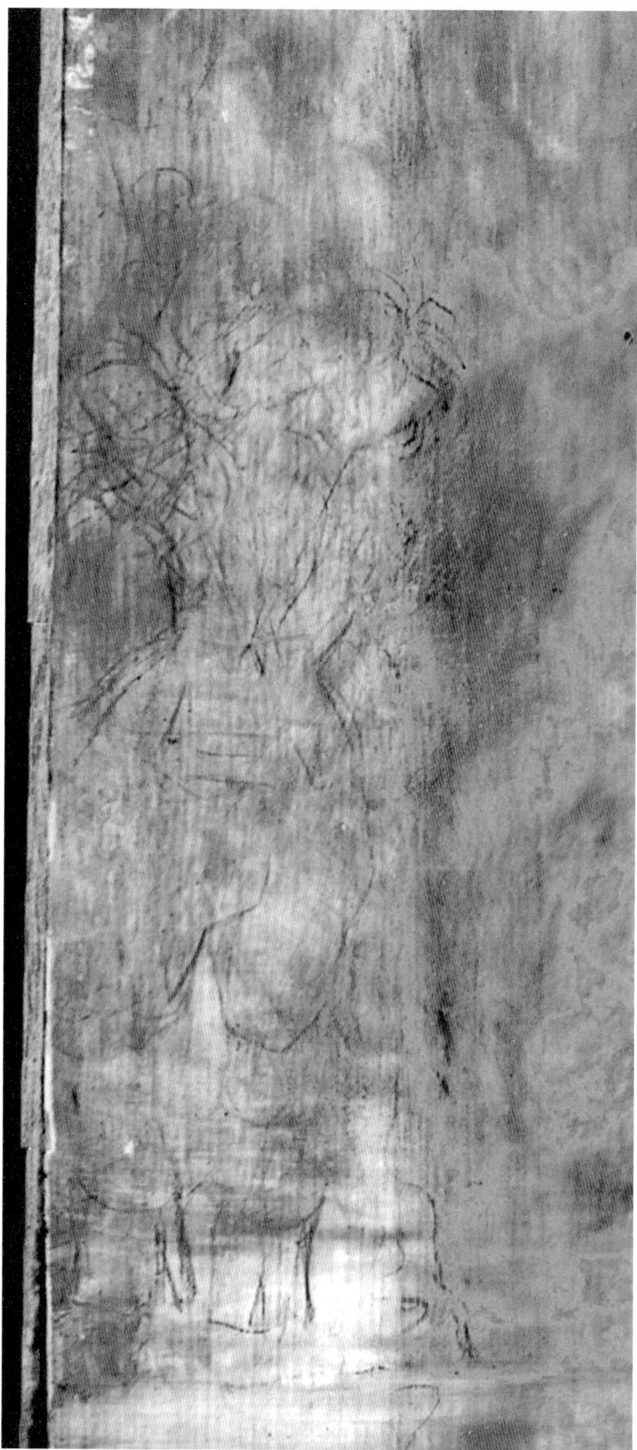

Fig. 9 *The Assumption of the Virgin* (Fig. 1): contrast-adjusted detail of the IRR showing a drawing of a man located in the left-side margin of the painting.

suggesting that the artist initially did not pull the paint to the edges of the panel. It seems that he left an unpainted margin while executing the main field of the composition. What makes this observation even more curious is that there is no panel join along the line where the thin-looking margin meets the more opaque main field of the composition. These two areas were laid on the same plank of wood.

The X-radiograph clearly shows the distinction between the main field and the left margin (Fig. 7). It is particularly visible in the sky, but less so in the darker lower area where

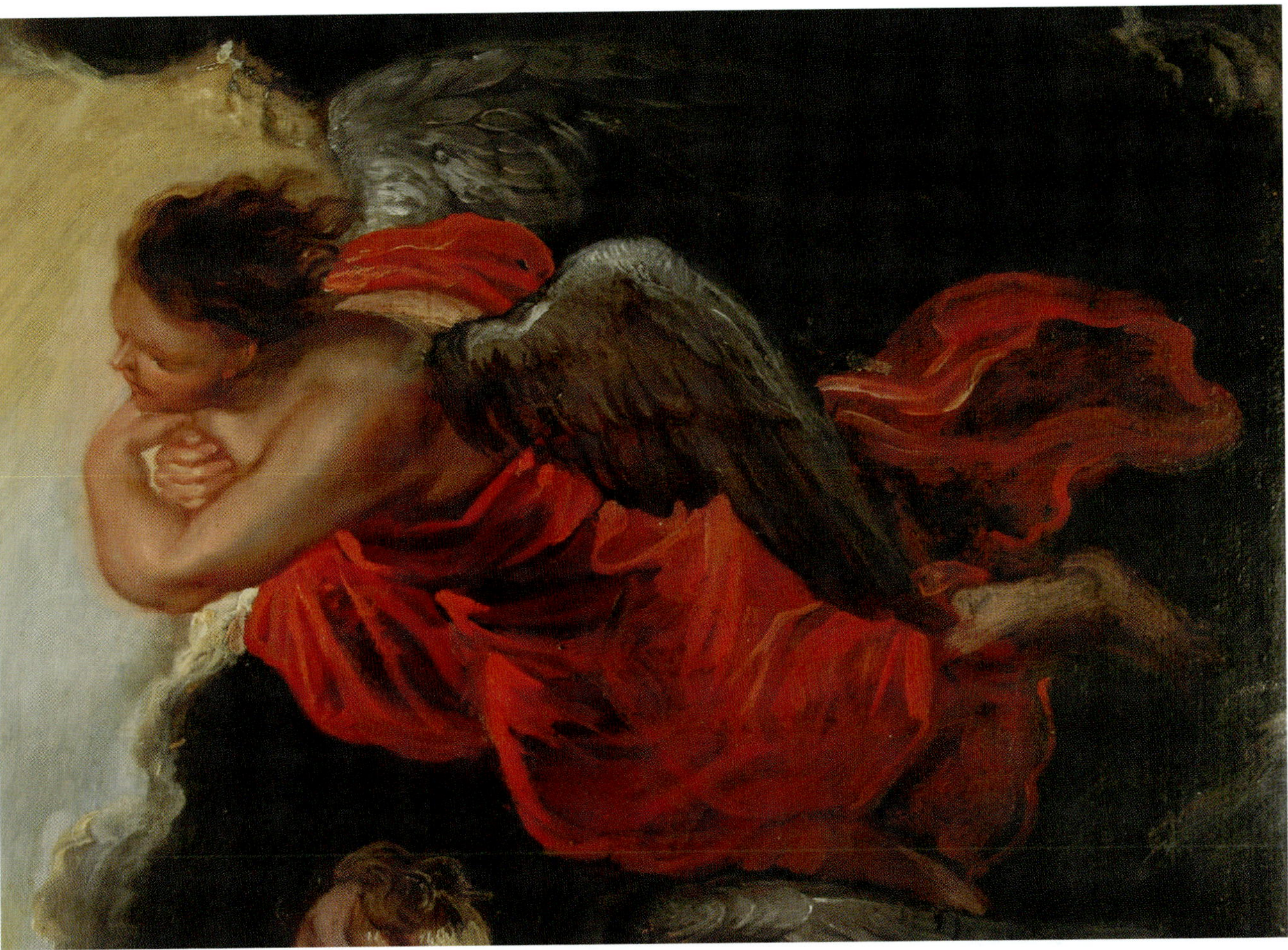

Fig. 10 *The Assumption of the Virgin* (Fig. 1): detail showing an angel in the upper right corner of the composition. Apparent, bright red additions observed on top of the angel's drapery suggest that some changes have been introduced, probably towards the completion of the painting. Note the sloppy execution of the angel's leg as compared to other areas of the painting.

lead white was not used so generously. For the same reason the 'band' along the right edge of the painting, where brown and black colours dominate, does not look distinctive in the X-radiograph. An IRR, however, shows that the right margin also differs from the central field of the composition as it appears lighter (Fig. 8). Curiously, the IRR also reveals a small drawing at the far left representing the figure of a man wearing 17th-century European garments. As this sketch is in the area of the sky it clearly is not part of the *Assumption* scene (Fig. 9). A cross-section taken from that area shows that the drawing was executed directly on the ground layer, with a black dry medium, possibly black chalk. It should be noted that there is no dry medium underdrawing present elsewhere in the painting. Since this small doodle occurs in the thinly painted margin, it is probable that the central field of the composition was already being painted when the drawing was made.

Besides the differences in the paint along the edges, technical examinations have revealed a number of other changes and additions to the paint layer. For instance, the red robe of the angel in the upper right corner was clearly reworked and extended towards the right edge of the composition. A bright red paint was spread over a velvety, dark red colour of the robe with quick, sloppy brushstrokes (Fig. 10). Also, small additions to the wing were made: the paint of the black feathers appears thin and beaded like an aqueous medium on top of an already dried oily layer. It also seems that the foot of this angel, as well as of the angel below, was painted without much care directly on top of the black clouds. Furthermore, the robe of the bearded man in a pink cloak standing on the far right of the composition was covered with a second layer of rather loosely applied dark pink paint. Finally, the hem of the yellow dress of the kneeling woman was extended, as can be observed both in visible light and in the IRR (Fig. 8).

Both side edges of the painting show evidence of hasty and sloppy work. Finger marks imprinted in wet paint are visible on the left side, both in the upper sky and near the foot of the man in the green cloak. They were left probably towards the end of the work, but some finishing was still done afterwards – a few blades of grass are pulled over the lower fingerprint, showing that no one had bothered to correct it.

The areas of different paint appearance and visible additions seem to be distributed around and beyond the borders of the painting's compositional model, the Mauritshuis oil sketch of *The Assumption* (Fig. 11). This suggests that the panel could have accommodated a composition larger than that of the *modello*. It also seems that the execution of the extended margins followed the execution of the main field.

Two cross-sections were taken from the main field of the painting and from the margin area (from the cloak of the man in pink on the right side of the painting) to compare the layer

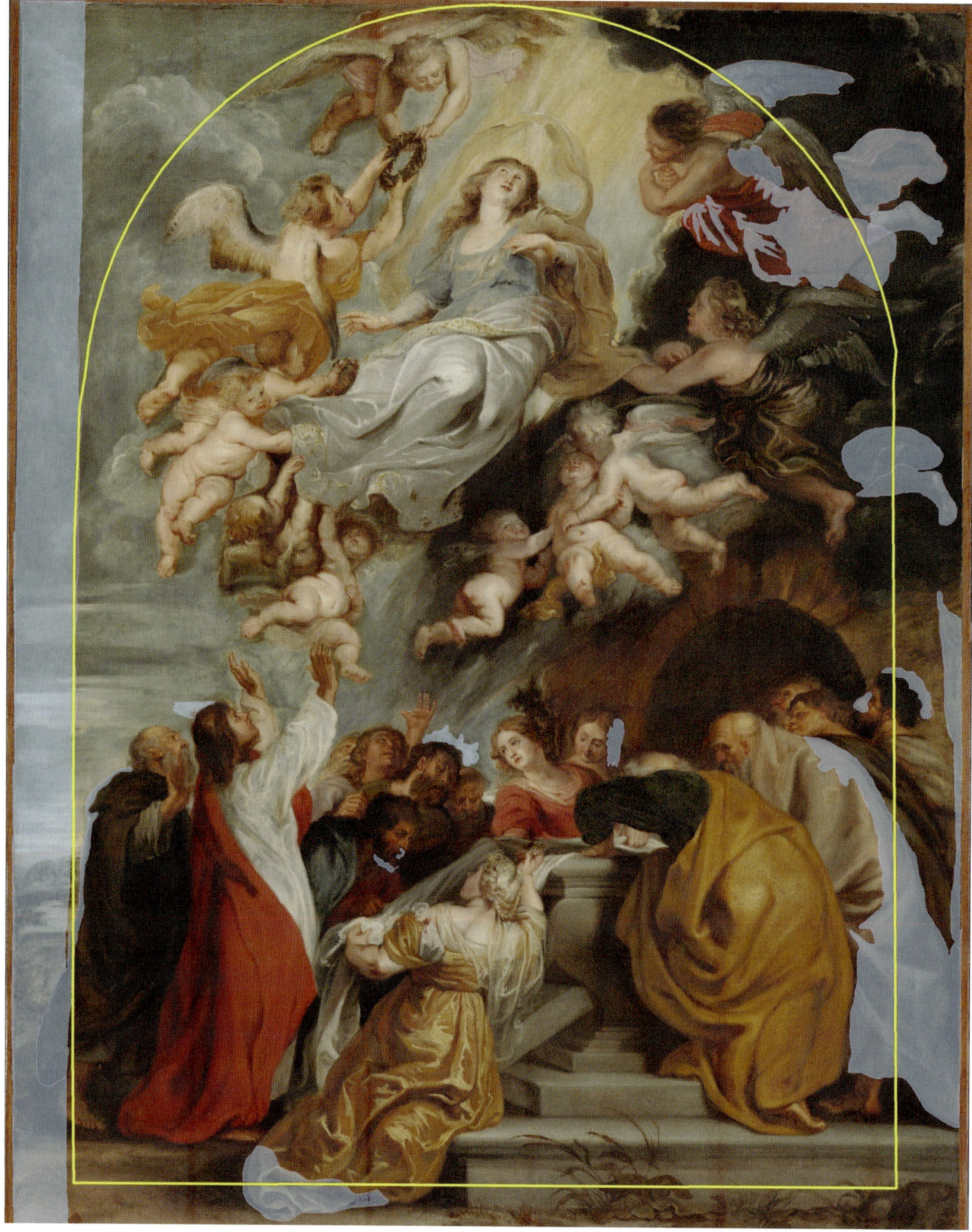

Fig. 11 *The Assumption of the Virgin* (Fig. 1): the blue colour indicates areas of different appearances of the paint layers and additions that were observed in the visible light, IRR and X-radiographs. The yellow line represents the boundaries of the composition of the Mauritshuis oil sketch (mapping made with metigoMAP software).

build-up of both areas. No apparent differences were observed in these two samples, except that the distribution of pigment particles in the pink paint layer seems to be somewhat less even in the sample from the margin (Fig. 4). Furthermore, no layer of varnish or grime was found between the paint layers of the margin sample, which suggests that the areas along the edges of the painting were completed shortly after the execution of the main field of the composition.

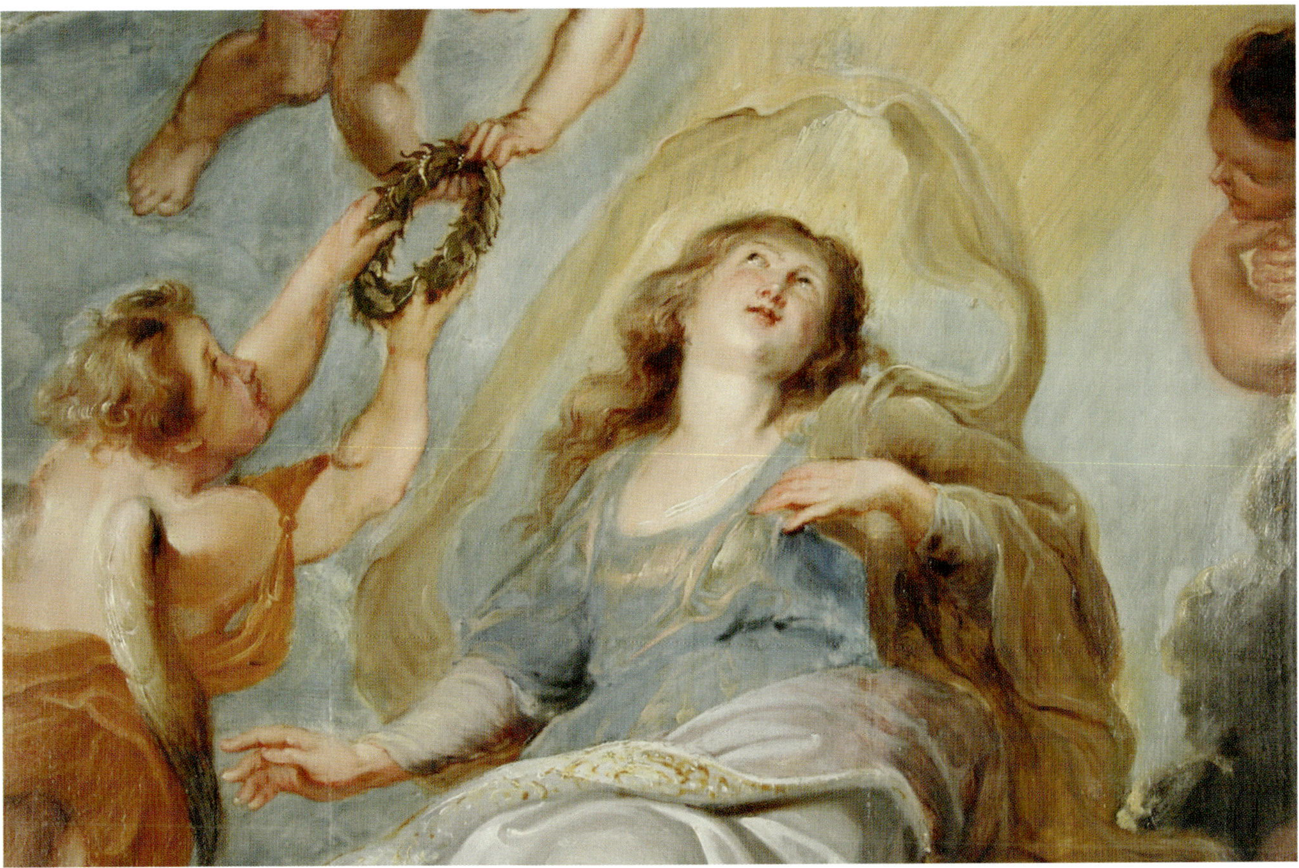

Fig. 12 *The Assumption of the Virgin* (Fig. 1): the most prominent figure of the composition, the Madonna, appears to be the most finely executed part of the scene.

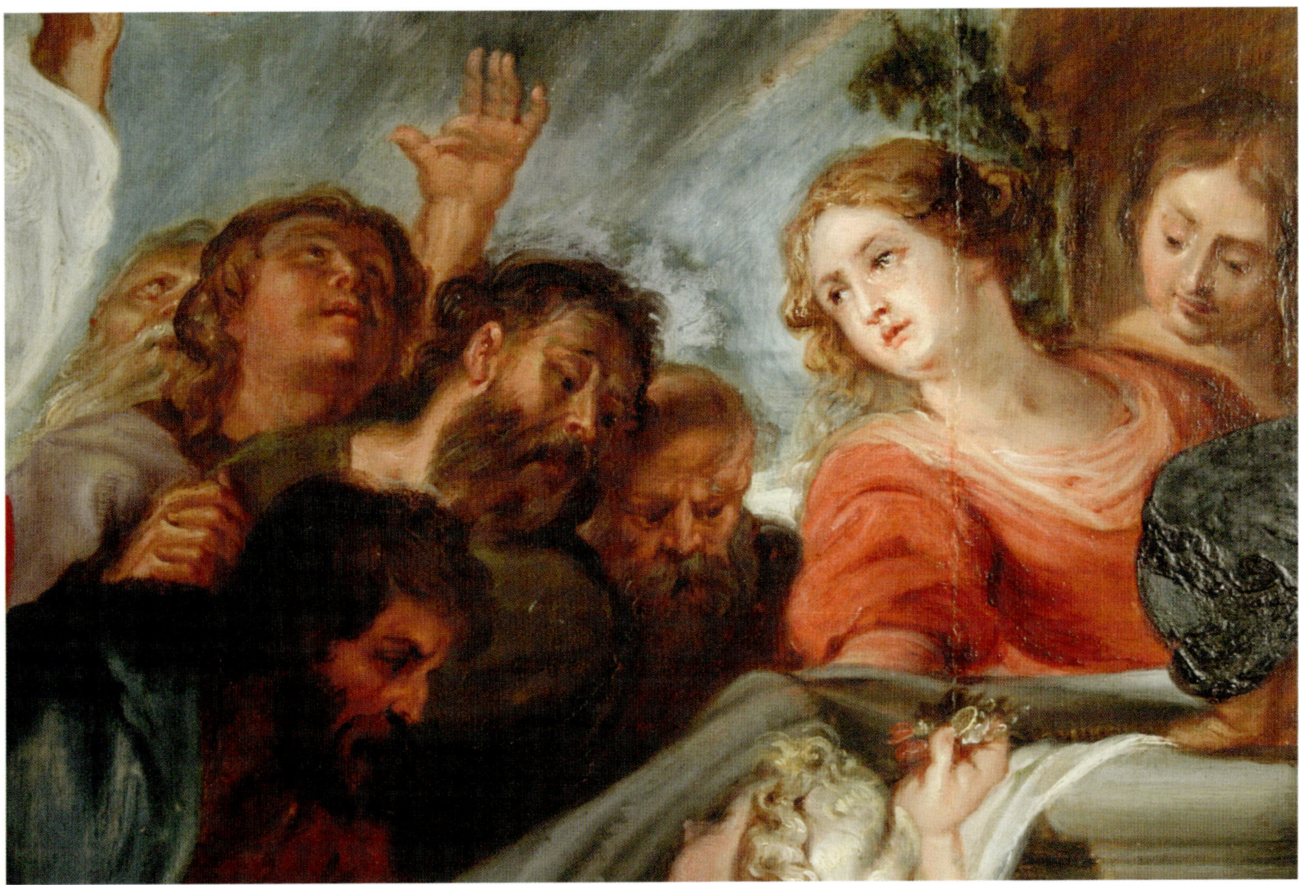

Fig. 13 *The Assumption of the Virgin* (Fig. 1): execution of the group of the mourning women and Apostles seems to be less skilful as compared to the Madonna.

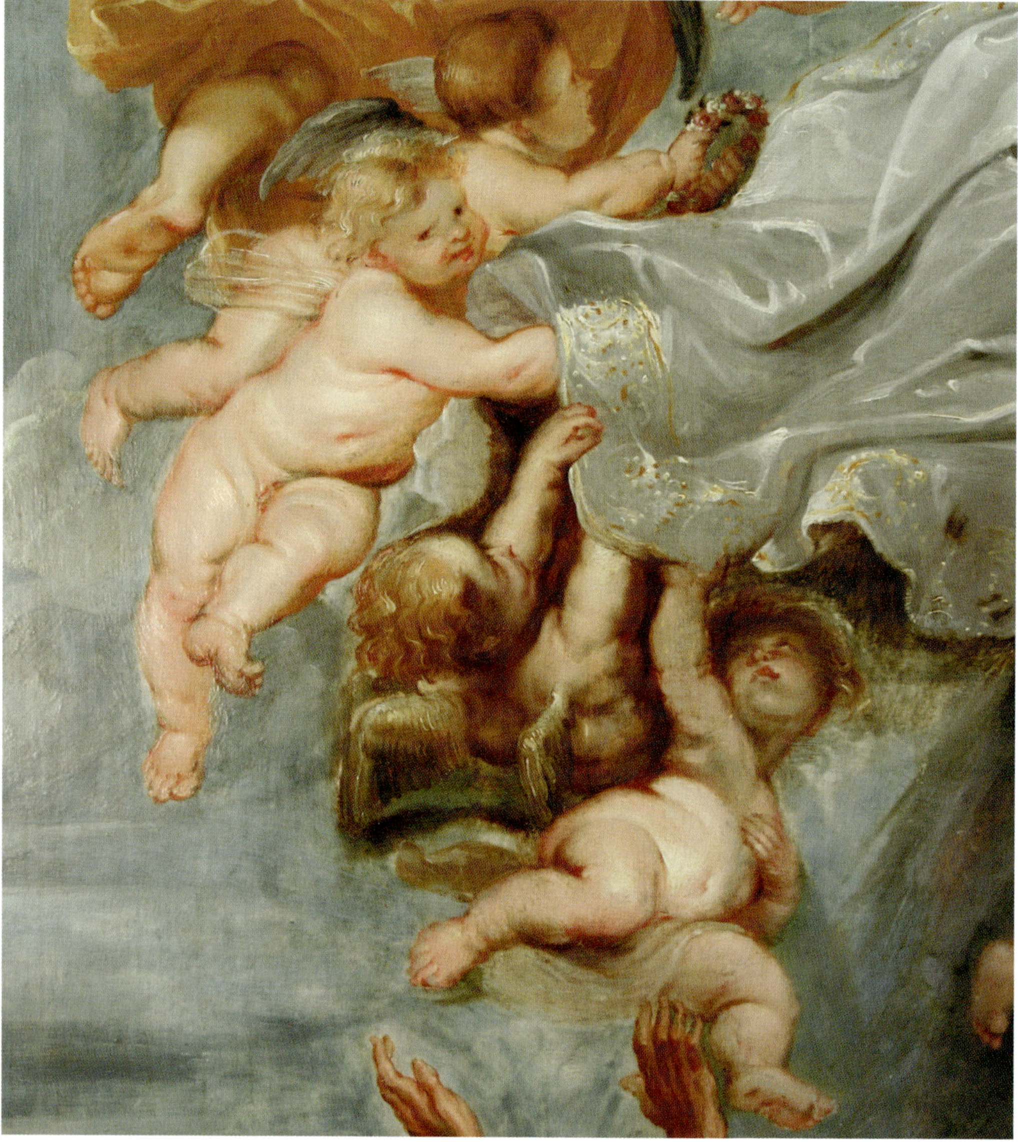

Fig. 14 *The Assumption of the Virgin* (Fig. 1): detail showing two groups of *putti*, apparently executed by two different artists.

It is possible that the NGA's *Assumption* was a commission from a private individual who wished to have a version of the *modello* executed in a larger scale and in a rectangular composition. Despite some rather loosely handled passages in the NGA painting, overall it seems to be more carefully executed than the *modello* and most likely was meant to be a completed painting, not a sketch. The fact that the NGA's *Assumption* is not as vigorous or spontaneous as the Mauritshuis sketch may result not only from the intended level of completion, but also from the fact that there was presumably more than just one hand working on this painting.

The authorship

In 1951 Ludwig Burchard signed a certificate of authentication for *The Assumption of the Virgin*, assuring the new owner, Samuel H. Kress, that the painting was entirely by Rubens' own hand.[15] However, two decades later, Rubens' authorship was questioned by Michael Jaffé, who found the painting 'very disappointing'.[16] The matter of how much Rubens was involved in the creation of this particular work has not been resolved since then and a 'studio of Rubens' term has been accepted.

In fact, the idea of identity of the artist becomes somewhat complicated in the case of old masters such as Rubens, who had a large studio and employed a number of artists to help create works that he would sell as his own.[17] But even though Rubens sold various works under his own general trademark, the concept of the 'artist's own hand' was meaningful to him. When pricing his paintings, he would pay great attention as to how much of his own input was involved in the creation of the painting. Surviving correspondence between him and his patrons testifies to the complexities of some of the transactions. These letters document a clever businessman who had very clear criteria for determining the value of his works.[18] For instance, a luxurious edition of a painting would be entirely by Rubens' own hand. A slightly less expensive version would involve some contribution by other artists in the studio, who sometimes specialised in adding very particular elements such as drapery or landscape to work primarily by Rubens. An affordable painting would either be started by Rubens and completed by his studio, or started by the studio and touched up by Rubens. A low value 'economy' option would involve a painting entirely by the studio, but still with the Rubens trademark, since it was painted after one of his original compositions and under his supervision.[19]

Some works leave little room for discussion on the authorship, but others, especially those that were executed in several versions and partially by other artists, make it difficult to isolate the master's hand from his students' efforts. In such cases, only a careful comparative art historical study, and scientific analysis of the materials and the technique of execution, could help establish an idea of relationship between various versions of the same composition and determine the extent of the engagement of the master himself. For example, such research was carried out on the occasion of an exhibition in the National Museum of Western Art in Tokyo (1994), where three versions of the *Flight of Lot and his Family from Sodom*,[20] all clearly executed in Rubens' workshop, were exhibited together. The study indicated similarities and revealed certain discrepancies between these works both in terms of artistic qualities and technical solutions.[21]

A careful examination of the execution of *The Assumption of the Virgin* from the NGA reveals that at least three or four hands could have been involved in the creation of this painting. The Madonna and the three *putti* below and to the right seem to have been painted by a very skilful artist. This area has the distinctive lightness and dynamism achieved by quick and confident brushstrokes, characteristic of Rubens' own work (Fig. 12). When compared to the same area in the Mauritshuis oil sketch, the group of the Madonna does not lose its appeal. Slight differences between these two areas can be explained by differences of scale (the NGA's painting is 140% larger than the Mauritshuis work) and of finish between the two compositions. The artistic quality in this part of the NGA painting is so much higher than the rest of the painting that an attribution to Rubens himself could be considered.

Aside from the areas along the edges, the largest part of the painting – the group of the mourning women and Apostles and the angels in the sky – although of good quality, is clearly less well executed than the Madonna (Fig. 13). Moreover, it is possible that these areas were painted by two different painters of comparable skill. This can be seen, for example, in the slightly different execution of the two groups of *putti* below and to the left of the Madonna (Fig. 14). The pair of *putti* holding the Madonna's hem on the left side is pinker overall and has a distinctive dark pink contour. The contours of the two *putti* below the figure of the Madonna are much softer, but the contrast between light and dark areas is stronger and the shadows have a dark brown tone.

Finally, there are areas that do surprise with their poor artistic quality and sloppy execution. These appear to coincide with the extended edges and include the feet of both angels in the upper right corner, the pink cloak of the man on the right, the two men beside him, and the entire left edge of the painting (the area with fingerprints in the wet paint).

Dating

It has been estimated that *The Assumption of the Virgin* was executed in the mid-1620s[22] but the question of the dating has never been fully answered. The only thing that seems certain is that it was painted when the *modello* already existed, that is in or after 1622, but there is no further evidence to help narrow the time of its execution. Although this research was not able to answer this question, one detail that came to light, the figure of a person sketched on the left edge of the painting, seems worthy of note. It appears that this doodle depicts a person in contemporary clothing, a man with rather short, so-called 'swollen' breeches, puffed quarter-sleeves and a very narrow waist.[23] This style of dress was in vogue in Spain in the early 17th century, as seen, for example, in a drawing Rubens made in Spain in the late 1620s of King Philip IV (Bayonne, Musée Bonnat, no. 1439).[24] Perhaps an artist working on *The Assumption* sketched it after seeing some of his master's drawings from his trip to Spain. If so, the date of the execution of this painting would have to be placed in the late 1620s or even in the 1630s. However, Rubens' apprentices could also have been familiar with this style simply through the Spanish presence in the southern Netherlands.

Conclusions

The question of dating as well as other aspects of the history of *The Assumption of the Virgin* still remains open. For now, it appears that the current research has helped to establish a few more facts. Strong similarities between the overall composition and specific details suggest that the NGA's *Assumption* was based on the *modello* from the Mauritshuis, which Rubens created around 1622. Moreover, the fact that the colours of the The Hague oil sketch and the Washington painting are identical, strongly suggest that the NGA's *Assumption* was painted when the *modello* was still in Rubens' workshop.

Technical study has also established that the panel for the NGA's *Assumption* was prepared in a larger format than the composition of the Mauritshuis painting, not only in terms of the size of the painting, but also the proportions: its composition was extended along both side edges and the bottom edge. It appears that even though the panel could have accommodated a larger composition than the *modello*, the extensions were initially left blank. For example, the way the sketched figure is squeezed into the left margin suggests that it was drawn there while the main part of the depiction was being painted but when the margins still remained unpainted. It is possible that the copying artist (or artists) did not have a clear idea of how to utilise the extra space and simply waited for further instructions from Rubens himself. In terms of authorship, it is plausible that the Virgin and the *putti* may have been executed or finalised by Rubens himself, whereas the figures of less importance and the surroundings were painted by one or two different studio assistants. The margins were eventually completed by another, less skilful associate or student, possibly working in haste.

Many questions concerning the history and authorship of this painting have yet to be answered but it is hoped that these discoveries could cast some more light on Rubens' studio practices and will be the subject of further discussion and research.

Acknowledgements

I would like to express my sincere thanks to colleagues in the National Gallery of Art for their valuable comments and help: Cathy Metzger (Senior Conservator of Paintings), Melanie Gifford (Research Conservator) and Arthur Wheelock (Curator of Dutch and Flemish Paintings).

Notes

1. C.T. Eisler, *Paintings from the Samuel H. Kress Collection: European Schools excluding Italian*, Oxford, Phaidon Press for the Samuel H. Kress Foundation, 1977, p. 111; A. Wheelock, *Flemish Paintings of the Seventeenth century: The Collections of the National Gallery of Art Systematic Catalogue*, Washington, DC, National Gallery of Art/ New York, Oxford University Press, 2005, pp. 218–222.
2. Examination of the painting before conservation treatment revealed that the panel was structurally sound and stable, and the paint and ground layers were in good condition. The treatment focused on removal of the discoloured and unsightly old varnish and retouchings. The cleaning revealed bright and rich colours; the losses, which were found predominantly along the joins of the panel, were painted in and the painting was varnished.
3. Eisler 1977 (cited in note 1), p. 111; Wheelock 2005 (cited in note 1), pp. 218–222.
4. From left: 17.7, 17.1, 16.1, 18.7, 22.7 cm.
5. P.T Sutton, M.E. Wieseman and N. Van Hout, *Drawn by the Brush: Oil Sketches by Peter Paul Rubens*, New Haven, CT, Yale University Press, 2004; J. Plesters, '*Samson and Delilah*: Rubens and the art and craft of painting on panel', *National Gallery Technical Bulletin* 7, 1983, pp. 30–50, p. 36.
6. Wheelock 2005 (cited in note 1), pp. 218–222.
7. P. Huvanne, *Rubens' "Assumption of the Holy Virgin" in the Cathedral of Our Lady in Antwerp*, C. Clapson (tr.), Antwerp, Openbaar Kunstbezit Vlaanderen, 1991, pp. 13–18.
8. Ibid., p. 13.
9. Ibid., pp. 14–18.
10. B. Broos, *Intimacies & Intrigues: History Painting in the Mauritshuis*, Ghent, Snoeck-Ducaju, 1993, pp. 293–305.
11. Ibid., p. 304; Wheelock 2005 (cited in note 1), pp. 218–222.
12. T. Nakamura, '*The Flight of Lot and his Family from Sodom*: Rubens and his studio', in T. Nakamura (ed.) and M.J. McClintock (tr.), *Rubens and his Workshop, 'The Flight of Lot and his Family from Sodom'*, Tokyo, The National Museum of Western Art, 1994, pp. 25–46, p. 32.
13. Broos 1993 (cited in note 10), p. 305.
14. N. Van Hout and A. Balis, *Rubens Unveiled: Notes on the Master's Painting Technique*, Antwerp, Ludion, 2012, pp. 102–109.
15. Letter dated 11 December 1951, Curatorial Files of the National Gallery of Art, Washington, DC.
16. A letter from Michael Jaffé to Professor Colin Eisler, Institute of Fine Arts, New York University, dated to 18 April 1972. Curatorial Files of the National Gallery of Art, Washington, DC.
17. Van Hout and Balis 2012 (cited in note 14), pp. 110–117.
18. Nakamura 1994 (cited in note 12), p. 30.
19. A. Balis, '"Fatto da un mio discepolo": Rubens' studio practices reviewed', in Nakamura 1994 (cited in note 12), pp. 97–128, pp. 97–98.
20. Paintings from the collections of the Ringling Museum in Sarasota, Florida, the Bass Museum.
21. N. Kamba, 'A comparison of the ground, pigment and painting techniques used in three versions of "The Flight of Lot and his Family from Sodom"', in Nakamura 1994 (cited in note 12), pp. 69–96; K. Kawaguchi, 'A comparison of three versions of "The Flight of Lot and his family from Sodom"', in *op. cit.*, pp. 47–68.
22. Wheelock 2005 (cited in note 1), pp. 218–222.
23. B. Reade, *The Dominance of Spain 1550–1660*, London, George G. Harra, 1951, pp. 10–12.
24. J.S. Held, *Rubens: Selected Drawings*, vol. II, London, Phaidon Publishers, 1959, p. 139, pl. 124.

Author's address

Julia Burdajewicz, Andrew W. Mellon Fellow in Painting Conservation, National Gallery of Art, Washington, DC, USA (julia.burdajewicz@gmail.com)

THE PROBLEM OF THE PORTRAIT COPIES PAINTED BY RUBENS IN MADRID, 1628–29

Jeremy Wood

ABSTRACT Rubens brought back at least 22 full-size painted copies of works by Titian from his visit to the court of Philip IV in Madrid in 1628–29. Only seven are widely accepted as having survived. This paper argues that three more – all portraits of men and associated with lost works by Titian – formed part of this group but were painted by assistants, not by Rubens himself. The entire group presents a different problem from the standard repetition of compositions in a workshop because Rubens kept these copies for his own collection. However, one of the examples examined survives in a prime example painted under Rubens's direction in Madrid and a studio repetition made in his Antwerp studio after his return and presumably for sale.

Introduction

Rubens was granted an exceptional favour in 1628–29 when, during his second visit to Madrid, Philip IV allowed him to copy many of the Titians in the royal collection. Making small versions would not have been a problem but Rubens wanted his replicas to be the same size as the originals, so it was necessary to take them down from the walls of the king's most private rooms in the Alcázar and move them to the artist's temporary studio nearby for copying. Despite the disruption caused to the inner sanctums of the palace, the surviving documentary and visual evidence establishes that Rubens painted no fewer than 22 copies of this kind during the visit.[1] Perhaps surprisingly, the majority of these works can no longer be traced and only seven survive that are generally accepted as from this date.[2] However, the following discussion examines whether three copies – all male portraits and based on Italian models – should be added to the group. The status of these works depends on whether Rubens delegated some of the work and how he organised his studio whilst he was in Madrid.[3]

Titian copies

Rubens's assistants

It has been assumed that Rubens took few assistants with him on his travels, yet the number of paintings produced in Madrid in 1628–29 suggests that he needed help from artists who had already worked with him, rather than general studio support available from the pool of Spanish artists at court. Admittedly, Francisco Pacheco was amazed at Rubens's industry during hisvisit to Madrid,[4] but this need not rule out delegation. There has been surprisingly little attempt to identify any studio assistance in the works of 1628–29, but it is worth recalling that Rubens tried to persuade the capable Jan Cossiers (1600–1671) to accompany him to Spain.[5] It seems that Rubens was looking for a skilled assistant since Cossiers was 28 years old at the time, an experienced artist and on the verge of joining the Antwerp painters' guild. The younger artist's parents were opposed to the idea, perhaps because he had only recently returned from travelling in Italy and France. But, if Rubens was frustrated in this, it seems reasonable to assume he found someone else to step into Cossiers's shoes or, more likely, several suitable assistants. Rubens's endeavours as a diplomat in Spain left a detailed paper trail, but unfortunately the size of his party and the names of his assistants was too insignificant a matter to be noted by his contemporaries. As far as courtiers were concerned, studio assistants were little more than servants and servants were invisible.

Copies

The topic outlined so far may seem different from the standard practice of producing several versions of the same original composition under the supervision of a master. This is because

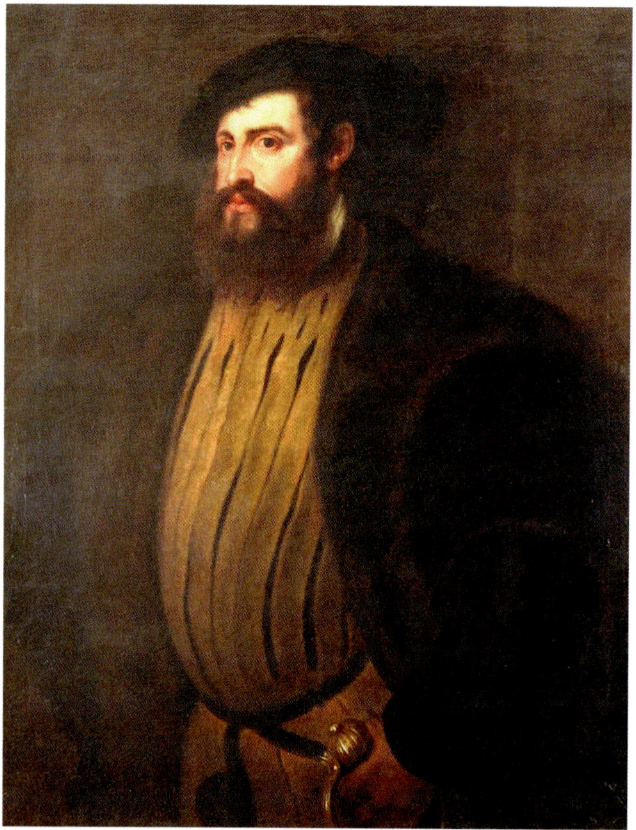

Fig. 1 Rubens and Workshop after Titian or a Venetian contemporary artist, *A Man in a Fur-trimmed Robe here identified as Philipp von Hessen*, oil on canvas, 97.5 × 76.5 cm. Courtauld Institute of Art, Princes Gate Collection (inv. P.19878.AS.354).

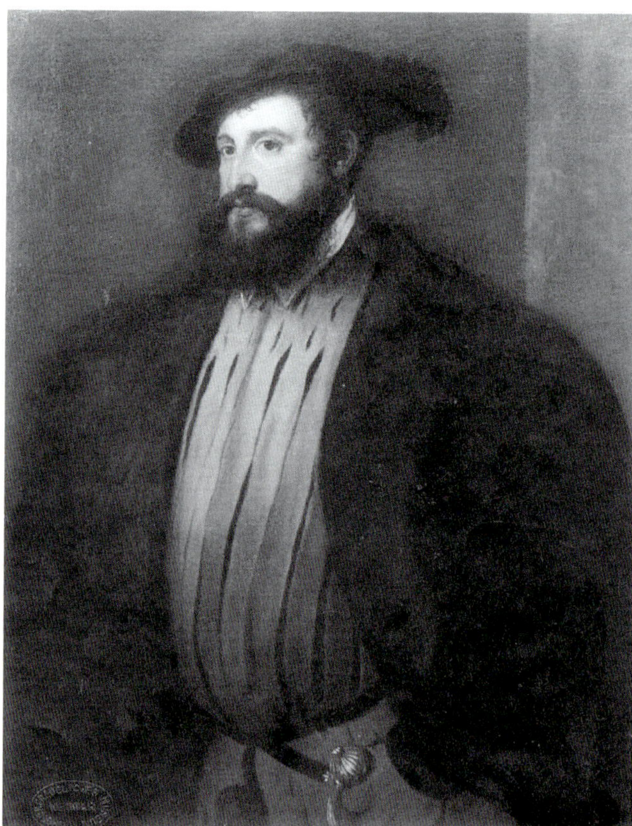

Fig. 2 Unidentified Flemish artist after Rubens and Workshop after Titian or a Venetian contemporary artist, *A Man in a Fur-trimmed Robe here identified as Philipp von Hessen*, oil on canvas, 96.5 × 74 cm. Klassik Stiftung Weimer, Museum (inv. G49).

Rubens's copies were not intended for sale and were kept by him for his own collection. On the other hand, these copies were sometimes replicated in his workshop, though admittedly very rarely. In these cases, subject matter was a factor since Rubens treated copies after portraits differently from those after history subjects. The latter were kept under close wraps, while he occasionally allowed portraits, particularly if they recorded a well-known figure, to be engraved or copied. As a result, this discussion will focus on the portraits as a coherent group to which specific questions of workshop practice relate.

A prime example is the copy from Rubens's workshop of a lost 16th-century Italian portrait. Two versions are known: one in the Courtauld Institute Gallery in London (Fig. 1) and the other in the Kunstsammlungen zu Weimar (Fig. 2).[6] It is worth considering whether one of these canvases could date from the 1628–29 visit, despite the traditional assumption that they look earlier in style.[7] If Rubens employed assistants while in Madrid, the old-fashioned look of the pictures could be explained since members of his workshop tended to be a step or two behind the master. The problem is made more complicated because the sitter has traditionally been identified as Hernán Cortéz (1485–1547), but no prototype has yet been found and the evidence provided by George Vertue in the 18th century was fanciful.[8] If the better of the two versions is to be dated to the second Madrid visit it must record a work that Rubens could have seen whilst at the Spanish court, but no corresponding portrait of Cortéz has been traced. However, if the identification is wrong, the most likely solution is that it records a lost portrait of *Landgrave Philipp von Hessen* by Titian that was recorded in Madrid in 1628–29 in the possession of the powerful courtier Diego Messia, marquis of Leganés (1585–1655), not the king. Early inventory descriptions establish that the sitter was depicted wearing a fur-trimmed coat and a Milanese cap, his left hand resting on his sword hilt,[9] and Rubens is known to have copied this prototype since his version is recorded in the 1640 inventory of his collection.[10] The Courtauld and Weimar paintings are the only works among Rubens's surviving copies that correspond. For present purposes it is helpful that both versions have been subject to technical investigation.

X-radiographs of both the Courtauld and Weimar paintings have been made. The latter were shown to me by Ulrich Haussmann in 2002 and the former some time after an investigation that was carried out by Hugo Platt in 1997.[11] Comparison of these two versions is limited because the technical examination of the Courtauld work was more thorough than that of the Weimar painting, but for present purposes, a simple point can be made, namely that the grounds of both versions were prepared differently.[12] In the case of the Courtauld version, the first ground layer is unusually thick and contains a large amount of lead white that was coarsely crushed and applied with a broad knife in fan-shaped movements.[13] These are visible to the naked eye and the texture carries through to the paint surface. The arcs of

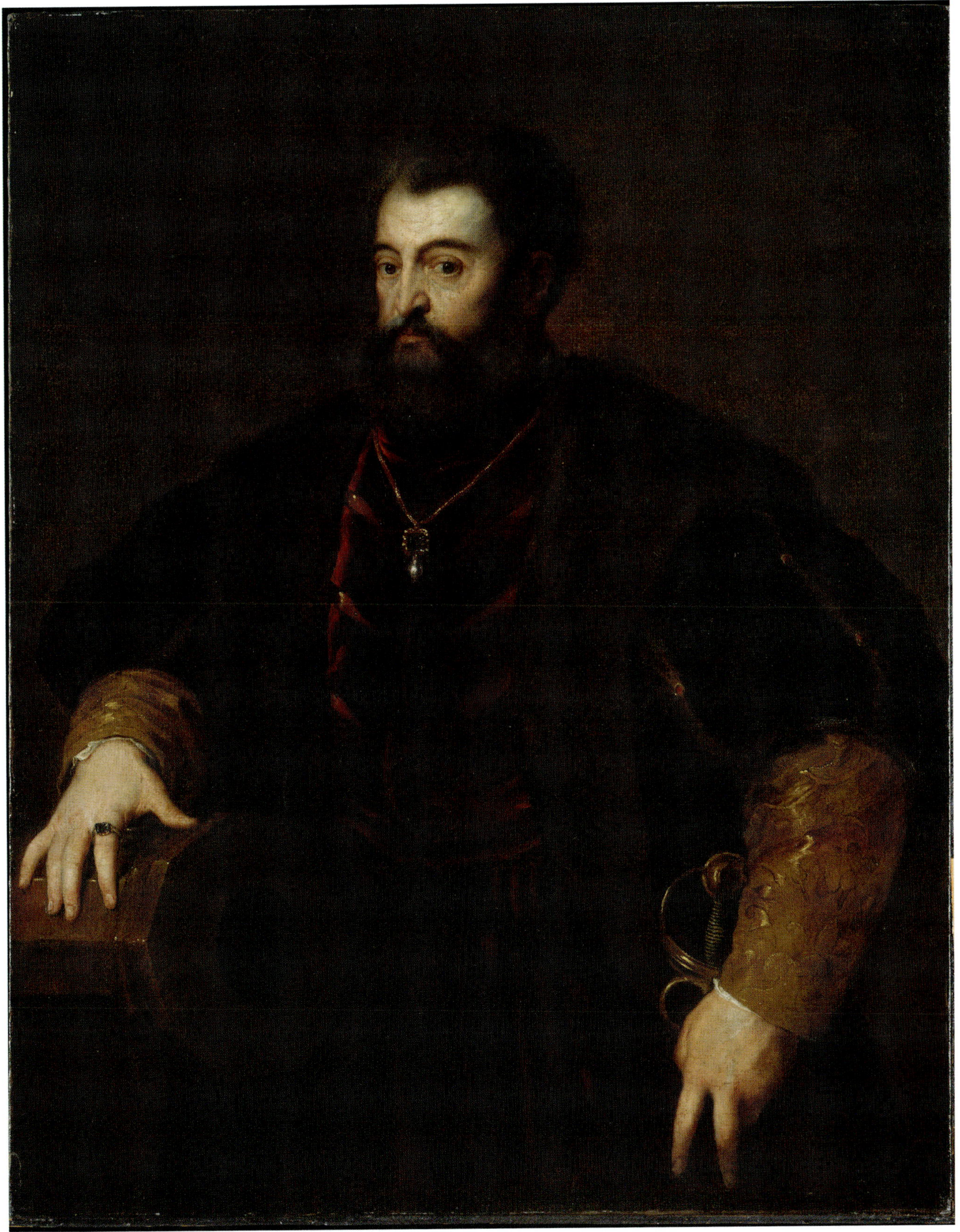

Fig. 3 Unidentified Flemish artist after Titian, *Alfonso d'Este, Marquess and Duke of Ferrara*, oil on canvas, 127 × 98.5 cm. Metropolitan Museum of Art, New York (inv. 27.56). (Metropolitan Museum of Art, New York. © Photo SCALA, Florence, 2013.)

white lead look much like those found in X-radiographs of Diego Velázquez's canvases of the 1630s.[14] The same vigorous application of lead white is apparent in unpublished X-radiographs of two of the most important and admired copies that Rubens painted from works by Titian in 1628–29: the *Adam and Eve* and the *Rape of Europa*, both in the Museo nacional del Prado, Madrid.[15] In the case of the former, the knife movements radiate from two corners of the canvas, while at the opposite edge the arc radiates from the centre, forming a distinctive and symmetrical pattern. Admittedly, this method is neither exclusively Spanish nor limited to the work of Velázquez, and the *imprimatura* on Rubens's canvases was sometimes applied with comparable fan-shaped movements that are visible in X-radiographs.[16] However, all examples known to me reveal a smoother, thinner ground and far less disruptive arcs of white lead. Of course, a large studio such as that run by Rubens would need several assistants to do menial work such as prime canvases and panels, and they may well have worked in different ways. As a result, thinness or thickness is not a matter of location.[17]

Nevertheless, Rubens's way of working was disrupted by his travels. A telling example is provided by the strips that Rubens added to his *Adoration of the Kings* of 1609, now in the Prado, Madrid, which he enlarged and reworked for Philip IV in 1628–29, an intervention that was subject to a thorough technical analysis in 2000–2002.[18] Carmen Garrido and Jaime García-Máiquez have demonstrated that the core of the canvas, dating from 1609, has a lead white ground, while the strips added in 1628–29 have an orange ground composed of red lead mixed with lead white, earth, quartz and carbon black.[19] Interestingly, Rubens did not use the red earth favoured by Madrid artists, *tierra de Esquivias*, but remained faithful to his Flemish training in his choice of pigments,[20] even though the way he prepared the second phase of work in Madrid was different from the way that he had begun this work in Antwerp. Garrido and García-Máiquez also plausibly suggested that Rubens obtained canvas from local suppliers whilst in Madrid.[21] So far as is known, he did not use orange-coloured grounds for the Titian copies so, at the very least, the Courtauld work is compatible with what is known about the preparation of Rubens's canvases in Spain.

So far, this discussion has implied that although the Courtauld work appears the stronger of the two (despite its abraded condition), the Weimar portrait was also produced during Rubens's lifetime. The reason for this is the close parallel in handling between the two. As already suggested, this duplication is unusual among Rubens's copies after earlier masters but there is another case, a canvas now in the Queensland Art Gallery, Brisbane,[22] that provides a faithful record of Titian's *Woman with a Fur Wrap* in the Kunsthistorisches Museum, Vienna. The Brisbane copy was not made during the Madrid trip but shortly afterwards in 1629–30 when Rubens visited the court of Charles I in London where he also made a few full-size copies after works by Titian. Several early versions of the Brisbane canvas survive, including one signed by Erasmus Quellinus II as late as 1673,[23] but a couple of the others could date from before Rubens's death. Unfortunately, the scattered locations of these works, several in private collections, make a technical assessment difficult. In addition, after Rubens's death in 1640 the Brisbane *Woman with a Fur Wrap* passed through the hands of several painters, notably Frans Snyders and Paul de Vos, and it was therefore accessible to – and admired by – Antwerp artists who had the opportunity to make further replicas of it in the middle years of the 17th century. In short, the rarity of workshop reproductions of Rubens's Italian copies makes the existence of the Courtauld and Weimar pictures more significant than might appear at first glance.

A different problem is presented by a Flemish copy in the Metropolitan Museum of Art, New York, that records Titian's famous lost portrait of *Alfonso I d'Este* (Fig. 3).[24] Rubens certainly made a replica of this prototype since *Vn pourtrait d'Alfonse d'Este Duc de Ferrare* by him after Titian was included in his 1640 inventory.[25] The crucial question is whether the New York *Alfonso d'Este* was this work and therefore, most likely, painted in Madrid where Rubens would have seen the original on the walls of Leganés's house.[26] Later in the discussion it will be argued that the entire group of copies made from works owned by Leganés was delegated to assistants for the good reason that even Rubens could not be in two places at once.

There has been a tendency to avoid discussing the picture since, while its Flemish character is undeniable,[27] it does not contain evidence of Rubens's own hand. The characteristics that set the *Alfonso d'Este* apart from Rubens's own handiwork need to be emphasised. The face and the hands are puffy and the figure has an unpleasant softness. Rubens's treatment of flesh tints shows considerable variety, as recently argued by Nico Van Hout,[28] and the structure of heads is often defined by the direction of his brushstrokes, the flesh being built up with impasto touches of ochre and light yellow and a warm brown glaze, so that opaque and translucent layers of paint are placed alongside each other. By comparison, cool blue-green shadows are far more evident in the face of Alfonso d'Este.

If the New York *Alfonso d'Este* is the work listed in 1640 it follows that the inventory may not be entirely reliable as regards authorship – but this needs caution. Rubens's will directed that Frans Snyders, Jan Wildens and Jacques Moermans should take charge of the sale of his collection.[29] They formed an expert team whose familiarity with Rubens's studio must give their opinions authority. But all three men were far less informed about the work that Rubens had produced abroad, and they treated the full-size painted copies as a homogenous group, which may have led to confusion between copies largely by Rubens and those that were all or in part by assistants, a distinction that seems vital today but was less pressing in the period. Recently Anna Tummers has questioned the modern search for fully autograph works and has reasoned that 'no seventeenth-century document lists a painting as by a *gesel* or paid assistant of a master, which suggests … that their share in the studio production must have commonly counted as "by the master" as long as it was done in the master's style'.[30] This argument fits the approach adopted by Snyders, Wildens and Moermans to the works by Rubens in the 1640 inventory, since they would have viewed the works painted by assistants in Rubens's style – and under his supervision – as being his authorial property.

To strengthen this argument it is useful to examine a work from the Madrid group that has long been identified as entirely by Rubens but was arguably prepared by an assistant. The work in question is now in the collection of the Duquesa de Berwick y Alba at the Palaçio de Liria, Madrid,[31] and it records Titian's lost double-portrait of Charles V and his wife Isabella of Portugal.

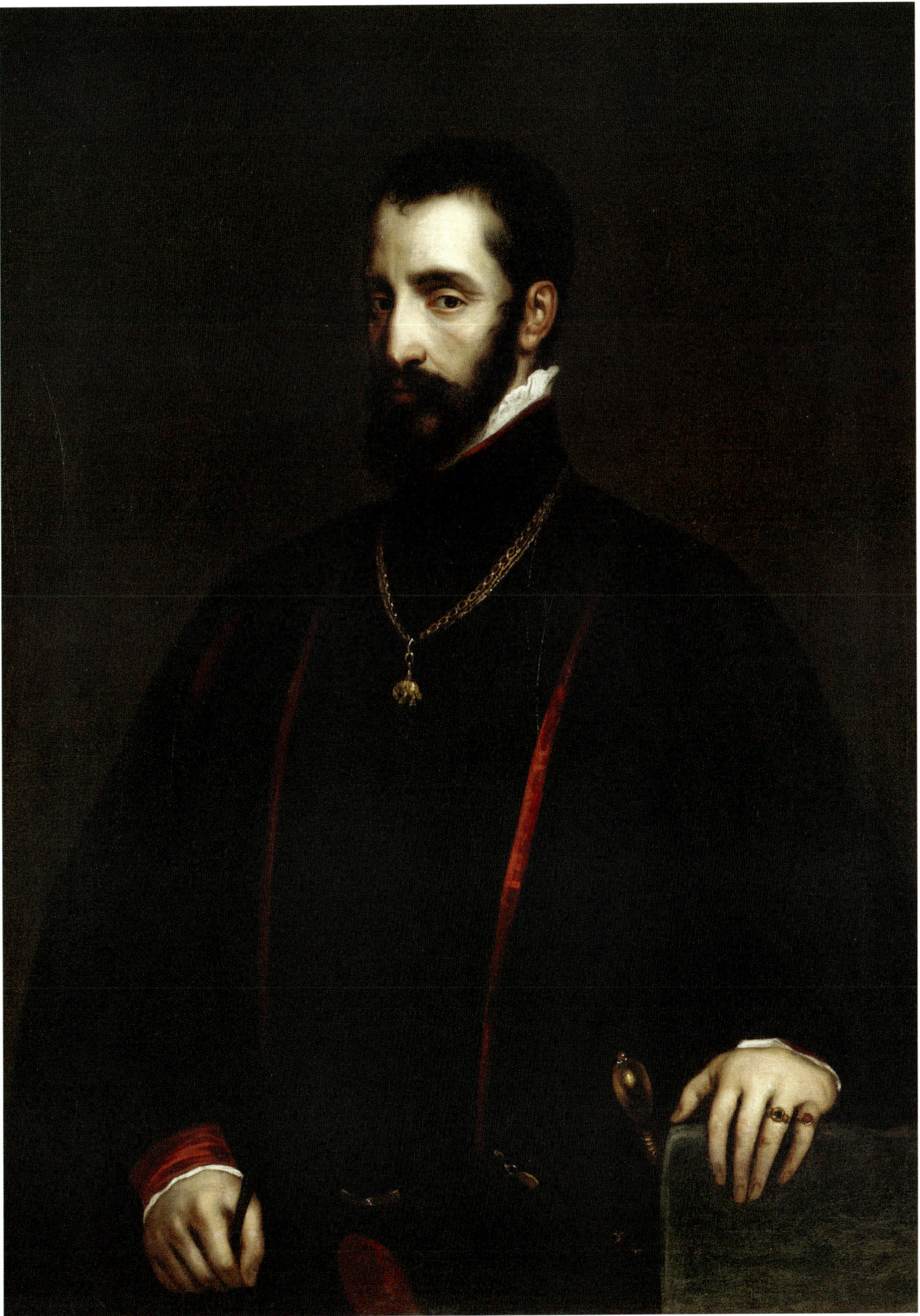

Fig. 4 Unidentified Flemish artist after Titian, *Fernando Alvarez de Toledo y Pimentel, Third Duke of Alba*, oil on canvas, 115.5 × 81 cm. Duquesa de Berwick y Alba, Palaçio de Liria, Madrid.

Rubens can only have made this replica in Madrid since the original had been kept very privately by the Habsburgs.[32] Rubens's version has been much admired, particularly in Spain where its documentary and historical resonance is obvious[33] but, in my opinion, there is a distinction to be made between its journeyman underpainting and the visible retouchings that bring it to life, in much the same way that the workshop repetitions of Rubens's own compositions were manufactured in the Antwerp studio under his supervision. Here the treatment of the subordinate areas is pedestrian, in particular the curtains (painted using a lake underpainting with dark carmine glazes), the puppet-like hands, and the treatment of ornament and embroidery. Rubens's additions, however, are clear and distinct. They can be seen on the faces of the emperor and his consort, and on Isabella's dress as, for example, on the puffed sleeves where Rubens drew in white lead with the brush to animate the forms. This is illuminating because on the whole Rubens's painted copies from earlier works of art are not easy to dissect in terms of different areas of responsibility and delegation. Logically it follows that if studio assistance can be found in this canvas then Rubens must have had help in making his painted copies while at the Spanish court.

Another problematic copy that should be added at this point is a portrait of Fernando Alvarez de Toledo y Pimentel, third duke of Alba (1508–1582) now also in the Alba collection at Palaçio de Liria (Fig. 4).[34] This copy has sometimes been published by Spanish scholars as entirely by Rubens; most recently, for example, by Matiás Díaz Padrón who wrote that: 'es dificil pensar en otro pintor de la época a tenor de la calidad'.[35] This is a matter of opinion, and few Rubens specialists outside Spain have accepted the attribution. The copy must date from 1628–29 however, since it is listed by Pacheco in his *Arte de la pintura* and it also appeared in Rubens's 1640 inventory.[36] As with the prototypes for some of the portraits already discussed, the original of Titian's portrait of the duke of Alba in court dress was in the collection of the marquis of Leganés.[37] This is a striking coincidence, but not all the Leganés copies are by the same assistant as one might expect. In the case of the Alba portrait it is hard to decide from looking at it in normal viewing conditions whether the deadness of the paint surface and weak drawing of the hands is characteristic of the copyist, or the result of later restoration and heavy varnishing. Provisionally, though, there is a plausible case to be made that this was not painted by Rubens, as claimed by Díaz Padrón, but for him.

Relatively few of the Titian – or supposed Titian – prototypes for the Rubens portrait copies have survived. In one case, however, replica and original can be compared. A copy by Rubens of Titian's full-length portrait of *Prince Philip of Spain, later Philip II, in Armour* is in the Devonshire collection at Chatsworth,[38] and the original survives in the Prado, Madrid.[39] The Titian measures 193 × 111 cm, but has probably been enlarged by 8 cm at the top, while Rubens's copy is 178 × 104 cm. From the pull of the stretcher pins on the canvas on the left it appears to have been cut at the top and on the right. The size is interesting since it raises the question of how precise Rubens wanted his copies to be. In some of his full-size painted replicas he was less punctilious in following the exact dimensions of the prototype, expanding the margins of space around a figure or an entire composition so as to let it breathe.

Few other painted copies by Rubens are as subservient to their model as the Chatsworth *Prince Philip*. It is thinly painted, fluent in handling and executed on a canvas with a fine grain. This speed of execution, however, did not lead to carelessness or approximation since the copy is attentive to detail, doing justice to the variety of ways in which Titian had described surfaces and textures. The reticence of the Chatsworth copy is probably why it was sometimes dated by earlier scholars to Rubens's first visit to Spain in 1603,[40] possibly because of a conventional assumption that artists, above all Rubens, should paint neatly when young and more freely when old, and that the making of copies is the job of the inexperienced. In fact, the degree of control found in the Chatsworth copy is not unique in Rubens's work of the late 1620s.

Conclusions

Art historians have claimed that Rubens modelled his technique in this period on Titian's example. Rubens's *Madonna with Saints* painted for the high altar of the Augustinian Church in Antwerp (now on loan to the Koninklijk Museum) is seen as pivotal in this respect[41] but, surprisingly, it was installed in June 1628, shortly before he left Antwerp for Madrid where Titian's example was to make such a demonstrable impact on him. It would follow that Rubens's move from a smooth and polished way of painting in the 1610s is not very well understood currently, and that the Madrid copies of 1628–29 were less about mastering technique than about recording subject matter. From that point of view, it would make sense to employ assistants to do some of the work when making the Titian copies.

When examined as a group, the full-size copies that Rubens painted in 1628–29 reveal varying levels of faithfulness to the originals, both in terms of treatment of detail and imitation of technique. When Rubens painted a copy of an earlier work at the same size as the prototype, he was forced to consider exactly how it had been made, as would any artist working in this way. Rubens's copies after Titian's mythologies, which have not been the focus of discussion here, also show the range of dependence and independence in his approach. For example, his *Rape of Europa* in the Prado, Madrid,[42] is more true to the composition of Titian's original (now in the Isabella Stewart Gardner Museum, Boston) than to its application of paint.[43] The Boston canvas has a white gypsum ground covered by a brownish layer mixed from glue, oil and white lead, which can give the misleading impression that Titian used a red ground.[44] Whether Rubens understood Titian's painting methods in this much detail is a matter of opinion, but for whatever reason he did not follow slavishly in the footsteps of the Venetian master, constructing his paint surface in a different way with the result that Europa has a whiter skin with an almost silken sheen because of Rubens's use of greyish half-tints. In short, Rubens's treatment of Europa's flesh tones make her look like a figure in one of his own works.

This discussion has focused on the possible intervention of several workshop assistants in Rubens's Madrid copies as well as the way that he may, or may not, have followed Titian's paint technique. It has emerged that the Madrid copies can be divided into three groups: some substantially by Rubens himself, some by workshop assistants and retouched by him, and some entirely by assistants with no intervention at all. None of these copies was intended for sale and all remained in his collection until his death, at which point Snyders, Wildens and Moermans treated them as one coherent group: the paintings made by Rubens after Titian.

Notes

1. See J. Wood, *Rubens: Copies and Adaptations from Renaissance and Later Artists. Italian Artists. Volume 1: Raphael and his School* (*Corpus Rubenianum Ludwig Burchard*, Part 26, 2), London/Turnhout, Harvey Miller, 2010, I, pp. 43–48.
2. For these works, all after works by Titian, see J. Wood, *Rubens: Copies and Adaptations from Renaissance and Later Artists. Italian Artists. Volume 2: Titian and North Italian Artists* (*Corpus Rubenianum Ludwig Burchard*, Part 26, 2), London/Turnhout, Harvey Miller, 2010. They are the *Adam and Eve* (*op. cit.*, I, pp. 111–119, no. 111) and the *Rape of Europa* (*op. cit.*, I, pp. 178–186, no. 122), both in the Museo Nacional del Prado; the *Diana and Callisto* in the collection of the earl of Derby at Knowsley Hall, Liverpool (*op. cit.*, I, pp. 171–178, no. 121); the *Venus and Cupid with a Mirror* in the Fundación Colección Thyssen-Bornemisza, Madrid (*op. cit.*, I, pp. 190–197, no. 124); the *Emperor Charles V and the Empress Isabella of Portugal* in the collection of the Duquesa de Berwick y Alba, Palaçio de Liria, Madrid (*op. cit.*, I, pp. 219–225, no. 129); the *Prince Philip of Spain, later Philip II, in Armour*, full length in the collection of the duke of Devonshire, Chatsworth (*op. cit.*, I, pp. 255–260, no. 137); and the *Woman Dressed in White holding a Fan* in the Kunsthistorisches Museum, Vienna (*op. cit.*, I, pp. 265–270, no. 140).
3. Unfortunately, technical data for only a few of the 1628–29 copies have been published. But at least the issues involved are becoming clearer following the recent technical investigations into Rubens's working methods led by Joost Vander Auwera at the Musées royaux des Beaux-Arts de Belgique, Brussels, and by Nico Van Hout and Arnout Balis in the Koninklijk Museum voor Schone Kunsten in Antwerp. For the former, see J. Vander Auwera and S. van Sprang, *Rubens: A Genius at Work. The Works of Peter Paul Rubens in the Royal Museums of Fine Arts of Belgium Reconsidered*, exh. cat., Musées royaux des Beaux-Arts de Belgique, Brussels, 2007–08; and for the latter, N. Van Hout and A. Balis, *Rubens Unveiled: Notes on the Master's Painting Technique*, Antwerp, Ludion, 2012.
4. F. Pacheco, *Arte de la pintura. Edición del manuscrito original, acabado el 24 de Enero de 1638*, F.J. Sánchez Cantón (ed.), 1–2, Madrid, Instituto de Valencia de Don Juan, 1956, p. 153.
5. See the letter from N.-C. Fabri de Peiresc to Adrien de Vries, 2 February 1629, in C. Ruelens and M. Rooses (eds), *Correspondance de Rubens et documents épistolaires concernant sa vie et ses oeuvres*, 1–6, Antwerp, Veuve de Backer, 1887–1909, vol. 5, p. 27, letter DLXX.
6. For these works, see Wood 2010 (cited in note 2), I, pp. 261–265, no. 139, where the possibility that the Courtauld version might date from 1628–29 and be a portrait of Philipp von Hessen is only raised speculatively.
7. See, for example, [A. Seilern], *Flemish Paintings and Drawings at 56 Princes Gate, London, SW7. Addenda*, London, Shenval, 1969, pp. 11–14, no. 299 (dated *c.*1608–12). The dating was upheld in M. Jaffé, *Rubens: Catalogo Completo*, Milan, Rizzoli, 1989, p. 171, no. 123.
8. The authority for this is an engraving by Vertue of 1724. For the identification of the sitter, see also E. Shaeffer, 'Ein Porträt und seine Tradition', *Monatshefte für Kunstwissenschaft* 6, 1913, pp. 27–29; and E. Schaeffer, 'Cortés in Weimar?', in *Von Bildern und Menschen der Renaissance*, Berlin, Julius Bard, 1914, pp. 168–171. Neither of these texts was cited by Seilern (see note 7), and, surprisingly, he made no mention of the Weimar version in his catalogue entry.
9. 'Ottro rretrato del mismo tamano del lantsgratte de hesen con un coletto acuchillado [en martas], la mano izquierda en la espada [y gorra de Milan] original de tiçiano'. See M.C. Volk, 'New light on a seventeenth-century collector: the marquis of Leganés', *The Art Bulletin* 62, 1980, p. 266, supplemented by C. Justi, 'Verzeichnis der früher in Spanien befindlichen, jetzt verschollen oder ins Ausland gekommen gemälde Tizians', *Jahrbuch der Königlich Preussischen Kunstsammlungen* X, 1889, p. 185, no. 43.
10. See Wood 2010 (cited in note 2), I, pp. 305–307, App. Titian 10. For the inventory reference see J.M. Muller, *Rubens: The Artist as Collector*, Princeton, NJ, Princeton University Press, 1989, pp. 106–107, no. 55.
11. Some information from Platt's research was discussed with me at a meeting in the Conservation Department at the Courtauld Institute in 2002. See H. Platt, *Observations on Four Portrait Paintings by Rubens: A Technical Examination*, final year dissertation, Diploma in the Conservation of Easel Paintings, Courtauld Institute of Art, London, 1997. I read the text of this dissertation on 14 May 2012 (my thanks to Fiona Rutka for making this possible).
12. I must now correct an error in my *Corpus Rubenianum* text where I wrote, mistakenly, that the Courtauld canvas did not have a double ground and that the conventional layer of calcium carbonate mixed with an oil-based vehicle was absent; Wood 2010 (cited in note 2), I, p. 236, under no. 139. This applies to another work in the Courtauld collection, the *Head of the Emperor Charles V* after Titian (see Wood 2010 (cited in note 2), I, pp. 236–241, no. 132). My mistake was based on a misunderstanding of the conversation mentioned in the previous note.
13. See Platt 1997 (cited in note 11), pp. 20, 55.
14. See, amongst others, J. Brown and C. Garrido, *Velázquez: The Technique of Genius*, New Haven, CT and London, Yale University Press, 1998, pp. 15–17, 81–84.
15. My thanks to Alejandro Vergara for making these X-radiographs available to me. Personal communication 4 September 2012.
16. As noted in Van Hout and Balis 2012 (cited in note 3), p. 48.
17. Nico Van Hout, personal communication, 14 May 2012.
18. See H. Cabrero, 'The restoration of Rubens' *Adoration of the Magi*', and C. Garrido, J. García-Máiquez, with E. Parra, 'Rubens' *Adoration of the Magi*: materials and pictorial technique', in A. Vergara *et al.*, *Rubens: The Adoration of the Magi*, exh. cat., Museo nacional del Prado, Madrid, 2004–2005, pp. 125–139, 141–154.
19. Garrido and García-Máiquez 2005 (cited in note 18), p. 145.
20. Ibid., p. 146.
21. Ibid., p. 144.
22. For this work, see Wood 2010 (cited in note 2), I, pp. 270–276, no. 141.
23. For brief details, see ibid., I, p. 271, Copy 2, under no. 141.
24. Ibid., I, pp. 241–246, under no. 133, where it is said that an autograph copy by Rubens is lost and that the New York version is a replica of it.

25. See Muller 1989 (cited in note 10), p. 107, no. 58.
26. See Volk 1980 (cited in note 9), pp. 258–259.
27. It was attributed to Titian himself in the early to mid-20th century by a number of scholars, including Berenson no less, but since then Italian specialists have tended to give it to Rubens while experts on Flemish painting are more sceptical. I am grateful to Andrea Bayer for showing me the canvas in 2005 and giving me access to the museum files that contain a great deal of correspondence on attribution. More detail on the differences of opinion about the author of this work can be found in Wood 2010 (cited in note 2), I, p. 244, under no. 133.
28. N. Van Hout, 'Reconsidering Rubens's flesh colour', *Bóletin del Museo del Prado* 19 (37), 2001, pp. 7–20.
29. P. Génard, 'Het laatste testament van P.P. Rubens', *Rubens-Bulletijn* 4, 1896, pp. 137, 139.
30. A. Tummers, *The Eye of the Connoisseur: Authenticating Paintings by Rembrandt and his Contemporaries*, Amsterdam, Amsterdam University Press, 2011, p. 92.
31. For this work, see Wood 2010 (cited in note 2), I, pp. 219–225, no. 129.
32. A dating to 1628–29 was proposed as early as the 1930s and has been widely accepted with the exception, amongst recent scholars, of Antoine Seilern, see [A. Seilern], *Corrigenda and Addenda to the Catalogue of Paintings at 56 Princes Gate, London, SW7*, London, Shenval, 1971, p. 22, under no. 13.
33. See, for example, the recent discussion by M. Díaz Padrón in *Colección Casa de Alba*, exh. cat., Museo de Bellas Artes, Seville, 2009–10, pp. 232–234, no. 4, which I saw too late to incorporate in my account of this painting in Wood 2010 (cited in note 2), I, pp. 219–225, no. 129.
34. See Wood 2010 (cited in note 2), I, pp. 216–219, no. 128, where it is said that an autograph copy by Rubens is lost and that the Palacio de Liria version is a replica of it.
35. Díaz Padrón 2009 (cited in note 33), p. 228, under cat. 3.
36. For Pacheco, see note 5 above. For the 1640 inventory, see Muller 1989 (cited in note 10), p. 106, no. 53.
37. Volk 1980 (cited in note 9), p. 266. Recently, both Díaz Padrón and I have argued independently that it was at Leganés's palace that Rubens saw the portrait of Alba in 1628–29; see Díaz Padrón 2009 (cited in note 33), p. 231.
38. For further details, see Wood 2010 (cited in note 2), I, pp. 255–260, no. 137.
39. For useful comparative details, see R. Baumstark, K. Lohse Belkin, G. Cavalli-Björkman, M. Neumeister, C. Quaeitzsch and J. Wood, *Rubens im Wettstreit mit Alten Meistern. Vorbild und Neuerfindung*, exh. cat., Bayerischen Staatsgemäldesamlungen, Alte Pinakothek, Munich, 2009–2010, pp. 186–195, under no. 9.
40. Credit for the re-dating is due to J. Müller Hofstede, 'Rubens und Tizian. Das Bild Karls V', *Münchner Jahrbuch der bildenden Kunst* 18, 1967, p. 90, n. 109, although he later changed his mind in *Peter Paul Rubens, 1577–1640*. I, *Rubens in Italien. Gemälde, Ölskizzen, Zeichnungen*, exh. cat., Kunsthalle, Cologne, 1977, pp. 308–310, no. 85.
41. For example, see J.S. Held, *The Oil Sketches of Peter Paul Rubens: A Critical Catalogue*, Princeton, NJ, Princeton University Press, 1980, p. 520: 'Even before his [Rubens's] celebrated "encounter" with Titian during the months he spent in Madrid, he had achieved a pictorial brilliancy unmatched even by the Venetians.' But how, exactly, was this achieved? More recently, the influence of Titian on this altarpiece is argued vigorously – and with good reason – by Van Hout and Balis 2012 (cited in note 3), pp. 82–86.
42. For basic references, see note 2 above.
43. For previous comments on this, see Wood 2010 (cited in note 2), I, pp. 44–45, 183.
44. See B. Mangum, 'Titian's *Europa*: comments on the condition and the artist's technique', in H.T. Goldfarb, D. Freedberg and M.B. Mena Marqués (eds), *Titian and Rubens: Power, Politics and Style*, exh. cat., Isabella Stewart Gardner Museum, Boston, Massachusetts, 1998, pp. 98–99.

Author's address

Jeremy Wood, Professor of Art History, Department of History of Art, Faculty of Arts, University of Nottingham, Nottingham, UK (Jeremy.Wood@nottingham.ac.uk)

AFTER RAPHAEL: THE HUNTERIAN *ENTOMBMENT* COPY EXAMINED IN THE CONTEXT OF COPYING PRACTICES IN EARLY 17TH-CENTURY ROME

Peter Black, Erma Hermens and Helen Howard

ABSTRACT The Hunterian Art Gallery, University of Glasgow, owns a full-scale copy of Raphael's famous *Entombment of Christ* composition (Rome, Galleria Borghese). The copy was purchased for the university in the 1750s as an original work by Raphael but more recently it was considered to date from the 18th century. Interdisciplinary research into its provenance, combined with a technical investigation into the materials and techniques used, has pushed its date of origin further back by at least one century. Raphael's original work has an interesting history of confiscation and reproduction. However, there are indications that in late 16th- and early 17th-century Italy, copies after Raphael's famous works were many in number, often produced by skilled artists and commissioned by important collectors. This paper looks at the provenance and making of the Hunterian copy, and employs the research results to re-evaluate its meaning and function.[1]

Introduction

Many museums own copies of well-known paintings, collected perhaps as originals at the time, or as faithful reproductions of works that would be difficult to obtain because of their scarcity or high prices on the art market. Although nowadays such copies tend to be ignored, for the history of art they can shed light on contemporary patterns of collecting, taste, as well as production methods. The status and function of a copy, once placed in its historical context varies from, for example, faithful reproduction of archetypal icons for devotional use to good quality copies after popular compositions produced to satisfy market demand or commissioned by established collectors to complement their collections, the latter also seen as creating comprehensive (art) historical documents.

In recent research, Peter van den Brink addressed the extensive copying practices of the Bruegel family studio, in the *Bruegel Enterprise* exhibition and publication (2001),[2] looking at the repetition of popular compositions for the art market, workshop involvement and methods of copying. In *On the Trail of Bosch and Bruegel*, four copies/versions of a Boschian/Bruegelian composition of *Christ Driving the Traders from the Temple* were addressed, discussing contemporary copying practices based on technical investigation, and demonstrating how the popularity and revivals of both Hieronymous Bosch and Pieter Bruegel the Elder, as well as the patronage of Philip II, who was an avid collector of Bosch's work, influenced collecting patterns leading to the production of such copies and versions.[3] The latter project addressed anonymous works with no clear provenance yet it provided insights into an area of art production and market that has so far received little attention.

It is likely that the full-scale copy of Raphael's *Entombment of Christ*, in the collection of the Hunterian Art Gallery, University of Glasgow (oil on canvas, 174.6 × 170 cm, GLAHA 43782, Fig. 1), belongs to the category of commissioned high quality copies made for a collector or for a keen market incentivised by the major collectors' taste for famous names. Bought as an original in 1753 as part of the study collection assembled by Robert Foulis for the Glasgow Academy of the Fine Arts, the painting in more recent times was considered to be an 18th-century copy with little attention paid to its provenance. In looking for the origins of this copy an important question was raised that cannot be answered definitively: what became of the earliest documented copy, painted by Giovanni Lanfranco

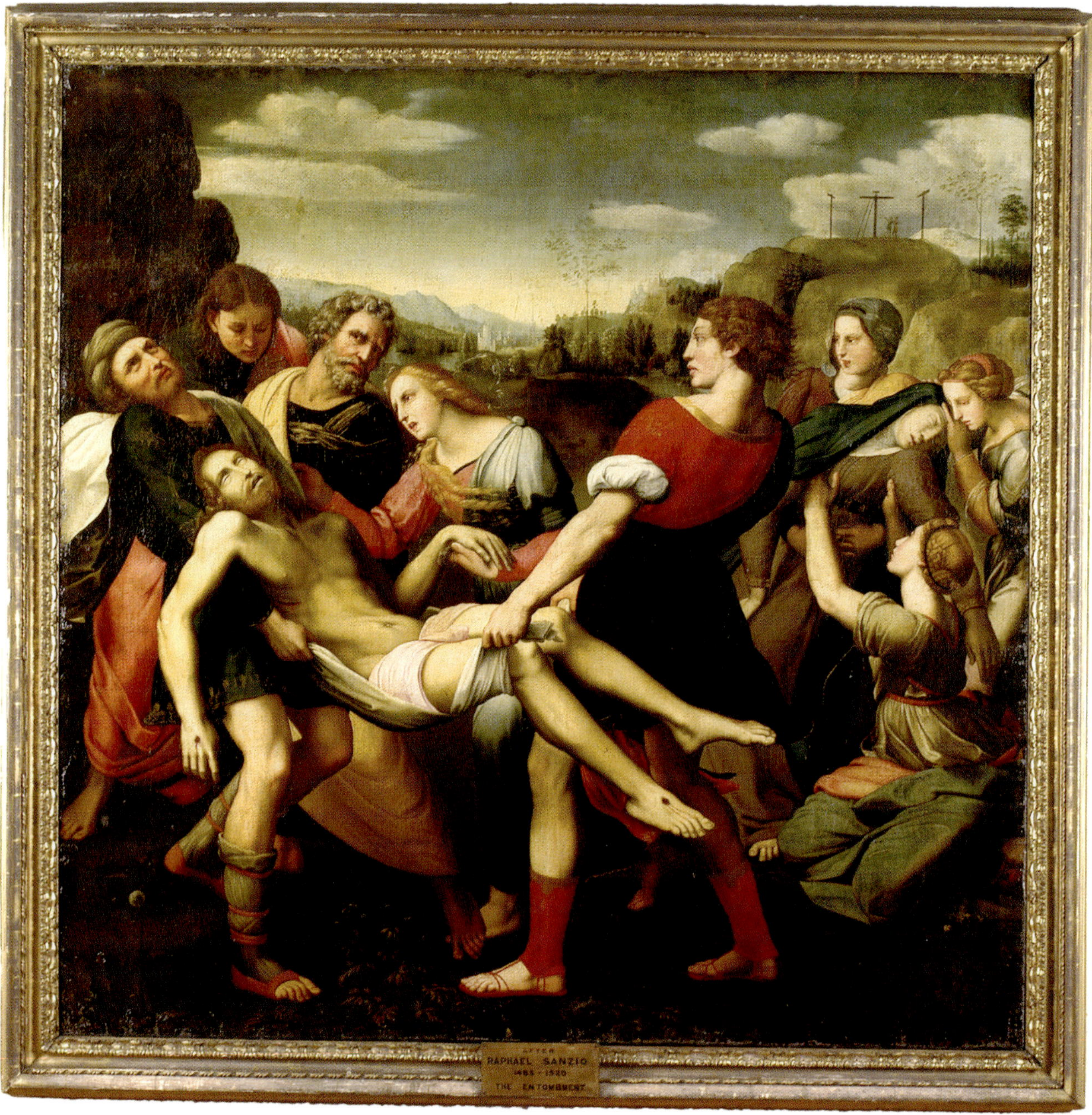

Fig. 1 Unknown Italian painter (after Raphael), *The Entombment*, *c.*1608–1620, oil on canvas, 174.6 × 170 cm, The Hunterian Art Gallery, University of Glasgow.

in Rome in 1608, and is the Hunterian copy identical to that painting? The combination of art-historical research with a focus on its provenance together with a technical examination of its methods and techniques looking for some 'markers' in terms of the time of execution and location, resulted in a new interpretation and further research questions.

Copies of Raphael's *Entombment*

Context

Not surprisingly, the Hunterian *Entombment* canvas is one of many copies after Raphael's compositions. As is well known, in 16th- and early 17th-century Italy, copying Renaissance masterpieces was an educational and inspirational exercise for young Italian artists as well as for aspiring painters from abroad. At the same time, there was a strong tendency to collect works by Titian and Raphael, regardless of their subject matter, but because of their famous makers.[4] The scarcity of Raphael's originals, their number limited because of his early death and because these works were already part of major collections, made the production of high quality copies to fill gaps in otherwise comprehensive collections desirable. For example, there is ample correspondence between Francesco Maria II Della Rovere, duke of Pesaro and Urbino (1578–1631), and his ambassadors and agents in various Italian cities, about obtaining works by Raphael, an 'Urbinato' like himself. His ambassador in Rome, Baldo Falcucci, wrote to the duke in 1581:

'It is true that these [Raphael originals] are very expensive ... it will be convenient to copy them.' Although the duke would have preferred an original, in further correspondence the option of a copy is frequently mentioned.[5]

The occurrence of copies is also discussed in contemporary texts with a focus on distinguishing between originals and reproductions, and addressing the specific qualities of both. For example, the writer Giulio Mancini (1558–1630), a well-known Roman collector and personal physician of Pope Urban VIII and thus well embedded in the Roman art scene, provides an example in his treatise *Considerazioni sulla pittura* (1620):

> And first one would need to recognize whether these [paintings] are copies or originals, which with regard to writings or books one names archetypes, as in first written and not copied, similarly with paintings, the first made or the originals as they say, or copied and thus a secondary work ... And it seems good to me to propose here a saying from a great prince who, delighting himself with painting, and wanting to buy one which was a copy, after he was made aware of this, said he wished to have the original; which they brought to him, and putting it next to the artefact which he had desired ... he took the original for the copy and the copy for the original; the prince added that in copies, when they are well made, one has two artefacts: the artefact made first, and a secondary work which imitates it.[6]

Mancini also points out the 'boldness and resolute manner' that will indicate the 'inventor', a manner which in copies, even 'intelligent and observant' ones, is inevitably lacking.[7]

Cardinal Borromeo, however, in his treatise the *Musaeum* (1625), provides a valid reason to make copies, as documentary evidence of famous artists from the past:

> How precious would the copy of any ancient painting by Apelles or Zeuxis be today! How useful to the progress of art! And at the same time how much pleasure would we draw from it! ... Therefore it is a praiseworthy thing to procure copies provided that they are worked with extreme diligence and taken from the most excellent models.[8]

Borromeo emphasises both the quality of the models as well as the skills of the copyist.

The Hunterian copy

A record exists of a copy by Raphael's assistant Giovanni Francesco Penni (*c.*1496–after 1528), signed and dated 'I F Penni MDXVIII', which is possibly the painting in the Galleria Sabauda in Turin.[9] Paola della Pergola lists 12 copies in her account of Raphael's original, most of them not full-scale but smaller.[10] Della Pergola's list begins with the painting commissioned by Scipione Borghese from Giovanni Lanfranco (1582–1647) in 1608, soon after his uncle, Pope Paul V, requested him to send a copy to Perugia to replace Raphael's original that Scipione had seized for the Borghese collection. The current location of Lanfranco's painting is not known, and it remains a possibility that it is identical to one of the surviving copies. Lanfranco was paid 57 *scudi* by Borghese to make a copy on 10 August 1608.[11]

Certainly, Borghese's removal of the painting from Perugia to Rome seems to have stimulated the making of copies in the 17th century. Raphael's original in the church of San Francesco in Perugia was replaced with a copy by Cavaliere d'Arpino (1568–1640), which is presumed, like the missing Lanfranco, to have been painted for the rapacious Borghese, who imprisoned Arpino in 1607 and appropriated numerous paintings from him for his own collection. Although Cavaliere d'Arpino's copy is, for whatever reason, not documented, the tradition that it is by D'Arpino dates back as far as 1676. It was mentioned in various guidebooks to Perugia. Baldassarre Orsini, for example, notes the copy in San Francesco: 'Above the corresponding door, is the painting with the dead Jesus carried to the grave. This is an exact copy made by Cav. D'Arpino after the original by Raphael, which used to be in this very church.'[12] If the painting sent by Borghese to Perugia to comply with the pope's demand was a copy by Arpino, one might ask: what did Borghese do with the painting he had made by Lanfranco? So far the Lanfranco painting has not been identified and may, indeed, be lost.

The Hunterian copy

Provenance

The history of the Hunterian *Entombment* copy, which has been in Glasgow since 1753, is at the least very interesting and hints at an illustrious provenance in France that would, if an old story is true, open up the possibility that it arrived in France as a diplomatic gift to Cardinal de Richelieu from an official in Rome before 1637.

In the period 1753–1776, the painting was part of the study collection of the Academy of the Fine Arts at the Old College in Glasgow (as the university was then known). The academy was established in a room obtained for the purpose from the university in 1753 by the printer and book dealer Robert Foulis (1707–1776), whose journeys to France to acquire books also provided opportunities to buy paintings appropriate for a study collection (Fig. 2). Students copied paintings as part of their training and copies were sold for profit to the academy's subscribers. For example, when visiting Glasgow in October 1767, the banker James Coutts paid £50 for a copy of the duke of Hamilton's monumental Rubens, *Daniel in the Lions' Den*.[13] Unfortunately the academy was short-lived, but because the director was an articulate correspondent and since printing was his main business, the paintings were well documented at the time of the academy's demise in 1776.

The Hunterian copy can be traced, with certainty, to the middle of the 18th century. It was purchased by the Old College in 1779, three years after the academy had closed.[14] At the time the painting was believed to be one of several original

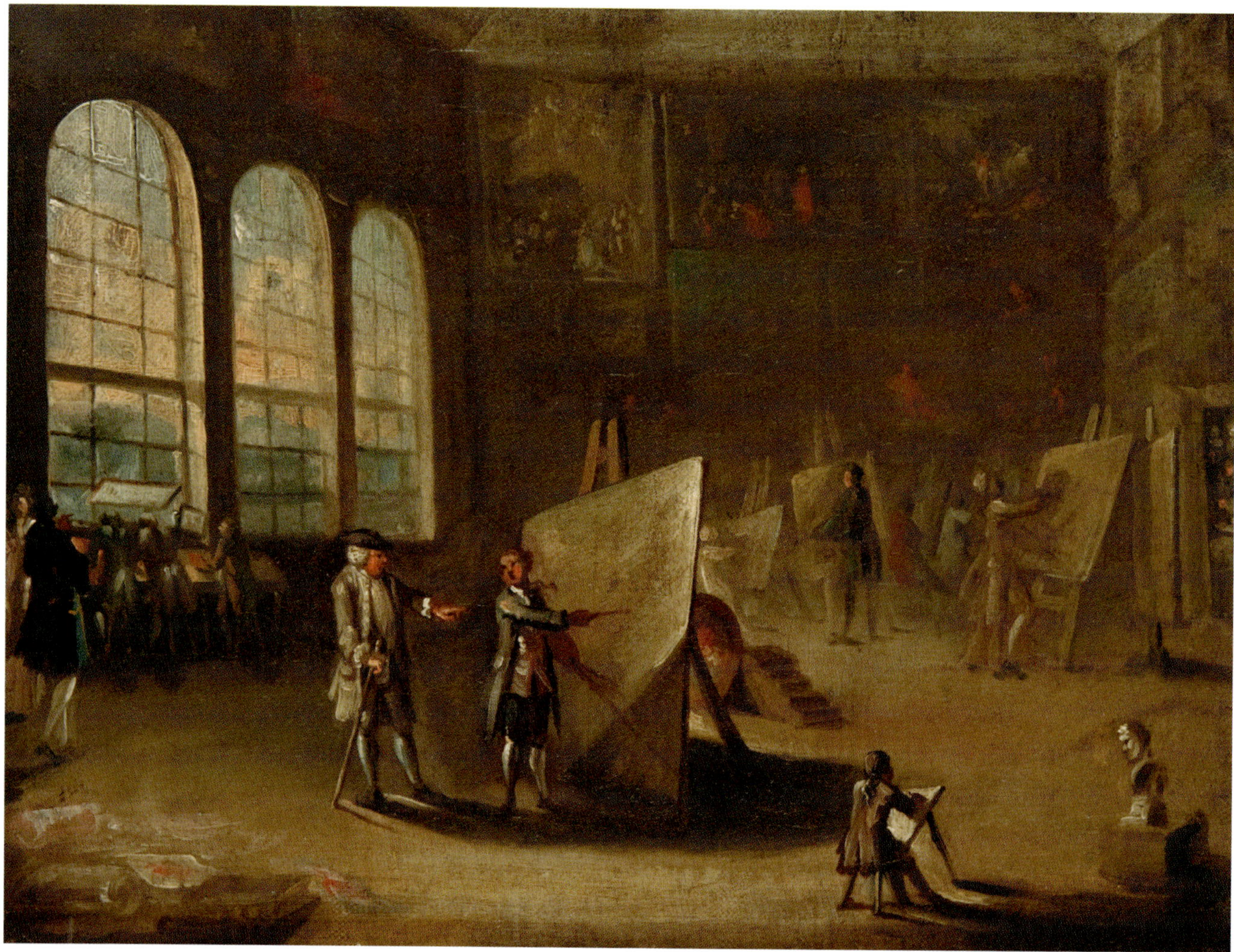

Fig. 2 David Allan, *The Academy of the Fine Arts*, *c.*1761, oil on canvas 36 × 44 cm, The Hunterian Art Gallery, University of Glasgow. In the background, among the paintings on the wall can be made out a copy of Raphael's *Transfiguration* and another of Rubens's *Adoration of the Magi*.

Raphael paintings in the collection, since this is how it was described in the three-volume catalogue that Foulis compiled for an exhibition in London that preceded the insolvency sale: 'An original and most capital picture, in his best colouring and manner; and of which there is no repetition, there being only one done prior to this, said to be rather less than half the size, in the Borghese palace at Rome.'[15] The description includes remarks about literature and reproduction by engraving that imply well-intentioned research into its history: 'It is described by Vasari in his life of Raphael, and by Raphael Borghini; and was engraved by Scalenberg at Paris.'[16] The painting was not listed in Christie's sale of 6–7 December 1776 presumably because it was held back for sale to the university.

The *Entombment* was first recorded in Glasgow in 1754, in the diary of a visiting American churchman, the Reverend Samuel Davies. He visited the Old College and noted that 'The most striking Curiosity I saw was a Collection of Pictures lately imported from France. One was the picture of the dead Body of Xt. Taken off the Cross and carrying to the Sepulchre.'[17] Davies does not tell the whole story, noting only that the paintings had come from France. The collection of which it had been part, however, is mentioned in letters from Robert Foulis to one of the academy's most important subscribers, the Honourable Charles Yorke (1722–1770), who was lord chancellor. Writing in 1758, about a painting that he had sold to Yorke's father, Philip, first earl of Hardwicke, Foulis insinuates the name of the former owner: 'The picture of the Virgin, Jesus, St John & an Angel in Lord Hardwicke's possession was painted by Leonardo da Vinci. I had the original with several others from a very old gentleman, whose father I was told by his friend, was a secretary of Cardinal de Richelieu's.'[18] The glamorous story of acquiring pictures connected with Cardinal de Richelieu was obviously one that Foulis loved to relate, since it is repeated in another letter to Yorke of 21 October 1762, making more concrete the connection with Richelieu: 'I had the good fortune to meet with some capital Pictures formerly the property of Cardinal Richelieu which were purchas'd at his sale by his Secretary.'[19]

If there were any such thing as an inventory of Richelieu's vast and important art collections it would be a simple matter to check Foulis's fascinating tale that his best paintings had belonged to the cardinal. In proportion to the sheer wealth of art that Richelieu acquired, the paucity of information about the contents of his many châteaux is extraordinarily disappointing.[20] There is no question that he owned some of the greatest paintings by Raphael, not to mention Mantegna and Leonardo. Not only did he have superb original works, but the inventories, such as they are, show that he also owned copies of major works such as the *Transfiguration*.

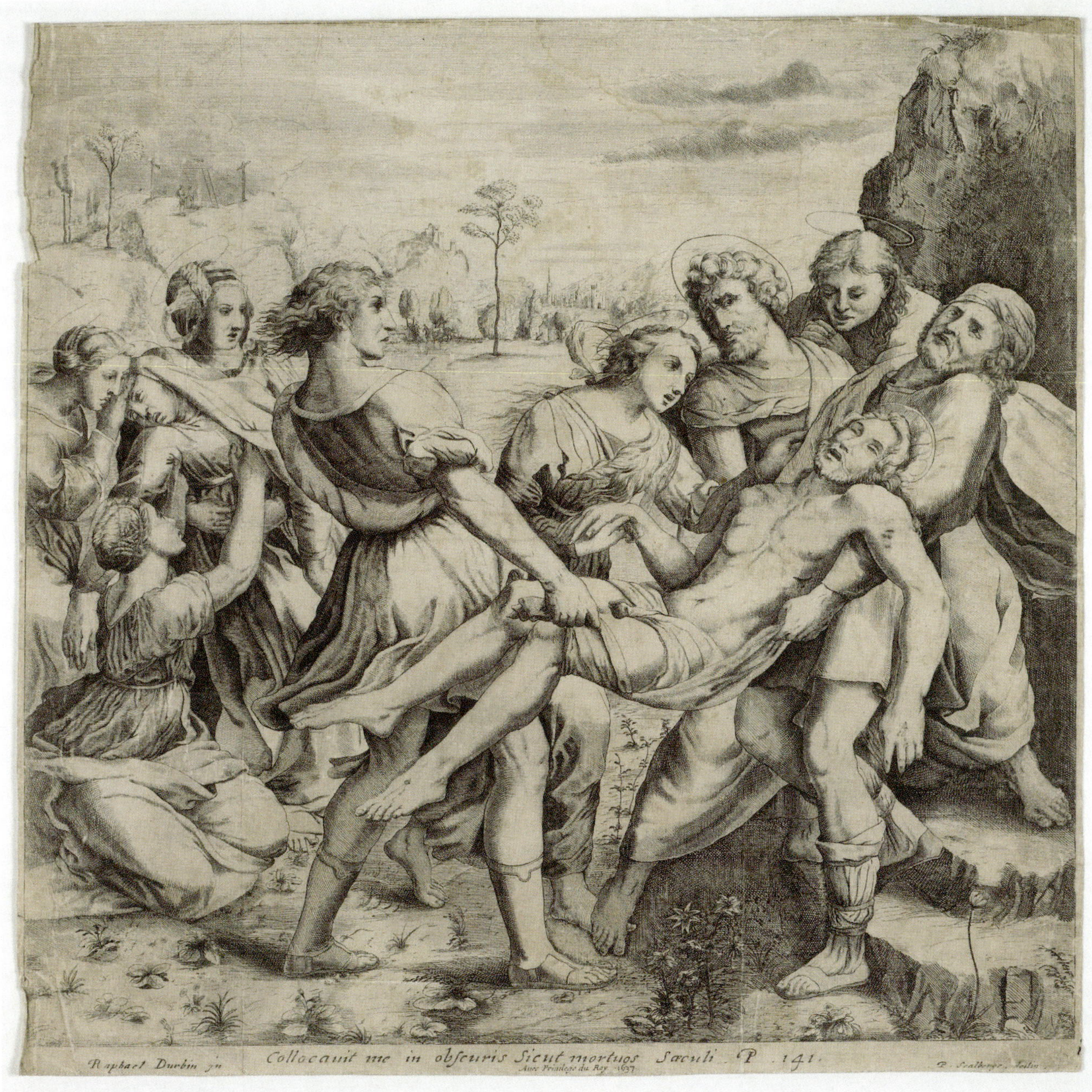

Fig. 3 Pierre Scalberge, *Entombment, after Raphael*, 1637, unfinished state (?) etching and engraving, 409 × 410 mm. Lettered with production detail: 'Raphael Durbin in (...) P. Scalberge dellin' (date and quotation in Latin). (© Trustees of the British Museum.)

Suffice it to say that no documentary record has yet been found that firmly connects the Glasgow *Entombment* with Richelieu. Visual documentation exists, however, which may cautiously be connected with the Glasgow painting. In his catalogue description of the painting, given above, Foulis mentioned a print by the French engraver and painter Pierre Scalberge (1592–1640) that reproduces the painting (Fig. 3).[21] It is not possible to state for certain whether it reproduces the Glasgow painting when it was in a French collection, or Raphael's original in Rome, although it is not known if Scalberge ever visited Rome. What can be said with certainty is that this visual document, made in France and dated 1637, places Scalberge in front of a painting of Raphael's *Entombment*, and possibly this was the Glasgow copy. A small amount of information on how he worked can be gleaned from the inscriptions of his prints, a number of which are opportunistically made reproductions of paintings in important French collections, including those of relatives of Cardinal de Richelieu. Selling such reproductions would have been a useful way of supplementing his income. This possible link with the Glasgow painting can be strengthened by consulting what the contemporary historian Félibien says in his *Entretiens* (1666–1668) about Scalberge's master, Simon Vouet. Félibien's account places Scalberge, with Vouet, at Richelieu's Château de Rueil, where the cardinal kept his favourite paintings. Talking about Vouet's reputation with the king, he states: 'The Ministers & the greatest lords of the kingdom, wished to have something of his hand. In 1632 he began to paint for Cardinal Richelieu, the gallery & the Chapel of his Palace in Paris, and a chapel in his house.' Going

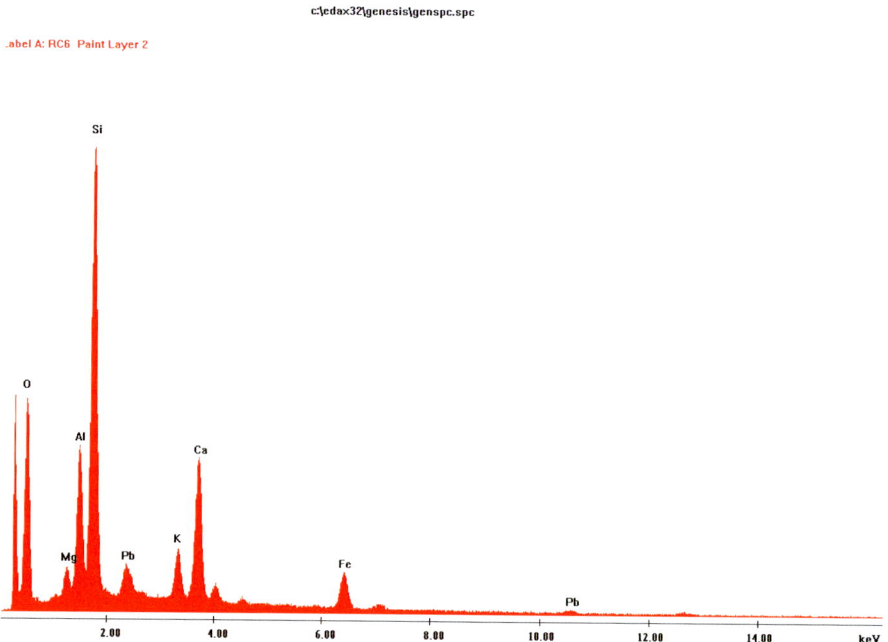

Fig. 4 SEM-EDX spectrum of the reddish-brown ground layer indicating the high silicon content.

on to mention the many decorative schemes in which Vouet was engaged, Félibien names Scalberge among the painters who assisted him: 'Juste d'Egmont & Vandrisse, Flamans; Scalberge, Pastel, Belin, Vanboucle, Bellange, Cotelle'.[22]

The starting point of this section on provenance is della Pergola's list of copies of Raphael's *Entombment*. This also includes a copy in France that was judged to be a 17th-century work by Passavant;[23] it was then in Caen and is now in the Musée des Beaux-Arts, Dôle.[24] At 101 × 101 cm it is about half the size of the original. Nonetheless, this smaller version has certain features in common with the Glasgow copy. For example, neither this painting nor the engraving by Scalberge reproduce the signature and date 'RAPHAEL. VRBINAS. M.D.VII', which appear in Raphael's panel on the stone step below left. Also, some interesting colour observations can be made. In the Glasgow painting the tunic of the young man who supports Christ by his knees, which is bright green in the original, appears as almost black in the Hunterian copy. The Dôle painting seems to repeat this, as was noticed by Passavant (1860).[25] Of course this could be an actual change caused by the materials used, however, it seems more likely that the dark tone was repeated at face value and may therefore have been copied from the Glasgow painting. Similarly the rather greyish stockings of the figure on the left, which are yellow in the original, are also rather greyish in the Dôle copy.[26]

Further research may confirm the Dôle copy to be a version based on the Glasgow painting rather than the original in Rome. It is therefore possible that both the Dôle painting and Scalberge's engraving record the Glasgow painting's presence in France in 1637. Certainly, these two French works taken together appear to strengthen the admittedly thin case made by Foulis in his correspondence that some of his best Italian paintings came from the collection of Cardinal de Richelieu.

Technical research

Painting technique

Research into the provenance of the Hunterian copy has shown that the assumed 18th-century date of origin should be reconsidered, as its extended provenance makes a 17th-century date plausible. Technical research was performed to gain insights into the materials and techniques used to find more evidence supporting or indeed contradicting an earlier date as well as an Italian origin.

Ground

Raphael's original composition is painted on panel and would have had a white preparation. In common with his other early works, a thin off-white *imprimatura* of lead white combined with lead-tin yellow would have been applied over the gesso ground.[27] By contrast, the Hunterian *Entombment* is painted on canvas and was prepared with a single layer of a rather dark ground, applied directly on the sized canvas, consisting of a silicon-rich mixture of earth pigments combined with small amounts of calcium carbonate and a few dark inclusions (Fig. 4). Dark reddish-brown grounds such as this, with a typical mixture of earth pigments with lead white and chalk sometimes added, were increasingly common in early 17th-century Italian painting.[28] Similar grounds are observed in paintings by, for example, Guido Reni, Guercino and Caravaggio. The latter used a dark ground of mixed earths and calcium carbonate, a little lead white and carbon black for *Salome Receiving the Head of John the Baptist* (London, The National Gallery, 1607–10, oil on canvas, 91.5 × 106.7 cm, NG6389). Here the warm colour of the ground has clearly been exploited, providing a mid-tone in much of the painting of flesh and hair. The ground would have been slightly veiled with darker paint to provide much of the half shadow in the modelling. The opacity of lighter colours is increased by the dark underlayer, while thinner and more transparent darker paint is given increased depth and luminosity by the ground.[29]

The dark inclusions found in the ground of the Hunterian *Entombment* were analysed by energy dispersive X-ray microanalysis in the scanning electron microscope (SEM-EDX) and found to be rich in sulphur and iron.[30] Such iron and sulphur-rich particles have been identified in the grounds of other paintings including Caravaggio's *Salome Receiving the Head of John the Baptist* c.1607–10 (London, The National Gallery, NG6389), Domenichino's, *Vision of St Jerome* (London, The National Gallery, oil on canvas, 51.1 × 39.8 cm, NG85) painted before 1603, and in *A Bearded Man Holding a Lamp* after Guercino *c.*1617–64 (London, The National Gallery, oil on canvas, 119.7 × 85.1 cm, NG5537). These particles are a black iron sulphide likely to be present as a natural mineral impurity of the earth pigments in the ground layer. However, there have been some indications that iron sulphide (naturally occurring pyrite) and a black iron oxide were used as actual black pigments.[31] Further detailed analysis is needed to establish the exact nature of the black inclusions.

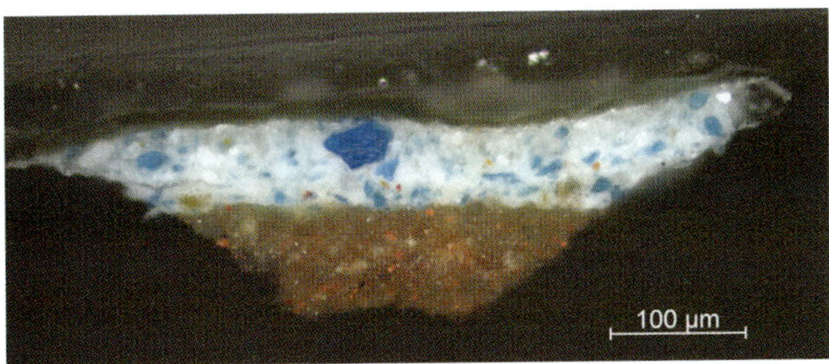

Fig. 5 Cross-section taken in the sky. The blue is applied in two layers on the reddish-brown ground, with the highest quality of azurite limited to the top layer. See also the presence of malachite and cuprite particles in the azurite and lead white mixture.

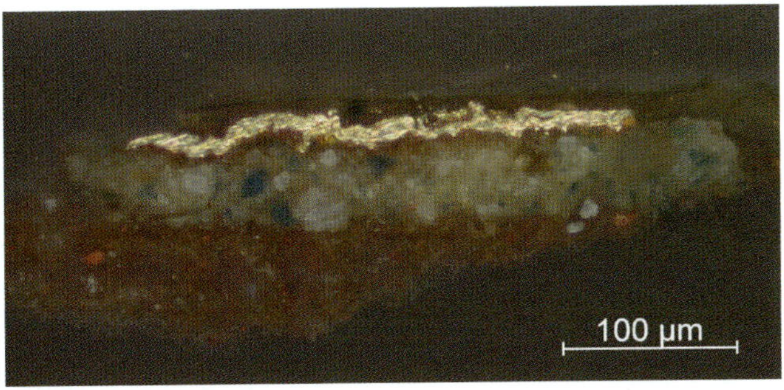

Fig. 6 Cross-section from the halo of the woman on the right behind Mary. The gold leaf was applied with an oil mordant on top of the background colour.

Palette

SEM-EDX analysis confirmed the presence of azurite, malachite, green earth, vermilion, red lake, red earth, lead-tin yellow, yellow earth, lead white, gold leaf and what appears to be the remains of a yellow lake pigment. This palette is typical for 17th-century Italian painting, though one might also have expected to see some ultramarine, red lead, smalt or indigo. The identification of azurite in the Hunterian *Entombment* is especially significant for its possible date, as azurite became scarce during the 17th century, principally in the second half. This and the high cost of ultramarine meant that smalt and indigo, neither of which is present in the Hunterian *Entombment*, were increasingly used in the late 17th century.[32] To extend the more expensive pigment, azurite was sometimes scumbled over other cheaper and more readily available blues such as indigo or smalt. However, in this instance, azurite was employed on its own, and in large quantities. Yet here too, economic factors were considered, as rather than using a cheaper pigment beneath the mineral blue, in a number of samples an underpaint of azurite combined with lead white was found, with the largest, darkest and thus most expensive blue particles of azurite reserved for the uppermost layer (Fig. 5). Such extensive use of high quality azurite, the only blue identified in the painting, is indicative of an early to mid-17th-century date.

A sample from the remnants of the gold halo of the woman behind Mary shows gold leaf (8 µm thick but clearly folded over and thus in multiple layers in some places) applied with an oil mordant over azurite combined with lead-tin yellow, lead white, a few particles of yellow earth and a large particle of burnt green earth (Fig. 6).

The presence of lead-tin yellow was confirmed by SEM-EDX analysis. There are two types of lead-tin yellow and the particle characteristics and conspicuous lack of silicon in samples taken from the Hunterian *Entombment* suggest the presence of lead-tin yellow type 1. This northern European synthetic yellow pigment was commonly employed by 17th-century painters but disappeared from the palettes of artists all over Europe by the early 18th century.[33] In addition to its use in mixed greens, the pigment was often combined with lead white to produce a beautiful luminous pale yellow colour such as that seen in the drapery of the male figure behind Christ.

Interestingly, malachite (identified by Fourier transform infrared (FTIR) spectroscopy) was extensively present, for example in the tunic of the male figure to the right of Christ. This drapery, which in the original *Entombment* is green, in the Hunterian copy appears almost black. SEM-EDX examination of the paint sample revealed a rich green paint layer consisting of malachite with a few inclusions of lead white and lead-tin yellow, applied over a dark green of azurite combined with yellow earth and carbon black. The medium in the green upper layer appears to have darkened which together with the surface accretions of dirt, a sulphated crust and varnish layers make this area now appear black.[34]

There are further inconsistencies in colour between the original and the Hunterian copy. For example, in the original, Nicodemus' stockings are yellow with red straps, while in the Hunterian copy they are a pale grey with red straps (Fig. 7). Analysis suggested that this discrepancy may be due to the fading of a yellow lake pigment. Large

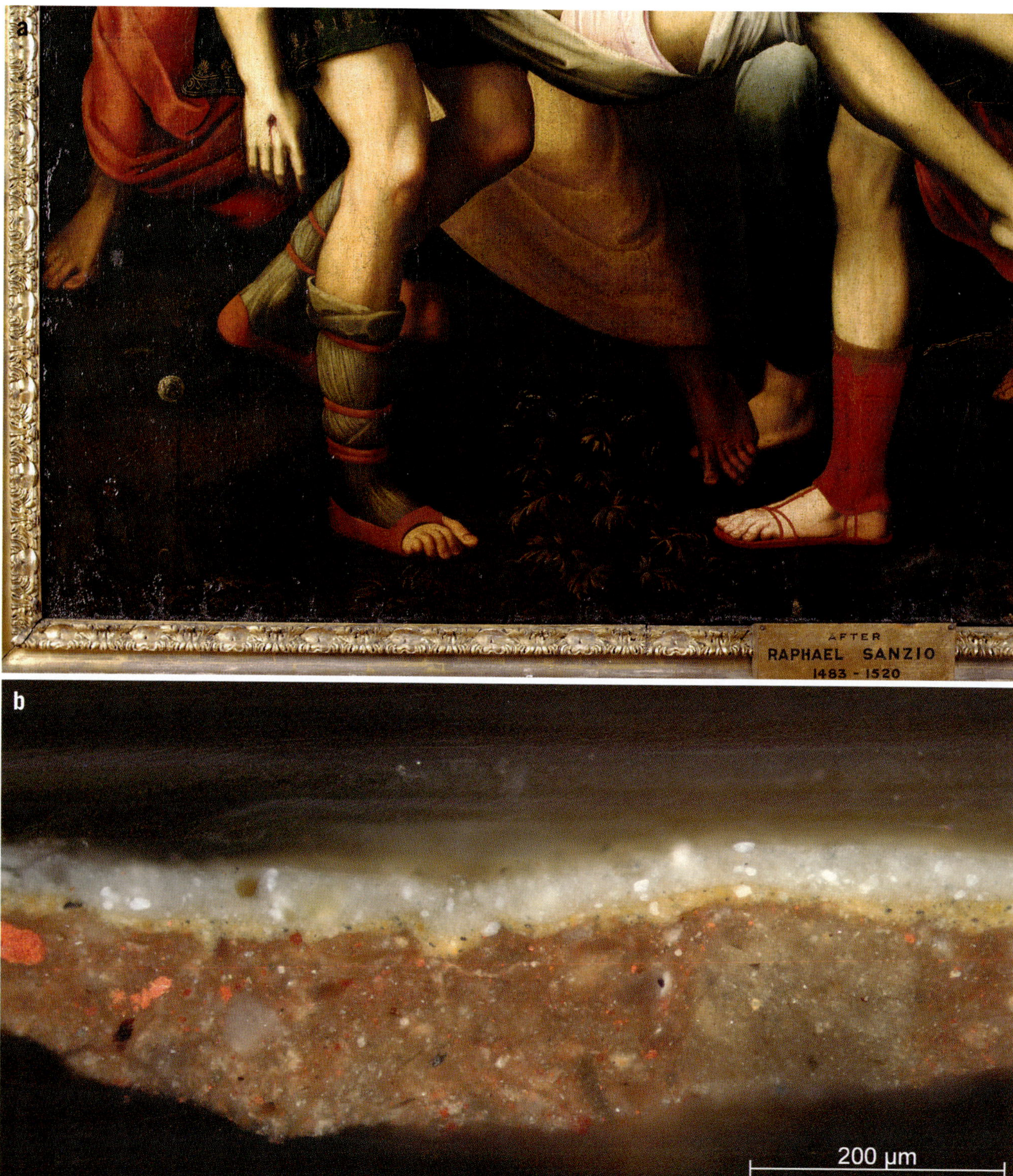

Fig. 7 (a) Detail of the discoloured stockings of the figure carrying Christ on the left. In the original the stockings are a warm yellow. (b) Cross-section of the grey coloured stockings of the figure carrying Christ on the left. The top layer contains lead white and chalk, the latter with some remnants of yellow visible. The chalk was most likely the substrate for a yellow lake. The slightly brownish particles are a green earth, possible a burnt green earth. This yellow layer was applied over a layer containing lead white, yellow earth and black.

translucent inclusions in the layer were found by SEM-EDX to be principally calcium, which may be the chalk substrate of a yellow lake, now faded. The translucent yellow brown particles also present were identified as green earth, possibly a burnt green earth pigment.[35] In addition, the garment of the woman on the right side now appears blue but was originally a purple colour. Examination of a paint sample from this area confirmed the presence of azurite combined with red lake and lead white, applied over a pink underpaint of lead white with red lake. The red lake pigment has faded substantially in both layers, resulting in an overall bluish colour.

Conclusions

If a painting has no signature or date that records authentically what it is, knowing its history helps a great deal in establishing its authorship. With paintings over 200 years old, we often know little and sometimes nothing at all about a work's early history, so even fragmentary records of its passage through time can be very helpful. Analysing the materials and methods used may also provide markers that support specific periods and locations in which the painting could have been made. The Hunterian *Entombment* was considered for a long time to be an 18th-century copy, used as a model for copying by students of the Glasgow Academy of the Fine Arts. However, its quality rewarded further investigation and both its provenance history and technical research make an earlier date in the first decade of the 17th century plausible; a time when such copies, and especially those made with 'extreme diligence' were valued as art-historical documents.

The ground layer and the palette found for the making of the Hunterian *Entombment* correspond with what is known of early 17th-century Italian painting. The technical evidence and its provenance history do not rule out a possible connection with the missing Lanfranco copy. More research, and especially a thorough comparison of materials and techniques used in documented Lanfranco works may shed further light on this.

To date, without a firm record of a painting of the Entombment by Raphael in the Richelieu collections it is not possible to construct any hypothesis about the route by which the painting might have arrived from Rome. Taken together, however, the insights gathered from provenance research and the technical investigation do make possible the unlikely sounding tale recorded by Robert Foulis that his best pictures came from the collection of 'a very old gentleman, whose father I was told by his friend, was a secretary of Cardinal Richelieu's'.

Notes

1. This research was made possible by a British Academy Grant (SG 37467). We are extremely grateful to the British Academy for its support.
2. P. Van der Brink (ed.), *Brueghel Enterprises*, exh. cat. (Bonnefantenmuseum, Maastricht, 13 October 2001–17 February 2002; Musées Royaux des Beaux-Arts de Belgique, Brussels, 22 March–23 June 2002), Amsterdam/Ghent, Ludion, 2001.
3. See E. Hermens (ed.), *On the Trail of Bosch and Bruegel: Four Paintings under Cross-examination*, London, Archetype Publications, 2012. The book presents the results from an EU Culture Fund, Strand 1.2.1 funded collaborative research project between the Kadriorg Art Museum (Tallinn, Estonia), The National Gallery of Denmark (Copenhagen) and the University of Glasgow with Glasgow Life.
4. C. Robertson, *Il Gran Cardinale: Alessandro Farnese Patron of the Arts*, New Haven, CT and London, Yale University Press, 1992, p. 6.
5. G. Gronau, *Documenti artistici Urbinati*, Florence, G.C. Sansoni, 1936, p. 255.
6. G. Mancini, *Considerazioni sulla pittura: pubblicate per la prima volta da Adriana Marucchi con il commento di Luigi Salerno*, Rome, Accademia Nazionale dei Lincei, 1956–1957, p. 327.
7. Ibid.
8. A. Quint Platt, *Cardinal Borromeo as a Patron and a Critic of the Arts and his Musaeum of 1625*, New York, Taylor & Francis, 1986, pp. 232–233.
9. Turin, Pinacoteca, no. 122 (according to della Pergola 1959 (cited in note 11)). The painting was in Milan when mentioned by Passavant in *Raphael d'Urbin et son Père Giovanni Santi*, Paris, 1860, vol. 2, p. 61. The Turin painting (oil on canvas) has a distinctive herringbone weave canvas, 173 × 170 cm.
10. Galleria Borghese, *I dipinti*, Rome, 1959, vol. II, pp. 117–121. For an account of Raphael's altarpieces in Perugia, see D. Cooper, 'Raphael's altar-pieces in S. Francesco al Prato, Perugia: patronage, setting and function', *The Burlington Magazine* 143(1182), 2001, pp. 554–561.
11. P. della Pergola, *Galleria Borghese: I dipinti*, Rome, 1959, vol. II, p. 213.
12. B. Orsini, *Guida al forestiere per l'augusta città di Perugia*, Perugia, 1784, pp. 303–304: 'Sopra all' altra porta corrispondente, è il quadro con Gesù morto portato al sepolcro. È un' esatta copia fatta dal Cav. D'Arpino d'all originale di Raffaello, che essisteva in questa medesima chiesa.' The earliest reference to the copy by Cavaliere d'Arpino is in O. Lancellotti, *Scorta Sacra*, fol. 320r, mss. B.4-B.5, Bibl. Augusta, Perugia, before 1676: H. Chapman, T. Henry and C. Plazzotta, *Raphael: From Urbino to Rome*, London, National Gallery, 2004, pp. 206–208.
13. R. Duncan, *Notices and Documents Illustrative of the Literary History of Glasgow*, Glasgow, 1831, p. 85, quoting Fleming's diary. Copies are listed for sale, with prices in R. Foulis, *A catalogue of pictures, drawings, prints, statues and busts in plaister of Paris, done at the Academy in the University of Glasgow*, Glasgow, 1758.
14. Glasgow College Faculty Minutes, 17 May 1779. It was purchased, together with the painting of the *Martyrdom of St Catherine* by Cossiers, for £50, 'by a friend for this college'.
15. R. Foulis, *A catalogue of pictures, composed and painted chiefly by the most admired Masters of the Roman, Florentine, Parman, Bolognese, Venetian, Flemish, and French schools ... Illustrated by descriptions, and critical remarks* ... London, 1776, vol. 1, pp. 93–143.
16. Ibid., p. 109.
17. G.W. Pilcher, *The Reverend Samuel Davies Abroad: The Diary of a Journey to England and Scotland, 1753–55*, Chicago, University of Chicago Press, 1967, pp. 101–102.
18. British Library, Add MS 35635 letter to the Hon. Charles Yorke (1722–1770), Lord Chancellor, 13 September 1758.
19. British Library, Add MS 35636.
20. Lizzie Boubli, in *Richelieu et le monde de l'esprit* (Sorbonne, Paris, Imprimerie nationale, 1985, p. 103) states: 'Dans ses diverses demeures, Richelieu avait constitué des cabinets de peintures, en particulier dans les appartements réservés au roi et à la reine. Mais de Rueil, de Bois-le-Viscomte, de Limours et d'autres résidences du cardinal, il n'existe aucune description précise.'
21. R. Dumensnil, *Le peintre-graveur français*, Paris, 1838, no. 5.
22. A. Félibien, *Entretiens sur les vies et sur les ouvrages des plus excellents peintres anciens et modernes*, Geneva, Minkoff, 1972, vol. IV, pp. 83–84.
23. Passavant 1860 (cited in note 9), vol. 2, p. 61.
24. Inv. 2004.0.7.
25. Passavant 1860 (cited in note 9), vol. 2, p. 61.
26. The painting in Dôle has not been inspected and is only known from a poor jpeg image on the French government database Joconde: www.culture.gouv.fr/documentation/joconde/fr/pres.htm.

27. Six paintings by Raphael in the National Gallery collection in London have this type of priming. See M. Spring, 'Raphael's materials: some new discoveries and their context within early sixteenth-century painting', in A. Roy and M. Spring (eds), *Raphael's Painting Technique: Working Practices before Rome*, Florence, Nardini Editore, 2007, pp. 77–86; and J. Dunkerton and M. Spring, 'The development of painting on coloured surfaces in sixteenth-century Italy', in A. Roy and P. Smith (eds), *Painting Techniques, History and Studio Practice*, London, IIC, 1998, pp. 120–130.
28. A.R. Duval, 'Les enduits de préparation des tableaux de Nicolas Poussin', *Techne* 1, 1994, pp. 35–43. Also M. Witlox, 'Grounds 1400–1900', in J. Hill Stoner and R. Rushfield (eds), *Conservation of Easel Paintings*, Abingdon/New York, Routledge, 2012, pp. 161–188, p. 173.
29. L. Keith, 'Three paintings by Caravaggio', *National Gallery Technical Bulletin* 19, 1998, pp. 45–47. Cleaning of the Hunterian *Entombment* may reveal a similar sophistication in the exploitation of the dark ground layer.
30. Analysis was undertaken with a Zeiss Evo MA10 variable pressure SEM with an Oxford X-max (80mm^2) EDX detector.
31. M. Spring, R. Grout and R. White, '"Black earths": a study of unusual black and dark grey pigments used by artists in the sixteenth century', *National Gallery Technical Bulletin* 24, 2003, pp. 96–114.
32. Hungary was the main source until the mid-17th century when the country was invaded by the Turks and the supply severely disrupted. See J. Kirby, 'The painter's trade in the seventeenth century: theory and practice. Painting in Antwerp and London: Rubens and Van Dyck', *National Gallery Technical Bulletin* 20, 1999, pp. 35–37; N. Costaras, 'Early modern blues: the smalt patent in context', in J. Kirby, S. Nash and J. Cannon (eds), *Trade in Artists' Materials: Markets and Commerce in Europe to 1700*, London, Archetype Publications, 2010, pp. 401–414, p. 405; R. Harley, *Artists' Pigments c. 1600–1835: A Study in English Documentary Sources*, London, Archetype Publications, 2001, p. 47.
33. See Roy and Smith 1998 (cited in note 27) and H. Kühn, 'Lead-tin yellow', in A. Roy (ed.) *Artists' Pigments: A Handbook of their History and Characteristics*, Washington, DC, National Gallery of Art, 1993, vol. II, pp. 83–112.
34. J. Dunkerton and A. Roy, 'The materials of a group of late fifteenth-century Florentine panel paintings', *National Gallery Technical Bulletin* 17, 1996, pp. 20–31. Further analysis is needed to establish the exact cause of the dark appearance of the green areas.
35. Because of the absorbency of the clay mineral, green earths were sometimes used as a substrate for dyes, particularly in the preparation of lakes with more intense shades of green. See A.C. Grissom, 'Green earth', in R.L. Feller (ed.) *Artists' Pigments: A Handbook of their History and Characteristics*, Washington, DC, National Gallery of Art and Cambridge University Press, 1986, vol. I, pp. 141–169.

Authors' addresses

- Peter Black, Hunterian Art Gallery, University of Glasgow, Glasgow, UK (Peter.Black@glasgow.ac.uk)
- Erma Hermens, History of Art, School for Culture and Creative Arts, College of Arts, University of Glasgow, Glasgow, UK (Erma.Hermens@glasgow.ac.uk)
- Helen Howard, Scientific Department, The National Gallery, London, UK (Helen.Howard@ng-london.org.uk)

MATERIALS AS MARKERS: HOW USEFUL ARE DISTINCTIVE MATERIALS AS INDICATORS OF MASTER OR COPYIST?

Libby Sheldon and Gabriella Macaro

ABSTRACT The identification of distinctive painting materials (pigments, grounds and supports etc.) as well as the particular handling of these materials can sometimes indicate a marker for a specific school or workshop. Moreover, the absence of such markers can suggest a follower or copyist at work. This paper discusses how far the discovery of unusual materials or techniques can help to define the difference between products of a workshop or those of a copyist; and it questions how reliable the initial finding of a material, such as vivianite, has been in the past. Based largely on surface microscopy, and analysis of pigments and paint cross-sections, this study has examined a variety of 16th- and 17th-century paintings associated with such artists as Holbein, Lavinia Fontana and Titian, in addition to past and current research on Cuyp, all of which has provided useful evidence on the issue of markers.

Introduction

Recent investigations into the materials of artists have unearthed some exciting findings. This paper argues not only that the identification of distinctive materials in paintings can prove useful as markers of workshops – such a premise has long been accepted – but also that the manner in which such materials have been employed can lead to a pattern of practice and provide evidence of the work of a master, follower or copyist. A selection of cases to substantiate this argument is presented together with cautionary tales about the pitfalls of first reactions on the discovery of an apparently idiosyncratic material. The methodology of research is important in determining the outcome, and needs to be taken into account when looking for clues about whether materials can be used as markers.

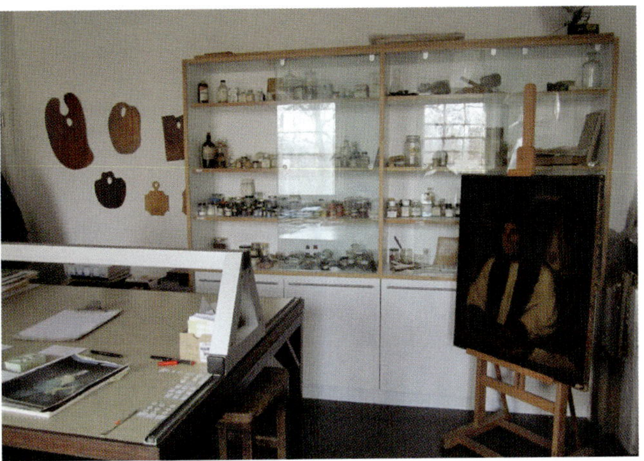

Fig. 1 The laboratory at UCL with the *William Warham* copy on an easel. (Photo: the author.)

One of the most common ways for pupils to train as artists was to copy their masters and masters they admired, and to copy and emulate past masters. At the beginning of the 15th century, Cennino Cennini's advice to aspiring artists was to 'take pains and pleasure in constantly copying the best things which you can find done by the hand of great masters' and that it would be 'against nature if you do not get some grasp of his style and spirit' in doing so.[1] Cennino's directions lead to the supposition that, in emulating the 'style and spirit', students would also imitate the methods and materials of the master if they were able. Such thorough emulation would make it difficult to distinguish the work of the accomplished apprentice from that of his master.

The same emulation can be seen in the pupils of later masters. Trainees during the 17th century in Rubens' studio had access not only to their master's work and local paintings on view, but to a much broader international selection of paintings. Even later, in the eighteenth and nineteenth centuries,

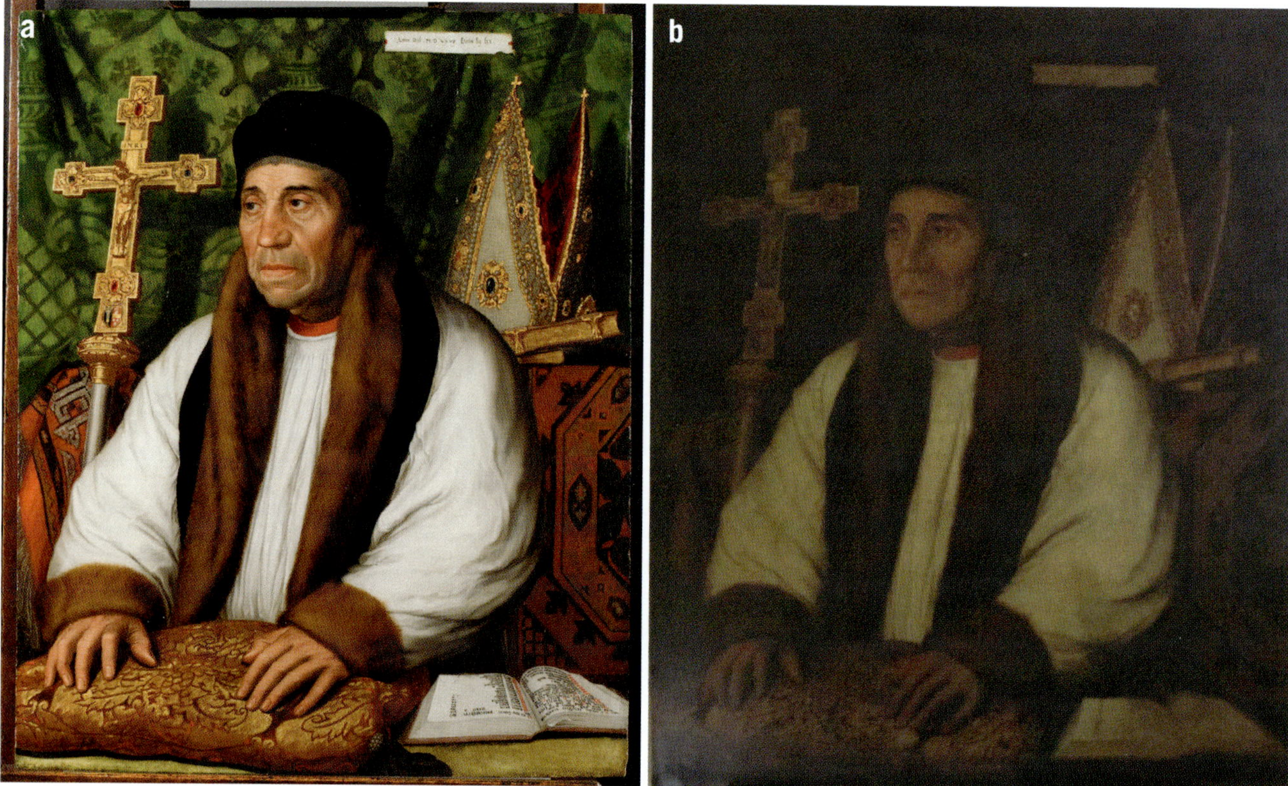

Fig. 2 (a) After Hans Holbein the Younger, *William Warham*, early 17th century, oil on oak panel, 82.2 × 66.3 cm, National Portrait Gallery (NPG 2094); (b) unknown artist, *William Warham*, late 17th century (?), oil on canvas, 87 × 71 cm (Darnley Fine Art).

with the breakdown of the apprenticeship system, young artists made countless painted copies of those works of past masters that they could access, either in private collections or in public galleries. There is a huge raft of paintings executed by later painters in direct imitation of earlier works, and much of this has ended up in the Painting Analysis laboratory (Fig. 1) at University College London (UCL). A frequent function of the lab is to examine the materials to try to differentiate a copy from an original work or a later copy from an earlier copy.

Two 17th-century copies of Holbein portraits

Two recent examples demonstrate the complications of making such distinctions. Hans Holbein has been mentioned in other papers in this volume, and the extraordinary esteem in which his work was held can be judged by the numerous copies made after him in almost all periods. The question prompted by one such painting, executed on canvas and recently submitted for analysis, was how early a replica it might be. It was clearly a copy of Holbein's portrait of *William Warham* (Paris, Musée du Louvre) dated 1527, but when was it executed, under what circumstances and at what date? Would a technical investigation into the materials be able to give us the answer to these questions?

The original portrait by Holbein had been painted on wood. Another later version exists in the National Portrait Gallery (NPG) in London (NPG 2094), the panel support having been dated by dendrochronology as early 17th century, and its colours seem to be in rather better condition than the original, especially the green damask drapery in the background (Fig. 2a). There is also a third version, belonging to Lambeth Palace in London, in which this same green cloth is a dull brown colour. The fact that the copy under examination (Fig. 2b) is on a canvas support immediately suggested a rather later date than the 16th century.[2]

Was this copy imitating the original painting, the NPG version or an even less well-preserved copy? The materials and condition of this copy on canvas was obscured by a heavily discoloured varnish, but analysis of the paint showed that the copied damask cloth did consist of copper green, albeit the artificial type, green verditer. However, the copyist seems to have interpreted the areas of darker green patterning, consisting of pure copper acetate in the earlier versions, as brown, since they are imitated with dark, mixed brown lines over the verditer. Does this provide evidence of the condition of the version that the copyist was replicating?

We can see the varied appearance of the three earlier versions today, and can imagine that chemical changes to the upper layer of copper green (on one of these), or a darkened varnish, or even misguided overpaint, might have added to the distortion of colours in the past. A cross-section of paint from a work of the late 16th century, *Robert Cecil* (NPG 107), gives some idea of the condition of a green that has been overpainted twice (Fig. 3). First the copper green has been retouched with a mixed green of smalt and ochre, and then, presumably with the deterioration of the blue smalt, a much browner retouch followed, perhaps in the 19th century.

With a considerable time lag between a prime painting and a copy, there is less likelihood of the painter being able or willing to employ the same materials or methods as the master painter. An examination of the green drapery behind the sitter of the NPG copy showed that this early 17th-century copyist seems to have been working in a different manner from that of Holbein, laying in darks and lights under a glaze of green in the manner of modelling typical of the later 16th- and early 17th-century painters. Although no firm evidence of date could be found in the materials, the use of verditer for green (rather than easier ways of achieving green in later periods, such as Prussian blue and yellow, viridian etc.), combined with employing an old-fashioned material such as gold leaf are perhaps reasons to suggest a late 17th-century work.

A second copy of a Holbein painting provided firmer evidence of date. A comparison of the brushwork of the NPG's version (NPG 4358) of a Holbein portrait of *Sir Thomas More* (New York, The Frick Collection, 1527, oil on panel) and yet another version of the same portrait (in a private collection) that was well executed, demonstrated the important difference that the use of canvas makes to the quality and manner of brushwork (Fig. 4a and b). The canvas weave disallows the fine delineation of form achieved on the panel by Holbein. However, the pigments in this copy included lead-tin yellow, which was mixed in with the copper green of the curtain, suggesting that it was executed not later than around 1700; while orpiment, also present, on the highlights of the chain, could relate to a possible origin in Italy, where orpiment seems to have been somewhat more common than in northern Europe.[3]

The original version of the Thomas More portrait was painted by Holbein in 1527, and after 1631 it was, for a time, in Rome with the Crescenzi family. Is it possible that the artist of this version copied it from the prime version while it was in Italy, where canvas was more common and red grounds more popular? The artist's purpose in copying the painting is not known, but the portability of canvas might have made the choice of support more suitable at this later date. Interestingly, the NPG version of this painting also has a red preparation, over the white chalk on a limewood panel. Could this be a sign that the privately owned *Thomas More* is imitating this version rather than the original Holbein? Does the combined use of canvas and red ground suggest a date? Those who had travelled abroad may have noted the prevalence of the red preparations used in Italian studios. However, Holbein himself did employ pink *primuersels* much earlier in the century.

With analysis, it has been possible to record patterns of usage and changing palettes, but for a 17th- or 18th-century copyist working in less than ideal circumstances, perhaps from a painting hanging on a wall, it must have been difficult to guess which materials had been used in the original, even if they were available and the copyist was concerned to employ those materials.

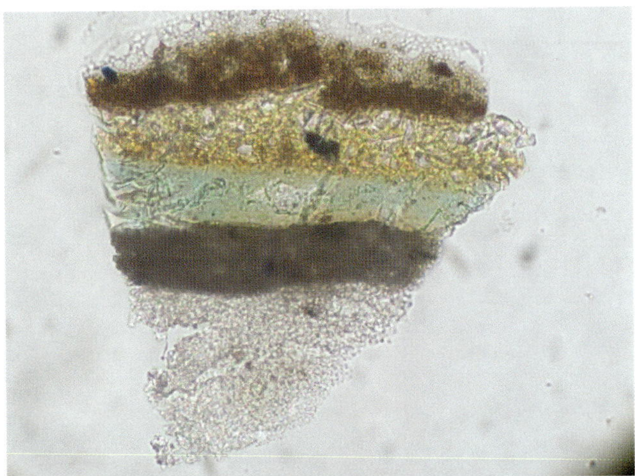

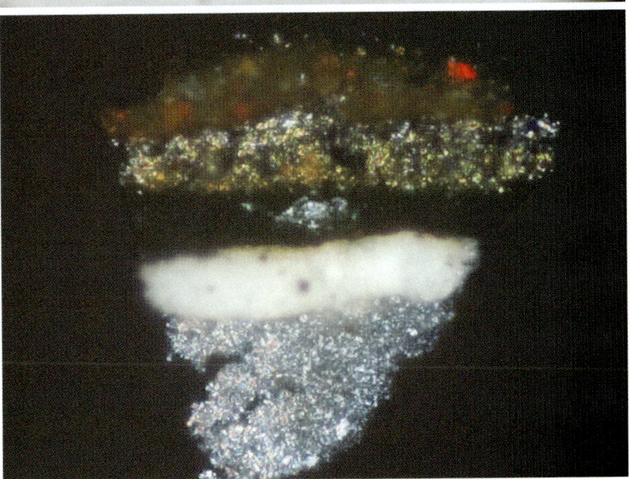

Fig. 3 Thin cross-sections of a copper green paint with two later stages of overpaint: an example of overpaint that might mislead the copyist. Sample from *Robert Cecil* by John de Critz (NPG 107).

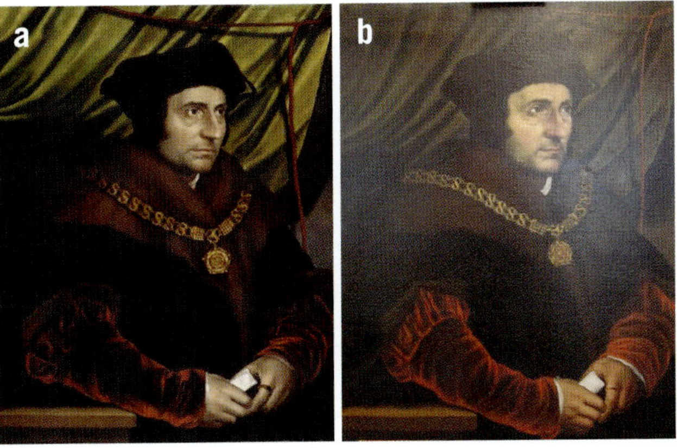

Fig. 4 (a) After Hans Holbein the Younger, *Sir Thomas More*, early 17th century, oil on panel, 74.9 × 58.4 cm, National Portrait Gallery (NPG 4358); (b) unknown artist, *Portrait of Thomas More*, late 17th century, oil on canvas, 71 × 57 cm (Darnley Fine Art).

Distinctive supports

The two examples described above have suggested that a variety of material components might be used to distinguish a later copy from an immediate follower or workshop imitation. Which of the painter's materials are most likely to be useful as secure markers for a workshop or an artist? Dendrochronological analysis allows many oak panels to be given at least approximate dates: the NPG portrait of Warham is now known to date from the 1570s to the 1580s.

Canvas is less easy to date by analytical means, but the unusual weave of a portrait by the Bolognese painter, Lavinia

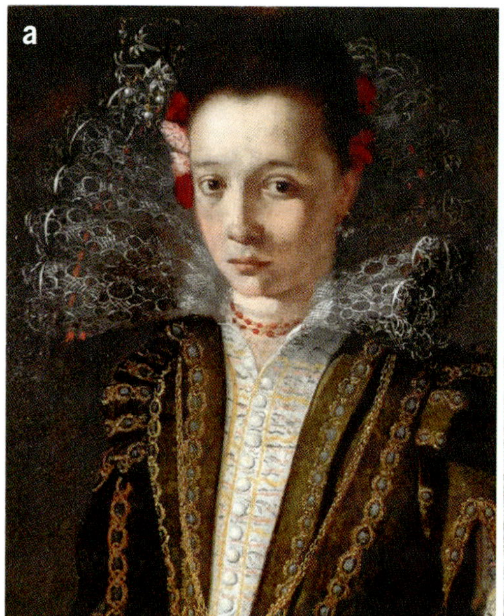

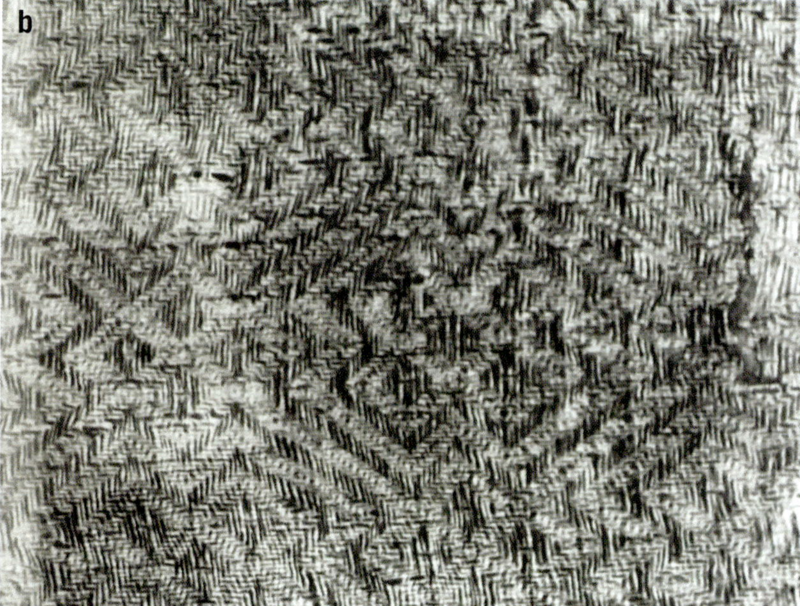

Fig. 5 (a) Lavinia Fontana, *Portrait of a Girl*, 1580s (private owner); (b) detail of the X-radiograph.

Fontana, which dates from the 1580s, may well connect it to a particular location and an approximate date (Fig. 5). The complex diamond-shaped weave of the canvas was obvious both in raking light and X-radiography and showed its unexpected zigzag patterns. A similar weave has been found by Claudio Seccaroni on paintings from both Spain and Italy, related to particular centres of production including Bologna.[4] For example, the same type of distinctive weave has been noted on a number of 16th-century paintings in Italy as well as on at least two works by El Greco and another by Velazquez.[5] Normally used for festive tablecloths, the wonderful sophistication of the weave indicates that it was an expensive cloth of high quality and status.[6] Such remarkable weaves could be said to provide a marker of a prime version of a work by any of these painters.

Ground layers

Aside from these uncommon weaves, it would not have been difficult for a copyist to identify the support of the original, but much harder to assess and imitate the nature of the ground layers. Titian's paintings in the 16th century inspired innumerable copies and pastiches throughout the three centuries that followed. It is often easy for the analyst to recognise 19th-century copies, where a different set of pigments imitated those of the earlier period, but an exacting task to determine whether a painting was made in Titian's workshop, while he was still active, or was an imitation created shortly afterwards. The palette would have changed very little, perhaps only malachite becoming less commonly used in the early 17th century. This is when identification of the preparation layers can sometimes help.

In the 1970s the conservation training at the Courtauld Institute of Art required the partial reconstruction of a painting by Titian. One surviving reconstruction demonstrates the state of knowledge about Titian's preparation layers at this time, when it was believed that the underlying ground on many of his late canvases was a red colour. This supposition had always been based on close inspection of paint surfaces. However, shortly after this imitation was made, Joyce Plesters' research at the National Gallery, London, established that Titian applied a thin layer of gypsum over his canvases rather than the reddish 'ground' that seemed to be visible, particularly on his later works where the coarser canvas weaves have tended to make it more visible.[7] The illusion of redness is created by both the degradation of the glue in the ground and the translucency of the calcium sulphate, so that the combination of darkened glue and the colour of saturated linen gives a reddish orange colour to the preparation.

Two decades later no firm evidence had been found to disprove these findings. A couple of paintings from a private collection, both ostensibly by Titian, were in poor condition and analysed prior to auction to determine whether either might be related to Titian's workshop or were later copies. In cross-section, one painting (*Venus and Adonis*) showed multiple layers of overpaint, but at the very bottom of those layers was the original paint, and underneath that, a gypsum ground.[8] The preparation of the other painting (*Diana and Callisto*) consisted of a double ground, with a reddish ground (mostly red ochre) over the canvas, followed by a grey upper ground: a double layering typical of the 17th century (Fig. 6a and b). Other than the ground layers, there was nothing about the pigments identified in this painting, or indeed its technique or style, to suggest it was not another 16th-century version from Titian's workshop.

Pigments as markers

It is the pigments that probably provide the most important and peculiar markers, signalling a copy or the original, both by their presence or lack of it. Dendrochronology had already confirmed the close relationship of two paintings attributed to the painter, Nicholas Hilliard, when surface examination and sampling took place.[9] An unusually bright, almost modern-looking green could be seen in small quantities in both paintings. It was identified as green verditer, and had been employed for specific parts of the costume or accessories, while verdigris and a mixed green of azurite and ochre were used elsewhere in the paintings. The verditer was certainly part of the original paint, and an odd find in that its known unreliability made it unpopular, perhaps a last resort with most painters in the Tudor-Stuart period.[10]

One of these paintings, *Elizabeth I*, known as *The Pelican Portrait* (Liverpool, Walker Art Gallery, WAG 2994, oil on panel), also showed traces of silver leaf used as highlights on two of the red jewels, one with only minor fragments remaining. It must be assumed that they have been lost from the other red jewels (Fig. 7). It was exciting therefore to find that this rather curious technique of highlighting with silver was also employed on an important late 16th-century painting being conserved by Katherine Ara, *Portrait of Catherine Carey*,[11] a painting which, at the time of analysis, was thought to be by either Peake or Hilliard. These issues relate to straightforward matters of attribution to a workshop, but they are included here since, though verditer and silver were not unusual materials to have in a painter's workshop, the particular *manner* in which they have been employed is certainly uncommon.

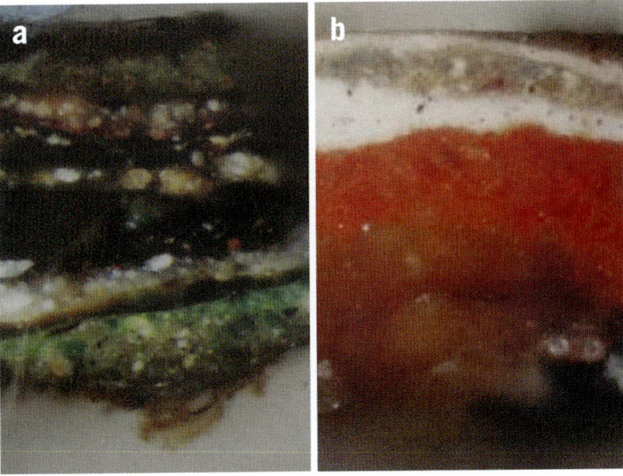

Fig. 6 (a) Cross-section of paint from *Venus and Adonis* attributed to Titian: green of the trees, showing multiple layers and the original paint and ground beneath; (b) cross-section of paint from the yellow bow in *Diana and Callisto*, attributed to Titian, showing a double ground of red earth lower layer and grey upper layer.

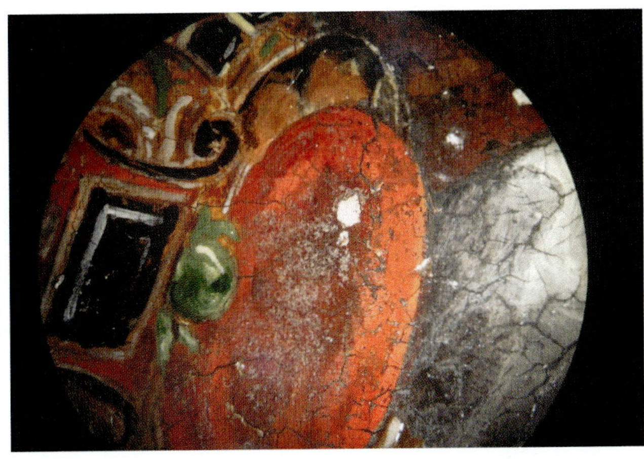

Fig. 7 Nicholas Hilliard, *Elizabeth I* (known as *The Pelican Portrait*), oil on panel, Walker Art Gallery, Liverpool: microphotograph showing traces of silver leaf used as highlights on the ruby on the sleeve.

Success and failure of markers: Vermeer and Cuyp

There were no especially distinctive pigments found in the small painting *Young Woman Seated at a Virginal* (*c*.1670, private collection), which was once a disputed Vermeer thought by many to be a 19th-century pastiche. Lead-tin yellow, vermilion, red lake, green earth and even the expensive ultramarine, for example, were all available and in use to some extent by painters other than Vermeer in Holland. However, the way ultramarine is employed in this little painting for the unimportant chair back and, more importantly, hidden from the naked eye, in the pale wall to the left of the woman's face, is highly distinctive and characteristic of Vermeer (Fig. 8).[12]

Much later, another hidden blue was discovered in a re-examination of the samples obtained from the same painting by Vermeer, several years after the picture had been acquired by a private collection in America.[13] This blue was vivianite, a blue that for a time was associated characteristically with the paintings of another Dutch painter. A current research project at UCL is investigating the materials and techniques of the 17th-century Dordrecht painter, Aelbert Cuyp (Fig. 9). One aim is to determine how far the types of painting materials and techniques of Cuyp and associated Dordrecht artists can be differentiated from each other, and from other contemporary schools of painters, as well as from later imitations. The focus has been mainly on paint and ground structure, pigments and close examination of brushwork using a range of analytical methods.

There has been a great deal of dispute over the years regarding the attribution of many of Cuyp's paintings. The artist's popularity in England from the mid-to-late 18th century onwards led to a great number of copies and imitations of his works being made. Signatures were often added to paintings in the style of Cuyp at a later date, and there have been numerous occasions in which the initials 'A C' have caused confusion since they belong to both Aelbert Cuyp and his pupil Abraham van Calraet. Close stylistic similarities could have been imitated by a copyist through careful study of the surfaces of Cuyp's paintings, such as distinctive facial features (the noses) and idiosyncratic brushstrokes: but observations beneath and within the paint layers would not have been possible for these copyists, and are more likely to provide some informative comparisons.

A significant study of the artist's materials and techniques was conducted at the National Gallery and published in 2001, when 11 of the artist's paintings were examined. At that time,

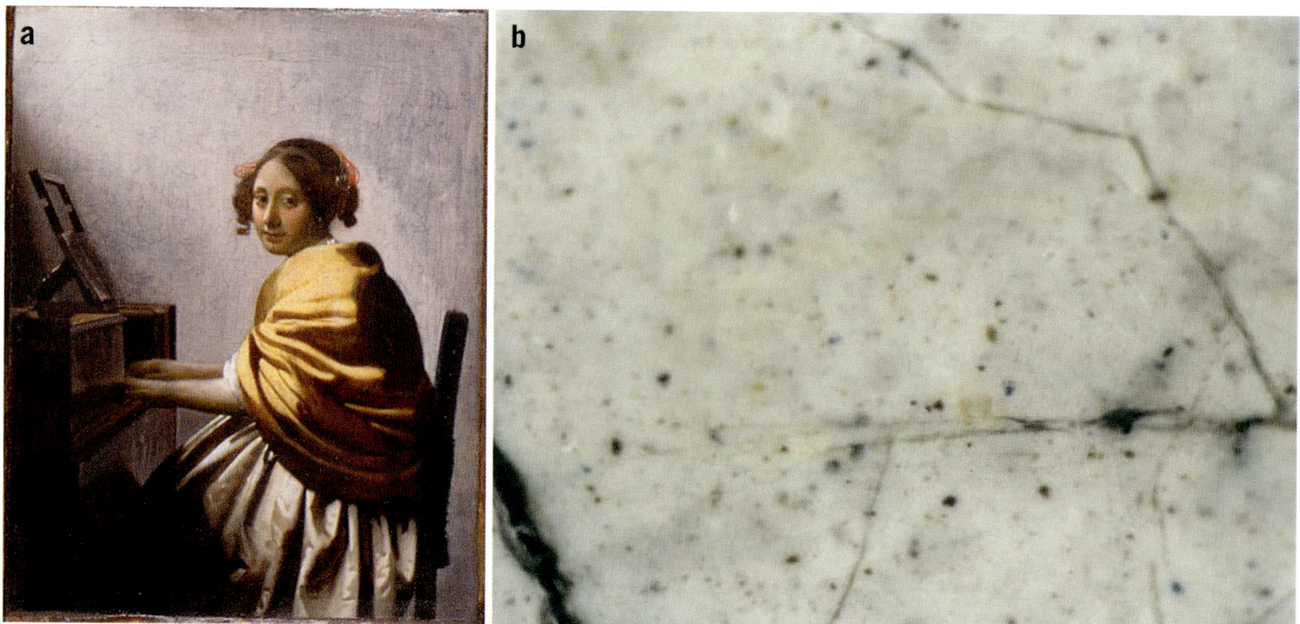

Fig. 8 (a) Johannes Vermeer, *Young Woman Seated at a Virginal*, c.1672, oil on canvas (private collection); (b) blue scattered in the wall next to the face of the woman.

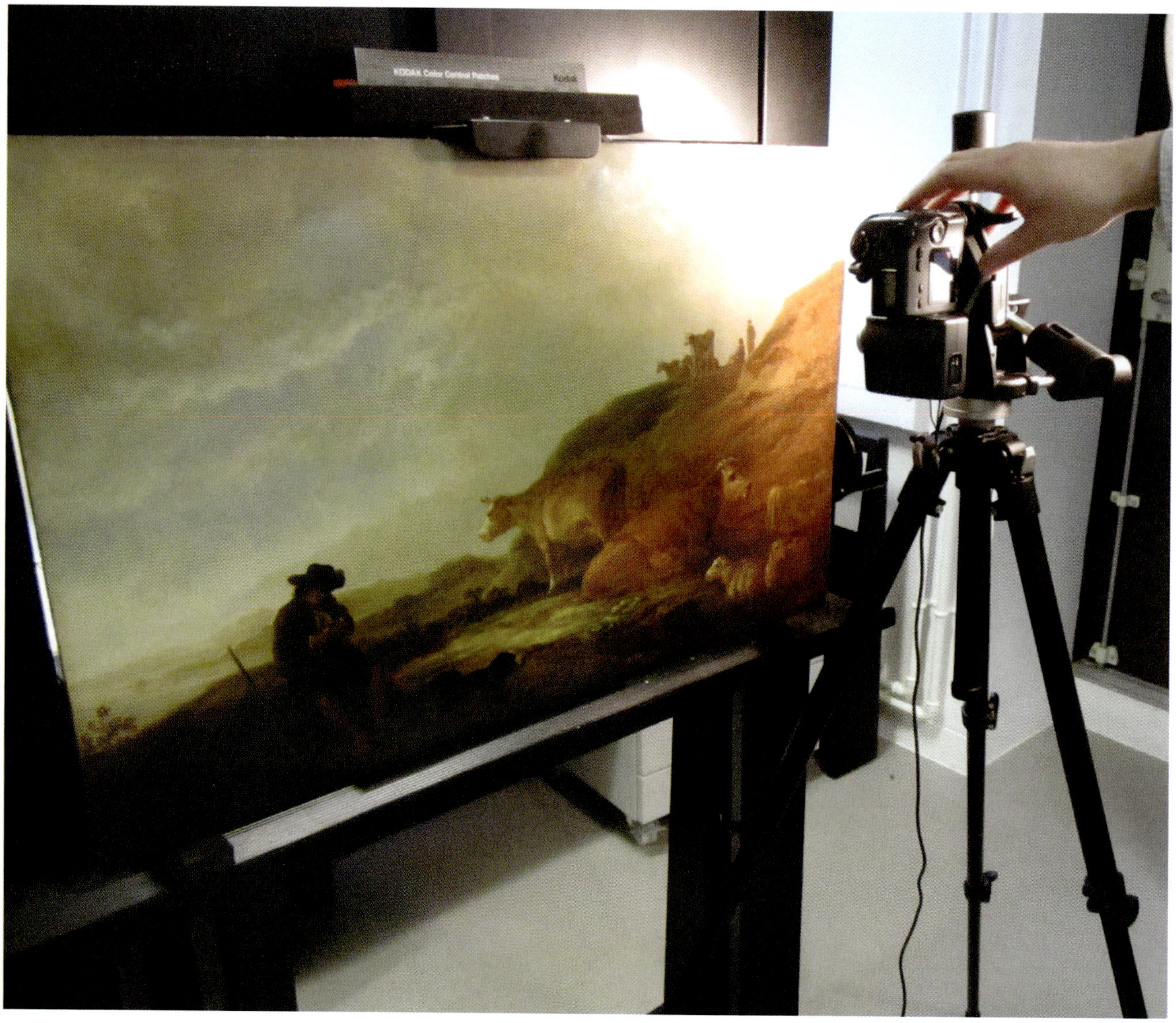

Fig. 9 Technical examination of paintings at the Ashmolean Conservation Laboratory.

Marika Spring made the surprising discovery of the little known pigment, vivianite, in eight of the 11 paintings examined, which suggested that the blue earth pigment (hydrated iron phosphate) could be considered a characteristic 'marker' of Cuyp's works.[14] Deposits of the pigment can be found in peat bog-iron ore, which would be a likely origin for the pigment in Cuyp's works since, as Spring describes, peat was not only abundant in the Netherlands but a very active peat bog was also located near his home town of Dordrecht.[15]

At this stage, vivianite had not been reported on any other Dutch 17th-century paintings and was therefore considered a distinct characteristic of Cuyp's paintings. This is no longer the case. Although the blue earth is a relatively difficult pigment to identify in paint samples, since these initial findings in 2001, various other cases of vivianite have been reported in 17th-century paintings from many different parts of the Netherlands, and elsewhere in Europe.[16] This has highlighted just how difficult it can be to establish characterising inferences about an artist's practices when, so often, the extant technical material is simply not sufficient.

Although still at the initial stages of the project, and with nothing as startling as a marker pigment emerging, some parallels and consistencies in the materials have been found in works studied so far. In the lead white and smalt of all the skies, the smalt is generally of high quality, often including large particles that have retained their bright blue colour. Analysis carried out using scanning electron microscopy with energy dispersive X-ray spectroscopy (SEM-EDX) has confirmed that vivianite is indeed present in some of the most recently examined paintings, predominantly in green and brown paint mixtures of the landscape, but as has been discussed, this may not be as significant as might once have been thought.

A more interesting finding in the landscape paint is the significant proportions of chalk that have been noted in upper paint layer mixtures. Although the chalk could have been added as an extender to the paint mixtures, it is more likely to be the substrate for a yellow lake, the latter having been identified on a number of paint samples from all the works examined. The presence of large proportions of chalk may relate to a yellow lake recipe typical of the period, which involved combining the yellow dye with '100 pounds of chalk

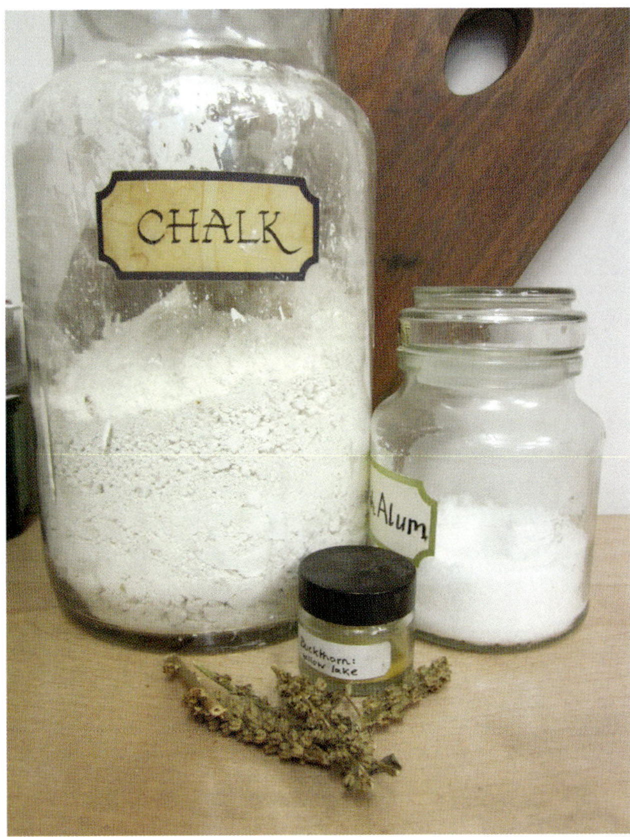

Fig. 10 Components of yellow lake pigment thought to have been used by Cuyp:' Buckthorn berries, weld, yellow wood (old fustic), 100 pounds of chalk and 20 pounds of alum'.

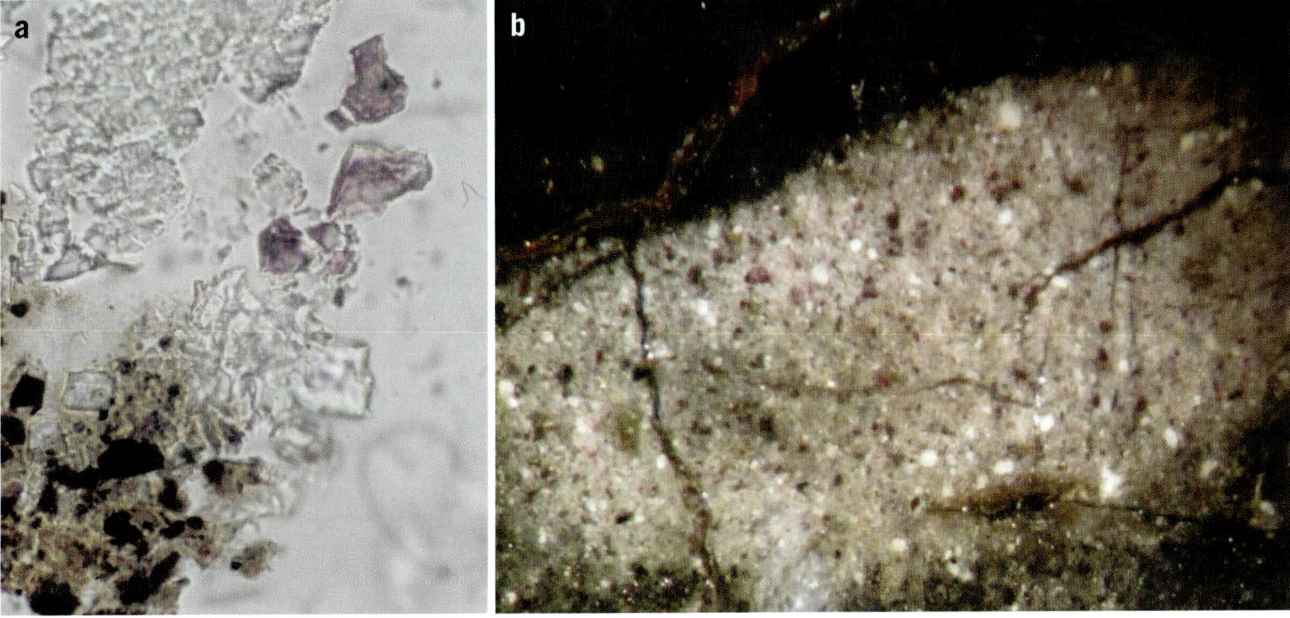

Fig. 11 (a) Dispersion of fluorite found on *Thomas Gresham*, c.1665 (NPG 352); (b) microphotograph of fluorite in lead white on the ruff on the same portrait.

and 20 pounds of alum' (Fig. 10).[17] This lake is only one of several yellows found in the greens of the landscape.

Where other artists might employ one yellow to create a green colour, Cuyp often combines numerous yellow pigments – lead-tin yellow, ochres and lakes – within the same paint mixture. So far, all cross-sections from Cuyp's landscape colours show comparable complex mixtures usually containing varying proportions of the same pigments combined to create subtle changes in hue for greens, yellows and browns. Such complicated paint mixtures may prove just as useful as the pigment 'marker'.

Nevertheless, one of the most exciting finds of the *Making Art in Tudor Britain* project at the NPG was the discovery of another rarely seen pigment: the purple-coloured fluorite. Found initially on a painting dating to the early part of the 16th century, and latterly on two paintings of Thomas Gresham, it is not always easy to identify on paintings from the late 16th century (Fig. 11). However, caution has to be exercised in considering the import of this find. Has it been more widely used than we think? Is the detection of fluorite likely to be a similar story to that of vivianite and will it be identified in many more paintings from different schools and locations?

Conclusions

As with stylistic analysis, a holistic view has to be taken with materials: it is usually the materials and techniques of the whole picture that present researchers with an idea of distinctive painting practice. The use of a particular pigment, ground or support can certainly characterise a workshop, but the manner in which materials have been manipulated and their purpose in the painting is just as likely to allow patterns to emerge. It is through both close studies and the accumulation and dissemination of information that patterns of usage will emerge and give us a better idea of who is copying, replicating or emulating whom.

Notes

1. C. Cennini, *The Craftsman's Handbook: 'Il Libro dell'Arte'*, D.V. Thompson, Jr. (tr.), New York, Dover Publications, 1960, p. 15.
2. English portrait painters in the 16th century seem to have been reluctant to abandon panels as a support and only at the end of the 16th century do canvases begin to come into use.
3. Van Dyck employed orpiment rather than lead-tin yellow while working in Italy on a portrait of a Genoese nobleman. Findings of orpiment on other paintings in his oeuvre have not been published. L. Sheldon, *Portrait of Tomaso Raggi*, Antony Van Dyck (private collection), unpublished painting analysis file no. C1599, UCL, 2001.
4. C. Seccaroni, 'A new survey of Caravaggio's canvases and preparatory layer: materials and aesthetic effects', in *Charisma International Workshop on the Painting Techniques of Caravaggio and his Followers, Florence, 2010*, forthcoming; J.M. Reifsnyder, 'Artist's canvas – or just an old tablecloth?', in *Paintings Techniques, History, Materials and Studio Practice, Summaries of the posters at the Congress of the IIC of Historic and Artistic Works*, Dublin, 1998.
5. C. Hale, 'Dating Velasquez's *Supper at Emmaus*', *Metropolitan Museum Journal* 40, 2005, pp. 67–78; F. Zuccari, Z. Veliz and I. Fiedler, '*St. John in the Wilderness*: observations on technique, style and authorship', *Art Institute of Chicago Museum Studies* 31(2), 2005, pp. 30–45, 100–108.
6. Seccaroni forthcoming (cited in note 4). Seccaroni has prepared a great deal of research in this field and his further conclusions are eagerly awaited.
7. J. Plesters (then Senior Scientific Officer, National Gallery London), lecture delivered in the late 1970s at the National Army Museum.
8. The substance was not readily recognisable in cross-section, but it had the characteristics of gypsum in polarising light microscopy (PLM) and energy dispersive X-ray (EDX) analysis confirmed the presence of calcium and sulphur.
9. Ian Tyres, dendrochronology reports for the *Making Art in Tudor Britain* project at the National Portrait Gallery, 2007–2012.
10. Hilliard himself decries its value when discussing miniature painting, calling it one of the 'unsweet' colours, unfit for use: N. Hilliard, *Art of Limning*, A.F. Kinney (tr.), Lebanon, NH, Northeastern University Press, 1983, p. 30.
11. *Portrait of Catherine Carey, Countess of Nottingham*, *c*.1597, oil on canvas, 78 × 54 cm, then the property of the Mark Weiss Gallery and now attributed to Studio of Robert Peake.
12. L. Sheldon and N. Costaras, 'Johannes Vermeer's *Young woman seated at a Virginal*', *The Burlington Magazine* CXLVIII, 2006, pp. 89–97.
13. L. Sheldon, 'Blue and yellow pigments: the hidden colours of light in Cuyp and Vermeer', *Art Matters* 4, 2007, pp. 97–101.
14. M. Spring, 'Pigment and color change in the paintings of Aelbert Cuyp', in *Aelbert Cuyp*, exh. cat., Washington, DC, National Gallery of Art, 2001, pp. 64–73.
15. Ibid., p. 66.
16. M. Spring and L. Keith, 'Aelbert Cuyp's *Large Dort*: colour change and conservation', *National Gallery Technical Bulletin* 30, 2009, pp. 71–85, p. 77.
17. Spring 2001 (cited in note 14). The yellow lake on three of the paintings at the National Gallery was analysed and found to derive from the weld plant (p. 65). All National Gallery paintings studied had yellow lake on a substrate consisting predominantly of chalk: 'The product is a brighter yellow color than it would be if only alum had been used, but it is more prone to fading' (p. 65); E. Hermens and A. Wallert, 'The Pepstock Papers, lake pigments, prisons and paint-mills', in E. Hermens (ed.), *Looking Through Paintings: The Study of Painting Techniques and Materials in Support of Art Historic Research*, London, Archetype Publications, 1998, p. 281: a recipe of 1666 is quoted using '14 or 15 Lb. of crushed buckthorn berries and 40 Lb. of clean yellow wood ... some 30 Lb of clean long weld', then '100 Lb. of fine chalk-white with 20–22 Lb. of clean good white alum'.

Authors' addresses

- Libby Sheldon, Honorary Senior Research Associate, History of Art, UCL, London, UK (l.sheldon@ucl.ac.uk; libbysheldon@hotmail.com)
- Gabriella Macaro, National Gallery Scientific Department and Freelance Paintings Conservator and Analyst (gabriella.macaro@ng-london.org.uk; gabriellamacaro@gmail.com)

JOSEPH BOOTH'S CHYMICAL AND MECHANICAL PAINTINGS

David Saunders

ABSTRACT The processes used by Joseph Booth and the Polygraphic Society to reproduce oil paintings in the final quarter of the 18th century are explored through technical examination of surviving examples and contemporaneous documentary evidence. Both point to a process that required considerable investment in time and resources to produce the first reproduction of any painting but which, thereafter, allowed straightforward replication. The process appears to have involved the blocking out of the main subject matter in areas of dead colour using block printing or stencilling, with no evidence of the transfer of a printed design or the presence of a print adhered to the support. The number of copies made of a particular painting was dictated not by the technicalities of reproduction but by the demand for the subject and the notion of exclusivity associated with limiting their number. During the 1770s and 1780s the Polygraphic Society and Booth produced copies of dozens of paintings, which were sold through exhibitions in their salerooms in London and by subscription. Following a fire at the manufactory in 1793 the business declined, and by the early 19th century the process seems to have been lost, save in the memory of those who had worked for Booth, including William Weaver, who marketed polygraphic reproductions in the United States.

Introduction

Between 2007 and 2009 the opportunity was taken to re-examine two so-called mechanical paintings in the collection of the British Museum to try to determine how and by whom they had been made.[1] These works were copies after two original oil paintings by Jacques de Loutherbourg that had been exhibited at the Royal Academy in London in 1775 and 1776. At the outset of the project, both copies – depicting 'summer' and 'winter' – were catalogued as mechanical paintings by Matthew Boulton and Francis Eginton (Fig. 1). Given that Eginton is best known as an aquatint printmaker, it had been inferred in an earlier study by Robinson and Thompson that these mechanical copies were prints that had subsequently been hand finished to simulate oil paintings.[2] This assumption was supported by a surviving group of seven monochrome and coloured aquatint prints held in the Science Museum in London that are known collectively as the 'sun pictures'. These came from Boulton's manufactory in Soho, Birmingham, and were thought to represent an intermediate state between the copper plate and the finished mechanical paintings.[3]

The study of the history and materials of *Summer* and *Winter* extended beyond the sun pictures and the British Museum copies to include a number of other versions of these same scenes after de Loutherbourg in various British collections. It became apparent from the materials used in the Science Museum and British Museum copies and their very different appearance – particularly when imaged in the infrared – that while the sun pictures may represent an intermediate step in Boulton and Eginton's process, the copies after de Loutherbourg were not made by the same method. Technical examination of the latter revealed a layer structure very similar to that of a traditional oil painting on canvas with no sign of an intermediate print adhered or transferred to the canvas or ground.[4]

Further evidence for this came from a label on the back of a version of *Winter*, from a pair of paintings virtually identical to those in the British Museum, which are preserved at Brodsworth Hall near Doncaster.[5] This label (Fig. 2) makes it clear that it was made by 'the polygraphic art of copying or multiplying Pictures in Oil Colours, by a chymical and mechanical process, [which] is the original invention of Mr Booth'. Although it seems likely – from the extensive surviving correspondence and records from Boulton's manufactory – that the original paintings of *Summer* and *Winter* were also available to Boulton and Eginton, a comparison of the seven mechanical paintings studied in 2007–2009 suggested that they were all made by the same method and, given the label on the Brodsworth *Winter*, that this was likely to be Joseph Booth's polygraphic, or chymical and mechanical, process.[6]

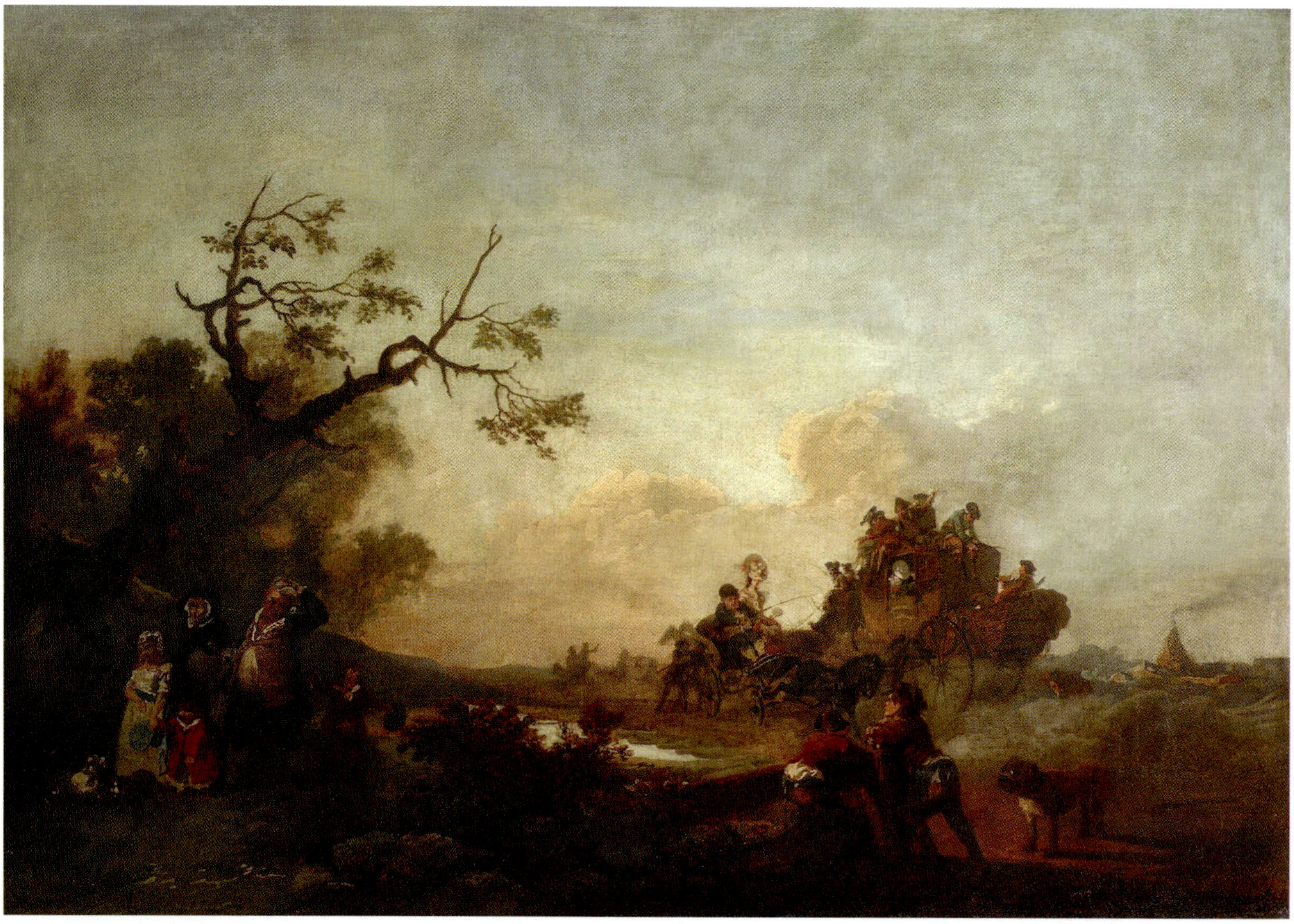

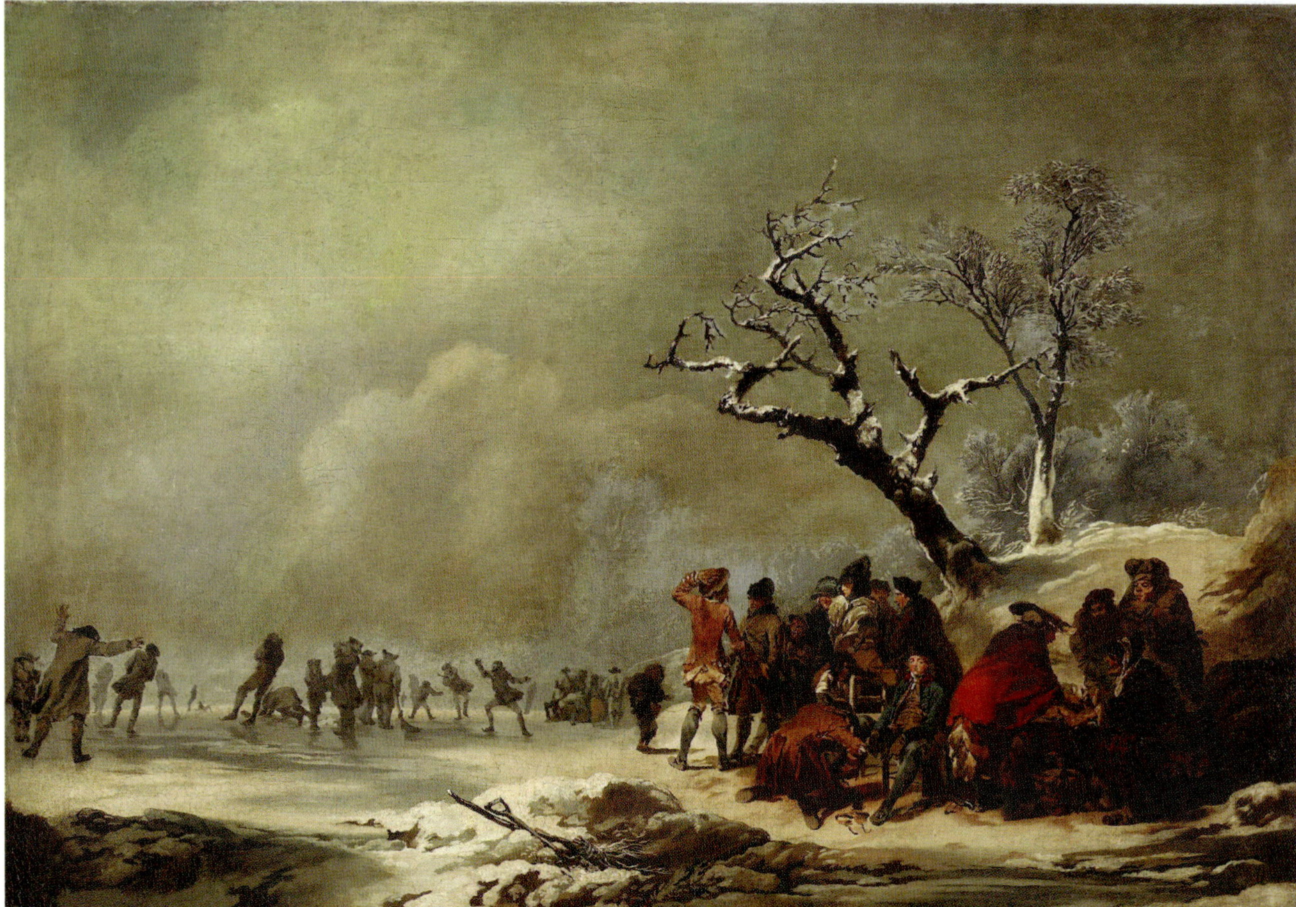

Fig. 1 Polygraphic reproductions of two paintings after Philip James de Loutherbourg: (top) *Summer* (BM 1982,0619.1) and (bottom) *Winter* (BM 1982,0619.2).

Joseph Booth and the Polygraphic Society

The early life of Joseph Booth is surrounded in an air of mystery. He appears to have started life as Joseph Martin, before changing his name to Booth around the time he fled his native Nottinghamshire for Dublin to pursue a career as a portrait painter, leaving a wife and young child.[7] In his *Artists and their Friends in England 1700–1799*, Whitley describes Booth as 'an itinerant portrait painter and theatrical manager',[8] while for the writer of one of his obituaries he was 'the ingenious inventor of the polygraphic art, and of the … art of manufacturing cloth by a perfectly original process'.[9]

The first mention of Joseph Booth in the context of the polygraphic process – or as it was first termed, 'pollaplasiasmos' – dates to 1784. According to Whitley, Booth had been unsuccessfully attempting to secure backing for an enterprise to replicate paintings for some time, before obtaining the necessary financial support from 'Mr Slade of Rochester … and one of the Derbys'.[10] To coincide with the display of a sample produced by his new method at his house at 6 Upper James Street, Golden Square on 28 May 1784, Booth published his *Treatise explanatory of the nature and properties of pollaplasiasmos; or, the original invention of multiplying pictures in oil colours …* The treatise concludes with a short proposal for a subscription for no more than 100 copies of the first picture to be reproduced – *Jupiter and Europa* – to be delivered on 1 August 1784.[11]

A series of exhibitions, designed to elicit further subscriptions, was held over the years that followed. An admission charge of one shilling was made that also secured a copy of an accompanying pamphlet, which generally contained a list of the works that could be purchased and often an essay, treatise or address by Booth.

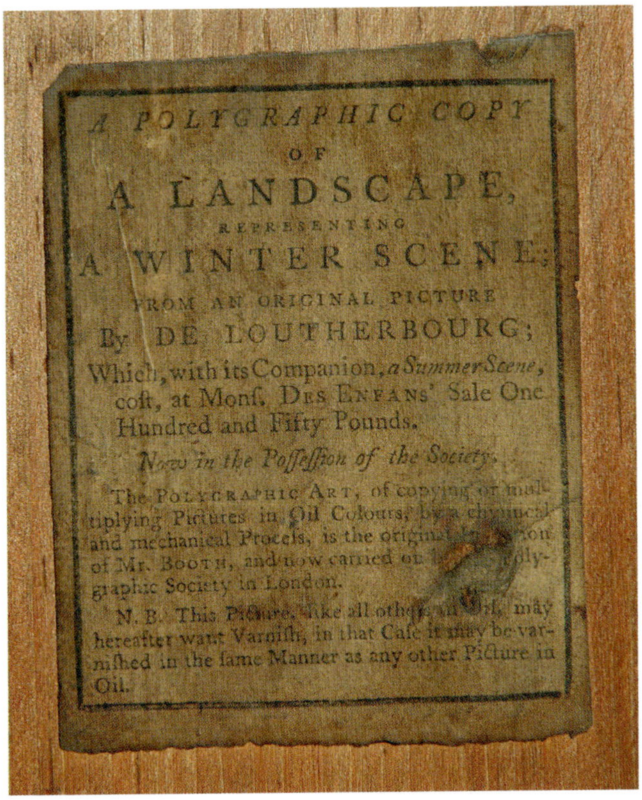

Fig. 2 The label attached to the rear of the frame of the version of *Winter* from Brodsworth Hall, Yorkshire.

In 1787 the 'Polygraphic Rooms' opened at No. 381 Strand, described as opposite Beaufort Buildings. The reproductions of the paintings of *Summer* and *Winter* after de Loutherbourg evidently formed part of the subscription as there is a report in *The World* that describes them hanging in that year's exhibition: 'the chief d'oeuvres of the art as it stands at present is his old man's head, by Piazzetta – next to this is a copy of a head from Guido, St John – and after that winter from Loutherbourg – the companion to it, summer, is very well'.[12] This fits well with the dates given on the label in Figure 2, since Monsieur Des Enfans' Sale, to which it refers, took place on 8 June 1786 and it can be presumed that the reason for their purchase was so that they could be copied. Although catalogues do not survive for every year, these de Loutherbourg copies were no longer among the list of pictures in the 1790 exhibition.

By 1787, not only had the site of the annual exhibitions moved to the Strand, but the term 'polygraphic' had replaced pollaplasiasmos, with the reproductions now offered by the Polygraphic Society rather than by Booth himself.[13] The newly termed Polygraphic Society continued to hold annual exhibitions of paintings and copies throughout the late 1780s and early 1790s, moving from the Strand in 1792 to more spacious rooms in 'the house in pall mall now occupied by Mr Cosway', which was No. 88, also known as Schomberg House.[14] Although this house had apparently been engaged in 1791, it was secured too late for the exhibition of that year to be staged there.

Despite the apparent success of the Society, Booth seems constantly to have worried about competition, either from those who might steal the 'secret' of the polygraphic process, or by the advent of other processes, notably the rather short-lived Mimeographic Company, which held its only exhibition in 1792. Such threats may have prompted Booth to propose, in 1793, that henceforth the Society would attach something slightly more substantial than a paper label to the back of its polygraphic copies; an announcement on 1 October declared that the Polygraphic Society would affix to its reproductions:

> a copper plate … at the back of each, indented with an allegorical figure neatly engraved, representing the art of painting, over which will be the name of the master the said picture was originally painted from, with the words 'By the Polygraphic Art, No. 88 Pall Mall' round the same, & the date the said picture was delivered out by the Society; which being indented & numbered, cannot be forged without being liable to be detected.[15]

However, as there are no reports of the survival of such plates attached to frames or stretchers, it may be that they were never actually produced.

Another threat to the success of the Polygraphic Society was the frequent criticism of the copies published in the press which, in addition to passing judgement on the price charged for mere copies, focused on two alleged shortcomings. First, it was said that the durability of the reproductions

A
CATALOGUE
OF
PICTURES,
Copied (for SALE)
BY A CHYMICAL AND MECHANICAL PROCESS;
EXHIBITED WITH THE
Capital ORIGINALS from which they have been taken,
BY THE
POLYGRAPHIC SOCIETY,
AT THEIR ROOMS, IN PALL-MALL,
BEING THEIR TENTH EXHIBITION:
Opened in FEBRUARY, 1793,
☞ Admittance One Shilling.
TO CONTINUE TILL FURTHER NOTICE,
FROM ELEVEN IN THE MORNING TILL FOUR.

∴ All ORDERS addreſſed by Letter to the POLYGRAPHIC SOCIETY, as above, will be executed in the ſame Manner as if the Parties were preſent.

[PRICE SIXPENCE.]

LONDON:
PRINTED BY A. GRANT, Nº 91, WARDOUR STREET, SOHO.

Fig. 3 Frontispiece of the Polygraphic Society's 1793 *Catalogue of pictures copied (for sale) by a chymical and mechanical process …*

A
TREATISE
EXPLANATORY OF THE
NATURE and PROPERTIES
OF
Pollaplaſiaſmos;
OR,
THE ORIGINAL INVENTION
OF
Multiplying PICTURES in Oil Colours, with all the PROPERTIES of the ORIGINAL PAINTINGS; whether in regard to Outline, Size, Variety of Tints, &c.
TOGETHER WITH A
PROPOSAL
FOR
A SUBSCRIPTION for forming a COLLECTION of PICTURES, truly ORIGINAL, on different Subjects.
INTERSPERSED WITH
Occaſional Remarks on the Utility of PAINTING—on the modern Improvements in that ART,—and on the Merits of the ENGLISH SCHOOL.
Magna eſt Veritas, et prævalebit.

By J. BOOTH.

A SPECIMEN of this Art may be now inſpected at the INVENTOR's Houſe, No. 6, *Upper James'-ſtreet*, North Corner of *Golden-ſquare.*
Admittance Gratis. *Price of the Pamphlet,* 1s.

Printed by J. ROZEA, No 91, Wardour Street, Soho, and ſold by J. BEW, No 28, Paternoſter-Row, and J. STRAHAN, near the Adelphi, Strand.

Fig. 4 Frontispiece of Booth's 1784 *A treatise explanatory of the nature and properties of pollaplasiasmos …*

was poor, particularly in the early years of the Society. Booth countered this in an advertisement in *The Critical Review* in 1792, acknowledging that 'in the infancy of the undertaking … some pictures were delivered, which did not preserve their colour so well as expected', but asserting and warranting that 'Pictures made by the Polygraphic art in its present state of improvement will be found in every respect equal in point of permanency and durability to the works of the most eminent masters'.[16]

The second criticism was that the paintings bore little resemblance to the paintings from which they derived. Perhaps the most stinging condemnation was contained in a review of the Society's 1789 exhibition published in the *Morning Herald*, which described the copies of *St John* by Guido as 'too palpable an evidence of the quackery of this scene to allow the most unpractised eye to be deceived for a moment. Neither the general form of the whole nor the particular markings of the several parts convey the most distant idea of the original'.[17]

The practice of hanging the original paintings alongside the copies in the annual exhibitions 'In order that an impartial Judgment may be formed of the Merit of this Discovery',[18] seems to have been counterproductive, offering the critics the chance to make direct, and clearly unfavourable, comparisons.

The beginning of the Society's decline can probably be traced to the fire at the polygraphic manufactory in Woolwich in January 1793 – most likely on 22 January.[19] Although the report of the fire given a few days later in the *Morning Herald* was brief, it seems that the fire was serious enough to elicit support from soldiers of the Royal Artillery whose barracks were nearby. The grave consequences of the fire for the Society – presumably through the loss of materials, equipment and perhaps stocks of copies – is emphasised by later correspondence (detailed below), which suggests that a number of those working for Booth before the fire were made redundant as a result of the disruption to the Society's business.[20] Another extract from this later correspondence indicates that 'After a short time the business was removed, and carried on by the same party, on a smaller scale, (at Walham Green, near Fulham, Middlesex) for a year or two longer, after which, I believe, it was quite relinquished'.[21]

Despite the fire the 1793 exhibition went ahead in February (perhaps the paintings and copies for the exhibition were already in Pall Mall: Fig. 3), but thereafter little is known about the Society until 1795. It seems to have broken up when Thomas Goddard, described as the acting manager of its affairs, died. By April 1795 Goddard's executors were offering 'polygraphic paintings made in the last two or three years' for sale through Mr. Christie,[22] while Mr. Cosway's house on Pall Mall was once again available to be let. (It is interesting that the executors stress that these were recent polygraphic copies given the criticism of the early reproductions mentioned above).

Notwithstanding the setbacks implied by these events, Booth continued to market polygraphic reproductions. Following the sale at Christie's, Booth placed an advertisement in the *Morning Chronicle* on 24 June in a bid to reinvigorate interest in the polygraphic paintings. In this advertisement he says that he will halve the price and set up rooms to show them in, but that meanwhile orders can be sent to him 'at his manufactory near Cumberland Gardens, Vauxhall'.[23] Following the loss of the factory and the sale of the Society's assets it seems likely that this was both his home and the address from which he sold polygraphic copies. There are no surviving records to indicate whether Booth ever secured rooms in which to exhibit, or sold more polygraphic paintings before his death in early 1797, when obituaries – including one in the *Freemason's Magazine* in March 1797 – confirm that he was still residing in Cumberland Gardens.[24]

The polygraphic process

Although the details of Boulton and Eginton's process are not completely understood, much can be pieced together from the original records and correspondence relating to Boulton's many business ventures that are now held in the Soho Archive and which have been very thoroughly investigated by Barbara Fogarty in her recent thesis.[25] At first sight, it might appear that understanding Booth's process would be much simpler; rather than reading between the lines of the Soho correspondence with its mentions of copper, presses and canvas, Booth produced at least two pamphlets that purport to describe the process, the first while the technique was still called pollaplasiasmos and the latter once he had coined the term polygraphic, and the catalogues for each Society exhibition had a foreword that offered some background to the method.

Booth's treatises, pamphlets and advertisements

As mentioned above, the first of Booth's 'treatises' was published in 1784 at the time that he was first setting out to sell copies by subscription, but it contains disappointingly few clues to how the reproductions were made. The *Treatise explanatory of the nature and properties of pollaplasiasmos ...* (Fig. 4) alludes to the original designs being executed either in black or slightly tinted, and claims they are 'as exquisitely painted as if the subject was first laboriously finished upon a piece of canvas'.[26] It mentions that this entirely new system is not subject to change, cracking or peeling, and stresses that because its principles are entirely new throughout, it cannot and should not be compared to print making. Indeed, the treatise is very dismissive of printmakers (who 'generally pay more attention to the gratification of the eye than the cultivation of the nobler faculties of the mind') and only marginally less dismissive of those who collect prints.

Across the first 60 pages of the 1784 treatise Booth makes clear his views on subjects from fashion to interior decorating in a series of polemics and anecdotes, reserving particular scorn for writers and artists whose works concern the fanciful rather than the concrete. He calls upon the patriotism of the reader to help promote British art through (his) British enterprise and explains that he has not patented the process, as this would allow foreigners to 'carry the invention out of the kingdom'.[27] At his most jingoistic Booth claims that he has 'lately refused a very advantageous offer made by a foreign power' because 'no terms can induce him to leave his native country'. Accordingly, he then throws himself 'on that candour and liberality which have been the characteristic of Britons',[28] with the implication that to support his patriotic enterprise is the mark of such a true Briton.

In the last two pages of the treatise, Booth finally comes to the crux of his argument and offers to the reader the first painting that is to be reproduced by subscription; this is *Jupiter and Europa*, and each of the 100 copies will sell for three guineas (£3.3s). But in introducing the painting and the subscription no more is revealed about the process by which it will be made.

The second of Booth's pamphlets, *An address to the public, on the polygraphic art, or the copying or multiplying pictures, in oil colours, by a chymical and mechanical process, the invention of Mr. Joseph Booth, portrait painter*, published in 1787, reveals nothing further about the process and everything about Booth's skill in marketing.[29] It takes up where the 1784 treatise left off, beginning 'Mechanical invention is one of the great pillars that support the grandeur of the British Empire'. The aims of the Society continue to be fervently patriotic, offering patronage of British artists (in increasing numbers as the years progress), commercial benefits for Britain (by this stage Booth is marketing the copies to ships' captains trading in the West Indies) and even 'improved morals'.

With no direct documentary evidence, we are left with the material evidence of the polygraphic copies and the inferences that can be drawn from advertisements or correspondence, many of which date to after Booth's death.

Evidence from polygraphic copies

The technical study of the British Museum's polygraphic paintings after de Loutherbourg in 2007–2009 revealed that they were probably made by some type of block, stencil or screen-printing technique (although the last of these, suggested by A.P. Laurie in 1934, seems the least likely) and then finished by hand.[30] The reasoning behind this was that while figure groups in the different versions that were examined are all identical in shape and scale, the distance between these groups varies slightly, suggesting that they had been applied independently, and the small touches of paint used to define the facial features and highlights on the clothes or landscape are much less consistent (Fig. 5). Although the technique has something in common with that of some Dutch *penschilderijen* of the mid-17th century, these earlier examples seem to have involved

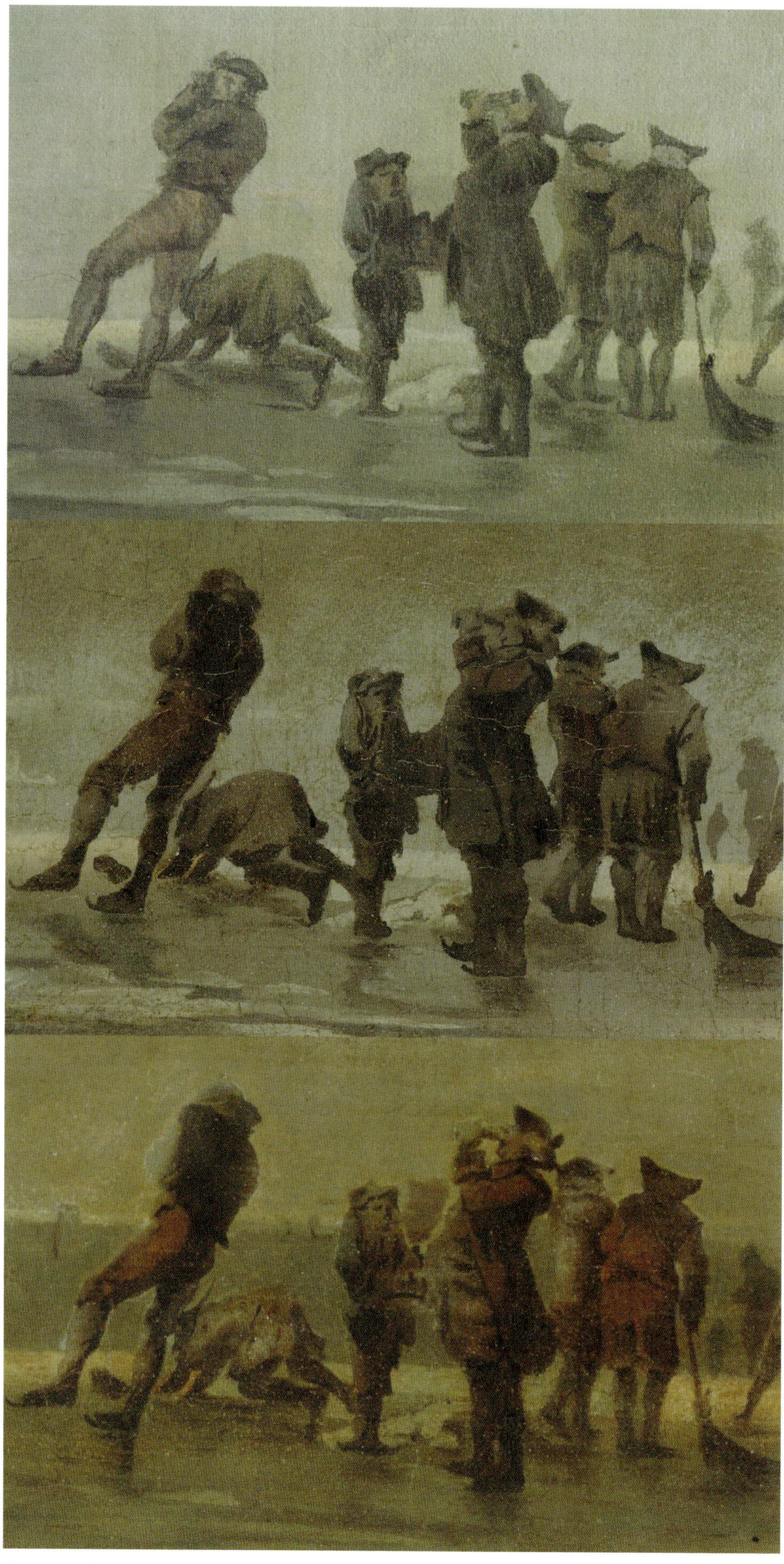

Fig. 5 Details of the group of skaters from the versions of *Winter* from (top) Brodsworth Hall, Yorkshire; (middle) British Museum; and (bottom) Birmingham Museum and Art Gallery.

THE

MONTHLY

MAGAZINE;

OR,

BRITISH REGISTER:

Including

MISCELLANEOUS COMMUNICATIONS FROM CORRESPONDENTS, ON ALL SUBJECTS OF LITERATURE AND SCIENCE.
MEMOIRS OF DISTINGUISHED PERSONS.
ORIGINAL LETTERS, ANECDOTES, &c.
POETRY.
LITERARY AND PHILOSOPHICAL INTELLIGENCE.
PROCEEDINGS OF LEARNED SOCIETIES.
REVIEW OF THE NEW MUSIC.
REVIEW OF THE FINE ARTS.
REVIEW OF ENGLISH, AND FRENCH LITERATURE.
ACCOUNT OF ALL NEW PATENTS.
LIST OF NEW BOOKS AND IMPORTATIONS.
REGISTER OF DISEASES IN LONDON.
RETROSPECT OF PUBLIC AFFAIRS.
LIST OF BANKRUPTCIES AND DIVIDENDS.
DOMESTIC OCCURRENCES CLASSED AND ARRANGED IN THE GEOGRAPHICAL ORDER OF THE COUNTIES.
MARRIAGES, DEATHS, BIOGRAPHICAL MEMOIRS, &c.
REPORT OF THE STATE OF COMMERCE, &c.
REPORT OF AGRICULTURE, &c.
REPORT OF THE WEATHER.

VOL. XXVI.

PART II. FOR 1808.

London:

Printed for RICHARD PHILLIPS, No. 6, Bridge-Street;
By whom Communications (Post-paid) are thankfully received.

(Price Twelve Shillings half-bound.)

Printed by J. Adlard, Duke-street, Smithfield.

Fig. 6 Frontispiece of *The Monthly Magazine or British Register* vol. XXVI, part II, 1808.

hand finishing an outline produced by transferring a still wet imprint from an etched plate onto a prepared panel.[31]

The application of solid areas of colour using stencils or, in particular, woodblocks would have been a familiar technique in the late 18th century for the production of wallpapers and fabrics, and it may be that Booth's acquaintance with cloth production might have introduced him to such methods. Applying large areas of oil colour to a relatively absorbent paper or cloth would have been rather different to applying the same process on a primed canvas. The study of the de Loutherbourg copies revealed that although the starting point for the paintings appeared to be a canvas primed with a traditional lead white ground in oil (perhaps a canvas preprimed by a specialist supplier), a secondary ground had been applied that contained a high proportion of pumice, a naturally occurring volcanic glass.[32] The role of this ground was probably to provide a rather more absorbent surface onto which to apply the blocks of oil colour, allowing individual areas to become 'touch dry' more quickly so that the next colour could be added without too great a delay.[33] Once the printed blocks were dry, the finishing touches were applied by hand. This proposed sequence is, however, based on the examination of few examples and is by no means proven; certain features that might be expected if block printing were used – such as raised paint at the edge of the blocks – have not been obvious on the polygraphic copies examined to date.

Other documentary sources

Clues to the nature of the polygraphic process come also from a number of other documentary sources. For an (at least partial) understanding of Booth's methods, most helpful is a brief published correspondence in *The Monthly Magazine* in 1808 to 1809 (Fig. 6). In September 1808, over a decade after Booth's death, an R. R--d of Bedfordshire wrote to the editor of *The Monthly Magazine* asking if any reader could inform him whether anything was still known of the polygraphic method used by Booth, whose 1797 obituary he had recently read. He (and it is here assumed that these various letter writers were men) also asked if anyone was still engaged in making such reproductions:

> I should be glad to be informed through the channel of your truly respectable publication, whether the process employed by Mr. Booth is now known, or whether it died with him, and if so lost, what is the supposed means he used to obtain copies from originals ... but if the secret is known at this time to any one, why is it not now practised?[34]

In November of the same year R. R--d received two responses. The first was from James Sillett, who was a painter who had once worked for Booth and was later a member of the Norwich Society of Artists. His reply first confirms that after the 1793 fire the business declined:

> the business carried on ... at Woolwich; having at the same time exhibition and sale rooms in Pall Mall, till February 1793 when a fire happened which destroyed the greatest part of the premises and materials, and of course caused stagnation of the business; the artists employed, myself being one, being then discharged and their engagements cancelled.[35]

It is from Sillett's letter to *The Monthly Magazine* that it is also known that – as mentioned earlier – Booth continued to produce copies after the fire:

> After a short time the business was removed and carried on by the same party, on a smaller scale, (at Walham Green, near Fulham, Middlesex) for a year or two longer after which, I believe, it was quite relinquished.[36]

Sillett then turns his attention to the polygraphic process, noting that: 'the art itself ... certainly did not die with Mr B. being still known to myself and some others, who I believe, are living.'[37] However, Sillett seems to have inherited from Booth not only the details of the process but also the art of obfuscation. He goes on to say that while he could produce copies at one-sixth or even one-tenth of the price of the original, 'the art is of such a nature, that it cannot conveniently (except partially) be put in practice so as to answer the purpose of any individual, who has not sufficient patronage and support to have the means of obtaining the use of the best and most valuable pictures'; and this is as near as he comes to revealing anything about the practices or processes used by Booth and the Polygraphic Society.

The second correspondent to the November issue of *The Monthly Magazine* – T.F––n of Peterborough – is a little more helpful. He says that the process is thoroughly known to him and that he has been practising it for 30 years, having learnt it from his father who in turn had been taught by his elder brother. If T.F––n, writing in 1808, is to be believed the process must, therefore, predate Booth's announcement in 1784. T.F––n implies that Booth merely formalised and named longstanding methods and indicates that these are far more mechanical than chemical, at which point he digresses into a hugely long, general and seemingly tangential list of chemicals.

On returning to the details of the polygraphic process, T.F––n proves to be nearly as evasive as Booth and Sillett. He comments that if he says 'more on this part of the subject, I may disclose more than I ought, because it may lessen its esteem and be of little or no value to the public'.[38] However, the final part of the correspondence offers the writer's view on why the process had not continued to be used and provides some hints that are helpful in trying to piece together the nature of the replication method:

> Because the speculation is not a good one, that is the preparation is tedious, (although the execution is rapid) requires a number of copies to be taken in order to render it profitable, and it is by no mean easy to dispose of many fac-simile oil paintings advantageously ... If R.R–––d, or any other person should wish to have forty, fifty, or one hundred, &c. copies of a picture, the writer would not object to execute such an order.[39]

Discussion and conclusions

Neither Booth's own writings nor the correspondence in *The Monthly Magazine* offer any concrete information about the nature of the polygraphic process or the materials employed in making these paintings. Examination of the British Museum polygraphic paintings has addressed the latter and offered some clues as to the way in which they might have been made. Combining these various sources of information, what can be said of the process, its economics and the marketing of the reproductions by Booth and the Society?

The letters from both James Sillett and T.F––n to *The Monthly Magazine* reinforce the comments made by Booth in the catalogues of the Polygraphic Society exhibitions, in which he stresses the need for a certain number of subscriptions. Although Booth often suggests that this is to afford the exclusivity associated with a limited edition, it might equally be interpreted as a means of assuring buyers for the minimum number of copies needed to make an edition economically viable. This in turn suggests that the process required an initial, complex set of steps but that thereafter copies could be produced quickly. As T.F––n, in his correspondence to *The Monthly Magazine*, puts it: 'the preparation is tedious, (although the execution is rapid)',[40] which probably rules out processes such as those based on systems of connected pens that found use copying documents, as these would require considerable effort to produce each additional copy.

However, it is evident that the copies of particular paintings were sold across a number of years: *A View of Mount Vesuvius by Moonlight* by Wright of Derby features in the 1790, 1792[41] and 1793 catalogues, so either those ordering in 1790 were kept waiting until a sufficient number of subscriptions was received, copies were held in stock against orders in future years, or – once an initial run sufficient to cover the set-up costs had been secured – reproductions were made as the orders came in.

Booth's copies clearly required a good deal of hand finishing and T.F––n notes as much:

> Another mistake exists as to its being complete, without any touch or finishing by the hand, inasmuch as that in one hundred cases, ninety-nine will indispensably require 'touching up', and that part of the process must be done by one who can paint, with or without polygraphics.[42]

In addition to Sillet and T.F––n, a third person who seems to have direct experience of the polygraphic process was William Weaver. Weaver is said to have worked in Booth's manufactory and may have been one of those 'discharged' after the fire at Woolwich in 1793. He emigrated to the United States and after working initially as a portrait painter – it is possible he was one of those employed by Booth to hand finish paintings – set up a business to reproduce paintings. He published notices in newspapers in Philadelphia, Norfolk, Alexandria, Charleston and Boston in which he proposed to make an edition of 200 copies of an allegorical painting by the process 'so long kept a secret and exclusively practiced by the Polygraphik Society in London ... now in the possession of a Citizen of the United States lately arrived from Europe'.[43]

Paul Schweizer, Director Emeritus, Museum of Art at the Munson-Williams-Proctor Institute (Utica, NY), has made a very thorough art historical study of Weaver and his series of portraits of Alexander Hamilton preserved in museums in the USA.[44] Schweizer believes that of the eight surviving portraits of Hamilton, three are original oil paintings and the remainder polygraphic copies. However, recent detailed examination of two of these copies (in the New York Historical Society and the Museum of the City of New York) and comparison with images of other versions identified clear differences in scale and composition that go beyond the variation observed in the hand finishing of Booth's polygraphs. Given that several of the portraits are already identified as versions rather than copies, the question arises whether they might all best be described as versions rather than copies and whether any chymical or mechanical process was involved in their creation; they might simply be 'hand made' copies marketed to appeal to a public fascinated by the modernity of mechanised production.

The supposedly radical and new process introduced by the Polygraphic Society may well predate the mid-1780s and have its roots in the block printing of textiles and paper, but Booth and those who had worked with him took advantage of a market for reproductions that, while inexpensive compared to oil paintings, were sufficiently similar to the originals to imply good taste in the purchaser. They also recognised a public thirst for novel and mechanical methods that somehow compensated for the lack of individuality in these copies, and this speaks volumes for the balance between the arts and the sciences in forming public taste around the turn of the 19th century.

Notes

1. D. Saunders and A. Griffiths, A. 2011. 'Two 'mechanical' oil paintings after de Loutherbourg: history and technique', in M. Spring (ed.), *Studying Old Master Paintings: Technology and Practice*, London, Archetype Publications, 2011, pp. 186–193.
2. E. Robinson and K.R. Thompson, 'Matthew Boulton's mechanical paintings', *The Burlington Magazine* 112, 1970, pp. 497–507.
3. Ibid.
4. Saunders and Griffiths 2011 (cited in note 1), p. 191.
5. This label was pointed out by Caroline Carr-Whitworth, Brodsworth Hall.
6. Saunders and Griffiths 2011 (cited in note 1), p. 191.
7. *The Monthly Magazine or British Register* XXXII(II), 1811, p. 556.
8. W.T. Whitley, *Artists and their Friends in England 1700–1799*, London and Boston, The Medici Society, 1928, p. 25.
9. *The Monthly Magazine or British Register* XXVI(II), 1808, pp. 315–316. The obituary first published in the *Freemason's Magazine* in March 1797 was reproduced verbatim in *The Monthly Magazine* in 1808.
10. *The World* 16 May 1787; W.T. Whitley, *The Whitley Papers*, London, Department of Prints and Drawings, The British Museum, 1784–1808, p. 1182.
11. J. Booth, *A treatise explanatory of the nature and properties of pollaplasiasmos; or, the original invention of multiplying pictures in oil colours, with all the properties of the original paintings*, London, J. Rozea, 1784.
12. *The World* 1787 (cited in note 10); Whitley 1784–1808 (cited in note 10), p. 1182.
13. J. Booth, *An address to the public, on the polygraphic art, or the copying or multiplying pictures, in oil colours, by a chymical and mechanical process, the invention of Mr. Joseph Booth, portrait painter*, London, Logographic Press, 1787.
14. *The Oracle* 21 June 1791; Whitley 1784–1808 (cited in note 10), p. 1178.
15. Whitley 1784–1808 (cited in note 10), p. 1181. The reviewer of this paper has helpfully pointed out that the reproductions might have been supplied with a paper label printed from an 'indented' copper plate rather than with a copper plate recessed (indented) into the rear of the frame or stretcher.
16. *The Critical Review or Annals of Literature*, London, A. Hamilton, vol. 5, May 1792, p. 3.
17. *Morning Herald* 23 May 1787; Whitley 1928 (cited in note 8), p. 26.
18. *The Critical Review* 1792 (cited in note 16), p. 3.
19. *Morning Herald* 25 January 1793; Whitley 1784–1808 (cited in note 10), p. 1180. The report in *The Morning Herald* is dated Friday 25 January 1793 and refers to a fire on Tuesday, which would be 22 January 1793.
20. *The Monthly Magazine* 1808 (cited in note 9), p. 516.
21. Ibid.
22. Whitley 1784–1808 (cited in note 10), p. 1181.
23. Ibid.
24. *The Monthly Magazine* 1808 (cited in note 9), pp. 315–316.
25. B. Fogarty, *Matthew Boulton and Francis Eginton's Mechanical Paintings: Production and Consumption 1777 to 1781*, MPhil thesis, Department of History of Art, University of Birmingham, 2010.
26. Booth 1784 (cited in note 11).
27. Ibid., p. 55.
28. Ibid., pp. 56–57.
29. Booth 1787 (cited in note 13).
30. Saunders and Griffiths 2011 (cited in note 1), p. 192.
31. D. Freedberg, A. Burnstock and A. Phenix, 'Paintings or prints? Experiens Sillemans and the origins of the *grisaille* sea-piece: notes on a rediscovered technique', *Print Quarterly* I(3), 1984, pp. 148–168. The main difference between the polygraphs and the *penschilderijen* by Experiens Sillemans lies in the evidence found in the latter for the transfer of printed outlines rather than the blocks of solid 'dead colour' found in the former.
32. Saunders and Griffiths 2011 (cited in note 1), pp. 190–191.
33. Ibid., p. 191
34. *The Monthly Magazine* 1808 (cited in note 9), p. 315.
35. Ibid., p. 516.
36. Ibid.
37. Ibid.
38. Ibid., p. 517.
39. Ibid.
40. Ibid.
41. Polygraphic Society, *Catalogue of pictures copied or multiplied (for sale) by a chymical and mechanical process*, London, A. Grant, 1792.
42. *The Monthly Magazine* 1808 (cited in note 9), p. 518.
43. P. Schweizer, 'William J. Weaver's secret art of multiplying pictures', in *Painting and Portrait Making in the American Northeast: Dublin Seminar for New England Folklife, Annual Proceedings 1994*, Boston, MA, Boston University, 1995, pp. 151–166.
44. Schweizer 1995 (cited in note 42); P. Schweizer, 'William J. Weaver and his 'chymical and mechanical' portraits of Alexander Hamilton', *American Art Journal* 30, 1999, pp. 82–101.

Author

David Saunders, Keeper, Department of Conservation and Scientific Research, British Museum, London, UK (dsaunders@thebritishmuseum.ac.uk)

THE STRAWBERRY GIRL: REPETITION IN REYNOLDS'S STUDIO PRACTICE

Alexandra Gent, Rachel Morrison and Rica Jones

ABSTRACT *The Strawberry Girl* is one of the best-known paintings of Reynolds's oeuvre. Two versions survive: in the collection at Bowood House in Wiltshire and the Wallace Collection in London. Technical analysis of *The Age of Innocence* at Tate revealed that this painting covers another version of *The Strawberry Girl*. The process of copying paintings was a well-known practice in Reynolds's studio. Technical analysis has shown that the copies often employ much simpler techniques than paintings by Reynolds's own hand. However there is documentary evidence that Reynolds sometimes worked simultaneously on more than one version of the same subject and *The Strawberry Girl* may be an example of this practice. This paper discusses the technical analysis of *The Strawberry Girl* in the Wallace Collection and the version hidden beneath *The Age of Innocence*. It also examines the two versions of this painting and how they relate to the development of this image.

Introduction

Reynolds's painting *The Strawberry Girl* in the Wallace Collection is one of his best-known works (Fig. 1). He himself described *The Strawberry Girl* as one of the most original paintings he had produced. As was often his practice, he made other versions of the composition – at least two in this instance – and his pupils and assistants may also have made copies of it. As part of the Wallace Collection 'Reynolds Research Project'[1] and from work done over many years in the Conservation Department at Tate, London, we have made a technical study of several pictures by Reynolds, including three paintings with a *Strawberry Girl* theme. In this paper we present some of the results of this work, relating them wherever possible to contemporary comment on Reynolds's practice of painting and to references to the paintings themselves.

Studio production

On his return to London in 1752, after spending almost three years in Italy, Reynolds quickly became one of the most fashionable portrait painters in Britain. During his most productive period in the late 1750s and early 1760s he was producing close to 100 paintings a year. In order to keep up with demand, Reynolds employed assistants and students in his studio. His principal assistant was Giuseppe Marchi, who returned with him from Italy and, apart from a short period where he worked independently as a portrait painter in Wales, continued to work for Reynolds until his death.[2] James Northcote, who trained with Reynolds from 1771 to 1776, was probably the most successful of Reynolds's pupils, and in the early 19th century wrote about his memories of his master, most notably in *Memoirs of Sir Joshua Reynolds* in 1813 that was revised and republished in a second edition as *The Life of Sir Joshua Reynolds* in 1818.

Several unfinished portraits by Reynolds show that during sittings he would complete the likeness and sketch out the rough placement of the body and limbs, as can be seen in, for example, the portrait of *Georgiana, Countess of Spencer and her Daughter*, now at Chatsworth in Derbyshire.[3] The paintings were often then passed to assistants or a drapery painter to fill in the costume and background, although there were exceptions: the unfinished portrait of *Lord Rockingham and Edmund Burke* in the Fitzwilliam Museum, Cambridge, shows that once the composition of a portrait was marked out, the background detail of a painting could be finished to a high degree by assistants, even before the figures were completed by Reynolds.[4]

In a letter to his brother, written while he was Reynolds's pupil, Northcote described working from a lay figure to paint a blue coat for a portrait of 'Mr Calthrop' (James Calthorpe) and painting a damask curtain and scenery for the background once Sir Joshua had finished the head.[5]

The use of specialist drapery painters was common practice in Britain at this period;[6] artists such as Hogarth and Gainsborough, who painted their own draperies, were the exception. Assistants and drapery painters allowed a much

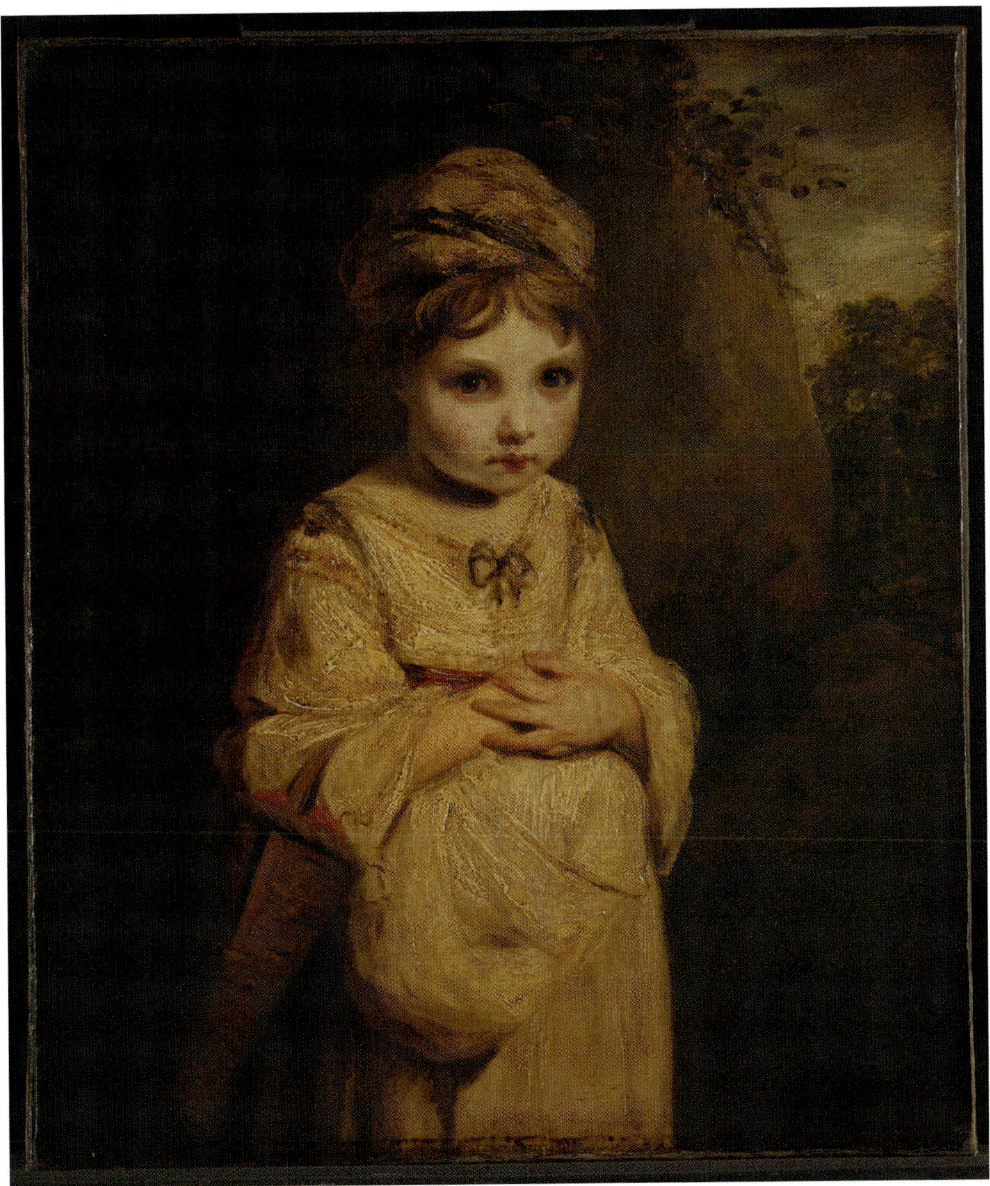

Fig. 1 Sir Joshua Reynolds, *The Strawberry Girl*, *c.*1773, oil on canvas, 76.6 × 73.7 cm, the Wallace Collection. (© By kind permission of the Trustees of the Wallace Collection, London. Photo: The National Gallery, London.)

higher output of paintings; as Reynolds himself said: 'No painter ever acquired a fortune by the work of his hands alone'.[7] In a letter from 1761, Lord Bath, who was sitting for his portrait, divulges Reynolds's use of a drapery painter and also comments that the same person was employed by Ramsey and Hudson.

> I was yesterday with Mr Reynolds & have fixed Fryday next at twelve, to finish the Picture. I have discovered a secret by being often at Mr Reynolds, that I fancy he is sorry I should know. I find that none of these great Painters finish any of their Pictures themselves. The same Person (but who he is, I know not) works for Ramsey, Reynolds & another called Hudson. my Picture will not come from that Person til thursday night, and on Fryday it will be totally finished, and ready to send home.[8]

As the earl of Bath suggests, once a painting was returned from the drapery painter it would be finished in Reynolds's studio. Northcote tells us that once a painting was nearing completion Reynolds would go over the whole painting himself, sometimes making changes and additions as he saw fit, so that although parts of the painting were executed by other hands, 'the whole together of the paintings was at last his own'.[9] In fact Northcote expressed his frustration and admiration when he described how 'with a few sweeps of his brush' Reynolds could transform the laboured drapery painting of a pupil.[10] It is also noteworthy that Northcote described one of Marchi's tasks in Reynolds's studio as 'partly painting his draperies'.[11]

Recent technical analysis of paintings from the Wallace Collection in London appears to support this anecdotal evidence. Examination of the portrait of *The 4th Duke of Queensberry ('Old Q') as Earl of March* shows that although the robes were probably executed by a different hand, Reynolds subsequently repainted parts of the drapery, moving the position of some of the ermine spots. The costume in the portrait of *Mrs Elizabeth Carnac* also appears to be the work of a drapery

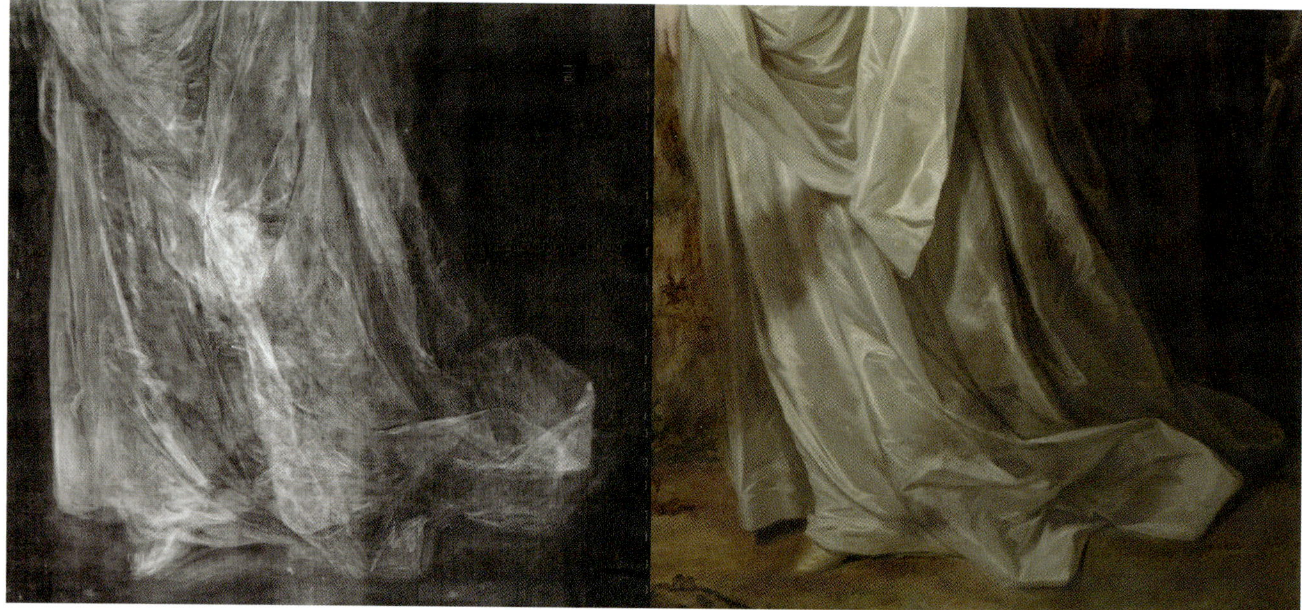

Fig. 2 Sir Joshua Reynolds, *Mrs Elizabeth Carnac*, the Wallace Collection: detail of the drapery of the skirt in X-ray (left) and visible light (right). (© By kind permission of the Trustees of the Wallace Collection, London. Photo: The National Gallery, London.)

painter, but significant changes have been made to the dress that are almost certainly the work of Reynolds. The proper left side of the skirt has been shifted and the folds at the back of the dress have been adjusted to produce a flatter draped form (Fig. 2). This has given the sitter a somewhat more dynamic appearance, as though she is moving through the landscape.

Copies

The production of copies was integral to Reynolds's studio and Mannings considers that 'replica' or 'studio replica' are better terms to use in relation to these paintings, the production of which would have been overseen by Reynolds at least, reserving the term 'copy' for those paintings produced at a later date from prints or by artists not associated with Reynolds's studio.[12]

Duplicate portraits were sometimes requested by sitters at the same time as the first version, as indicated by a note in a letter to Luke Gardiner, Lord Mountjoy, in which Reynolds states 'I shall send away your picture (the best of the two)'.[13] Northcote lists making copies as one of Marchi's responsibilities in the studio.[14] Reynolds's students also developed their painting skills by producing copies. This was not limited to portraits: Northcote recalled preparing a groundwork in black and white for a copy of *The Infant Jupiter* for the duke of Rutland.[15] Farington observed that students were almost solely employed in copying pictures and painting drapery and backgrounds, so that his studio 'resembled a manufactory'.[16] In fact, in later life Northcote complained that he did little else during his time with Reynolds: 'I learnt nothing from him while I was with him: and none of his scholars (if I may except myself) ever made any figure at all. He only gave us his pictures to copy'.[17] Paintings were also sent to independent copyists working outside of the Reynolds studio.[18]

To date, technical analysis of studio replicas has revealed a generally simplified technique in comparison with the first versions. During treatment of the studio version of *Lord Ligonier* at Tate, Helen Brett found that the painting is a faithful rendition of the original, however the paint is very flat with just wet-in-wet work but no glazing or impasto. On the other hand in the first version, now at Fort Ligonier, Pennsylvania, details such as the costume and horse's saddlebags were worked up with elaborate impasto and glazes.[19]

There are three versions of the celebrated portrait of *Mrs Siddons as the Tragic Muse* (San Marino, The Huntington Library; London, Dulwich Picture Gallery; private collection). Technical analysis of the Huntington painting revealed it to be the prime version with numerous *pentimenti* and a complex layer structure as a result. In contrast, the Dulwich copy emulates the appearance of the rich paint surface of the original by using a layer of resinous material over which thin paint layers were applied. Details of the composition, such as the pearls and headdress, show a much freer application in the original than the copy.[20]

Multiple versions in Reynolds's studio practice

In addition to making copies to satisfy his clients' demands, Reynolds also seems to have produced multiple versions of the same subject simultaneously as part of his method of painting. Northcote recalls that Reynolds painted several versions of *The Strawberry Girl*:

> for he always advised, as a good mode of study, that a painter should have two pictures in hand of precisely the same subject and design, and should work on them alternately; by which means, if chance produced a lucky hit, as it often does, then, instead of working upon the same piece, and perhaps by that means destroy that

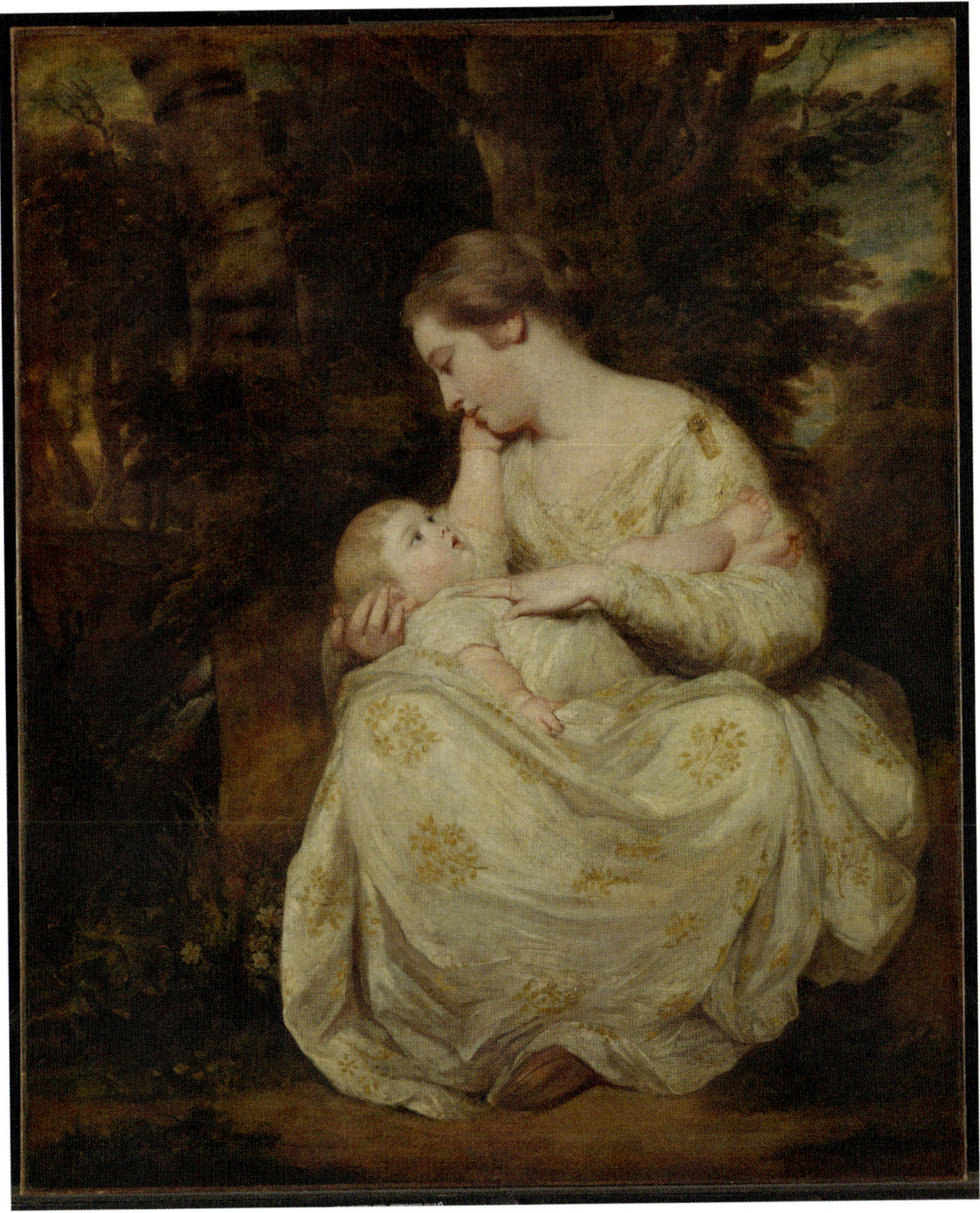

Fig. 3 Sir Joshua Reynolds, *Mrs Susanna Hoare and Child*, *c*.1763–4, oil on canvas, 132.5 × 101.6 cm, the Wallace Collection. (© By kind permission of the Trustees of the Wallace Collection, London. Photo: The National Gallery, London.)

> beauty which chance had given, he should go to the other and improve upon that. Then return again to the first picture, which he might work upon without any fear of obliterating the excellence which chance had given it, having transposed it to the other.[21]

It is generally accepted that Reynolds experimented to a greater extent with his materials and technique when painting fancy pictures such as *The Strawberry Girl*, for which there was not generally a commission.[22] However, the process of working on two pictures simultaneously does not appear to be restricted solely to elaborate pictures. The portrait of *Mrs Susanna Hoare and Child* in the Wallace Collection (Fig. 3) and the unfinished oil sketch now in the collection of the Museum of Fine Arts in Boston (Fig. 4) seem to be examples of this working process.[23] The Boston sketch is smaller than the Wallace Collection painting with the composition more tightly framed, but the design of the figure group, although more freely executed and not complete, is remarkably similar. The relationship between these two paintings has previously been discussed, in particular with the view to establishing which of these two paintings was produced first. On the one hand it has been suggested that the Boston sketch was made by Reynolds after the painting to capture an element of the composition with which he was particularly pleased.[24] Conversely, the *pentimenti* around the shoulders of the Wallace Collection picture have been interpreted as evidence that the sketch was made first in preparation for the finished painting.[25] Originally the shoulders in the Wallace Collection picture were positioned in the same way as in the Boston sketch; the drapery on Mrs Hoare's proper right shoulder was visible between the child's head and outstretched arm. This was later covered but the impasto of the underlying drapery is clearly visible through the overlying background colour, which was applied to adjust the composition.[26]

A recent X-radiograph of the Wallace Collection painting, however, shows that the relationship between the sketch and the finished painting is not straightforward and one painting does not strictly follow the other. The new discovery of further *pentimenti* in the finished Wallace Collection painting has revealed that the composition was not completely worked out before the painting was started. The proper right hand of the child was originally depicted with all four fingers extended and the index finger hooked into the folds of the fabric, a design rather different from that shown in the Boston sketch. This was later changed to show a protruding thumb and only two outstretched fingers as the surrounding drapery was adjusted. The final appearance of the hand is much closer to the design in the Boston sketch. It seems most likely that the two paintings were executed concurrently with the sketch used to develop the composition at the same time that the full-size painting was being worked on. The earlier position of the child's hand, revealed by the X-radiograph of the Wallace Collection painting, seems to indicate that the Boston sketch was not produced first, as it corresponds with a later stage in the image's progress. However, the *pentimenti* at the shoulders in the Wallace Collection painting indicate that the sketch was produced before the finished painting was completed.

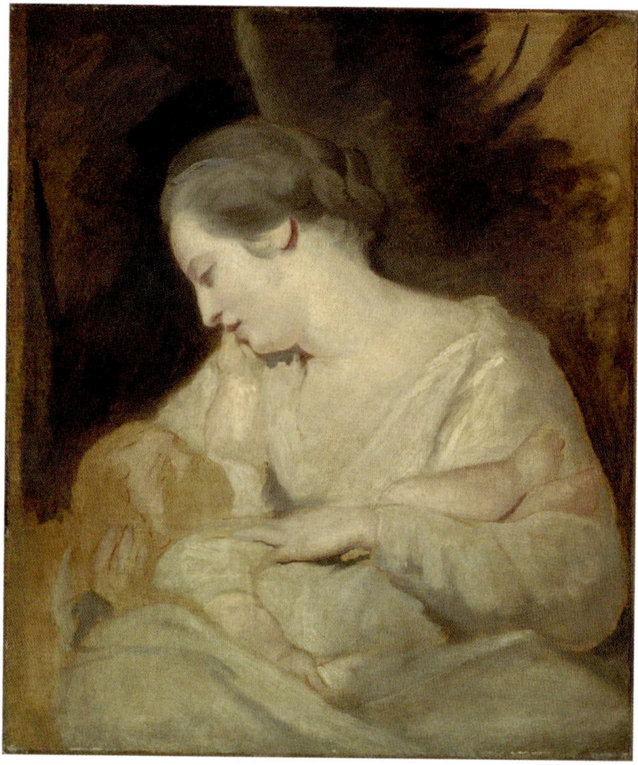

Fig. 4 Sir Joshua Reynolds, *Mrs Richard Hoare Holding her Child*, c.1763, oil on canvas, 75.9 × 63.5 cm, Museum of Fine Arts, Boston. (Photo © 2013 Museum of Fine Arts, Boston.)

The Strawberry Girl

The image of *The Strawberry Girl* was developed from a portrait, thought to be of Reynolds's niece, Theophila Palmer, and to date from around 1767. This painting shows a bare-headed girl, standing facing the viewer, with her hands in a muff.[27] A version of *The Strawberry Girl* was exhibited at the Royal Academy in 1773.[28] The following year Lord Carysfort bought a version of *The Strawberry Girl*, the payment being recorded in Reynolds's ledger on 8 June 1774; this painting is now at Bowood House.[29] In the same year, an engraving of *The Strawberry Girl* by Thomas Watson was published (Fig. 5). The version of *The Strawberry Girl* in the Wallace Collection was sold in Reynolds's sale at Greenwood's after his death and so must have remained in his studio since the time of its creation (see Fig. 1). A print of this version was not made until 1873, when it was engraved by Samuel Cousins.[30] There is also a technical note in Reynolds's ledger dated 1778 that states: 'Strawberry Girl. Cera sol [wax only]'.[31] In addition to the two surviving versions there is a version of *The Strawberry Girl* beneath the painting *The Age of Innocence* at Tate, as shown in the X-radiograph (Fig. 6).[32] Although Reynolds rarely made preparatory drawings, there is a small rough sketch, now in the Hershel Album, of a girl with crossed arms in a fringed cap that relates to *The Strawberry Girl* composition.[33] Graves and Cronin list six studio versions of *The Strawberry Girl*.[34] However, the Bowood and Wallace Collection paintings are the only two versions of *The Strawberry Girl* listed as autograph works by Martin Postle in the more recent Reynolds catalogue raisonné, described as 'type A' and 'type B' respectively.[35] These two variants are distinguished by differences in the head scarves and the girl's fringe of hair. The pose is slightly altered between the two versions with the 'type A' figure appearing more hunched, with raised shoulders. There are also differences in the landscape background at the right of the composition.

Recent technical analysis of the Wallace Collection painting, the 'type B' image, shows that it originally bore a closer resemblance to the 'type A' composition. The X-radiograph reveals that the scarf the girl is wearing on her head originally had fringing at the front. The hair has been painted over this and some impasto from the underlying paint layers is visible on the paint surface, especially where the paint has been damaged by lining. There is also a vertical line visible in the infrared reflectogram, on the proper right side of the forehead above the eye, which seems to relate to the fringing. The proper left side of the face has been widened over the background to give the sitter fuller cheeks and the original narrower shape can be seen in the infrared image. The X-radiograph indicates that the shoulders have been adjusted to make them slightly lower and less rounded (Fig. 7).

There has been some speculation as to which version of *The Strawberry Girl* was exhibited in 1773, with both the Bowood House and Wallace Collection versions being considered by different authors.[36] The existence of Watson's engraving (see Fig. 5) shows that the 'type A' composition was publicly known during Reynolds's lifetime, which suggests that the exhibited painting resembled this composition. It is clear that the Bowood painting more closely resembles the contemporary engraving. However, recent analysis has shown that the

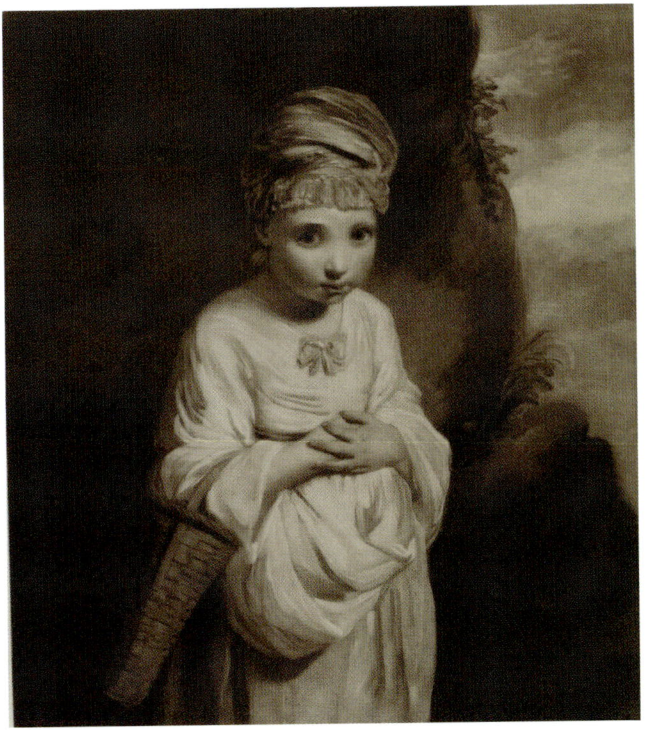

Fig. 5 *The Strawberry Girl*: print engraved by Thomas Watson after Sir Joshua Reynolds, 1774. (© Trustees of the British Museum.)

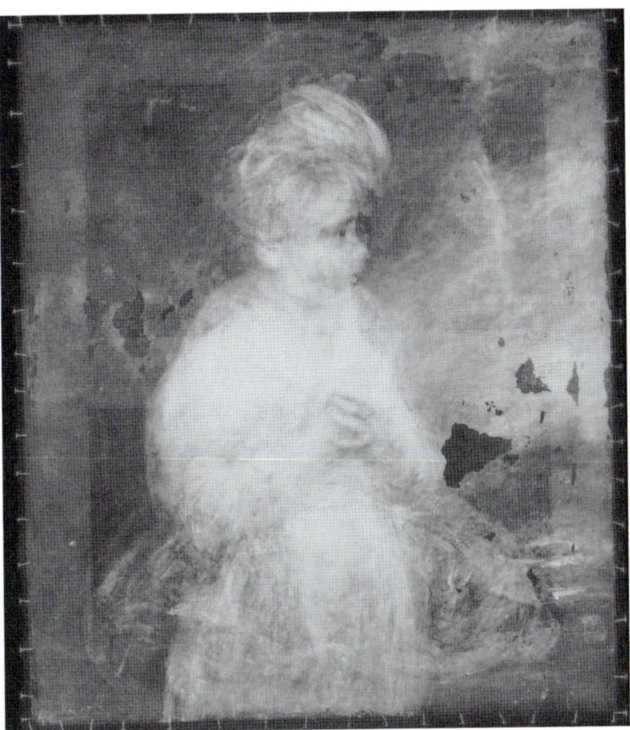

Fig. 6 Composite X-ray image of Sir Joshua Reynolds, *The Age of Innocence*, Tate. (© Tate, London 2013.)

Wallace Collection painting was a 'type A' composition at an earlier stage of its development. In addition, close comparison of *The Age of Innocence* X-radiograph with that of the Wallace Collection picture suggests that the underlying version of *The Strawberry Girl* was also a 'type A' composition. The shoulders appear to be in the raised position and the sitter's cap sits well beyond the proper left side of her face.

Paint analysis

The thick layers of degraded varnish on the Wallace Collection painting give the whole surface and particularly the figure an extremely yellowed appearance. It is difficult to read the original colour values of the drapery and any intended colour difference between the underskirt and the thickly painted apron, caught up over the girl's arm, is now impossible to discern. However, in the Bowood version of *The Strawberry Girl* there is a clear difference in colour between these two areas. The apron is certainly intended to appear white while the skirt has an ochre hue.[37] Analysis of the Wallace Collection painting has shown that in this version there may also have been a more discernible difference between these areas. The apron seems to consist of white paint and lead white was identified, with no evidence of other pigments, in a small scraping from one of the ridges of textured paint in an area of highlight. The underskirt originally had a pink colour. A cross-section sample taken from the lower edge shows a pale pinkish paint applied over a darker, mixed underlayer (Fig. 8).[38] The pink layer consists of lead white with some very fine particles of an iron oxide earth pigment and a few particles of smalt.[39] There is some evidence that the pinkish tonality may have faded as the upper part of this paint layer seems paler in colour, although no analytical evidence of a lake pigment within this layer has been found. However, the large brown particles in the medium-rich glaze layer over the surface, seen more clearly in ultraviolet light, appear to be faded particles of a red lake pigment (see Fig. 8).[40] Examination of an unmounted fragment of the surface layers in transmitted light showed that non-faded parts of these lake particles still have a strong red colour (see Fig. 8). The particles are sparsely distributed through this translucent layer, which could perhaps be described as a tint rather than a red lake glaze. Nonetheless, this must have produced a significant visual effect on the underlying paint, which may once have been a deeper pink colour and therefore more visually distinct from the apron.

A comparable sample was also taken from *The Age of Innocence* below the child's right foot (Fig. 9). The X-ray image (see Fig. 6) indicates that this area should contain the underskirt of the original *Strawberry Girl* composition and in the cross-section there is a distinct pink layer of paint below the greenish-yellow paint that was subsequently applied for the foreground of *The Age of Innocence*. In this version of *The Strawberry Girl*, the original skirt is more strongly coloured and consists of lead white with two types of red earth pigment.[41] As in the Wallace Collection *Strawberry Girl*, there is also a little blue pigment included in the pink paint layer, in this instance Prussian blue.

As noted above, a technical entry in Reynolds's ledgers dated 1778 reads 'Strawberry Girl. Cera sol', implying that the picture was worked on using a binding medium of wax only. It is not clear from this entry whether this refers to an entirely new picture, a reworking or a further adaptation of a painting already in existence. Some of the other technical

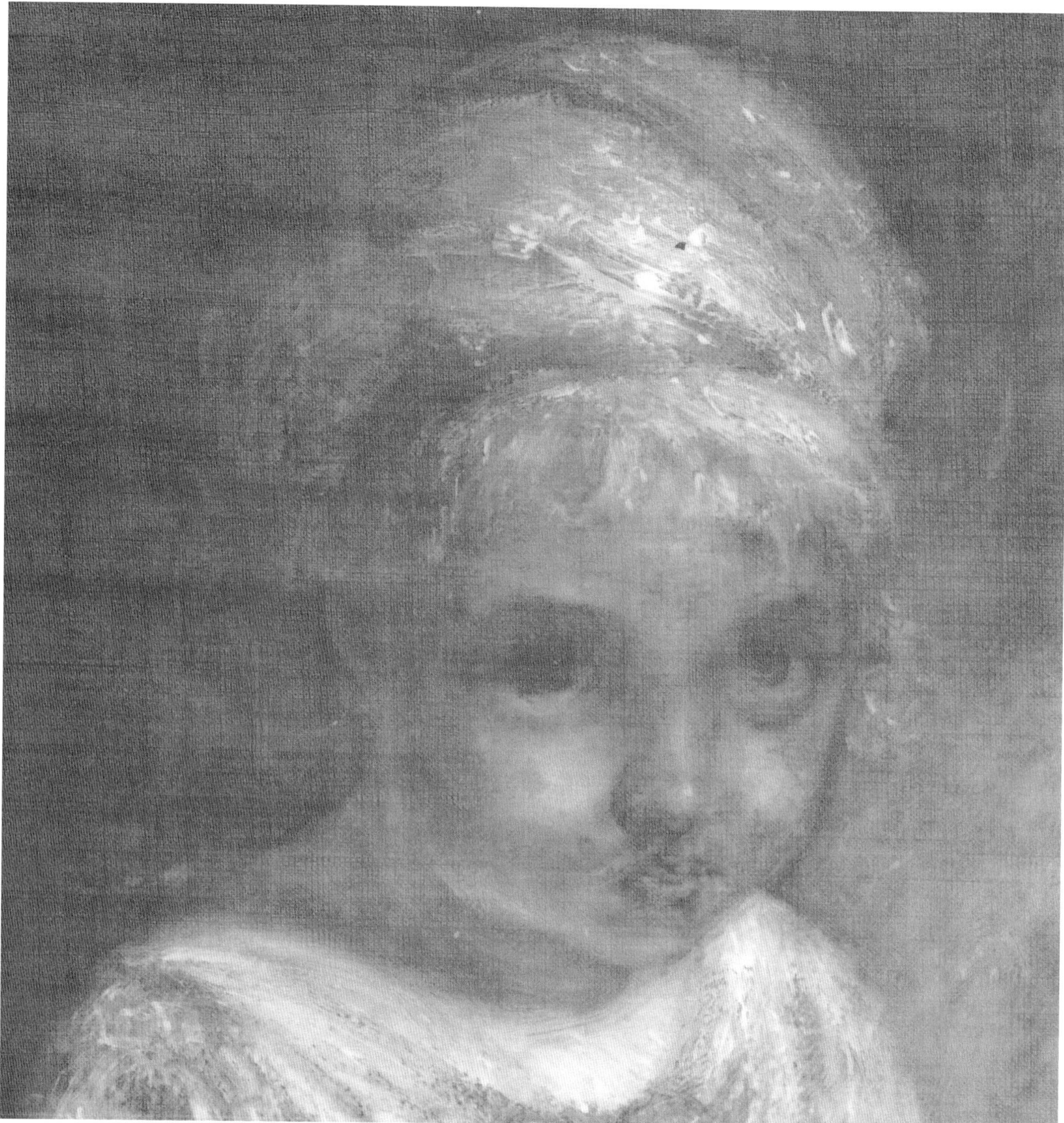

Fig. 7 Detail of the X-ray image of *The Strawberry Girl* from the Wallace Collection. (© By kind permission of the Trustees of the Wallace Collection, London. Photo: The National Gallery, London.)

notes clearly refer only to one specific stage in the execution of a painting. However, binding medium analysis of both the Wallace Collection version of *The Strawberry Girl* and *The Age of Innocence* has found little evidence of wax, and neither of these paintings can be firmly connected to this entry.[42] In the Wallace Collection version of *The Strawberry Girl*, heat-bodied walnut oil was identified as the medium in the white paint of the apron and the blue paint from the sky, whereas heat-bodied linseed oil was found in the dark paint from the background.[43] The pink paint from the skirt of *The Strawberry Girl* composition lying beneath *The Age of Innocence* is also based on oil – heat-bodied walnut oil – in this case with the addition of some mastic and pine resin.

The Strawberry Girl and *The Age of Innocence* are both painted on plainly woven canvas and each was prepared with a white ground consisting of a mixture of chalk and lead white. As Postle has noted, it is impossible to attach a strict chronology to the development of Reynolds's fancy pictures.[44] Although we do not have a firm date for Reynolds's start on either of the paintings under discussion, we can propose a possible date for one stage of painting on *The Age of Innocence* canvas. Several cross-section samples show that some of the lower layers associated with *The Strawberry Girl* composition contain the unusual pigment Indian yellow.[45] A letter from Reynolds to Charles Smith dated 3 December 1784 refers to a 'yellow colour' that Smith had sent him from Calcutta: 'I

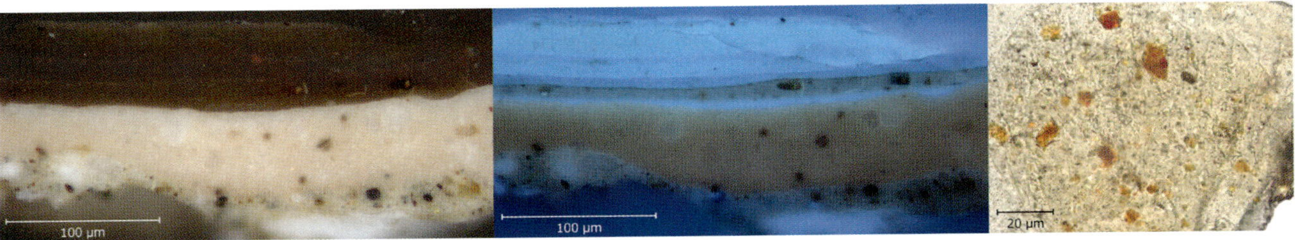

Fig. 8 Cross-section taken from the skirt of the Wallace Collection version of *The Strawberry Girl* photographed in visible (left) and UV (centre) light, and an unmounted sample of the surface layers only from an adjacent area showing the lake particles, photographed in transmitted light with extended focus (right). (© By kind permission of the Trustees of the Wallace Collection, London. Photo: The National Gallery, London.)

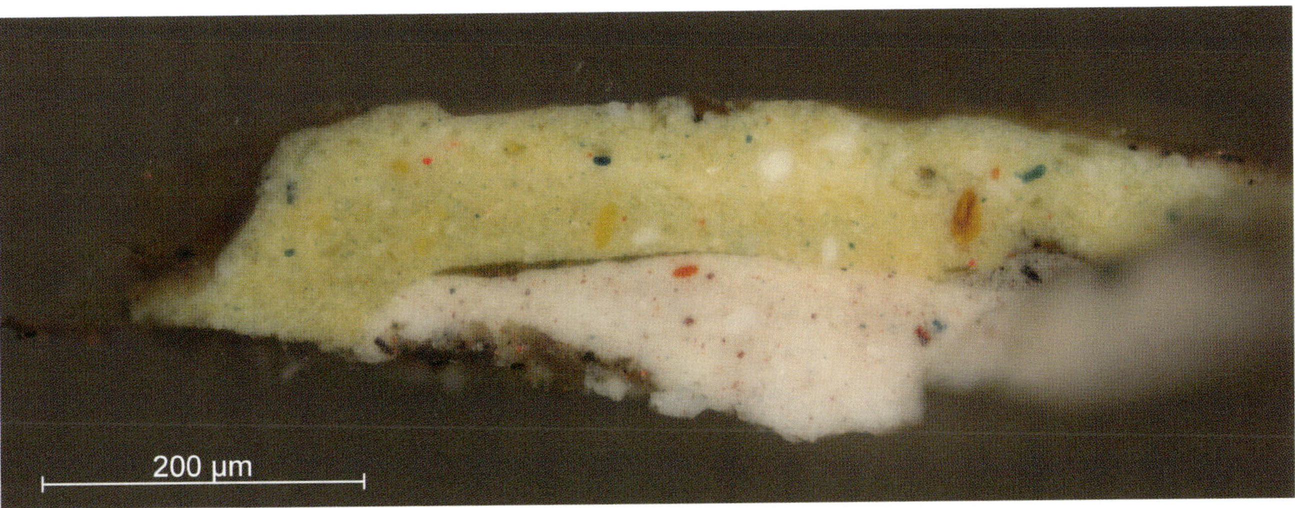

Fig. 9 Cross-section taken from the lower edge of *The Age of Innocence* in the area of the skirt of the underlying *Strawberry Girl* composition. Photographed in visible light. (© Tate, London 2013. Photo: The National Gallery, London.)

take this opportunity of returning you my sincere thanks for the present you was so obliging as to send me of the yellow colour, which is certainly very beautiful, and I believe will do very well in oil, though perhaps better with water.'[46] This is almost certainly Indian yellow and Reynolds's wording makes it clear he has not used it before, giving us therefore a dating post December 1784 for these paint layers in *The Strawberry Girl* that lies hidden beneath *The Age of Innocence*. This date is more than 10 years after the painting called *The Strawberry Girl* was first exhibited, and rather later than the reference in Reynolds's ledgers dated 1778.

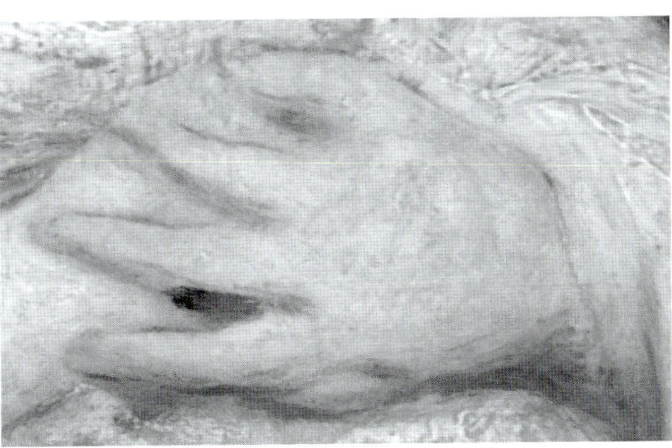

Fig. 10 Detail of the infrared reflectogram of *The Strawberry Girl* from the Wallace Collection showing the outlines visible around the hands. (© The National Gallery, London.)

Underdrawing

Infrared reflectography (IRR) of the Wallace Collection painting revealed a brushed underdrawing. Thin lines, that appear to have been applied with a small brush, have been used to mark out features in the composition: the fingers and thumb of the hand (Fig. 10); the line of the drapery at the proper left wrist (although not the final position); the edge of the proper left sleeve; the major folds of the skirt draped over the sitter's arm; the sitter's philtrum; and the handle of the basket. Fainter lines are visible around the sides of the nose and eye sockets.

In the unfinished oil sketch of *Mrs Hoare and Child* thin, painted, dark red lines are visible around the limbs and features of the child and Mrs Hoare's hands (see Fig. 4). The style of the lines bears a close resemblance to those observed in the IRR of *The Strawberry Girl*, especially in the area of the hands, where the outlines of the fingers are not completely closed. However, it is unlikely that the same pigments were used for both paintings as it is doubtful that the red lines seen in the portrait of *Mrs Hoare and Child* would be visible under IR examination. It would seem that in both cases the underdrawing was applied to transfer an established composition to a second canvas. This may relate to Reynolds's simultaneous working process described by Northcote.

A similar narrow red line can also be seen at the edge of Burke's head in the unfinished painting of *Lord Rockingham and Edmund Burke*. In this instance the line does not appear to be part of a copying or simultaneous working process as the painting was not completed and no other version is known to exist. However, there is a related chalk drawing in the collection of the Yale Center for British Art (New Haven, CT),[47] so the lines could relate to the transfer of the image once the composition had been devised.

These brushed lines of underdrawing have not been observed on any of the other 11 paintings examined in the 'Reynolds Research Project' and are markedly different from the loose-sketched brushstrokes used for broadly laying in the composition from life. A completely different sort of outline underdrawing was observed on a replica of Reynolds's portrait of *Mrs Baldwin*, examined at Tate. The X-ray image revealed precise outlining composed of broken lines, unlike those seen in other paintings, that most probably relate to the transfer of the image.

Conclusions

The technical examination of the Wallace Collection version of *The Strawberry Girl* has revealed new insights into Reynolds's working methods and replication procedures within his studio. Examination of the Wallace Collection *Strawberry Girl* and comparison of the two versions of *Mrs Hoare and Child* has indicated that Reynolds sometimes made use of a brushed underdrawing when marking out his compositions. This seems to relate to the transfer of a pre-planned design, such as when working on two versions of a composition, and is different from the sketched brushstrokes seen in other unfinished paintings. As the passage from Northcote suggests, the Wallace Collection picture was probably developed in conjunction with another version of *The Strawberry Girl* and the type of underdrawn lines visible in infrared light may relate to this process.

However, Reynolds's practice of making multiple versions was not simply to produce replica images. Comparison of paint samples from the Wallace Collection painting and *The Age of Innocence* has revealed that similar passages may have been executed with different materials and using different painting techniques. The Bowood House version shows that the coloration of the images may also vary. We cannot specify which version of *The Strawberry Girl* was exhibited in 1773, but the existence of Watson's print of 1774 probably indicates that it was a 'type A' composition. However, each of the extant versions, including the version revealed in the X-ray of *The Age of Innocence*, started with a composition closer to 'type A'. The X-radiograph of the Wallace Collection painting revealed changes to the fringing of the sitter's head scarf and the position of the shoulders. The adjustments to the Wallace Collection painting may have occurred at a later date, since the painting remained in Reynolds's studio until his death. The presence of Indian yellow in a paint layer from *The Strawberry Girl* concealed below *The Age of Innocence* indicates that Reynolds returned to this iconic image as late as 1784. The note in Reynolds's ledgers from 1778 shows that he also returned to this composition at this time, but we have not been able to identify wax in the medium analysis and so, tantalisingly, another version of *The Strawberry Girl* may remain still to be discovered.

Acknowledgements

We would like to thank The Paul Mellon Centre for Studies in British Art, whose funding has made the Wallace Collection 'Reynolds Research Project' possible. We are grateful to Lord Lansdowne for allowing us to examine the Bowood House version of *The Strawberry Girl* and the curator Kate Fielden for her assistance during our visit. We thank our colleagues at the Wallace Collection, the National Gallery and Tate. We would especially like to thank Ashok Roy, who prepared the cross-sections from the Wallace Collection *Strawberry Girl*, and Marika Spring and Kate Stonor for the SEM-EDX analysis. We are grateful to Rachel Billinge for capturing the infrared reflectogram and for helpful discussions about the underdrawing. Joseph Padfield's invaluable help with technical imaging is also acknowledged. Thanks to Helen Brett for sharing her insights into Reynolds's technique and to Anna Sanden for allowing us to visit her studio while she was treating the portrait of *Mrs Carnac*.

Notes

1. The Wallace Collection 'Reynolds Research Project' is a four-year undertaking funded by The Paul Mellon Centre for Studies in British Art. The project is investigating the techniques and materials used by Reynolds through examination of the 12 paintings by Reynolds held in the Wallace Collection. The examination will inform the conservation treatment of the paintings.
2. J. Northcote, *The Life of Sir Joshua Reynolds, comprising original anecdotes of many distinguished persons, his contemporaries and a brief analysis of his discourses*, 2nd edn. rev. and augmented, 2 vols, London, Henry Colburn, 1819, vol. I, p. 57; M.K. Talley, 'All good pictures crack': Sir Joshua Reynolds's practice and studio', in N. Penny (ed.), *Reynolds*, London, Royal Academy of Arts, 1986, p. 57.
3. D. Mannings, *Sir Joshua Reynolds: A Complete Catalogue of his Paintings / David Mannings; The Subject Pictures Catalogued by Martin Postle*, 2 vols, New Haven, CT and London, published for the Paul Mellon Centre for Studies in British Art by Yale University Press, 2000, vol. 1, p. 428 and vol. 2, fig. 465.
4. An image of the unfinished portrait of *Lord Rockingham and Edmund Burke* in the Fitzwilliam Museum, Cambridge can be found at: http://www.fitzmuseum.cam.ac.uk/opac/search/cataloguedetail.html?&priref=3796&_function_=xslt&_limit_=10#1.
5. J. Northcote, Letter to his brother Samuel Northcote dated 8 April 1772, London, GB/0397 NOR/9.
6. Talley 1986 (cited in note 2), p. 57; S. Bennett and M. Leonard, '"A sublime and masterly performance": the making of Sir Joshua Reynolds's *Sarah Siddons as the Tragic Muse*', in R. Asleson (ed.), *A Passion for Performance: Sarah Siddons and her Portraitists*, Los Angeles, The J. Paul Getty Museum, 1999, p. 110.
7. Northcote 1819 (cited in note 2), vol. I, p. 85.
8. Mannings 2000 (cited in note 3), vol. 1, p. 387. An image and a transcription of W. Pultney, Letter from the Earl of Bath to Mrs Montague dated 15 October 1761, London, NPG 337 (1c) are available on the National Portrait Gallery website: http://www.

npg.org.uk/collections/about/primary-collection/documents-relating-to-primary-collection-works/npg-337a.php .

9. Northcote 1819 (cited in note 2), vol. II, p. 27.
10. C.R. Leslie and T. Taylor, *Life and Times of Sir Joshua Reynolds*, 2 vols, London, John Murray, 1865, vol. I, p. 418.
11. Northcote 1819 (cited in note 2), vol. I, p. 57.
12. Mannings 2000 (cited in note 3), vol. 1, p. 7.
13. Northcote 1819 (cited in note 2), vol. I, p. 293; Mannings 2000 (cited in note 3), vol. 1, p. 208.
14. Northcote 1819 (cited in note 2), vol. I, p. 57.
15. Ibid., p. 285, n.
16. J. Farington, *Memoirs of the Life of Sir Joshua Reynolds*, London, T. Cadell and W. Davies, 1819, p. 69.
17. W. Hazlitt, *Conversations of James Northcote Esquire RA*, London, Henry Colburn and Richard Bentley, 1830, p. 32.
18. There is a note in Reynolds's ledgers in relation to the portrait of Mrs Shirley 1758–9: 'send Mrs Shirley's picture to be copied' (Mannings 2000 (cited in note 3), vol. I, p. 413). Northcote relates an anecdote referring to a Mr Powell who was returning a work after copying; Northcote 1819 (cited in note 2), vol. II. p. 83.
19. Helen Brett, paintings conservator, Tate, personal communication. An account of the conservation treatment of this painting can be found on the Tate website: http://www.tate.org.uk/about/projects/john-schaeffer-nevill-keating-conservation-project.
20. Bennett and Leonard 1999 (cited in note 6), pp. 113–136.
21. Northcote 1819 (cited in note 2), vol. II, p. 7.
22. M. Postle, *Sir Joshua Reynolds: The Subject Pictures*, Cambridge, Cambridge University Press, 1995, p. 60.
23. The Museum of Fine Arts, Boston refers to its sketch as *Mrs Richard Hoare Holding her Child*. However in this paper both the finished painting in the Wallace Collection and the sketch in Boston will be referred to with the shortened title *Mrs Hoare and Child*.
24. N. Penny (ed.), *Reynolds*, London, Royal Academy of Arts, 1986, pp. 219–220.
25. Mannings 2000 (cited in note 3), vol. I, p. 258.
26. J. Ingamells, *The Wallace Collection Catalogue of Pictures I: British, German, Italian, Spanish*, London, The Trustees of the Wallace Collection, 1985, p. 142.
27. Mannings 2000 (cited in note 3), vol. I, p. 363 and vol. II, fig. 935.
28. Postle 1995 (cited in note 22), pp. 79–82.
29. Mannings 2000 (cited in note 3), vol. I, p. 565 and vol. II, fig. 1702.
30. Ibid., vol. I, p. 656.
31. M. Cormack, 'The ledgers of Sir Joshua Reynolds', *The Walpole Society* XLII, 1968–70, pp. 105–169, p. 168.
32. R. Jones, 'Sir Joshua Reynolds (1723–1792) *The Age of Innocence* c.1788', in S. Hackney, R. Jones and J. Townsend (eds), *Paint and Purpose: A Study of Technique in British Art*, London, Tate Gallery Publishing Ltd, 1999, pp. 60–65, pp. 60–62.
33. L. Herrmann, 'The drawings of Sir Joshua Reynolds in the Herschel Album', *The Burlington Magazine* 110(789), 1968, pp. 650–658, p. 654.
34. A. Graves and W.V. Cronin, *A History of the Works of Sir Joshua Reynolds*, 4 vols, London, 1899–1901, vol. III, pp. 1213–1216.
35. Mannings 2000 (cited in note 3), vol. I, pp. 564–566.
36. Ibid., pp. 564–565; Ingamells 1985 (cited in note 25), p. 151.
37. No technical analysis of the Bowood House painting was undertaken during this study but the surface of the painting was closely examined.
38. SEM-EDX analysis of this cross-section identified lead white, bone black, Naples yellow and earth pigments in the mixed underlayer.
39. The smalt particles now have a rather grey appearance and there is evidence from SEM-EDX analysis that they have altered, as the potassium content of the particles is low. However, the cobalt content is also rather low and the particles may never have been very strongly coloured.
40. SEM-EDX analysis showed that the lake particles contain aluminium and sulphur and the ATR-FTIR spectra obtained from the cross-section indicate that the lake substrate contains a proportion of sulphate in addition to the alumina. This is consistent with the method of lake preparation commonly in use during the latter part of the 18th century and throughout the 19th century; J. Kirby, M. Spring and C. Higgitt, 'The technology of red lake pigment manufacture: study of the dyestuff substrate', *National Gallery Technical Bulletin* 26, 2005, pp. 71–87, pp. 80–81.
41. SEM-EDX analysis identified particles of a haematite-type red earth consisting largely of iron oxide whilst the brighter orange particles contained a larger proportion of aluminium and silicon.
42. A previous study reported that some beeswax was identified in the medium of samples from *The Age of Innocence* (Jones 1999 (cited in note 32), pp. 63–64). However, it seems unlikely that any of the samples analysed at this time related to the lower paint layers associated with the underlying *Strawberry Girl* composition. In addition this analysis was carried out before the painting was cleaned and it is possible that material from subsequent surface coatings and past restorations may also have contributed to the results. Some additional analysis was carried out during the recent conservation treatment. The medium-rich paint in the foliage from the background of *The Age of Innocence* was analysed and the medium was found to consist of heat-bodied linseed oil with additions of pine resin and mastic. There was some indication that a trace of beeswax may be present but this appeared to be connected to the remaining surface coating rather than the paint.
43. The oil was identified by GC-MS of paint samples. In addition, ATR-FTIR analysis of a cross-section from the dark background also determined that a proteinaceous material is present in the dark paint. This is visible in the cross-section as a rounded, fluorescent inclusion when examined under UV light, but it is not clear if this represents an addition to the medium and the source of the protein has not been determined.
44. Postle 1995 (cited in note 22) p. 60.
45. Jones 1999 (cited in note 32), p. 63.
46. J. Ingamells, and J. Edgecumbe, *The Letters of Sir Joshua Reynolds*, New Haven, CT, Yale University Press, 2000, p. 136.
47. R. Prochno, *Joshua Reynolds*, Weinheim, VCH, Acta Humanoria, 1990, p. 96.

Authors' addresses

- Alexandra Gent, The Wallace Collection, London, UK (Alexandra.Gent@wallacecollection.org)
- Rachel Morrison, The National Gallery, London, UK (Rachel.Morrison@ng-london.org.uk)
- Rica Jones, Freelance Paintings Conservator and Researcher (formerly Tate Gallery) (rica.jones@ymail.com)